Principles for Interrogating Sources

Every object produced by human beings is a potential so   tion about the past. Historians must coax the past out of   asking it the right questions. In *Going to the Source,* you will interrogate sources by asking the same questions historians ask:

- When was this source produced and under what circumstances?

- Who produced this source? And why? What purpose was this source created to serve?

- Who was the audience for this source? Who was meant to use it?

- What is the point of view in this source? What does the inherent bias of the source reveal about this source's past and purpose?

Principles for Interpreting Sources

After interrogating sources, historians must provide an *interpretation* of the sources to make an argument about what these sources mean and what story they reveal. In *Going to the Source,* you will interpret evidence by following the same principles that historians follow:

- Sources are incomplete. You will never have all the sources for any single moment, and no single source can tell the whole story.

- Sources have limits to what they can tell you. You must consider what you can and cannot logically conclude from a source.

- Sources have biases, which must be accounted for. Do not dismiss the source's bias or adopt it in your interpretation. Instead, identify the bias and use it as evidence of one viewpoint.

- Sources can conflict. Never hide or dismiss sources that complicate or contradict your interpretation. Either revise your interpretation or explain why conflicting evidence does not alter your interpretation.

Brief Contents

Going to the Source
The Bedford Reader in American History

SECOND EDITION

Going to the Source

The Bedford Reader in American History

VOLUME 1: TO 1877

Victoria Bissell Brown

Grinnell College

Timothy J. Shannon

Gettysburg College

Bedford / St. Martin's

Boston ◆ New York

To our students, who have taught us so much

For Bedford/St. Martin's
Executive Editor for History: Mary Dougherty
Director of Development for History: Jane Knetzger
Senior Developmental Editor: Sara Wise
Senior Production Editor: Bridget Leahy
Production Supervisor: Jennifer Peterson
Executive Marketing Manager: Jenna Bookin Barry
Associate Editor: Marissa Zannetti
Copyeditor: Linda McLatchie
Text Design: Claire Seng-Niemoeller
Indexer: Steve Csipke
Cover Design: Billy Boardman
Cover Art: Louisiana Soldiers. J. W. Petty portrait of Confederate soldiers from Louisiana in 1861.
   © CORBIS. Letters from Lincoln's widow. Six hitherto unprinted letters by Mary Todd Lincoln
   have been found in her doctor's family. © STATE JOURNAL REGIS/CORBIS SYGMA.
Cartography: Mapping Specialists, Ltd.
Composition: Pine Tree Composition, Inc.
Printing and Binding: R.R. Donnelley & Sons Company

President: Joan E. Feinberg
Editorial Director: Denise B. Wydra
Director of Marketing: Karen Melton Soeltz
Director of Editing, Design, and Production: Marcia Cohen
Managing Editor: Elizabeth M. Schaaf

Library of Congress Control Number: 2007927403

Copyright © 2008 by Bedford/St. Martin's

Manufactured in the United States of America.

1   0   9   8   7
f   e   d   c   b   a

For information, write: Bedford/St. Martin's, 75 Arlington Street, Boston, MA 02116
(617-399-4000)

ISBN-10: 0–312–44822–8
ISBN-13: 978–0–312–44822–6

Acknowledgments
   Page xiv (Chapter 2 thumbnail): Detail from the cover of a 1773 Boston Edition of *A Narrative of the Captivity, Sufferings, and Removes of Mrs. Mary Rowlandson.* Courtesy of the Rosenbach Museum & Library, Philadelphia.

Chapter 1
   Page 6 (Figure 1.1): Untitled engraving depicting of Sir Walter Ralegh entering the Orinoco River. Courtesy of Neil L. Whitehead.
   Pages 10–11 (Source 1): *Succarath.* Image from André Thevet, *Cosmographie universalle,* fol. 1002r. Courtesy of The John Carter Brown Library at Brown University. Caption text from *André Thevet's North America: A Sixteenth-Century View,* edited by Roger Schlesinger and Arthur P. Stabler. Reprinted with permission of McGill-Queen's University Press.
   Pages 10–11 (Source 2): *Hoga.* Image from André Thevet, *Cosmographie universalle,* fol. 1002r. Courtesy of The John Carter Brown Library at Brown University. Caption text from *André Thevet's North America: A Sixteenth-Century View,* edited by Roger Schlesinger and Arthur P. Stabler. Reprinted with permission of McGill-Queen's University Press.

Acknowledgments and copyrights are continued at the back of the book on pages 349–51, which constitute an extension of the copyright page. It is a violation of the law to reproduce these selections by any means whatsoever without the written permission of the copyright holder.

Preface for Instructors

In the course of writing and revising *Going to the Source*, we have heard from many instructors about how they use primary and secondary documents in their history classes. Many instructors focus on the goal of providing lively historical content; they appreciate the way in which a letter from a Lowell mill worker, for example, can bring to life the feel of nineteenth-century New England. We were looking for something more. We wanted students to move beyond empathizing with folks in the past to engaging in *analysis* the way that historians do. However, we wanted to train our students in critical thinking by addressing them not as historians-in-the-making, but as consumers of information; as people who have to think about the reliability of sources of information all the time. Most survey students will never become historians, but they will have to act on sources to cast a vote or make a major decision.

We provide a range of sources for students to examine. The sources in each volume are personal and public; they run the gamut from popular to official, from obvious to obscure. In satisfying our own interest in Americans' struggle to realize democratic ideals out of undemocratic realities, we have provided sources from the margins of society as well as the centers of power. By including documents that balance a bottom-up with a top-down approach to U.S. history, we seek to remind students that the nation's conflicts over democratic ideals have not been confined to marginal communities or anonymous voices. By exposing students to elite or official documents as well as private or anonymous ones, we seek to remind them that influence can arise from humble communities in America, that centers of power cannot be ignored when writing the history of American democracy, and that marginal people have had to learn about elite institutions in order to influence the powerful. We also seek to remind students of the range of sources a historian can draw upon to capture U.S. history and to convince them of their ability to understand—and their right to access—a vast array of documentary material so that they can become more critical consumers of all types of information.

In *Going to the Source* we hope to provide students and instructors with a way to discuss historical content while experiencing hands-on work in historical source analysis. Our goal in writing this reader is to provide consideration of a particular topic while blending in a healthy portion of historical thinking about the nature of different types of sources, be they newspapers, letters, paintings, statistical data, or scholars' secondary writing. To achieve these aims, we've designed each chapter around one historical topic and one type of source in order to allow for focused student reading and engaging assignments and to enrich classroom discussion on the various processes that go into researching and reconstructing the past.

Each chapter in *Going to the Source* is designed to expose students to historians' processes and to encourage active interrogation of the sources at hand. Each chapter begins with an introduction that sets the stage for the case study that will unfold in the documents. Following the introduction, a "Using the Source" section examines the advantages and disadvantages inherent in the particular type of source on display and provides pertinent questions to ask of all sources of the type under discussion. A "Source Analysis Table" follows, providing students with a template for organizing the evidence they glean from the documents. The central portion of each chapter is "The Source," the documents or images that draw from a single source or single type of source. It is followed by a set of questions for analysis that include ideas for written assignments or class discussion. To provide closure on the case study, "The Rest of the Story" explains later developments in the chapter's story and connects it to larger themes in U.S. history. The concluding section, "To Find out More," points students to additional primary, secondary, and online sources for further study.

NEW TO THE SECOND EDITION

This new edition of *Going to the Source* reflects several changes in the book's content and structure inspired by feedback we received from instructors and students who used the first edition. Many instructors liked the reader but wanted it to mesh more fully with their survey course. With that goal in mind, we have revised and rewritten each chapter extensively. Every chapter makes explicit links to important survey topics and themes, and each volume includes several all-new chapters that introduce students to additional popular types of sources, such as political cartoons, biographies, and diaries.

The new chapters cover topics that instructors commonly teach and that are certain to capture the attention of students taking a U.S. history survey course. For example, in responding to requests for a chapter on environmental history, we discovered that some of the most interesting recent work written by environmental historians on early America deals with human–animal relations. We coupled that idea with the plan for an opening chapter that dealt with visual sources so that students would have a comparatively lighter reading load for the first week of the semester. The new chapter examines the precolonial environment of the New World through European depictions of animals. Their visual interpretations of an exotic new world reveal as much about Europeans' own mental framework as about the landscape itself. As the first chapter it also eases students' way into the book's methods and purposes by using an accessible but especially engaging source. Other new chapters in Volume 1 address Indian captivity and John Brown's raid on Harpers Ferry.

In Volume 2, we have written a new chapter on World War I soldiers' diaries and we have completely revised the post-1945 section. Chapter 10 uses transcripts of the presidential recordings from the Cuban Missile Crisis to underscore Cold War tensions; in Chapter 13, student protest manifestos provide a window into the tumult of the 1960s; and the chapter on the Reagan-Gorbachev era uses political cartoons as a fun and creative way to examine cracks in the Cold War order—they combine presentations of Ronald Reagan that range from lovable leader to foolish ideologue. At the end of the semester, when everyone is feeling a bit weary, we hope the editorial cartoons will provide a welcome stimulus to class discussion.

We have also increased our emphasis on helping students understand why each type of document works well for each topic under examination. The sections explaining the advantages and disadvantages of a particular source prompt students to think about what types of sources might best suit their own research and help them become more critical consumers of all types of information—skills that are important not just for budding historians, but for all productive citizens.

To make it easier for students to navigate each chapter, we have streamlined the reader's prose and heading structure. In addition, we added a new subsection, "Questions to Ask," which comes at the end of each "Using the Source" section to summarize key issues in bulleted points for students just before they delve into the source material. The Source Analysis Tables have also been redesigned and expanded to provide more room for note-taking.

A new appendix on avoiding plagiarism augments the popular "Documenting the Source" appendix, which shows students how to document the sources included in these volumes according to the *Chicago Manual of Style.*

The second edition of *Going to the Source* also features a supporting Web site where students or instructors can download the Source Analysis Tables for each chapter to complete electronically and email back to their instructor. Students will also find links to Web-based resources mentioned in the chapters, additional links, and related research and documentation aids. Instructors who wish to arrange homework or research assignments around the book's chapters will find these tools especially useful for integrating their students' use of *Going to the Source* with the rest of their coursework.

ACKNOWLEDGMENTS

We would like to thank the following reviewers who guided us in our revisions with their suggestions and comments: Jonathan Bass, Samford University; Steven Boyd, University of Texas at San Antonio; Rowland Brucken, Norwich University; Marius Carriere, Christian Brothers University; Paul Clemens, Rutgers University; Kendrick Clements, University of South Carolina; Elizabeth Crosman, University of Delaware; Douglas Cupples, University of Memphis; Suzanne DeLuca, Northern Kentucky University; Darren Dochuk, Purdue University; Douglas Dodd, California State University, Bakersfield; Vicki Eaklor, Alfred University; Van Forsyth, Clark College; George Geib, Butler University; Terrell Goddard, Northwest Vista College; Larry Dana Goodrich, Northwest Vista College; Joseph Hawes, University of Memphis; Dwight Henderson, University of Texas at San Antonio; Kurt Hohenstein, Hampden-Sydney College; John Johnson, University of Northern Iowa; Carol Keller, San Antonio College; Kevin Kern, University of Akron; Daniel Kotzin, Kutztown University; Jessica Kross, University of South Carolina; David Krugler, University of Wisconsin–Platteville; Michelle Kuhl, University of Wisconsin–Oshkosh; Janice

Leone, Middle Tennessee State University; Sheila McIntyre, The State University of New York at Potsdam; John Mack, Labette Community College; Gordon Marshall, Brock University; Lawrence Mastroni, University of Oklahoma; Eric Morser, University of New Mexico; Earl Mulderink, Southern Utah University; James O'Donnell, Marietta College; Ami Pflugrad-Jackisch, University at Buffalo; Richard Pointer, Westmont College; Louis Potts, University of Missouri–Kansas City; Caroline Pruden, North Carolina State University; Sandra Pryor, University of Delaware; Yasmin Rahman, University of Colorado at Boulder; Sonya Ramsey, University of Texas Arlington; Roger Robins, Marymount College; Thomas Rust, Montana State University Billings; Brett Schmoll, California State University, Bakersfield; Jeff Seiken, Ohio State University; Ashley Sousa, West Valley College; Joan Supplee, Baylor University; Paul Sutter, University of Georgia; Sean Taylor, Minnesota State University Moorhead; Melissa Teed, Saginaw Valley State University; Vincent Vinikas, University of Arkansas at Little Rock; John Gregory Whitesides, University of Colorado; Cynthia Van Zandt, University of New Hampshire; and four reviewers who chose to remain anonymous.

We extend our thanks to the editorial staff at Bedford/St. Martin's: Joan E. Feinberg, president; Mary Dougherty, publisher for history; Jane Knetzger, director of development for history; Sara Wise, our appropriately named editor for this edition; Marissa Zanetti, our deft editorial assistant; and Bridget Leahy, our efficient production editor. We continue to thank Laura Arcari, our developmental editor on the first edition; Heidi Hood, the developmental editor who guided the plan for the second edition; our copyeditor, Linda McLatchie, and the book's designer, Clare Seng-Neimoeller. A very special thanks also to Katherine Kurzman, our original sponsoring editor. This book never would have happened without her impetus and the sponsorship of Charles H. Christensen, former president of Bedford Books.

We were greatly aided in our endeavors by the librarians at Gettysburg College, including Chris Amadure, Karen Drickamer, Linda Isenberger, and Susan Roach, as well as the Government Documents librarians at the University of Iowa, Marianne Mason and John Elson, and the staff in the archives section of the Minnesota Historical Society. Staff assistance from Carla Pavlick, Rebecca Barth, and Linda Ludwig is gratefully acknowledged, as is the advice we received from colleagues who answered questions and read drafts of chapters. We are particularly grateful to Gabor Boritt, Joe Coohill, Brendan Cushing-Daniels, William Farr, Keith Fitzgerald, Matt Gallman, Jim Jacobs, Mary Lou Locke, Gerald Markowitz, Barbara Sommer, Mark Weitz, and Robert Wright. The assistance of students and former students was invaluable in this project, and we owe much to Maggie Campbell, Katie Mears, Amy Scott, Jason Stohler, Matthew Raw, and Lauren Rocco.

Finally, of course, we owe thanks to our families, who encouraged us throughout this process and regularly offered much-needed relaxation from our labors. Thanks to Jim, Colleen, Caroline, Daniel, and both of our Elizabeths.

Victoria Bissell Brown
Timothy J. Shannon

About the Editors

Victoria Bissell Brown is the L.F. Parker Professor of History at Grinnell College, where she teaches Modern U.S. History, U.S. Women's History, and U.S. Immigration History. She is the author of *The Education of Jane Addams* (2003) and the editor of the Bedford/St. Martin's edition of Jane Addams's *Twenty Years at Hull-House* (1999). Her articles have appeared in *Feminist Studies*, *The Journal of Women's History*, and *The Journal of the Illinois State Historical Society*. She has served as a Book Review Editor for *The Journal of the Gilded Age and Progressive Era* and for the Women and Social Movements website.

Timothy J. Shannon is an associate professor at Gettysburg College, where he teaches Early American and Native American History. His other books include *Atlantic Lives: A Comparative Approach to Early America* (2004) and *Indians and Colonists at the Crossroads of Empire: The Albany Congress of 1754* (2000), which received the Dixon Ryan Fox Prize from the New York State Historical Association and the Distinguished Book Award from the Society of Colonial Wars. His articles have appeared in the *William and Mary Quarterly*, *Ethnohistory*, and the *New England Quarterly*, and he has been a research fellow at the Huntington Library and John Carter Brown Library.

Contents

8   Family Values: Advice Literature for Parents and Children in the Early Republic   156

12   Martyr or Madman? Biographies of John Brown   254

13   The Illustrated Civil War: Photographers on the Battlefield   273

14   Political Terrorism during Reconstruction: Congressional Hearings and Reports on the Ku Klux Klan   303

Using the Source: Congressional Hearings and Reports   306

The Source: Testimony and Reports from the Joint Select Committee to Inquire into the Condition of Affairs in the Late Insurrectionary States   312

Analyzing Congressional Hearings and Reports   327

The Rest of the Story   328

To Find Out More   329

Going to the Source

The Bedford Reader in American History

Monsters and Marvels

Images of Animals from the New World

Sir Walter Ralegh was in deep trouble in 1595. An expedition he had led to South America in search of Manoa, a fabled city of gold in the continent's interior, had not exactly gone as planned. Instead of finding a civilization with wealth and numbers to rival that of the Incas, he had sailed fruitlessly around the Orinoco River basin (in present-day Venezuela and Guyana), bumping into people who kept telling him that what he was looking for was around the next bend. As he returned home, Ralegh must have known that Queen Elizabeth I, who had authorized his expedition, and the investors who had financed it were not going to be happy. In order to keep the political and financial backing necessary to continue his search for New World riches, Ralegh would have to put the best possible spin on a bad situation.

Fortunately, he was up to the task. Shortly after returning to England, Ralegh published a narrative of his voyage titled *The Discoverie of the Large, Rich and Bewtiful Empyre of Guiana*. Ralegh might not have found Manoa, but he did capture the imagination of his readers. Within a few years, *The Discoverie* had been published in five languages and circulated throughout western Europe. Part of its appeal no doubt came from images that a German publisher named Theodore de Bry used to illustrate Ralegh's story. Readers could see Indians casting gold, decorating their bodies with the precious metal, and greeting Ralegh as their lord and friend. In word and image, the New World depicted by Ralegh was a ripe piece of fruit just waiting to be picked.

The Discoverie also included images of some of the animals and fantastical creatures that inhabited the New World. As with the scenes of the gold-laden Indians, these pictures illustrated passages from Ralegh's text. One scene depicted deer grazing in abundance along a riverbank, while man-eating *lagartos* (alligators) swam nearby. Other exotic creatures included monkeys, manatees, and parrots, but the strangest of all were the *Ewaipanoma*, headless men "reported to have their eyes in their shoulders, and their mouths in the middle of their breasts . . . [with] a long train of haire grow[ing] backward between their shoulders." Ralegh admitted that he had not seen the *Ewaipanoma* himself, but he believed them to be real because so many of the local Indians "affirme the same." Nor had he personally met any *Amazones*, the tribe of warlike women who lived near the river named after them, but he relayed reports he had heard, perhaps a bit enviously, about their annual mating ritual with male neighbors. A map of Guiana included in Ralegh's narrative included depictions of the *Ewaipanoma* and *Amazones*, along with pictures of the armadillos, tigers, lions, deer, and "other sortes of beastes [fit] eyther for chace [i.e., hunting] or foode."

As Ralegh's book indicated, early European descriptions of the New World liberally blended fact with fiction. It comes as no surprise that explorers and colonizers trying to enrich their own reputations and line their own pockets exaggerated the wealth of the land or the docility of the natives they encountered. They commonly depicted the oceans, rivers, and forests of the Americas as a new Eden teeming with natural bounty, but more was at work here than tall tales and outright lies. In some instances, Ralegh and his contemporaries described the creatures they found in the New World with the careful observation of a modern biologist, detailing an animal's anatomy, diet, and habits. At other times, they exhibited the pragmatism of an experienced survivalist: Could you eat this animal? What did it taste like? In other passages, these same writers appeared as gullible as children, ascribing to the creatures they encountered magical powers or mythical origins. It is easy for modern-day readers to understand why someone like Ralegh might have fabricated stories about Indians covered in gold; it is much harder to explain why his book also included pictures of headless warriors and man-eating sea monsters.

When Ralegh and his contemporaries wrote about the New World's environment, they relied on a mental framework inherited from Europe's medieval past. The best way to begin understanding that framework is to examine its vocabulary. Early explorers and colonizers used a common set of words to describe what they found in America; these words are familiar to us today but had different meanings in their era. While we use "wonderful" and "marvelous" as synonyms for "good" and "pleasing," they used these words to describe things or events of such jaw-dropping strangeness that they could only be the handiwork of God. We tend to describe only positive things as a "marvel" or a "wonder," but Ralegh and his contemporaries applied these terms more broadly to mean anything extraordinary, be it good or bad. They also used "monstrous" to describe strange and grotesque deviations in the natural world, such as odd combinations of different animals into a single creature. What marvels, wonders, and monsters had in common was that they all testified to God's continuing intervention in his creation.

Another important component of Ralegh's mental world was the revival of classical learning in late medieval Europe. The artistic and intellectual movement known as the Renaissance began in Italy in the fourteenth century and dramatically changed how Europeans thought about the natural world. A key element of this transformation was the recovery, translation, and publication of ancient Greek and Roman texts on geography, biology, and philosophy that formed the foundation of the natural sciences in the Western world. Columbus's voyages to the New World were inspired by his reading of the Greek geographer Ptolemy, whose maps and writings were made available in print for the first time in 1477. Likewise, the Roman scholar Pliny the Elder's *Natural History* provided Renaissance Europeans with their most complete encyclopedia of the world's plant and animal life. When Columbus, Ralegh, and others sailed across the Atlantic, they relied on these ancient authorities to make sense of what they found there, but also recognized for the first time the limits of what the Greeks and Romans had known about the natural world. Pliny, for example, had described monstrous peoples very similar to the *Ewaipanoma* and *Amazones*, but nowhere did he mention an armadillo or many of the other exotic animals Ralegh found in South America.

Folklore also shaped how Europeans perceived the New World's environment and the forms of life it sustained. Greek and Roman mythology provided plenty of examples of mythical creatures whose bodies combined different animal and human parts and who were endowed with magical powers: Medusa, the snake-headed woman who could turn men to stone; the hydra, which could regenerate and multiply its heads; the chimera, a fire-breathing combination of goat, lion, and serpent. Many European explorers, when confronted with the strange anatomies and habits of American animals, described them as amalgams of different Old World animals that resembled these mythological beasts. Thus, one early description rendered an opossum as a "strange Monster, the foremost part resembling a Fox, the hinder a Monkey, the feet were like a mans, with ears like an owl, under whose Belly hung a great Bag, in which it carry'd the young." There was also a tradition in European travel literature of placing monstrous races of people at the edge of the known world. The most widely circulated travel narrative of Ralegh's time (he cited it as an authority) was authored by a thirteenth-century English knight known as Sir John Mandeville, who claimed to have traveled to the far corners of Asia, India, and Africa during the Crusades. Mandeville told of encountering many of the same monstrous peoples described centuries earlier by Pliny: Amazons, pygmies, cannibals, dog-headed men, and men with heads in their chests. Historians are now certain that Mandeville never existed, but the anonymous writer who fabricated his travels exerted a tremendous influence on Europe's imaginative perception of the New World.

Ancient scholarship, mythology, and folklore could go only so far in helping Ralegh and his contemporaries make sense of what they encountered in the Americas. Here was a world that boggled the mind in its very strangeness and that contained marvels that Ptolemy, Pliny, and Mandeville had not known. Even Holy Scripture, Renaissance Europe's most authoritative text on creation, did not offer an explanation for America. If all humans had inherited the original sin of Adam and Eve, then why did Native Americans walk around naked without shame? If Noah's three sons and their wives had repopulated Africa, Asia, and Europe after the flood, then who were the biblical ancestors of the Americans? And how could the story of Noah's Ark account for the innumerable new species of animals found on the other side of the Atlantic? The mere existence of America threw the inherited wisdom of the ages into question and encouraged a new spirit of inquiry and observation. The monsters and marvels of the New World were a wonder in their own right, one that challenged the very foundations of all that Europeans knew about the world around them.

Using the Source: Images of Animals

The first images of the New World seen by Europeans were made possible by technological innovations in book publishing that had occurred in the decades preceding Columbus's first voyage to the Americas in 1492. Before the invention of the printing press in the mid-fifteenth century, books were a rare commodity in Europe. Monks and other trained copyists painstakingly produced copies of important works one at a time. Such books are known as illuminated manuscripts because of the elaborate and colorful inkwork that filled their pages, but they were rare and expensive, available to only the wealthy and learned.

The invention of the printing press changed all that. Movable type meant that books, maps, and other printed materials could be produced in greater quantities and at lower cost than previously imaginable. Furthermore, the efforts of religious reformers to translate the Bible from Latin into vernacular languages encouraged the growth of literacy, especially in those regions where the Protestant Reformation took root. The expansion of Europe's trade with the outside world also created a market for consumer goods among merchants and other people with disposable income. All of these changes brought books out of the monasteries and university libraries and into the retail stalls of urban printers and booksellers, and a growing number of people had the financial means and intellectual ability to make use of them.

Even the illiterate and semiliterate were drawn to these texts, especially if they contained images. In the medieval era, the Catholic Church had relied on all sorts of visual images and artifacts—paintings, sculptures, relics, stained glass—to convey spiritual messages to the faithful. That same visual tradition carried over into early book illustrations, which often borrowed symbols and scenes from religious art to convey their messages. Early book illustrations were generally of two types, woodcuts and engravings. As the name implies, a woodcut was manufactured by carving an image into a block of wood, inking it, and then pressing it to a piece of paper. Such images tended to be rudimentary, lacking detail and color, but unlike the illuminated manuscripts of the medieval era, they could be mass-produced; the same woodcut would produce hundreds, even thousands, of copies. In a similar manner, printers and artists engraved images on copper plates that could be inked and reproduced on paper. Copperplate engravings featured greater detail than woodcuts and gradually supplanted them as book illustrations. Some were hand-colored before being bound into books, creating images that rivaled illuminated manuscripts for their beauty.

Illustrating the New World animal life that Ralegh and other explorers described in their books presented a special problem to printers. Generally speaking, they had no models from which to work. Live animals rarely survived the voyage back to Europe, and preserved dead ones usually ended up in the "cabinets of curiosities" maintained by wealthy collectors of such exotica. Some expeditions did include artists who drew or painted New World scenes, and if such works survived, they were occasionally reproduced as engravings for books. Most often, however, the artist producing a woodcut or engraving had to apply his imagination to the words he read in a traveler's account, much like a police sketch artist who creates a visual image from a witness's spoken recollections. The results could be startling to the eye: grotesque or exaggerated features, monstrous combinations of human and animal body parts, even some beasts utterly unrecognizable then or now. These images, when examined alongside some of the written descriptions that inspired them, open a fascinating window into the European imagination as it struggled to make sense of the New World's environment.

What Can Images of Animals Tell Us?

If, as the old saying goes, a picture is worth a thousand words, then it demands the same critical eye and careful attention that a historian brings to a written source. But images also have their own particular strengths and weaknesses as historical sources. Consider for example the following image (Figure 1.1), which appeared in an edition of Ralegh's *Discoverie* published by de Bry. The image was used to illustrate a passage from Ralegh's narrative, in which he described the basin of the Orinoco River as "the most beautifull countrie that ever mine eies beheld." Ralegh wrote of deer "feeding by the waters side," so tame that they seemed "used to a keepers call," as well as a "great store of fowle . . . of many sorts" and "divers sorts of strange fishes . . . of marvellous bignes." He also warned his readers about the "*lagartos*" (alligators). According to Ralegh "thousands of those uglie serpents" lived in the river, and he had watched in horror as one "devoured" a member of his party who fell into the water.

While derived from a passage in Ralegh's text, this image elaborates on it in ways that show the imaginative license taken by de Bry, one of Europe's most prolific publishers of American scenes. De Bry has taken Ralegh's verbal description of a New World Eden and rendered it visually, with grazing deer and plumb turkeys standing idly by as Ralegh's men move upriver. De Bry has also inserted some exotic animals not mentioned in Ralegh's narrative. The monkey was commonly associated with South America, but the ostrich was

Rows of trees create an open, parklike landscape

Turkey and deer suggest plentiful hunting

A monkey and ostriches indicate exotic animal life

A fish of "marvellous bignes"

What is this long-eared creature?

The *lagarto* who consumed one of Ralegh's men

Figure 1.1 *Untitled engraving from a Latin edition of Ralegh's* Discoverie, *depicting Ralegh and his men entering the Orinoco River.* *Source:* Theodore de Bry, *Americae pars VIII* (Frankfurt, 1625).

native to Africa (in other engravings, de Bry used ostriches to represent peacocks). The long-eared beast tucked behind a tree on the right appears to be a figment of de Bry's imagination. De Bry has rendered the left bank of the river as a landscaped park, with trees planted in parallel rows. Most interesting of all, de Bry has chosen to present the *lagartos* as legless sea monsters. In earlier engravings, he had depicted alligators more realistically; perhaps his aim in this print was to link Ralegh's description of Guiana even more closely to the biblical account of Eden, in which evil took the form of a serpent.

When read as closely as Ralegh's text, de Bry's image tells us something about the artistic conventions used to present the New World to Europeans, about the pervasive influence of biblical themes in this art, and about the artists' willingness to play fast and loose with the facts in order to achieve a desired end. In such images, realism took a backseat to eliciting awe, terror, or excitement from the viewer. Images of animals in early accounts of the New World also served as a sort of visual shorthand for conveying geographic information. Animals on maps indicated what natural resources were available to colonial enterprises. Plumb turkeys, tame deer, and fish of "marvellous bignes" would help fill the bellies of hungry colonists, while beaver, bear, and deer would supply European markets with a new source of furs.

The disadvantages of using images of animals to study the European encounter with the New World derive mainly from the manner in which these images were produced. Europe's printing industry at the time of Ralegh and de Bry was centered in Germany and the Netherlands. Spain, which dominated the exploration and colonization of the Americas for the first two centuries after Columbus, carefully guarded its growing knowledge of the New World. Much of what was published about the Americas during this period came to printers as hearsay, exaggeration, and fabrication (Ralegh being an excellent example). Images of New World animals show evidence of this loose grip on reality. They could also be heavily derivative of other sources. Making new woodcuts and copperplates was expensive and time-consuming; many printers cut costs by using old prints to illustrate new books or by borrowing willy-nilly from previous publications for their models. De Bry's work, most of which was published in the 1590s, was so influential that it was still being used by printers to illustrate books about the Americas two centuries later. Finally, it is worth noting that the people who knew the New World best, the Native Americans, never participated in the production of these images. In many respects, this source tells us much more about what Europeans hoped to find in the New World than about what was actually there.

Questions to Ask

To get the most out of these images, you need to approach them critically and to take the same time with them that you would with a written source. Start by gathering as much information as you can about how the image was produced. When and where was it published? What source did the artist use for the image, a painting or drawing or a written account? Once you have asked these basic questions, turn your attention to the subject of the image. How would you describe the presentation of this animal or creature: realistic, grotesque, fantastic? What attributes does the image or its accompanying text ascribe to the beast? Finally, think about the image's wider context. What do you know about the book or map in which the image appeared? Are there other elements in the image (background, detail, perspective) that affect what it tells you about its subject? Does the image or its accompanying text convey a particular use for the animal, such as food, transportation, or medicine? What does the information conveyed in this image tell you about how Europeans perceived the New World's environment?

- Where did the image come from? Who produced it? When?
- What are the physical characteristics and attributes of the animal presented in the image?
- What are the animal's potential uses or dangers?
- What does the image tell you about how Europeans viewed nature, animals, and the New World?

Source Analysis Table

Source	Origin of the Image: Author/Artist, Date, Region the Animal(s) Inhabits	Distinguishing Characteristics of the Animal(s)	Potential Uses and Dangers of the Animal(s)
1. Succarath			
2. Hoga [Manatee]			
3. Whale			
4. Alligator			
5. Llama			
6. Birds and Fish of New England			

(continued)

Source	Origin of the Image: Author/Artist, Date, Region the Animal(s) Inhabits	Distinguishing Characteristics of the Animal(s)	Potential Uses and Dangers of the Animal(s)
7. Animals of the Carolinas: *Buffalo*			
Opossum			
Rattlesnake			
8. Beaver			
9. The Vampire, or Spectre of Guiana [Vampire Bat]			
10. Aboma Snake [Anaconda]			

To download and print this table, visit the book companion site at **bedfordstmartins.com/brownshannon**.

The Source: Images of Animals from the New World

The images you are going to examine come from books published in Europe about the Americas between 1550 and 1800. They are arranged chronologically so that you can look for changes over time in the way European writers and artists described New World animals and their environment. Each image is also accompanied by some descriptive text about its subject excerpted from the source in which the image appeared.

1 | *Succarath* (above right)

One of the earliest illustrated books about the New World was French geographer André Thevet's *Cosmographie universelle*, published in 1575. Thevet had traveled extensively in Turkey, Arabia, and Egypt, but his firsthand experience with the Americas was limited to a brief visit to Brazil in 1555, most of which he spent incapacitated by illness. He claimed to have visited North America on his voyage home from Brazil, but many of his peers thought him little more reliable than the fabled medieval traveler Sir John Mandeville. Thevet probably relied on reports and stories he gathered from sailors and fishermen for his descriptions of Mexico, Florida, and Canada.

Cosmographie universelle included descriptions of several exotic beasts of the New World, illustrated with woodcuts. One such creature was the succarath, which may have been a species of sloth. According to Thevet, it lived in Florida.

> There is also found another kind of beast (which for its rarity as well as for its deformity I should much dislike to omit) named by this people [local Indians] *Succarath* and by the cannibals *Su*. That animal mostly inhabits the banks of rivers and is rapacious, and is very strangely built, such as you see pictured above. If it is pursued, it takes its young on its back and covers them with its tail which is rather long and wide, and flees.

Source: André Thevet, *André Thevet's North America: A Sixteenth-Century View,* edited by Roger Schlesinger and Arthur P. Stabler (Kingston and Montreal: McGill-Queen's University Press, 1986), 140–41.

2 | *Hoga [Manatee]* (below right)

In his material on Mexico, Thevet included this description of a *Hoga*, an aquatic mammal. It was probably a manatee.

> It has a head and ears little different from a terrestrial pig, and five moustaches a half-foot long or thereabouts. . . . Its flesh is as tasty as that of the albacore of which I have already spoken. Formerly I had the skin of one in my cabinet, but because it was badly cured it was spoiled by vermin, which gave me the occasion to picture it for you here as I saw it from life. . . . This *Hoga* gives birth to its young alive as do whales and some others, which I have discussed previously. . . . If you look at it when it is frolicking [and] swimming in the water you would say that it is sometimes green, sometimes yellow, and then red like a chameleon. . . . It has many teeth and is ferocious, killing and devouring the other fish, even those twice as large as it is.

Source: André Thevet, *André Thevet's North America: A Sixteenth-Century View,* edited by Roger Schlesinger and Arthur P. Stabler (Kingston and Montreal: McGill-Queen's University Press, 1986), 196–97.

3 | *Whale*

Whalers and fishermen working off the coast of Canada and Newfoundland were some of the first Europeans to become familiar with the American environment. In his commentary on Canada, Thevet offered the following description to accompany an illustration of a female whale being slaughtered:

> The female of this Behemoth has only one little one at a time, to which she gives birth as do the quadrupeds, without eggs, contrary to the nature of all other fishes. Furthermore, the whale gives milk to her little whalelet once he is on the outside: and for this reason she has breasts on her stomach under the navel, which no other fish does either in the sea or in fresh-water. . . .
>
> Moreover the whale is a dangerous beast for sailors to meet up with because of its hugeness. . . . I remember that when I was in the Antarctic it happened that a merchant who was going by boat from one land to another with fourteen sailors to trade was sunk by meeting up with this sea animal, which struck the boat with his tail and upset it in the depths of the sea, so that all of the men who were in it were lost except one who survived on a plank, who told us his story.

Source: André Thevet, *André Thevet's North America: A Sixteenth-Century View*, edited by Roger Schlesinger and Arthur P. Stabler (Kingston and Montreal: McGill-Queen's University Press, 1986), 55–57.

4   *Alligator*

This engraving is based on one originally published by the German engraver Theodore de Bry, who never visited the New World, but whose monumental *Historia Americae*, published in fourteen volumes between 1590 and 1634, provided Europeans with their most widely circulated images of America before the eighteenth century. When possible, de Bry used paintings and drawings done by artists who had visited America as his models, but he also worked from textual descriptions and his own imagination.

De Bry's engraving and description of an alligator were based on the artwork and account of Jacques le Moyne, a Frenchman who had participated in an aborted attempt by French Protestants to colonize Florida in the 1560s. Europeans were familiar with African crocodiles, but those beasts seemed to pale in comparison to their monstrous American cousins.

These creatures, driven by hunger, climb up out of rivers and crawl about on the islands in search of prey. When they find none they make such a ghastly noise that it can be heard half a mile away. At this moment the watchman calls the hunters who are in readiness. Grasping a pointed tree trunk ten or twelve feet long, they advance toward the animal, who usually crawls along with open mouth, and when he opens his mouth they quickly plunge the thinnest part of the pole into it in such a way that he cannot get it out because of the roughness and irregularity of the bark. Turning the crocodile over, they pound and pierce his belly, which is the softest part of his body, with blows from clubs and arrows. The backs of these animals, particularly those of the old ones, are impenetrable, covered as they are with hard scales. Such is the Indians' method of hunting the crocodile. These animals trouble them so much that they have to keep a watch against them at night and sometimes even in the day, as if they were guarding against some dreadful enemy.

Source: Erasmus Francisci, *Erasmi Francisci Guineischer und americanischer Blumen-Pusch* (Nuremberg: Christoph Gerhard, 1669), plate 1, and Michael Alexander, ed., *Discovering the New World: Based on the Works of Theodore de Bry* (New York: Harper & Row, 1976), 43.

5 *Llama*

De Bry's *Historia Americae* included an illustrated account of Peru, adapted from the narrative of Spanish missionary José de Acosta. Like many European visitors to South America, Acosta was intrigued by the llama and its cousin the alpaca, both of which had been domesticated by native Peruvians, who used them for their wool and as beasts of burden. This description accompanied de Bry's engraving.

> A very particular sort of sheep exists in Peru, which the Indians called *llamas*. They used these animals to transport goods and silver from the mines, they ate their meat and used their wool for making blankets. These sheep were not expensive to keep because saddles were not necessary and they ate whatever they found in the fields. However, the llamas were supposed to be very stubborn. If they did not want to advance, nothing could be done save lie next to them for two or three hours until they were prepared to continue. If sometimes they refused to come down a mountain, and it was necessary to regain the merchandise they were transporting, they were shot so they would fall down the mountain.

Source: Michael Alexander, ed., *Discovering the New World: Based on the Works of Theodore de Bry* (New York: Harper & Row, 1976), 157.

6 | *Birds and Fish of New England*

De Bry died in 1598, but his sons and grandsons continued publishing narratives and engravings under the family name. One author with whom they worked was Captain John Smith, the Englishman who had played an instrumental role in the founding of Jamestown, Virginia. Smith left Virginia in 1609, but he returned to North America several years later to map the coast of the region he named "New England." The de Bry family published Smith's travel narratives with engravings that illustrated his verbal descriptions of America's natural splendor.

> Here, in New England, nature and liberty furnish us freely that which in England costs us dearly. Men, women, and children, with a small hook and line, may take many kinds of excellent fish. . . . [H]e is a very bad fisher who cannot kill in a day with his hook and line one, two, or three hundred cod.
>
> For gentlemen, what exercise should more delight them than ranging daily these unknown parts for fowling, fishing, and hawking. And taking pleasure from seeing the wild hawks stoop six or seven times after one another in an hour or two at the fish in their fair harbours as those ashore at the fowl. For hunting, also, the woods, lakes, and rivers afford not only sufficient chase for those that enjoy such pleasure, but such beasts as not only are their bodies delicate food but also their skins are so rich that they will recompense a day's work with captain's pay.

Source: Michael Alexander, ed., *Discovering the New World: Based on the Works of Theodore de Bry* (New York: Harper & Row, 1976), 202.

Animals of the Carolinas

John Lawson, a native Englishman, arrived in Charles Town (present-day Charleston), South Carolina, in 1700 and spent the next ten years traveling throughout the Carolina backcountry, working as a surveyor, land speculator, and fur trader. In 1709, he returned to London, where he published a narrative titled *A New Voyage to Carolina*. It included a long section on the insects, reptiles, and mammals of North America, several of which were illustrated in an engraving for the book. He returned to Carolina in 1710 but was captured by Indians in a war that broke out shortly thereafter and was killed.

Lawson wrote with the detached tone of a scientist, but he was also fascinated by some of the oddities of New World animal life, including the buffalo, opossum, and rattlesnake.

Today we associate the buffalo with the American West, but in the colonial era, this beast ranged east of the Mississippi. Among other uses, Lawson believed it might be successfully cross-bred with European cattle.

> 1. The *Buffelo* is a wild Beast of *America*, which has a Bunch on his Back. . . . I have eaten of their Meat, but do not think it so good as our Beef; yet the younger Calves are cry'd up for excellent Food, as very likely they may be. It is conjectured, that these Buffelos, mixt in Breed with our tame Cattle, would much better the Breed for Largeness and Milk, which seems very probable. . . . The *Indians* cut the Skins into Quarters for the Ease of their Transportation, and make Beds to lie on. They spin the Hair into Garters, Girdles, Sashes, and the like, it being long and curled, and often of chesnut or red Colour. These Monsters are found to weigh (as I am informed by a Traveller of Credit) from 1600 to 2400 Weight.

The opossum is the only marsupial indigenous to the Americas, and it was the first such animal encountered by Europeans. Travelers were fascinated by this animal's singular anatomy, which seemed to be such an odd amalgam of other beasts.

> 2. The *Possum* is found no where but in *America*. He is the Wonder of all the Land-Animals, being the size of a Badger, and near that Colour. The Male's Pizzle [penis] is placed retrograde; and in time of Coition, they differ from all other Animals, turning Tail to Tail, as Dog and Bitch when ty'd. The Female, doubtless, breeds her Young at her Teats; for I have seen them stick fast thereto, when they have been no bigger than a small Rasberry, and seemingly inanimate. She has a Paunch, or false Belly, wherein she carries her Young, after they are from those Teats, till they can shift for themselves. . . . They have no Hair on their Tails, but a sort of a Scale, or hard Crust, as the Bevers have. If a Cat has nine Lives, this Creature surely has nineteen; for if you break every Bone in their Skin, and mash their Skull, leaving them for Dead, you may come an hour after, and they will be gone quite away, or perhaps you meet them creeping away. They are a very stupid Creature, utterly neglecting their Safety. They are most like Rats of any thing.

p. 115.

p. 133.

p. 132.

2　p. 120.

p. 118.

p. 119.

3

p. 116.

p. 121.

The rattlesnake was another singular creature to Europeans. Observers such as Lawson were fascinated by how it gave a warning before striking by rattling its tail, and so it acquired a reputation for attacking only when provoked. Like his contemporaries, Lawson also believed that this snake had hypnotic powers, which it used to charm its prey.

3. The Rattle-Snakes are accounted the peaceablest in the World; for they never attack any one, or injure them, unless they are trod upon, or molested. . . . They have the Power, or Art (I know not which to call it) to charm Squirrels, Hares, Partridges, or any such thing, in such a manner, that they run directly into their Mouths. This I have seen by a Squirrel and one of these Rattle-Snakes; and other Snakes have, in some measure, the same Power. . . . They cast their Skins every Year, and commonly abide near the Place where the old Skin lies. These Skins are used in Physick [medicine], and the Rattles are reckon'd good to expedite the Birth. The Gall [bile] is made up into Pills, with Clay, and kept for Use; being given in Pestilential Fevers and the Small-Pox. It is accounted a noble Remedy.

Source: John Lawson, *A New Voyage to Carolina* (London: n.p., 1709), 115–16, 120–21, 128–29.

8   *Beaver*

The beaver was indigenous to the Old World as well as the New, but by the time of Columbus it had been hunted to near extinction in many regions of Europe. Travelers' accounts from North America, therefore, made much of this creature's appearance and behavior. Europeans valued beaver fur, but they also saw these industrious creatures as model colonizers of the animal world because they worked cooperatively to alter the environment to their use, building comfortable homes and achieving group security.

Herman Moll, a German geographer and engraver living in London, captured this impression perfectly in an illustration he completed for a map of British North America in 1715. Moll based his description of the beavers' engineering skills on the accounts of French missionaries in the Great Lakes region.

A View of ye [the] Industry of ye Beavers of Canada in making Dams to stop ye Course of a Rivulet, in order to form a great Lake, about which they build their Habitations. To Effect this: they fell large Trees with their Teeth, in such a manner as to make them come Cross ye Rivulet, to lay ye foundation for the Dam; they make Mortar, work up, and finish ye whole with great order and wonderfull Dexterity. The Beavers have two Doors to their Lodges, one to the Water and the other to the Land side. According to ye French Accounts.

Source: Herman Moll, "A New and Exact Map of the dominions of the king of Great Britain on ye Continent of America," 1715, in *The World Discovered* (London, 1708–20).

The Cataract of NIAGARA, some make
this Water-Fall to be half a League while
others reckon it no more than
a hundred Fathom.

9 The Vampire, or Spectre of Guiana [Vampire Bat]

John Gabriel Stedman was a Scottish mercenary who spent five years fighting rebellious slaves in Surinam, a South American sugar colony in the region Ralegh had originally called the "Empyre of Guiana." Like Ralegh before him, Stedman published a narrative of his South American sojourn, lavishly illustrated by engravings based on his own drawings. The quest for a city of gold was long dead; sugar and slaves had long since replaced *Ewaipanoma* and *Amazones* in European designs for this region. Yet, Stedman still had a keen eye for the monsters and marvels of the New World, one of which was the vampire bat.

> Waking about 4 OClock in my Hammock, I was Extremely Alarmed at Finding Myself . . . Weltering in Congealed Blood. . . . In Short the Mystery Was that I had Been Bit by the *Vampire* or *Spectre of Guiana* Also Call'd the *Flying Dog* of New Spain Which is no Other than a Monstrous Large Bat, that Sucks the Blood from Men and Cattle When they are a Sleep Sometimes till they Die; and as the Manner in Which they Proceed is Truly Wonderful I Will give an Account of it—Knowing by instinct that the Person they intend to Attack is in a very Sound Slumber they Pitch Generally near the Feet, Where, While they keep Fanning with theyr Enormous Wings to keep them Cool, they Bite a Small Piece out of The Tip of the Great Toe, Which Orifice is so Very Small that the Head of a Pin Could not be Received into it, And Consequently not painful, yet through which Opening they keep on Sucking Blood till they Degorge it, then begin Again and thus Continue Sucking And Degorging till they are Scarce Able to Fly and the Sufferer Sometimes Sleeps from time into Eternity.

Source: John Gabriel Stedman, *Narrative of a Five Years Expedition against the Revolted Negroes of Surinam*, edited by Richard and Sally Price (1796; Baltimore: Johns Hopkins University Press, 1988), 427–29.

10 *The Aboma Snake [Anaconda]*

Stedman also described and illustrated several kinds of snakes he encountered in Surinam. The largest of these was the *aboma*, or anaconda. After shooting one from his canoe, Stedman told of how a group of slaves slaughtered the beast.

The negroe David having climb'd up a Tree with the end of a rope, let it down over a strong forked branch, and the other Negroes hoisted the Snake up in the Suspence, this done David with a sharp knife between his teeth now left the Tree, and clung fast upon the Monster, which was still twisting, and began his Operations by ripping it up and stripping down the Skin as he descended, which though the Animal could now do him no hurt, I acknowledge had a terrible appearance . . . to See a Man Stark naked, black and bloody, clung with Arms and legs around the Slimy yet living Monster— however, his labour was not in vain since he not only dextrously finished the operation, but provided me with, besides the Skin, above 4 Gallons of fine Clerified fat or rather Oil . . . which I delivered to the Surgeons . . . for the use of the wounded Men in the Hospital . . . it being deem'd, particularly for Bruises, a verry excellent Remedy—at Signifying my Surprize to see the Snake still living after he was deprived of his Intestines and Skin, *Cramaca* the old Negro assured me, he would not die till after Sun Set.

Source: John Gabriel Stedman, *Narrative of a Five Years Expedition against the Revolted Negroes of Surinam,* edited by Richard and Sally Price (1796; Baltimore: Johns Hopkins University Press, 1988), 147–48.

Analyzing Images of Animals

1. What types of animals attracted the attention of European writers and artists? Judging from the examples you have seen here, what characteristics of an animal were most likely to catch a writer's or artist's attention?

2. What were some of the practical reasons Europeans had for paying attention to the animals of the New World? How do you think their perceptions of animals affected their overall interest in colonizing a particular region of the New World?

3. Which of the animals you have examined here reflect the European folklore of monstrous creatures? Do any of the verbal or visual depictions of these animals call to mind creatures from biblical accounts or ancient Greek and Roman lore? Which of these animals were believed to have special powers? Were these powers generally helpful or harmful to humans?

4. Which of these creatures have anthropomorphic (humanlike) features or qualities? Why do you think early explorers and writers tended to anthropomorphize the new creatures they encountered?

5. Do these images reflect change or consistency in European perceptions of the New World and its natural environment over time? Does the tone of description or the visual presentation of animals change in any significant way between 1550 and 1800?

6. Imagine yourself as a semiliterate European contemplating migration to the New World in 1650. Explain how your exposure to these images would affect your decision. Based on these images, would you find one region more attractive than another? Why?

The Rest of the Story

Shifting political fortunes kept Ralegh from returning to South America for quite some time. In fact, he spent more than ten years locked up in the Tower of London after falling out of favor with Elizabeth I's successor, James I. Never one for small projects, Ralegh used the time to write another book, *The History of the World*. In 1616, Ralegh was freed from the Tower so that he could lead another expedition in search of Manoa, but the king forbade him from engaging in any hostilities with the Spanish. Nevertheless, Ralegh spent most of the expedition in the unsuccessful pursuit of Spanish plunder. When he returned home empty-handed, he was arrested and executed for treason.

Monsters and marvels in the New World died much more slowly. As the images you have just examined indicate, the animal life of the Americas remained a source of European fascination throughout the colonial era. However, the new science inspired by the Enlightenment changed the manner in which Europeans approached such phenomena. The rhetoric of monsters and marvels gradually gave way to more clinical descriptions by observers trained in the scientific methods of observation and experimentation. Swedish botanist Carl Linnaeus's system for classifying plant and animal life encapsulated a revolution in the way Europeans thought about nature, taking a world of wonders and turning it into an orderly universe in which every creature was somehow linked to another in a grand design. In the Linnaean system, there were no monstrous races or magical beasts living on the edge of the known world, only organisms awaiting their proper identification and classification by perceptive humans.

An orderly environment was also one that could be mastered and manipulated by humans. From the moment of their arrival, Europeans began altering the natural world they were observing, introducing intentionally and inadvertently new plants and animals that had a profound effect on native species. In particular, large domestic animals brought over by Europeans—cattle, horses, pigs, sheep, and goats—reproduced rapidly in an environment where they had few natural predators. The colonizers' search for "merchantable commodities"—goods that could be exported for a profit—also had a negative impact on indigenous animals. Codfish, whales, beaver, and deer were all hunted almost to the point of extinction for their value in the marketplace, while other species, such as the wolf, alligator, and rattlesnake, were attacked whenever possible because they threatened the newly arrived species, including humans. In some cases, local governments encouraged the destruction of such creatures by paying cash bounties, making them another source of the gold that had proved so elusive to Ralegh and his contemporaries.

Then again, the monsters and marvels of Europe's first contact with the Americas have never entirely left our consciousness. Thomas Jefferson, one of America's great Enlightenment thinkers, had his imagination set afire by the eighteenth-century search for the "American *incognitum* or Mammoth," an elephant-like beast that some of his contemporaries believed roamed the interior of the continent. Reports of its existence can be traced to the discovery of mastodon fossils in the Ohio Valley in the 1730s. More recently, we have sought our monsters and marvels in our own new worlds. As any number of science fiction films will attest, the beasts we conjure from the farthest reaches of space or the deepest depths of the ocean occasionally bear more than a passing resemblance to Thevet's succarath or Stedman's Vampire.

To Find Out More

The best place to find images from Europe's early exploration and colonization of the Americas is "The Archive of Early American Images," sponsored by the John Carter Brown Library in Providence, Rhode Island, and available online at **www.brown.edu/Facilities/John_Carter_Brown_Library/pages/ea_hmpg .html**. Another useful Web site, featuring Theodore de Bry's work, is "Early Images of Virginia Indians," sponsored by the Virginia Historical Society, available online at **www.vahistorical.org/cole/debry.htm**. Useful book collections for such images include Wilma George, *Animals and Maps* (London: Secker and Warburg, 1969); Michael Alexander, editor, *Discovering the New World: Based on the Works of Theodore de Bry* (London: London Editions, 1976); and Hugh Honour, *The New Golden Land: European Images of America from the Discoveries to the Present Time* (London: Allen Lane, 1975).

For discussions of the language of discovery and Europe's mental picture of the Americas, see Stephen Greenblatt, *Marvelous Possessions: The Wonder of the New World* (Oxford: Clarendon Press, 1991); Anthony Grafton, *New Worlds and Ancient Texts: The Power of Tradition and the Shock of Discovery* (Cambridge, Mass.: Belknap Press, 1992); and J. H. Elliott's brief but provocative *The Old World and the New, 1492–1650* (1970; Cambridge: Cambridge University Press, 1992). For European perceptions of New World animals, see Angus K. Gillespie and Jay Mechling, editors, *American Wildlife in Symbol and Story* (Knoxville: University of Tennessee Press, 1987), and Jon T. Coleman, *Vicious: Wolves and Men in America* (New Haven: Yale University Press, 2004). Susan Scott Parrish explores the intersection of science and nature in the New World in *American Curiosity: Cultures of Natural History in the Colonial British Atlantic World* (Chapel Hill: University of North Carolina Press, 2006). The impact of Old World species on the colonization of the Americas is described in Virginia DeJohn Anderson, *Creatures of Empire: How Domestic Animals Transformed Early America* (Oxford: Oxford University Press, 2004), and Alfred W. Crosby, *Ecological Imperialism: The Biological Expansion of Europe, 900–1900*, second edition (Cambridge: Cambridge University Press, 2004).

CHAPTER 2

Tales of Captivity and Redemption

North American Captivity Narratives

I n the winter of 1675–1676, war raged across the New England frontier. Metacomet, a Wampanoag Indian known to the English as King Philip, led an uprising of several Algonquian tribes against English colonists in Massachusetts, Connecticut, and Rhode Island. The Indians had a number of long-standing grievances that led to this violence, including encroachment on their lands, attempts to subject them to English law, and unfenced colonial livestock destroying their cornfields. Indian war parties attacked frontier settlements, killing their inhabitants, burning homes and barns, and taking away as many captives as possible. Colonial militias responded with search-and-destroy missions against Indian communities. They, too, killed noncombatants, burned homes and crops, and took captives, most of whom they sold into slavery in the West Indies.

At sunrise on the morning of February 10, 1676, this brutal war came to the isolated town of Lancaster, Massachusetts. It was poorly prepared for the attack because many of the local men were off fighting with the militia elsewhere. Residents took refuge in their homes, but the Indians set the buildings on fire, forcing the occupants out into the open. Of the thirty-seven people who crowded into the home of the local minister Joseph Rowlandson, twelve were killed in the raid and twenty-four were taken prisoner. Only one escaped. Among the captives were the minister's wife, Mary, and her three children. She was immediately separated from the older two children, but the third, who had been wounded by a bullet that also passed through Mary's side, remained in her arms. She described it as "the dolefullest day that ever mine eyes saw."

Plenty more doleful days lay ahead of her. For the next eleven weeks, Mary remained a captive of the Narragansetts who had raided her town. Her wounded child died not long after the attack, and she was forced to leave the corpse unburied. The pain from her own wound was compounded by hunger and physical exhaustion as her captors moved constantly to avoid the pursuing English. She sought consolation among other captives and read a Bible given to her as a piece of discarded loot, but her captors threatened her with beatings and death and occasionally tormented her with false news of her husband's and other children's deaths. Mary's circumstances put her religious faith and identity to the test. She found herself eating food she had considered repellent before, at one point sinking so low as to steal a horse's hoof from the mouth of a small child. Denied the chance to worship among fellow Christians, she lamented time previously wasted smoking her pipe rather than engaged in prayer. Finally, she was sold back to the Massachusetts authorities, in exchange for cash and goods raised by family and friends. Six years later, she told her story in a short book titled *The Soveraignty and Goodness of God . . . Being a Narrative of the Captivity and Restauration of Mrs. Mary Rowlandson.*

Hundreds of other Europeans experienced Indian captivity in colonial America. Many, like Mary, were able to return to colonial society, either by escaping or by being ransomed by their captors. Others never returned. Some were quickly murdered for being too much of a burden to their captors on the trail home. Others survived the trek back to their captors' village, only to be tortured and executed before its inhabitants. Still others were adopted into

Figure 2.1 Title Page of a 1773 Edition of Mary Rowlandson's Captivity Narrative
Rowlandson's narrative first appeared in 1682, but it remained popular with New England readers throughout the colonial era. This 1773 edition featured an illustration depicting the Indians' attack on Rowlandson's home. The image of Rowlandson brandishing a musket is in sharp contrast to her self-portrait in the pages that follow as a patient and passive sufferer of God's will. Source: Rosenbach Museum and Library, Philadelphia.

Indian families, in which they acquired new names and clothes, worked alongside their neighbors, and married Indian spouses. Although the use and fate of captives varied from one Indian culture to the next, captivity was the chief method by which native peoples converted enemies into members of their own communities.

North American Indians practiced captivity long before they encountered Europeans, but the newcomers' arrival altered this practice in important ways. Captivity was part of the customs that governed Indian warfare. Indians warred to gain control of people, not territory or plunder. A successful war party returned home with minimal casualties of its own but many captives, who could be distributed among the families of the community. Adult male captives could expect to be tortured to death in a ritualized process that allowed the community to vent its rage against its enemies or to mourn the loss of its own dead. Captives who were women or young children were prime candidates for adoption to replace deceased kin. Women capable of bearing children would be expected to take husbands and help replenish the community's numbers. Children would find themselves living among new relations, all of whom contributed to their upbringing as members of an extended family. Indians did not attach the same meaning to skin color and other physical differences as did Europeans, and so race did not affect how they dealt with colonial captives. Europeans, however, did pay ransoms to have captives returned, creating a financial incentive for Indians to take them. European diseases and warfare also caused increased mortality among Indians, which in turn led them to rely even more heavily on captivity to replenish their populations.

In brief, Indians had many reasons for taking captives and many uses for them. While some were tortured and killed and others were ransomed, many others were put to work and in time became productive members of Indian society. Rowlandson literally knit herself into her captors' community by sewing shirts and other articles of clothing for them. European observers were struck at how effectively Native Americans were able to turn colonial captives into "white Indians," so much so that when given the chance for repatriation to their former families and friends, some captives chose to remain with their newly adopted kin. Rowlandson may have described her captivity as a divine judgment ordained by God, but it may also be interpreted as her captors' cultural response to the European colonization of their homelands.

Using the Source: Captivity Narratives

Indian captivity narratives like Mary Rowlandson's were one of the most influential and enduring forms of popular literature in early America. They had precedents in Old World tales of Christians held against their will in strange lands, such as Crusaders taken prisoner in the Holy Land or sailors enslaved in the Islamic kingdoms of northern Africa. Like those Old World tales, Indian captivity narratives emphasized the spiritual as well as the physical trials of captivity. Pain suffered at the hands of an infidel enemy was only the physical manifestation of a soul in imminent peril of renouncing God or succumbing to despair. The moment of redemption, when the captive was finally delivered out of captivity, had a twofold meaning. Not only did it return the captive to the safety and security of home, but it also represented a renewed and strengthened faith. Indian captivity narratives provided American women with their first acceptable avenue of literary expression. Although both men and women penned such narratives, those featuring female captives were the best sellers and achieved the greatest notoriety for their authors.

Like any literary genre, Indian captivity narratives followed a format determined by a shared set of expectations between authors and readers. The narrative typically began, as Rowlandson's did, with a detailed description of the attack that resulted in the captivity. Plots then followed captives on a journey into the wilderness, where they experienced more violence, ate disgusting food, and contemplated escape. The farther the captive moved from home, the more she became familiar with her captors' way of life, shedding old clothes for new ones, learning a new language, and acquiring skills for survival. The author would periodically temper a newfound appreciation for the Indian way of life with professions of Christian faith and more evidence of Indian savagery. Variations in this format did occur. Some narratives were unrelenting in the hatred they expressed for Indians, while others offered stinging criticism of Christian hypocrisy. No two were exactly the same, and the genre varied between time and place. Oftentimes, a historian may be convinced of a captivity narrative's value by its differences from others of its kind: Does it offer unique insight into the Indian method of assimilating captives? Is its narrator more reliable than others because of the circumstances of his or her captivity?

What Can Captivity Narratives Tell Us?

There are two great advantages to using captivity narratives as a source for studying the European-Indian encounter. First, they offer an insider's view of Indian cultures undergoing the profound stress and change of colonization. Captives were of course far from objective in their observations about Indian culture. For the most part, they shared the same prejudices and stereotypes of Indians as did other Europeans, but their experiences also offered uncommon insight into Indian communities. Some captives, especially those held for months or years, developed the language skills and kinship ties necessary to gain a deeper understanding of Indian life, and in their narratives they tried to correct misperceptions and biases Europeans held against native peoples. Others offered detailed descriptions of Indian rites of adoption seldom witnessed by other Europeans.

The second advantage to working with captivity narratives is the insight they provide into the captives' own cultures. Captivity narratives were the best sellers of their day, and they helped shape colonial American attitudes about Indians, the frontier, and history. What became known in the nineteenth century as Manifest Destiny — a God-given mandate to white Protestants to conquer North America and the other races that inhabited it (see Chapter 11)— first found expression in captivity narratives from the colonial era. Overwhelmingly, colonial captives interpreted their experiences through the lens of their religious beliefs, relating their suffering to the captivity of the Jews in the Old Testament, describing Indians as agents of the devil, and attributing all to God's divine plan. Even Spanish and French captives, whose Catholic beliefs differed sharply from those of English Protestants, used their identities as Christians to explain their sufferings at the hands of their captors.

In other words, a close reading of a captivity narrative will reveal as much about the author's culture and beliefs as it will about the Indians he or she is observing. Consider, for example, this passage from Mary Rowlandson's narrative, which offers insight into not only the Narragansetts' marriage practices but also the Puritan values at the core of Rowlandson's identity.

The Indian male who claimed Rowlandson as his captive

Belts and sashes made from marine shells and trade beads

Rowlandson's distaste for Wettimore's dress and bodily decorations

Rowlandson's captors intend to ransom her

My master had three Squaws, living sometimes with one, and sometimes with another one. This old Squaw at whose Wigwam I was, and with whom my Master had been those three weeks. Another was Wettimore, with whom I had lived and served all this while; A severe and proud Dame she was, bestowing every day in dressing her self neat as much as any of the Gentry of the land, powdering her hair, and painting her face, going with Neck-laces, with Jewels in her ears, and Bracelets upon her hands. When she had dressed her self, her work was to make Girdles of Wampum and Beads. The third squaw was a younger one, by whom he had two Papooses. . . . I understood that Wettimore thought that if she should let me go and serve with the old Squaw, she would be in danger to lose not only my service but the redemption-pay also. And I was not a little glad to hear this, being by it raised in my hopes that in Gods due time there would be an end of this sorrowfull hour.

In this passage, Rowlandson's observations tell us something about the practice of polygamy among her captors. Her master had three wives, varying in age from old to young. Although most Indians in New England at this time would have had only one marriage partner at a time, such polygamous relationships were not uncommon so long as the husband had the resources to support multiple wives and their children. This arrangement may also have reflected the Indians' adaptation to an imbalance in their sex ratios, possibly caused by an increased mortality rate among young males from warfare. Of course, a historian would need more evidence to support such a conclusion, but when read in conjunction with other sources, captivity narratives provide important clues about how Native American lives changed in the wake of European contact. Rowlandson's Puritanism is also evident in this passage. Note how she equates Wettimore's "severe and proud" character with her elaborate clothing, bodily decoration, and jewelry. The Puritan notion of "providential affliction," a period of trial imposed by God to test the faith of his chosen people, is also evident in the way Rowlandson phrases her hope for redemption ("in Gods due time there would be an end of this sorrowfull hour").

Reading even a small sample of captivity narratives reveals some common disadvantages to working with them as a source. First, some narrators and editors are more reliable than others. Many captives were barely literate, and so told their tales through editors or journalists who took considerable liberty with the text, inventing speeches or dialogue as if such words were remembered verbatim or massaging the details in order to maximize dramatic effect. Some narratives were published years after the experience of captivity, when the passage of time may have dulled some memories or exaggerated others. Separating fact from fiction in captivity narratives can be difficult. As with any source, a historian will seek other materials, such as Indian oral traditions or archaeological data, to corroborate conclusions derived from them.

Another significant disadvantage to working with captivity narratives concerns the type of captives who wrote them. Historians value the eyewitness accounts that these narratives provide of Indian life, but those captives who were most assimilated into Native American communities—the ones who never returned to colonial society—rarely wrote narratives of their experiences. The longer a captive stayed with her captives, the more immersed she became in Indian life, learning a new language, acquiring new kin, and ultimately learning to view the world through Indian eyes. These same captives were the ones most likely to forget their native language, never acquire literacy, and gradually lose connection with colonial society. Unless they were purposely sought out by journalists or publishers, their stories were not likely to be told in print. Conversely, many captivity narratives were published by escaped or ransomed captives who never spent more than a few weeks in Indian company. Compared to what long-term captives underwent, their experience amounted to little more than that of tourists on a particularly bad trip.

Questions to Ask

When reading captivity narratives, you might want to collect and compare information about the captives' backgrounds, such as their age, sex, hometown, and length of time in captivity. You may not be able to determine this information for every captive, but it will help you construct a "group portrait" of the captives. You can then compare and contrast their experiences as captives: Were they treated kindly or harshly? What types of physical trials did they endure? Did their captors use them for labor, adoption, torture, or ransom? Having assembled this information, you can contemplate what the narratives tell you about the culture and values of both the captives and their captors.

- Where, when, and at what age was the captive taken? How long did the captivity last?
- What use did the captive serve for his or her captors?
- What does the narrative tell you about Indian culture and society?
- What does the narrative tell you about the captive's values and attitudes?

Source Analysis Table

Source	Date, Region, Duration of Captivity	Indians' Treatment and Use of the Captive	Information about Indian Culture	Captive's Values, Attitudes toward Indians
1. Cabeza de Vaca				
2. Jogues				
3. Rowlandson				

To download and print this table, visit the book companion site at **bedfordstmartins.com/brownshannon**.

The Source: North American Captivity Narratives

The following sources are from three of the earliest North American captivity narratives. Although the vast majority of published captivity narratives were Anglo-American in origin, examples from Spanish and French sources will allow you to compare and contrast the experience of captivity across ethnic, religious, and regional lines.

 ## *Alvar Nuñez Cabeza de Vaca,* 1542

Alvar Nuñez Cabeza de Vaca sailed from Spain in 1527 as part of an expedition to Florida. After a storm-tossed passage through the Caribbean and losses sustained from desertion and a hurricane, about three hundred men reached Tampa Bay in April 1528. They immediately fell prey to poor leadership, hostilities with Indians, and disease. Living at times as captives and slaves of local Indians, an ever-dwindling remnant of the expedition made its way along the Gulf Coast, until eight years later, Cabeza de Vaca and three other survivors crossed paths with Spanish slave raiders in northern Mexico. Cabeza de Vaca returned to Spain in 1537 to seek rewards from the king. He told his story in a book published five years later.

Cabeza de Vaca's story shows the Indian captivity narrative in its infancy. In some passages, it reads like a medieval travel tale, full of fantastic adventures, while in others it resembles the field notes of an anthropologist visiting a foreign culture. Cabeza de Vaca's treatment as a captive also varied as he traveled. In some instances, he was beaten and starved, while in others he was treated with respect and generosity. Throughout his ordeal, he remained dependent on Indians for food, shelter, and security. The passage below describes his life and work among the Karankawan Indians on the Texas Gulf Coast.

On an island of which I have spoken,[1] they wished to make us physicians without examination or inquiring for diplomas. They cure by blowing upon the sick, and with that breath and the imposing of hands they cast out infirmity. They ordered that we also should do this, and be of use to them in some way. We laughed at what they did, telling them it was folly, that we knew not how to heal. In consequence, they withheld food from us until we should practice what they required. Seeing our persistence, an Indian told me I knew not what I uttered, in saying that what he knew availed nothing; for stones and other matters growing about in fields have virtue, and that passing a pebble along the

---

[1] Cabeza de Vaca was at this time stranded on an island off the coast of Texas, probably near Galveston Bay.

Source: "The Narrative of Cabeza de Vaca," in *Spanish Explorers in the Southern United States, 1528–1543,* edited by Frederick W. Hodge (New York: Charles Scribner's Sons, 1907), 52–54, 76–78, 81–82.

stomach would take away pain and restore health, and certainly then we who were extraordinary men must possess power and efficacy over all other things. At last, finding ourselves in great want we were constrained to obey; but without fear lest we should be blamed for any failure or success.

Their custom is, on finding themselves sick, to send for a physician, and after he has applied the cure, they give him not only all they have, but seek among their relatives for more to give. The practitioner scarifies[2] over the seat of pain, and then sucks about the wound. They make cauteries[3] with fire, a remedy among them in high repute, which I have tried on myself and found benefit from it. They afterwards blow on the spot, and having finished, the patient considers that he is relieved.

Our method was to bless the sick, breathing upon them, and recite a Paternoster and an Ave-Maria,[4] praying with all earnestness to God our Lord that He would give health and influence them to make us some good return. In His clemency He willed that all those for whom we supplicated, should tell the others that they were sound and in health, directly after we made the sign of the blessed cross over them. For this the Indians treated us kindly; they deprived themselves of food that they might give to us, and presented us with skins and some trifles. . . .

The next morning, many Indians came, and brought five persons who had cramps and were very unwell. They came that Castillo[5] might cure them. Each offered his bow and arrows, which Castillo received. At sunset he blessed them, commending them to God our Lord, and we all prayed to Him the best we could to send health; for that He knew there was no other means, than through Him, by which this people would aid us, so we could come forth from this unhappy existence. He bestowed it so mercifully, that, the morning having come, all got up well and sound, and were as strong as though they never had a disorder. It caused great admiration, and inclined us to render many thanks to God our Lord, whose goodness we now clearly beheld, giving us firm hopes that He would liberate and bring us to where we might serve Him. For myself I can say that I ever had trust in His providence that He would lead me out from that captivity, and thus I always spoke of it to my companions.

. . . The Indians told me to go and heal them, as they liked me; they remembered that I had ministered to them in the walnut grove when they gave us nuts and skins. . . . Coming near their huts, I perceived that the sick man we went to heal was dead. Many persons were around him weeping, and his house was prostrate,[6] a sign that the one who dwelt in it is no more. When I arrived I found his eyes rolled up, and the pulse gone, he having all the appearances of death. . . . I removed a mat with which he was covered, and supplicated our

[2] Makes shallow cuts.

[3] Instruments to burn the wound.

[4] Our Father and Hail Mary, Christians prayers.

[5] A fellow survivor of Cabeza de Vaca's expedition.

[6] Torn down.

Lord as fervently as I could, that He would be pleased to give health to him, and to the rest that might have need of it. After he had been blessed and breathed upon many times, they brought me his bow, and gave me a basket of pounded prickly pears.[7]

The natives took me to cure many others who were sick of a stupor, and presented me two more baskets of prickly pears, which I gave to the Indians who accompanied us. We then went back to our lodgings. Those to whom we gave the fruit tarried, and returned at night to their houses, reporting that he who had been dead and for whom I wrought before them, had got up whole and walked, had eaten and spoken with them and that all to whom I had ministered were well and much pleased. This caused great wonder and fear, and throughout the land the people talked of nothing else. All to whom the fame reached, came to seek us that we should cure them and bless their children. . . .

I bartered with these Indians in combs that I made for them and in bows, arrows, and nets. We made mats, which are their houses, that they have great necessity for; and although they know how to make them, they wish to give their full time to getting food, since when otherwise employed they are pinched with hunger. Sometimes the Indians would set me scraping and softening skins; and the days of my greatest prosperity there, were those in which they gave me skins to dress. I would scrape them a very great deal and eat the scraps, which would sustain me two or three days. When it happened among these people, as it had likewise among others whom we left behind, that a piece of meat was given us, we ate it raw; for if we had put it to roast, the first native that should come along would have taken it off and devoured it; and it appeared to us not well to expose it to this risk; besides we were in such condition it would have given us pain to eat it roasted, and we could not have digested it so well as raw. Such was the life we spent there; and the meagre subsistence we earned by matters of traffic[8] which were the work of our hands.

[7] Fruit of a cactus that was Cabeza de Vaca's main source of food.
[8] Trade.

2　*Father Isaac Jogues, S.J.,* 1647

Father Isaac Jogues, S.J., was a Catholic missionary in Canada. In 1642, he was taken captive by Mohawk Indians while traveling with a party of Indian converts to a religious mission among the Hurons. Jogues spent several months among the Mohawks before escaping to the Dutch settlement at Fort Orange (present-day Albany). From there he made his way back to France. His story was told in the 1647 edition of the *Jesuit Relations,* an annual publication devoted to raising support for the French Catholic missionary effort in the New World. This passage describes the treatment Jogues and his fellow captives received en route to and on arrival at their captors' village.

All their men being assembled, and the runners having come back from their hunt for men, those barbarians divided among themselves their booty, rejoicing in their prey with great shouts of mirth. As I saw them engrossed in examining and distributing our spoils, I sought also for my share. I visit all the captives; I baptize those who were not yet baptized; I encourage those poor wretches to suffer with constancy, assuring them that their reward would far exceed the severity of their torments. I ascertained, on this round of visits, that we were twenty-two captives, without counting three Hurons killed on the spot. An old man, aged eighty years, having just received holy Baptism, said to the Hiroquois[1] who were commanding him to embark: "It is no more for an old man like me to go and visit foreign countries; I can find death here, if you refuse me life." Hardly had he pronounced these words when they beat him to death.

　　So there we were, on the way to be led into a country truly foreign. Our Lord favored us with his Cross. It is true that, during thirteen days that we spent on that journey, I suffered in the body torments almost unendurable, and, in the soul, mortal anguish; hunger, the fiercely burning heat, the threats and hatred of those Leopards, the pain of our wounds—which, for not being dressed, became putrid even to the extent of breeding worms—caused us, in truth, much distress. But all these things seemed light to me in comparison with an inward sadness which I felt at the sight of our earliest and most ardent Christians of the Hurons. I had thought they were to be the pillars of that rising Church, and I saw them become the victims of death. The ways closed for a long time to the salvation of so many peoples, who perish every day for want of being succored, made me die every hour, in the depth of my soul. It is a very hard thing, or rather very cruel, to see the triumph of Demons over whole nations redeemed with so much love, and paid for in the money of a blood so adorable.

---

[1] Iroquois. The Mohawks were the easternmost of the five Iroquois nations, who inhabited modern upstate New York.

Source: Reuben G. Thwaites, editor, *The Jesuit Relations and Allied Documents: Travels and Explorations of the Jesuit Missionaries in New France, 1610–1791,* 73 volumes (Cleveland: Burrows Brothers, 1896–1901), 31:29–35, 39–45, 49–51.

Eight days after our departure from the shores of the great river of saint Lawrence, we met two hundred Hiroquois, who were coming in pursuit of the French and Savages, our allies. At this encounter we were obliged to sustain a new shock. It is a belief among those Barbarians that those who go to war are the most fortunate in proportion as they are cruel toward their enemies; I assure you that they made us thoroughly feel the force of that wretched belief.

Accordingly, having perceived us, they first thanked the Sun for having caused us to fall into the hands of their Fellow-countrymen; they next fired a salute with a volley of arquebus[2] shots, by way of congratulation for their victory. That done, they set up a stage on a hill; then, entering the woods, they seek sticks or thorns, according to their fancy. Being thus armed, they form in line—a hundred on one side and a hundred on the other—and make us pass, all naked, along that way of fury and anguish; there is rivalry among them to discharge upon us the most and heaviest blows; they made me march last, that I might be more exposed to their rage. I had not accomplished the half of this course when I fell to the earth under the weight of that hail and of those redoubled blows. I did not strive to rise again—partly because of my weakness, partly because I was accepting that place for my sepulchre. . . . Seeing me prostrate, they rush upon me; God alone knows for how long a time and how many were the blows that were dealt on my body; but the suffering undertaken for his love and his glory are filled with joy and honor.

Seeing then, that I had not fallen by accident, and that I did not rise again for being too near death, they entered upon a cruel compassion; their rage was not yet glutted, and they wished to conduct me alive into their own country; accordingly, they embrace me, and carry me all bleeding upon that stage they have prepared. When I am restored to my senses, they make me come down, and offer me a thousand and one insults, making me the sport and object of their reviling; they begin their assaults over again, dealing upon my head and neck, and all my body, another hailstorm of blows. I would be too tedious if I should set down in writing all the rigor of my sufferings. They burned one of my fingers, and crushed another with their teeth, and those which were already torn, they squeezed and twisted with a rage of Demons; they scratched my wounds with their nails; and when strength failed me, they applied fire to my arm and thighs. My companions were treated very nearly as I was. . . .

After they had glutted their cruelty, they led us in triumph into that first village; all the youth were outside the gates, arranged in line—armed with sticks, and some with iron rods, which they easily secure on account of their vicinity to the Dutch.[3] Casting our eyes upon these weapons of passion, we remembered what saint Augustin says, that those who turn aside from the scourges of God, turn aside from the number of his children; on that account, we offered ourselves with great courage to his fatherly goodness, in order to be

---

[2] A seventeenth-century gun.

[3] The Mohawks acquired iron and other metal goods from their trade with the Dutch at Fort Orange (present-day Albany).

victims sacrificed to his good pleasure and to his anger, lovingly zealous for the salvation of these peoples.

Here follows the order that was observed at that funereal and pompous entry. They made one Frenchman march at the head, and another in the middle of the Hurons, and me the very last. We were following one another at an equal distance; and, that our executioners might have more leisure to beat us at their ease, some Hiroquois thrust themselves into our ranks in order to prevent us from running and from avoiding any blows. The procession beginning to enter this narrow way of Paradise, a scuffling was heard on all sides; it was indeed then that I could say with my Lord and master, *Supra dorsum meum fabricaverunt peccatores* — 'Sinners have built and left monuments and marks of their rage upon my back.' I was naked to my shirt, like a poor criminal; and the others were wholly naked, except poor René Goupil,[4] to whom they did the same favor as me.

The more slowly the procession marched in a very long road, the more blows we received. One was dealt above my loins, with the pommel of a javelin, or with an iron knob, the size of one's fist, which shook my whole body and took away my breath. Such was our entrance into that Babylon. Hardly could we arrive as far as the scaffold which was prepared for us in the midst of that village, so exhausted were we; our bodies were all livid, and our faces all stained with blood. But more disfigured than all was René Goupil, so that nothing white appeared in his face except his eyes. I found him all the more beautiful as he had more in common with him who, bearing a face most worthy of the regards and delight of the Angels, appeared to us, in the midst of his anguish, like a leper. Having ascended that scaffold, I exclaimed in my heart, *'Spectaculum facti sumus mundo et Angelis et hominibus propter Christum'* — 'We have been made a gazing-stock in the sight of the world, of Angels, and of men, for Jesus Christ.' We found some rest in that place of triumph and glory. The Hiroquois no longer persecuted us except with their tongues — filling the air and our ears with their insults, which did us no great hurt; but this calm did not last long.

A Captain exclaims that the Frenchmen ought to be caressed. Sooner done than it is said — one wretch jumping on the stage, dealt three heavy blows with sticks, on each Frenchman, without touching the Hurons. Others, meanwhile drawing their knives and approaching us, treated me as a Captain — that is to say, with more fury than the rest. The deference of the French, and the respect which the Hurons showed me, caused me this advantage. An old man takes my left hand and commands a captive Algonquin woman to cut one of my fingers; she turns away three or four times, unable to resolve upon this cruelty; finally she has to obey, and cuts the thumb from my left hand; the same caresses are extended to the other prisoners. This poor woman having thrown my thumb on the stage, I picked it up and offered it to you, O my God! Remembering the sacrifices that I had presented to you for seven years past, upon the Altars of your Church, I accepted this torture as loving vengeance for the want of love

---

[4] A fellow Frenchman taken captive with Jogues.

and respect that I had shown, concerning your Holy Body; you heard the cries of my soul. One of my two French companions, having perceived me, told me that, if those Barbarians saw me keep my thumb, they would make me eat it and swallow it all raw; and that, therefore, I should throw it away somewhere. I obey him instantly. They used a scallop or an oyster-shell for cutting off the right thumb of the other Frenchman, so as to cause him more pain. The blood flowing from our wounds in so great abundance that we were likely to swoon, a Hiroquois—tearing off a little end of my shirt, which alone had been left to me—bound them up for us; and that was all the dressing and all the medical treatment applied to them. . . .

Word was brought that some warriors, or hunters of men, were conducting thither some Hurons, recently taken. I betook me to the place as best I could. I consoled those poor captives, and having sufficiently instructed them, I conferred upon them holy Baptism; in recompense, I am told that I must die with them. The sentence decreed in the Council is intimated to me; the following night is to be (as they say) the end of my torments and of my life. My soul is well pleased with these words, but not yet was my God—he willed to prolong my martyrdom. Those Barbarians reconsidered the matter, exclaiming that life ought to be spared to the Frenchmen, or rather, their death postponed. They thought to find more moderation at our forts,[5] on account of us. . . . Life being granted us, they did us no more harm. . . . Some women, more merciful, regarded us with much charity and were unable to look at our sores without compassion.

[5] The Mohawks believed they could use Jogues and his compatriots as bargaining chips with the French.

 ## *Mary Rowlandson,* 1682

Mary Rowlandson's narrative, first published in 1682 with the encouragement of Puritan clergyman Increase Mather, was the most famous Indian captivity of the colonial era. It was the first North American captivity narrative with a female as the central character and the first to be published as a book of its own, rather than as part of a larger travel narrative or collection of stories. It quickly went through several editions in Massachusetts and London. Today, scholars regard it as a classic of early American literature. The following passages describe the Indian attack on Rowlandson's home, her relationship with her captors, and her spiritual reflections on the ordeal.

Source: Mary Rowlandson, *The Soveraignty and Goodness of God . . . Being a Narrative of the Captivity and Restauration of Mrs. Mary Rowlandson . . . The second Addition, Corrected and amended* (Cambridge, Mass.: Samuel Green, 1682), in *Narratives of the Indian Wars,* edited by Charles H. Lincoln (New York: Charles Scribner's Sons, 1913), 119–22, 130–31, 150–51, 166–67.

Now is the dreadfull hour come, that I have often heard of (in time of War as it was the case of others), but now mine eyes see it. Some in our house were fighting for their lives, others wallowing in their blood, the House on fire over our heads, and the bloody Heathen ready to knock us on the head, if we stirred out. Now might we hear Mothers and Children crying out for themselves, and one another, "Lord, what shall we do?" Then I took my Children (and one of my sisters, hers) to go forth and leave the House; but as soon as we came to the door and appeared, the Indians shot so thick that the bullets rattled against the House as if one had taken an handfull of stones and threw them so that we were fain to give back.[1] . . . But out we must go, the fire increasing and coming along behind us roaring, and the Indians gaping before us with their Guns, Spears, and Hatchets to devour us. No sooner were we out of the House, but my Brother in Law (being before wounded, in defending the house, in or near the throat) fell down dead, whereat the Indians scornfully shouted, halloed,[2] and were presently upon him, stripping off his cloaths, the bullets flying thick, one went through my side, and the same (as would seem) through the bowels and hand of my dear Child in my arms. One of my elder Sisters children, named William, had then his Leg broken, which the Indians perceiving, they knockt him on the head. Thus were we butchered by those merciless Heathen, standing amazed, with the blood running down to our heels.

My eldest Sister being yet in the House and seeing those woefull sights, the infidels hailing mothers one way and children another and some wallowing in their blood, and her elder Son telling that her Son William was dead and my self was wounded, she said, "And, Lord, let me die with them." Which was no sooner said, but she was struck with a Bullet, and fell down dead over the threshold. I hope she is reaping the fruit of her good labours, being faithfull to the service of God in her place. . . . The Indians laid hold of us, pulling me one way, and the Children another, and said, "Come go along with us." I told them they would kill me. They answered, if I were willing to go along with them they would not hurt me. . . .

I had often before this said that if the Indians should come, I should chuse rather to be killed by them than be taken alive, but when it came to the tryal, my mind changed; their glittering weapons so daunted my spirit, that I chose rather to go along with those (as I may say) ravenous beasts than that moment to end my dayes. . . .

A certain number of us[3] got over the river that night, but it was the night after the Sabbath before all the company was got over. On the Saturday they boyled an old Horse's leg which they had got, and so we drank of the broth as soon as they thought it was ready, and when it was almost all gone, they filled it up again.

---

[1] Wished to retreat.

[2] Gave the war cry.

[3] Rowlandson is traveling with a band of her captors and fellow captives, including mostly women and children.

The first week of my being among them I hardly ate anything; the second week, I found my stomach grow very faint for want of something; and yet it was very hard to get down their filthy trash, but the third week, though I could think how formerly my stomach would turn against this or that, and I could starve and die before I could eat such things, yet they were sweet and savoury to my taste. I was at this time knitting a pair of white cotton stockins for my mistriss[4] and had not yet wrought[5] upon a Sabbath day; when the Sabbath came they bade me go to work; I told them it was the Sabbath day, and desired them to let me rest, and told them I would do as much more to morrow, to which, they answered me, they would break my face. And here I cannot but take notice of the strange providence of God in preserving the heathen. They were many hundreds, old and young, some sick, and some lame, many had Papooses[6] at their backs, the greatest number at this time with us were Squaws, and they travelled with all they had, bag and baggage, and yet they got over this River aforesaid. And on Munday they set their Wigwams on fire, and away they went. On that very day came the English Army after them to this River and saw the smoak of their Wigwams, and yet this River put a stop to them. God did not give them courage or activity to go over after us; we were not ready for so great a mercy as victory and deliverance; if we had been, God would have found out a way for the English to have passed this River, as well as for the Indians with their Squaws and Children and all their luggage. *"Oh that my People had hearkened to me, and Israel had walked in my ways, I should soon have subdued their Enemies and turned my hand against their Adversaries,"* Psal. 81:13, 14.[7] . . .

My master[8] had three Squaws, living sometimes with one, and sometimes with another one. This old Squaw at whose Wigwam I was, and with whom my Master had been those three weeks. Another was Wettimore, with whom I had lived and served all this while; A severe and proud Dame she was, bestowing every day in dressing her self neat as much as any of the Gentry of the land, powdering her hair, and painting her face, going with Neck-laces, with Jewels in her ears, and Bracelets upon her hands. When she had dressed her self, her work was to make Girdles of Wampum and Beads.[9] The third squaw was a younger one, by whom he had two Papooses. By that time I was refresht by the old Squaw with whom my master was. Wettimore's Maid came to call me home, at which I fell a weeping. Then the old Squaw told me, to encourage me, that if I wanted victuals, I should come to her, and that I should lie there in her Wigwam. Then I went with the maid and quickly came again and lodged there. The Squaw laid a Mat under me and a good Rugg over me; the first time I had any such kindness shewed me. I understood that Wettimore thought that if she should let me go and serve with the old Squaw, she would be in danger to lose

---

[4] One of the wives of the Indian who took Rowlandson captive.

[5] Worked.

[6] Infants and young children.

[7] Rowlandson's narrative often cited biblical passages as commentary on her experiences.

[8] The Indian male who had taken Rowlandson captive.

[9] Belts and sashes made from marine shells and trade beads.

not only my service but the redemption-pay[10] also. And I was not a little glad to hear this, being by it raised in my hopes that in Gods due time there would be an end of this sorrowfull hour. Then came an Indian and asked me to knit him three pairs of stockins, for which I had a Hat and a silk Handkerchief. Then another asked me to make her a shift,[11] for which she gave me an Apron.

[10] At this point, colonial agents were negotiating with Rowlandson's master a price for her return.

[11] A loosely fitted dress.

Analyzing Captivity Narratives

1. How does the information you have assembled on each of these captives affect your judgment of them as sources? Which narrator—Cabeza de Vaca, Jogues, or Rowlandson—do you consider most truthful or reliable? Why?

2. What roles did each of these captives play in the Indian communities they encountered? Why do you think those roles differed from one time or place to another? How do you think the personal background of the individual captive affected his or her treatment and incorporation into Indian society?

3. What do these captivity narratives tell you about the Indians' practice of taking captives? What purpose did captives serve in their communities? Do you see any evidence in these sources of how contact with Europeans changed the Indians' practice of captivity?

4. How did gender shape the captivity experience? Does Rowlandson's narrative differ from that of Cabeza de Vaca or Jogues in any significant way because she is a woman? Why do you think female captivity narratives came to dominate this literary genre?

5. In these narratives, do you see any significant differences in the way Spanish, French, and English captives interpreted their experiences? What role did religion play in shaping the captives' interpretation of their experiences?

6. Imagine that the Indians who held Cabeza de Vaca, Jogues, or Rowlandson captive had the opportunity to tell their story. Explain how their version might have differed from the one you have read.

The Rest of the Story

Captives who returned to their society of origin often faced a difficult transition, depending on the age at which they were taken and the length of time they stayed among their captors. Young children assimilated quickly into Indian society, forgot European languages, and were reluctant to leave adopted parents and kin. Captive women who took Indian husbands were also less inclined to seek repatriation because they correctly suspected that former friends and neighbors would view them as sexually polluted and any children they had by Indian husbands as racially degenerate.

Some former captives used skills and knowledge they had acquired from Indians to work as traders, interpreters, and go-betweens. Jogues, for example, returned to North America after a short stay in France. His familiarity with the language and customs of his former captors led the governor of Canada to send him as an envoy to the Mohawks. Jogues's adopted Mohawk kin welcomed him back, but others blamed him for a crop failure that coincided with his return and murdered him. Like Jogues, Cabeza de Vaca returned to America after an interlude in Europe, but not to the site of his captivity. He acquired a commission from the Spanish king to serve as a governor in South America. His career as a colonial administrator was almost as disastrous as his first American expedition. Political rivals had him jailed and sent back to Spain, where he died under house arrest in 1557. Of the three captives featured in this chapter, we know the least about what happened to Mary Rowlandson after her redemption. Her husband died not long after her return, after which she remarried and slipped quietly back into colonial life, a fate indicative of her status as a Puritan woman, but also ironic for the most famous Indian captive of the colonial era.

During the eighteenth century, the captivity narrative grew in popularity. Initially, Puritan captives like Mary Rowlandson dominated the genre, telling tales of spiritual trial and physical torment along the New England frontier. During the French and Indian War (1754–1760), the captivity narrative shed some of its regional distinctiveness. Tales of captivity from the Pennsylvania and Virginia frontier did not place the same emphasis on spiritual introspection as had those that originated in New England. Instead, the narratives became more secular in content. They also became much more graphic and violent, lingering over descriptions of torture, scalpings, and hair-raising escapes. By the 1790s, frontier warfare in the Ohio region had given rise to hundreds of sensationalistic accounts of captivity that demonized Indians and mixed fact with fiction. The success of these sensationalistic accounts inspired early American novelists such as Charles Brockden Brown and James Fenimore Cooper to incorporate captivity stories into their plots. As the nation's Indian wars moved westward, so too did the setting for captivity narratives, real and imagined. From dime-store novels of the Old West to film classics such as *The Searchers,* the "white Indian" has remained a stock character in American arts and literature, used to illustrate the gap between Indian and European cultures as well as the constant desire to pass between them.

To Find Out More

Colonial-era captivity narratives are available in several online and published collections. The Web site "Early American Captivity Narratives" at **wsu.edu/ ~campbelld/amlit/captive.htm** includes literary analysis and links to online versions of several narratives. "Women Captives and Indian Captivity

Narratives," at **womenshistory.about.com/library/weekly/aa020920a.htm**, provides similar information and links, with an emphasis on female captives and authors. The *Jesuit Relations,* an indispensable source for European-Indian relations in northeastern America, is available online from the Library and Archives of Canada at **collectionscanada.ca/jesuit-relations/index-e.html.** Published collections of captivity narratives are also widely available. *Women's Indian Captivity Narratives,* edited by Kathryn Zabelle Derounian-Stodola (New York: Penguin Books, 1998), offers examples from the colonial era through the late nineteenth century. *Puritans among the Indians: Accounts of Captivity and Redemption, 1676–1724,* edited by Alden T. Vaughan and Edward W. Clark (Cambridge, Mass.: Belknap Press, 1981), is a collection of narratives from the New England–Canada frontier.

Historians and literary critics have written volumes about Indian captivity. Fortunately, a number of articles provide excellent introductions to this scholarship. For the experience of colonial captives, see James Axtell, "The White Indians of Colonial America," *William and Mary Quarterly,* third series, 32 (1975): 55–88; for the role captivity played in Indian warfare, see Daniel K. Richter, "War and Culture: The Iroquois Experience," *William and Mary Quarterly,* third series, 40 (1983): 528–59; and for a literary overview, see Roy Harvey Pearce, "The Significance of the Captivity Narrative," *American Literature* 19 (1947): 1–20. Longer works that address captivity as a cross-cultural experience include John Demos, *The Unredeemed Captive: A Family Story from Early America* (New York: Knopf, 1994); Evan Haefeli and Kevin Sweeney, *Captors and Captives: The 1704 French and Indian Raid on Deerfield* (Amherst: University of Massachusetts Press, 2003); and June Namias, *White Captives: Gender and Ethnicity on the American Frontier* (Chapel Hill: University of North Carolina Press, 1993). Richard Slotkin's *Regeneration through Violence: The Mythology of the American Frontier, 1600–1860* (Middletown, Conn.: Wesleyan University Press, 1973) examines the role that Indian captivity played in forging American national identity.

Most scholarship on captivity narratives has focused on the experiences of English-speaking captives, but there are works that take Spanish-American and French-American approaches to this topic. For the former, see James F. Brooks, *Captives and Cousins: Slavery, Kinship, and Community in the Southwest Borderlands* (Chapel Hill: University of North Carolina Press, 2002), and Susan Migden Socolow, "Spanish Captives in Indian Societies: Cultural Contact along the Argentine Frontier, 1600–1835," *Hispanic American Historical Review* 72 (1992): 73–99. For a French perspective on captivity, see William Henry Foster, *The Captors' Narrative: Catholic Women and Their Puritan Men on the Early American Frontier* (Ithaca, N.Y.: Cornell University Press, 2003).

CHAPTER 3

Colonial America's Most Wanted

Runaway Advertisements in Colonial Newspapers

Between 1759 and 1766, a man named Bood appeared three times in runaway advertisements placed by his master in the *New-York Gazette*, a colonial newspaper. The first advertisement, from June 21, 1759, described Bood as a "Mulatto" who ran away with "three Negroe Men." The four fugitives took with them extra shirts, breeches, shoes and stockings, two guns, two or three hatchets, and several blankets. William Hunt, who claimed Bood and one of the other runaways as his property, believed that the four men had planned their escape together and would likely head for "the Indian Towns upon the Sasquehannah [Susquehanna River]" in frontier Pennsylvania, because Bood had lived among the Indians there for "several months, some years ago."

Bood showed up next in a runaway advertisement on May 26, 1763. His owner, Wilson Hunt (the same William Hunt as before, or perhaps a relative?), described Bood as "of a yellowish Complexion," and this time he ran away without accomplices or goods other than the clothes on his back. Hunt warned anyone who apprehended Bood that he was a "smooth Tongued Fellow" who would surely try to escape again "if not well secured."

On December 25, 1766, Bood made his last appearance in the *New-York Gazette* (see Figure 3.1 on p. 45). This time Wilson Hunt added to his physical description of Bood, noting that the runaway "has had the Small Pox" and "his great Toes have been froze, and have only little Pieces of Nails on them." Hunt repeated his warning about Bood's penchant for evading capture, "as he is a remarkable stout, cunning, artful Fellow."

The historical record is silent as to whether Bood was caught again, and we do not know if he lived the rest of his life in bondage or freedom. These three advertisements, however, paint a fascinating portrait of a man who constantly resisted another person's effort to claim him as property. When read in con-

THIRTY DOLLARS REWARD:

RUN-AWAY from the Subfcriber, the 16th of September laft, a Negro Man named BOOD, about 38 Years old, 5 Feet 10 Inches high, yellow Complexion, thin Vifage, has had the Small Pox; his great Toes have been froze, and have only little Pieces of Nails on them : He is much addicted to ftrong Liquor, and when drunk very noify and troublefome. Whoever takes up faid Slave, and brings him home, or fecures him in Gaol, fo that his Mafter may get him again, fhall be intitled to the above Reward of THIRTY DOLLARS, paid by   WILSON HUNT.

Any Perfon who takes up faid Negro, is cautioned to be particularly careful that he does not make his Efcape, as he is a remarkable ftout, cunning, artful Fellow.

Hunterdon-County,
Maidenhead, December 20, 1766. }

Figure 3.1 Runaway Advertisement from the **New-York Gazette** *This runaway advertisement appeared in the* New-York Gazette *on December 25, 1766. It is the last one in which Bood, a runaway from New Jersey, appeared. We do not know if he was recaptured or remained free.* Source: Graham Russell Hodges and Alan Edward Brown, editors, *"Pretends to Be Free": Runaway Slave Advertisements from Colonial and Revolutionary New York and New Jersey* (New York: Garland, 1994).

junction with similar runaway advertisements, they tell us about the material circumstances of slavery and servitude in colonial America as well as about the physical and psychological tensions between masters and their human property. In Bood's record, we can glimpse instances of collective and individual resistance to a master's authority. The advertisements also tell us something about how masters viewed their human property, what physical characteristics and personality traits they attributed to them, and the techniques they relied upon to recapture runaways and keep them in line.

Most important, Bood's story challenges the typical image of runaway slaves in American history, which depicts them as fugitives from cotton plantations in the Deep South running north to freedom. Nineteenth-century slave narratives and novels such as Harriet Beecher Stowe's *Uncle Tom's Cabin* have indelibly printed this image in the American mind, associating fugitive slaves with the coming of the Civil War. The Underground Railroad, with its secret network of "conductors" and "stations" that ferried runaway slaves to freedom, played an important role in the sectional crisis, but its story belongs to the nineteenth century. Before the American Revolution, slavery and servitude were legal throughout the colonies, and no clear geographic line or barrier separated freedom from bondage. When slaves such as Bood stole themselves, they were just as likely to run east, west, or south as north.

Bood's story also raises questions about the intersection of race, slavery, and servitude in eighteenth-century America. In each of the three advertisements placed for Bood, his master claimed him as property, sometimes referring to him as a slave, other times not. Many people lived and worked in eighteenth-century America in a state of bondage; some were African slaves, but others were white indentured servants, apprentices, or convicted felons transported from the British Isles. The institutions of slavery and servitude were universal, and unfree laborers, whether servants or slaves, dominated the workforce. Black slaves and white servants toiled in the swamps of lowland Georgia, in the tobacco fields of Virginia, in workshops and iron forges in Pennsylvania, and in the homes and on the docks of Boston. Both called their bosses "master" and endured whipping as the most common form of discipline.

On the other hand, a clear racial barrier separated black slaves and white servants and made the conditions of their bondage different. Slavery was a hereditary, lifetime status that passed from mother to child. Servitude was contractual, and people entered into it voluntarily, even convicts who chose it over the noose, for a fixed number of years. It was much harder for a runaway slave to pass unmolested into free society, and a suspected runaway slave faced much more severe punishment and fewer legal protections when apprehended. A master could "outlaw" a runaway slave, giving license to others to kill the fugitive, but no such legal sanction existed for the murder of a runaway servant. While the working lives of servants and slaves could be similar in many ways, race made the experience of running away much different for an African slave than for a white servant.

Advertisements for runaway servants and slaves were a common feature of colonial newspapers published from Boston, Massachusetts, to Savannah, Georgia. These advertisements numbered in the thousands. Individually, they provide snapshots of men, women, and children who sought at least temporary respite from a life of working for others. Collectively, these advertisements provide scholars with a database that they can use to quantify the age, sex, place of origin, occupation, and destination of thousands of discontented workers who otherwise left no discernible trace in the historical record. By sampling runaway advertisements from a number of regions, you can recover the dynamics of unfree labor in colonial America: the living and working conditions of the slaves and servants, their relations with each other and their masters, and their masters' efforts to control their lives.

Using the Source: Runaway Advertisements

Few sources offer a more comprehensive or interesting look inside colonial American society than its newspapers. The first colonial newspaper appeared in 1690 in Boston, but it folded after one issue; a successful newspaper did not appear until the *Boston News-Letter* in 1704. Boston sustained its preeminence in newspaper publication throughout the colonial era, but during the 1720s newspapers appeared in New York and Philadelphia as well. The most significant growth in colonial newspapers occurred in the 1760s and 1770s. In 1764, there were twenty-three colonial newspapers; on the eve of the American Revolution, that figure had increased to thirty-eight.

Colonial newspapers were typically published once a week, on long sheets of paper that when folded in half, divided into columns, and printed on both sides, made for four pages stuffed with information. Their publishers included local and international news they copied from other papers or that they received from private correspondents. As with modern newspapers, an important source of the newspaper's revenues was advertising. In columns of notices similar to the modern classifieds section, readers found announcements for the arrival and departure of ships, the importation and sale of goods, public auctions, and the like. Seaports such as Boston, New York, Philadelphia, and Charleston were the nerve centers of colonial trade, and merchants and other business folk relied heavily on newspapers for this information. The smudged and tattered state of surviving editions of colonial newspapers testifies to their wide circulation and readership.

Runaway advertisements in colonial newspapers were found among other advertisements for lost or stolen goods, for debt collections and foreclosures, or for the sale of real estate, servants, slaves, or livestock. One of the great advantages to reading these advertisements in their original context is to comprehend how casually colonial Americans bought and sold human laborers, subjecting them to public inspections and sales in the same way that they traded livestock or any other goods. No one in colonial America thought it out of the ordinary to read an advertisement for a runaway servant or slave alongside one for a stray horse, or to see a monetary reward offered for both.

A review of even a small sample of runaway advertisements reveals a consistent pattern in their composition. This advertisement placed by Virginia slave owner Archibald Cary for three runaways in the *Virginia Gazette* on March 7, 1766, is typical of the style used in such ads. A close reading reveals important clues about the runaways' background, their relationship to one another, and their relationship with their master.

These runaways worked at an iron forge	RUN away from the subscriber's forge, on the 22d instant, at night, three Negro men; one of them named STEPHEN, by trade a carpenter, Virginia born, a black fellow, about 5 feet 8 or 9 inches high, very brisk and active, speaks quick, has a pleasant countenance, and walks very nimbly. Also NED, a	**Born into slavery in North America and therefore assimilated into colonial society**
A skilled slave	fellow fire-man, a black fellow, remarkably well made for strength, about 5 feet 7 or 8 inches high, generally laughs	**Runaway advertisements often included details about the speech patterns of runaways, such as their proficiency with English or foreign languages, accents, or speech impediments**
Born in coastal West Africa and therefore less familiar with colonial society	when he speaks, has a large mouth, which is seldom shut, Virginia born, inclinable to be fat, has a sluggish walk, and broad shoulders. Also BRUMALL, a Gold Coast Negro, about the size and height of Ned; he is a fire-man, has remarkable broad shoulders, a roll in his walk, and had a hurt on his knee	

The physical hazards these slaves faced in their work may have motivated their flight

Cary believes these slaves may have intended to run far from home

lately, from which he was lame a day or two before he went off; but whether any scar on it, I know not. Both the last mentioned fellows, have scars on their arms, from burns which they got by melted cinders flying on them when at work. Brumall is a yellow Negro, and has a very pleasant countenance. I can give no particular description of their clothes; I do not know of their carrying any more than their suits of cotton and osnabrugs. I will give £5 reward for each slave, if taken up in Virginia, and delivered to me; if in Carolina, £10 for each.

ARCHIBALD CARY

Suggests biracial parentage

Suggests that someone other than Cary supervised these slaves

Details commonly found in runaway advertisements included the name, age, sex, ethnicity, and race of the fugitive, along with a description of his or her physical appearance and disposition followed by a description of the clothing he or she was wearing when last seen. Advertisements typically concluded with the offer of a reward for the return of the fugitive and a warning against assisting the person in flight. More detailed advertisements provided a wealth of other information: occupations and skills; aliases, disguises, and motivations for running away; potential destinations or plans; distinctive habits or vices.

What Can Runaway Advertisements Tell Us?

There are many advantages to working with runaway advertisements when studying slaves and servants in colonial America. First, the detailed descriptions of the runaways' physical appearance offer important clues about the day-to-day lives and material circumstances of the "lower sort" in colonial society: slaves and servants who lived and worked under the authority of someone else. The coarseness of the clothing these runaways wore serves as a metaphor for the hand-to-mouth existence so many of them endured. Likewise, descriptions of scars and physical disabilities are evidence of the dangers they endured from the elements, disease, malnutrition, hazardous working conditions, and brutal discipline meted out by their masters.

Runaway advertisements also offer a glimpse into the runaways' strategies and motives for resisting their masters. In many such advertisements, the master speculates as to why the slave or servant ran away. Was the fugitive seeking a reunion with family members or perhaps trying to preserve a family that was about to be driven apart by the sale of a spouse or child? Labor was very scarce in colonial America. Many runaway advertisements hint that a servant or slave with a marketable skill—such as blacksmithing, woodworking, or seafaring—left to find more satisfactory work, perhaps at the instigation of another potential employer. Some advertisements, such as the one for Bood from the June 21,

1759, edition of the *New-York Gazette,* also indicate that runaways found living among neighboring Indians or backcountry settlements more appealing; others suggest that runaways headed for seaports where they hoped to find work in shops or on ships.

One of the disadvantages of working with runaway advertisements derives in part from the medium in which they appeared. Relatively few colonial newspapers existed before 1760, and those that did tended to be in northern seaports, such as Boston, New York, and Philadelphia. Southern newspapers lagged behind northern ones in their founding and readership because the southern colonies lacked the urban centers and printshops necessary to sustain newspapers. New England had few servants and slaves but many newspapers; the colonies of the Chesapeake and Lower South had many slaves but few newspapers. The Middle Colonies had many servants and slaves as well as an active printing industry. Thus, historians interested in runaway advertisements have often focused their attention on New York, New Jersey, and Pennsylvania. While this geographic bias shortchanges the southern colonies, especially before 1760, it does help shed light on the experience of northern and urban slaves and servants.

Another disadvantage is that runaway advertisements accounted for only a small portion of slaves and servants who ran away. Placing a newspaper advertisement cost money and required a master to post a reward and pay the charges of anyone who apprehended the runaway. Capturing a fugitive slave or servant was an expensive proposition, and many masters chose to wait a considerable period before placing a runaway advertisement in hopes that they would recover their property by some other means. Some slaves and servants used running away for short periods of time as a way of protesting their treatment or negotiating better working and living conditions. Such fugitives were less likely to be documented in runaway advertisements than those who absconded with stolen goods or left evidence that they were seeking permanent freedom. Masters were also less likely to post advertisements for runaways whom they did not consider worthy of the expense of retrieving. Therefore, runaway advertisements were more likely to describe valuable, skilled slaves and servants than old, sick, or unskilled ones.

Finally, in weighing the disadvantages of this source, one must consider that the advertisements' descriptions of the runaways came from the masters rather than the fugitives themselves. In composing advertisements, masters were anxious to dismiss any suggestion that a runaway's actions reflected mistreatment or abuse on their part. They were also inclined to attribute negative personality traits to the runaways in question. In the master's eyes, any servant or slave who ran away was by definition a person of questionable moral character. The standard words and phrases that masters used to describe runaways' personalities sound like a roll call of seven dwarfs Snow White would not want to meet: Surly, Insolent, Cunning, Lusty, Sour, Impudent, and Artful. In this respect, the advertisements do not tell us about the runaways themselves so much as they tell us about what their masters thought of them.

Questions to Ask

To get the most out of using runaway advertisements as a source, it is helpful to devise a plan for classifying the information they contain. You can start by keeping track of the name, age, sex, and race of each runaway described. You can then look for more specific biographical information, based on what you want to know about the runaways: What were their places of origin? Did they speak any languages other than English? Did they have specific occupations or work skills? Keep an eye out for information about the runaways' personalities and motives for pursuing freedom. Does the advertisement shed light on grievances between servant and master? After collecting information from many advertisements, you can begin to draw defensible conclusions about the experience of servitude and slavery in colonial America.

- What is the runaway's name, age, sex, and race?
- What are the runaway's distinguishing traits in appearance or personality?
- What generalizations can you draw from the advertisements about servitude and slavery?

Source Analysis Table

The first two advertisements have been completed as examples.

	Number of Runaways	Runaway's Name	Servant or Slave	Ethnicity or Race	Sex	Age	Physical Features, Personality Traits, Occupational Skills, or Other Significant Information	Notes
Source 1	1	Quomino	servant	African	M	21	head half-shaved; speaks good English; carried away clothes and a scythe	carrying scythe as a weapon?
Source 2	1	Cuff	?	African	M	45	facial scars in "Negro Fashion"; could be carrying a forged pass	born in Africa?
Source 3								
Source 4								
Source 5								
Source 6								
Source 7								
Source 8								

(continued)

	Number of Runaways	Runaway's Name	Servant or Slave	Ethnicity or Race	Sex	Age	Physical Features, Personality Traits, Occupational Skills, or Other Significant Information	Notes
Source 9								
Source 10								
Source 11								
Source 12								
Source 13								
Source 14								
Source 15								
Source 16								

To download and print this table, visit the book companion site at **bedfordstmartins.com/brownshannon.**

52

The Source: Runaway Advertisements from Colonial Newspapers, 1747–1770

These runaway advertisements are reprinted in their entirety. They are arranged by region: New England, the Middle Colonies, the Chesapeake, and the Lower South.

As you will see, all runaway advertisements promised rewards, but it is hard to convert eighteenth-century values into their modern equivalents. The colonies used a bewildering combination of monetary units they borrowed from British and Spanish precedents, not to mention their own paper currencies. Exchange rates varied substantially over time and between regions. The table below offers a roughly estimated conversion guide to help you get a sense of the modern equivalent of the reward amount most commonly cited in the advertisements you will read.

In 1766	1 pound (£) = in 1991 Dollars	£5 Reward = in 1991 Dollars
New England	$ 43.25	$216.25
Middle Colonies	$ 28.38	$141.90
Chesapeake	$ 48.54	$242.70
Lower South	$153.52	$767.60

Table based on values of local currency in 1766–1772 for Massachusetts, Pennsylvania, Virginia, and South Carolina listed in Table A-3 in John J. McCusker, *How Much Is That in Real Money? A Historical Price Index for Use as a Deflator of Money Values in the Economy of the United States* (Worcester, Mass.: American Antiquarian Society, 1992).

NEW ENGLAND

 ### *Boston Evening-Post,* August 1, 1748

RAN away from his Master, John Allen, Merchant of Newton, a Negro Man named Quomino, about 21 Years of Age, a likely Fellow, of middling Stature, his Head shav'd half over, and speaks good English. Carried away with him, an Olive coloured Cloth Coat with Buttons of the same Colour, a new Jacket and Breeches, dark Cloth Colour, homespun, with Pewter Buttons on, two pair of Trousers, two Tow[1] Shirts, two Linnen Shirts, an old Bever Hat, and large Brass Buckles in his Shoes, &c. He also carried with him a Scythe.

Whoever shall take him up and return him to his said Master, shall receive of him the Sum of Five Pounds, and all necessary Charges, in Old Tenor

---

[1] Fabric made from flax or hemp fibers.

Money;[2] and all Masters of Vessels are upon their Peril forbid concealing or carrying off said Servant.

NEWTON, JULY 26, 1748.

[2] Paper currency used in Massachusetts.

2   *Boston Evening-Post,* May 19, 1755

RAN away from his Master William Bucknam, a Negro Man named Cuff, about 45 Years old, and pretty tall and slender, and has Scars on each Side of his Face, Negro Fashion,[1] and had on a streaked blue and white woollen Shirt, an under Jacket and Breeches, homespun woollen Cloth, streaked black and white about an Inch wide, mill'd Cloth; outside Jacket, homespun Kersey[2] grey colour'd, and grey yarn-Stockings, thick [illegible], worsted Cap, Felt Hat, and is suspected to have a forged Pass or Freedom for his Protection with him. Any Person that shall take up said Negro, and commit him to Gaol,[3] and secure the Papers, if any, and send me Tidings of the same, or to Messieurs Samuel Hewes and Son, Merchants in Boston, shall have Five Dollars Reward, and all necessary Charges paid. This likewise is to forbid all Masters of Vessels from carrying said Negro away.

FALMOUTH, APRIL 22, 1755   WILLIAM BUCKNAM

[1] A reference to ritual scarification found on slaves born in West Africa (also described as "country marks" in Source 14 on p. 60).
[2] Coarse woolen cloth from Yorkshire, England.
[3] Jail.

3   *Boston Evening-Post,* March 29, 1762

SIXTY DOLLARS Reward

RUN-away from Messi'rs Bodkin & Ferrall, of the Island of St. Croix,[1] on the 1st Day of July, 1760, a Negro Man named Norton Minors, is by Trade a Caulker and Ship-Carpenter, was born & bred up at Capt. Marquand's at Newbury,[2] who sold him to Mr. Craddock of Nevis,[3] from whom the above Gentleman

[1] A Caribbean island.
[2] A Massachusetts port town.
[3] A Caribbean island.

bought him, is about 5 Feet 10 Inches high, about 30 Years of Age, speaks good English, can read and write, is a very sensible, smart, spry Fellow, has a remarkable bright Eye, he has been seen at and about Newbury sundry Times since his Elopement.[4] Whoever takes up and secures the said Negro Man, so that he may be delivered to the Subscriber,[5] shall receive SIXTY DOLLARS Reward, and all necessary Charges paid by

BOSTON, MARCH 29, 1762   HENRY LLOYD

N.B. All Persons whatever are cautioned against harbouring or concealing said Negro, or carrying him off, as they may depend on being prosecuted with the utmost Rigour of the Law.

[4] Disappearance.
[5] The person placing the advertisement.

MIDDLE COLONIES

| 4 | *Pennsylvania Gazette*, November 26, 1747 |

RUN away the 22d instant, from James Greenfield, of Newlin township, Chester county, an Irish servant man named Robert Clinton, a weaver by trade. He is of middle stature, with black curled hair, swarthy complexion, and about twenty years of age. Had on when he went away, a new felt hat, a dark brown coat, green jacket, flaxen shirt, and fine stock, tow trowsers, black stockings, footed with brown worsted,[1] old brass shoes, with large brass buckles. He was enticed away by one Sylvester Eagon, an Irishman, by trade a weaver, and speaks very brogueish, but no servant. Whoever secures said servant, and sends word to his master, so as he may have him again, shall have Five Pounds reward, and reasonable charges, paid by

JAMES GREENFIELD

[1] Woolen fabric made in Worstead, England.

| 5 | *Pennsylvania Gazette*, July 8, 1756 |

RUN away on the 23rd of June last, from the subscriber, living in Vincent township, Chester county two Dutch[1] servants, husband and wife; the man named Jacob Hakaliver, about 24 years of age, 5 feet 4 inches high, has a pale complexion, and a down look: Had on and took with him, a coarse shirt and

[1] When used in runaway advertisements from the eighteenth century, this ethnic designation usually refers to German-speaking servants from the Rhine River Valley.

trowsers, a black coat, with white metal buttons on it, the fore skirts lined with red, an old blue jacket, old felt hat, and has no shoes; he has brown bushy hair. His wife is named Magdalen, a lusty woman, about 30 years of age, has fair hair and a sour look: Had on and took with her, an orange coloured linsey² bed-gown, three petticoats, one of linsey, striped red and brown, another of brown cloth, bound about the tail with black, and the third of black linen, a coarse shirt and apron, three black Dutch laced caps. She has with her a male child, named Michael, five months old, little of his age. They carried with them some bed clothes, and some Dutch books. Whoever takes up and secures said servants, so as their master may have them again, shall have Forty Shillings reward, and reasonable charges, paid by

ABRAHAM SMITH

²A wool-flax blend.

6   *Pennsylvania Gazette,* July 22, 1756

RUN away from the subscriber, living in Kent County, Maryland, two convict servant men; the one named Benjamin Shotton, a shoemaker by trade, about 5 feet 8 or 9 inches high, of a tawney complexion, large black beard, and curled hair; he is a talkative, pert, well-made fellow: Had on when he went away, An ozenbrigs¹ shirt, coarse country made trowsers, old brown cloth coat, with a cuff and slash sleeve, and broad metal buttons, old swanskin jacket, with red stripes, and an old beaver hat. He also got with him a pair of old fine blue broadcloth breeches, and probably has other clothes with him. He is a notorious villain, and this is the third time he has run away without the least reason. The other one is a young fellow, named Edward Phelps, about 22 years of age, a smooth faced fellow, about 5 feet ten inches high, slim made and thin faced, has light colour'd short hair, and a down look: Had on when he went away, An old white linen shirt, a country kersey jacket, a half-worn, dark colour'd, and almost black coat, trimmed with brass buttons with wood bottoms, ozenbrigs trowsers, and a pair of old pumps² much too big for him. He also took with him two new shirts, made of country linen. They have forged two passes; probably will change their names and cut their hair. Whoever takes up and secures abovesaid fellows, shall have Four Pistoles³ reward, or two for each, paid by

THOMAS SMYTH

¹Cheap linen made in Oznaburg, Germany.
²Thin-soled shoes.
³A Spanish coin commonly used in colonial North America.

7   *Pennsylvania Gazette,* August 11, 1757

Middletown, Monmouth County, East New Jersey, Aug. 1. 1757.
RUN away from the Subscriber the First of January, twelve Months past, a Negroe Man, named Cato, who has since his Elopement changed his Name several times: Had on when he went away, a Pair of Buckskin Breeches, fine brown Linen Shirt, a plain made whitish Camblet[1] Coat, dark Yarn Stockings, new Shoes, and a Wool Hat. He is a stout well set Fellow, understands Husbandry in all its Parts, an excellent Hand with a Scythe in Grass or Grain, speaks English as well as if Country born, and pretends to be free. Underneath his right-shoulder Blade he was branded in Jamaica when a Boy with the Letters BC, which are plain to be seen. He plays poorly on the Fiddle, and pretends to tell Fortunes. It is supposed he has a forged Pass. Whoever secures the said Negroe, so that his Master may have him again, shall receive a Reward of FIVE POUNDS and reasonable Charges, paid by

RICHARD STILLWELL

[1] A fabric made from different materials, including wool and silk.

8   *Pennsylvania Gazette,* November 29, 1764

RUN away from the Subscriber, in King and Queen, Virginia, two white indented Servants, a Man and his Wife. The Man is English, about 5 Feet 5 Inches high, of a red Complexion, wears his Hair, is much Sun-burnt, steps short and quick in his Walk, is a Brickmaker by Trade, and has a sett of Shoemaker's Tools; had a short red Coat, red Breeches with Metal Buttons, an old green lapelled Jacket, a Flannel Jacket with red Stripes, new Osenbrigs Trowsers, with other Clothes, as he stole Part of mine; his Name is James Marrington. His Wife is about 30 Years of Age, about 5 Feet high, very thick, looks well, and has got good Clothes; she is an Irish Woman, and her Name is Mary Marrington.

Run away likewise 4 Negroes, viz. Jack, a black thick Fellow, about 30 Years old, about 5 Feet 6 Inches high, speaks broken English, has been used to go by Water, but of late to Plantation Business; had on a blue Cotton Jacket and Breeches, Petticoat Trowsers, Stockings, Shoes with Buckles, and has a Whitemetal Button in his Hat. Dick, a dark Mulattoe, very lusty, about 25 Years old, about 5 Feet 8 Inches high, a Carpenter and Painter by Trade; had on Cotton Clothes, with Petticoat Trowsers, and he has got a red Jacket and Breeches, a good Felt Hat, and Buckles in his Shoes. Daniel, a well set black Fellow, about 5 Feet 10 Inches high, has been used to Plantation Business, and had on Cotton Clothes. Dorcas, a small Wench, about 5 Feet high, has been used to House Business, has got a new brown Linen Jacket and Petticoat, and sundry other Things that she stole. They have all large Bundles, as they stole several

Sheets and Blankets, with other Things. They are supposed to be seen crossing from Point Comfort to Little River, in a small Boat, with a Blanket Sail, Last Saturday Morning, and I imagine will make for North-Carolina. Whoever apprehends the above Servants and Slaves, and delivers them to me, shall have Ten Pounds Reward, if taken in Virginia, if out thereof Twenty Pounds.

EDWARD VOSS

If the above Runaways are taken in Pennsylvania, and conveyed to Philadelphia, the above Reward will be paid by RITCHIE and CLYMER.

CHESAPEAKE

9   *Virginia Gazette,* April 11, 1766

WARWICK county,
April 8, 1766.
RUN away from the subscriber, on or about the 10th of February last, a Virginia born Negro man named GEORGE AMERICA, about 5 feet 8 or 9 inches high, about 30 years old, of a yellow complexion, is a tolerable good shoemaker, and can do something of the house carpenters work, walks quick and upright, and has a scar on the back of his left hand; had on a cotton waistcoat and breeches osnbrugs shirt, and yarn stockings. As the said slave is outlawed,[1] I do hereby offer a reward of £5 to any person that will kill and destroy him, and 40s.[2] if taken alive.

THOMAS WATKINS

[1] An "outlawed" runaway slave was considered a threat to public safety, and he or she could be killed by another person without fear of legal prosecution.
[2] 20 shillings (s.) equaled 1 pound (£). Thus, in this advertisement, the reward for returning the runaway slave alive is £2, but the reward for killing him is £5.

10   *Virginia Gazette,* April 25, 1766

RUN away from the subscriber in Louisa county, the 24th of February last, 2 Negroes viz. POMPEY, a short thick fellow, 36 years old, Virginia born, very apt to wink his eyes quick, contract one corner of his mouth, and stammer in his speech when under any apprehension of fear; had on when he went away a cotton waistcoat and breeches, died of 2 brown colour, Virginia shoes and stockings; he carried with him some other clothes, but of what sort is not known; he pretends to something of the tailor's business, and sews well. ALICE, a tall slim wench, about 20 years old, and clothed in Negro cotton when she went away. Whoever secures them, or either of them, shall have 20s. reward, besides what the law allows, if taken in the colony and if out thereof 40s. They are both outlawed.

R. ARMISTEAD

 ### Virginia Gazette, August 10, 1769

RUN away from the subscriber, in King & Queen county, a Negro man named BEN about six feet high, a very black fellow, his right knee so much bent in, that when he walks it knocks much against the other. Also, a Negro woman named ALICE, about five feet eight inches high, of a yellow complexion; and has remarkable large eyes. A few years ago she made an elopement, and passed for a free woman, in Williamsburg, and I suspect she may now do the like, or both of them attempt to get on board some vessel; if [this] should be the case, I beg of all persons they may apply to, to forward them (or either of them) to the most convenient gaol, and the gaoler is also begged to send an express immediately to the subscriber, which he will defray. As neither of those slaves have been ill used at my hands, I have had them outlawed in this county, and for their bodies without hurt, or a proper certificate of their death, a proper reward will be given; the fellow I suppose (for many reasons) will not be taken easily, as he has formerly made several overseers fear him.

EDWARD CARY

 ### Virginia Gazette, May 31, 1770

RUN away from the subscriber, the first day of November last, (under pretence of suing for his freedom) a likely young fellow, named Bob, of a yellow complexion, slim made, near six feet high, has a remarkable down look, is a very good blacksmith, and, as supposed, is harboured by some white man of that trade. Whoever will bring the said fellow to my house in Dinwiddie county, near the court-house, shall receive a reward of FIVE POUNDS.

JOHN HARDAWAY

LOWER SOUTH

13   Georgia Gazette, May 26, 1763

Run away in January last, from my plantation near Savannah,
A NEGROE called Primus, belonging to James Skirving, Esq; of Ponpon. As he has not been heard of since, I am apprehensive he might have gone away with

a gang of Creek Indians which were down at that time, or that he may be taken up by some of the back settlers, who, I am informed, frequently conceal runaway Negroes, and work them in their own fields, or change them in some of the northern colonies for horses; whoever delivers the said negroe to me, or gives information of his being concealed, shall be well rewarded; and whoever conceals him may expect to be prosecuted by

JOSEPH GIBBONS

N.B. He is a slim fellow, speaks tolerable good English, and had when he went away a new blanket, jacket and breeches.

14   *Georgia Gazette,* March 7, 1765

RUN AWAY FROM THE SUBSCRIBER
A YOUNG NEW NEGROE WENCH, named SIDNEY, has her country marks[1] on her breast and arms, and a mole under her left eye, talks no English, wore a blue negroe cloth gown and coat, a new oznaburg shirt, a cheque handkerchief on her head and another about her neck. A reward of TEN SHILLINGS will be given to any person who takes her up and delivers her in Savannah to

ELIZABETH ANDERSON

[1] See note 1 with Source 2, p. 54.

15   *Georgia Gazette,* January 14, 1767

RUN AWAY from the subscriber's brick-yard, the 19th August last, ONE NEW NEGROE MAN, named DAVID, of the Gambia country, about 5 feet nine inches high, can speak no English, has a large hole in each ear, had on when he went away a blanket, a hat, a pair of broad, cheque trowsers, and an old cheque shirt. Whoever takes up said negroe, and delivers him to me, or to the warden of the work-house, shall receive 40s. reward.

THOMAS LEE

16   *Georgia Gazette,* August 31, 1768

RUN AWAY from Mr. Robert Bradley's plantation at Pansacola, THREE NEW NEGROE MEN, called NEPTUNE, BACCHUS, and APOLLO, that can speak no English, and one STOUT SEASONED FELLOW called LIMERICK, speaks good

English, and is very much marked on the back, &c. by severe whipping. It is imagined he has taken the conduct of the rest, and that they may have found their way through the Creek nation. Whoever takes up and will deliver the said Negroes, or any of them, to the Warden of the Work-House in Savannah, shall receive TWENTY SHILLINGS STERLING REWARD for each over and above all reasonable charges for bringing them any considerable distance from Savannah.

11TH AUGUST, 1768   T. NETHERCLIFT

Analyzing Runaway Advertisements

1. One striking feature of these advertisements is the detail they devoted to the physical appearance and dress of the runaways. Describe the composite portraits these advertisements paint of slaves and servants. What were the typical visual or spoken clues that indicated a person's status (slave, servant, or free)?

2. What evidence do these advertisements present of the techniques and strategies runaways used to make their way into free society? What skills or traits were helpful for doing so? Judging from the information conveyed in Sources 4, 12, and 13, who was likely to assist a runaway slave or servant, and why?

3. What types of racial and ethnic diversity are evident in the slaves and servants described in these advertisements? How does information about a runaway's place of origin (that is, born in America or elsewhere?) contribute to your understanding of his or her motive and method for running away?

4. Are there any significant differences in the structure and content of runaway advertisements from one region to another? If so, what do these differences tell you about regional variations in slavery and servitude in colonial America?

5. Where in these advertisements do you see evidence of different methods used to apprehend runaway slaves versus runaway servants? How was a runaway's race likely to affect the punishment he or she faced if caught?

6. Using what you have learned from these advertisements, compare the institutions of servitude and slavery in colonial America. In what ways were the worlds of servants and slaves similar? What were the most significant differences between them?

The Rest of the Story

The American Revolution changed the nature of unfree labor in North America. Indentured servitude gradually fell out of use in all regions after independence from Britain, in part because it was considered contrary to the democratic values of the new nation. Also, after 1790 the economy of the northern states began to industrialize, and wage labor gradually replaced other forms of labor in urban areas. Apprentices and journeymen, who in the colonial era typically received room, board, and clothing from their masters, now received cash payments instead. These wages allowed apprentices and journeymen to live outside of their masters' homes and independently of their authority when not at work, but the wage economy also led to greater social and geographic segregation between employers and workers in the cities of nineteenth-century America.

The nature of slavery in the new nation also changed dramatically. Between 1780 and 1830, every state north of the Mason-Dixon Line, which divided Maryland and Pennsylvania, prohibited slavery within its borders. New York and New Jersey were the slowest in this regard, passing gradual emancipation laws that freed only slaves born after a certain date. As late as 1840, advertisements appeared in New Jersey newspapers for runaway slaves. Nevertheless, in the wake of the Revolution, slavery receded along with indentured servitude in the North.

Labor relations took a different course in the South. Southern states experienced a hemorrhaging of runaway slaves during the Revolution, but the invention of the cotton gin and expansion into new western territories after the war reinvigorated the plantation system. Rather than melting away as it had in the North, unfree labor in the South became the cornerstone of the economy. Runaway slaves remained a problem for their masters, who continued to place runaway advertisements in southern newspapers through the era of the Civil War.

During the 1840s and 1850s, runaway slaves became a political wedge between North and South. Free blacks and abolitionists encouraged Southern slaves to seek their freedom by fleeing north, and slave owners insisted that the federal government help them recover such human contraband. The Constitution included a fugitive slave clause (Article IV, Section 2) that prohibited states from passing laws that would confer freedom upon runaways from other states. In 1850, the federal Fugitive Slave Law strengthened the hand of slaveholders by denying accused runaways the right to trial by jury and by requiring U.S. citizens to assist federal marshals in apprehending runaways. Abolitionists and free blacks decried this law as a blatant violation of civil liberties, and even people unsympathetic to the plight of slaves found the law's extension of federal power repugnant. Yet, so long as there was slavery in America, slaves continued to challenge the institution by stealing themselves. While the decision to run away was as singular as the person making it, the collective impact of runaways on the slave system is undeniable. Runaways made slavery less efficient and more costly, and their masters' efforts to recover them caused political repercussions that were not resolved until the Civil War.

To Find Out More

Students wishing to conduct research in colonial newspapers should begin with Clarence Brigham, *History and Bibliography of American Newspapers, 1690–1820,* two volumes (Worcester, Mass.: American Antiquarian Society, 1947), a reference work that can help identify a newspaper appropriate to the region and period you wish to study. Original copies of colonial newspapers are very rare and fragile, making it hard for researchers to access them unless they live near a rare books library, but several colonial newspapers are available on microfilm, which can be accessed at university libraries or via interlibrary loan. The online database "Accessible Archives" (**accessible.com**) provides full-text articles from eighteenth- and nineteenth-century American newspapers, including the *Pennsylvania Gazette*. This database is available by subscription only, so you will want to check with a reference librarian to see if you can gain access to it.

If you cannot access a colonial newspaper but still want to research runaway advertisements, there are several published collections. The "Geography of Slavery" project at **www.vcdh.virginia.edu/gos/** has an archive of more than 4,000 runaway advertisements from Virginia and Maryland. For the Middle Colonies, see Graham Russell Hodges and Alan Edward Brown, editors, *"Pretends to Be Free": Runaway Slave Advertisements from Colonial and Revolutionary New York and New Jersey* (New York: Garland, 1994), and Billy G. Smith and Richard Wojtowicz, editors, *Blacks Who Stole Themselves: Advertisements for Runaways in the* Pennsylvania Gazette, *1728–1790* (Philadelphia: University of Pennsylvania Press, 1989). For the southern colonies, see Lathan A. Windley, editor, *Runaway Slave Advertisements: A Documentary History from the 1730s to 1790*, four volumes (Westport, Conn.: Greenwood, 1983). As their titles indicate, these collections focus on runaway advertisements for slaves, but *Blacks Who Stole Themselves* contains a small selection of runaway advertisements for servants.

Noteworthy studies of colonial slavery that make use of runaway advertisements include Gerald W. Mullin, *Flight and Rebellion: Slave Resistance in Eighteenth-Century Virginia* (New York: Oxford University Press, 1972), and Michael A. Gomez, *Exchanging Our Country Marks: The Transformation of African Identities in the Colonial and Antebellum South* (Chapel Hill: University of North Carolina Press, 1998). For a study of runaway advertisements that focuses on their production and significance as part of colonial print culture, see David Waldstreicher, "Reading the Runaways: Self-Fashioning, Print Culture, and Confidence in Slavery in the Eighteenth-Century Mid-Atlantic," *William and Mary Quarterly*, third series, 56 (April 1999): 243–72. Robert E. Desrochers Jr. examines the role newspaper advertisements played in the business of slavery in "Slave-for-Sale Advertisements and Slavery in Massachusetts, 1704–1781," *William and Mary Quarterly,* third series, 59 (July 2002): 623–64. For studies that focus on the experience of servants, see Sharon V. Salinger, *To Serve Well and Faithfully: Labor and Indentured Servants in Pennsylvania, 1682–1800* (Cambridge: Cambridge University Press, 1987), and Jonathan Prude, "To Look upon the 'Lower Sort': Runaway Ads and the Appearance of Unfree Laborers in America, 1750–1800," *Journal of American History* 78, no. 1 (1991): 124–59.

Sylvia Frey discusses the impact of runaways on the southern states during the American Revolution in *Water from the Rock: Black Resistance in a Revolutionary Age* (Princeton, N.J.: Princeton University Press, 1991). For studies that look at runaway advertisements from the American South in the nineteenth century, see Daniel Meaders, editor, *Advertisements for Runaway Slaves in Virginia, 1801–1820* (New York: Garland, 1997), and John Hope Franklin and Loren Schweninger, *Runaway Slaves: Rebels on the Plantation, 1790–1860* (New York: Oxford University Press, 1999).

CHAPTER 4

Germ Warfare on the Colonial Frontier

An Article from the Journal of American History

During the summer of 1763, the northern colonial frontier erupted in a paroxysm of violence known as Pontiac's War. Three years earlier, the British had conquered Canada and taken over forts surrendered by the French in the Great Lakes and Ohio Country. The Indians who lived in this region were not pleased with the manner in which the British newcomers conducted themselves. The commander in chief, General Jeffery Amherst, ordered his officers to stop giving presents of material goods to Indians who had traditionally received such gifts from the French. Amherst also severely curtailed the gunpowder and ammunition available to Indians who needed these supplies for hunting. In May 1763, Ottawa Indians led by the war chief Pontiac laid siege to Fort Detroit to protest the British presence there. A month later, Delawares, Shawnee, and Iroquois did the same to Fort Pitt at the headwaters of the Ohio River, where the British had built fortifications despite their promise to leave the area after they had dislodged the French.

As Fort Pitt endured its siege, Amherst corresponded with one of his subordinates about the possibility of using smallpox as a weapon against the Indians. Amherst wrote from his headquarters in New York City to Colonel Henry Bouquet, who was marching west from Philadelphia with an army to relieve Fort Pitt. In their letters, Amherst and Bouquet discussed the latest news from the Ohio Country, and with each succeeding exchange, their rhetoric in regard to the Indians grew more vicious, declaring (in Bouquet's words) their intention to "extirpate that Vermine from a Country they have forfeited."

In a postscript to a letter he sent to Bouquet on July 7, Amherst raised the possibility of using germ warfare against the Indians: "Could it not be contrived to Send the *Small Pox* among those Disaffected Tribes of Indians? We must, on this occasion, Use Every Stratagem in our power to Reduce them." Bouquet's reply came in a postscript to a letter he wrote on July 13, while still en route to Fort Pitt: "I will try to inocculate the Indians by means of Blankets that may fall in their hands, taking care however not to get the disease myself." An undated postscript found among Bouquet's papers appears to be Amherst's response to Bouquet's idea: "You will Do well to try to Innoculate the Indians by means of Blanketts, as well as to try Every other method that can serve to Extirpate this Execreble Race."

While Amherst and Bouquet were exchanging these letters, the civilians and soldiers inside Fort Pitt had already taken matters into their own hands. Six hundred people, practically the entire population of the new town of Pittsburgh, had sought refuge in the fort. Smallpox soon broke out among them, and the fort's commander, Captain Simeon Ecuyer, ordered a hospital built to quarantine the victims. On June 24, several weeks before Bouquet arrived with his force at Fort Pitt, a trader at the fort named William Trent recorded in his journal that a council had occurred between Ecuyer and two Delaware Indians. The Indians had asked for the customary diplomatic presents before leaving, and according to Trent, "we gave them two Blankets and an Handkerchief out of the Small Pox Hospital. I hope it will have the desired effect." In an account entry, Ecuyer approved reimbursing Trent for two blankets and two handkerchiefs "taken from people in the Hospital to Convey the Small-pox to the Indians."

Smallpox was a deadly disease feared by colonists and Indians alike in the eighteenth century. It spread quickly, especially among previously unexposed populations, and killed with frightening efficiency, as many as one-third of those infected. The most common method of dealing with smallpox was to quarantine its victims. Inoculation, a medical procedure in which a person was deliberately infected with the smallpox virus, was also used; if successful, it caused a milder form of the disease that resulted in lifelong immunity. However, people who were inoculated had to be quarantined during their treatment; otherwise, they could spread the disease among the general population. Despite such measures, the disease spread easily among neighboring populations. In April 1764, a former Indian captive named Gershom Hicks described for British officers at Fort Pitt smallpox cases he had witnessed among his captors in the Ohio Country the previous year. Whether this outbreak was related to Trent's infected blankets and handkerchiefs is impossible to tell, but it is evidence of smallpox's presence among the Indians who lived in that area.

Historians have been in general agreement about this reconstruction of what has become known as the Fort Pitt incident since the 1950s, but they continue to argue about what it means. Were Amherst and Bouquet aware that Trent and Ecuyer had given infected goods to their Delaware guests on June 24, or did they conduct their correspondence without any knowledge of this exchange? Did Bouquet act upon the ideas he had discussed with Amherst once he arrived at Fort Pitt in August 1763? Did the blankets and handkerchiefs that Trent retrieved from the hospital cause the smallpox cases observed by Hicks, or did the contagion come from another source? Was this an isolated incident, or was it symptomatic of a wider use of smallpox as a biological weapon?

Figure 4.1 An Anglo-Indian Council during Pontiac's War *The scene depicted here helps us visualize what happened at Fort Pitt in June 1763. Delaware Indians from the Ohio Country are delivering a speech to a group of British military officers. At such diplomatic councils, the Indians expected to receive presents of trade goods from their counterparts as material evidence of their generosity and good faith. After one such council during the siege of Fort Pitt, the post's commander gave blankets and handkerchiefs "out of the Small Pox Hospital" to the Indians.* Source: Library of Congress.

The Fort Pitt incident drives home an important point about how historians go about their work. Facts do not write history; historians do. And they don't just organize the facts; they interpret them. Historians will, and often do, come to different conclusions based on their interpretation of the same evidence. When you read a book or an article written by a historian, it is important to bear in mind this relationship between facts and interpretation. What evidence is the historian presenting to support the argument? Based on that evidence, does the historian's interpretation appear sound and reasonable or speculative and unwarranted? How should you weigh and compare contradictory interpretations? All history is an interpretation of the past, but not all interpretations are equally valid. When you encounter a historian's interpretation of the facts, what methods or standards will you apply to determine its worth?

Using the Source: Journal Articles

Within the historical profession, journals have long served the role of featuring the "breaking news" of the field, highlighting new scholarship, calling attention to new books, and providing a forum for current debates. Most of these journals are quarterlies, meaning that they are published four times a year. They typically feature two to three articles, book reviews, and sometimes roundtables in which historians offer opinions about a common topic. Articles in scholarly journals are the front lines of new historical interpretations, and a provocative article can often generate more excitement and controversy in the profession than a book, which takes much longer to reach its intended readership. If you want to jump into the middle of an argument between historians or to learn what the most recent scholarship has to say about a long-standing topic, reading an article in a history journal is a great place to start.

The article excerpted in this chapter first appeared in the *Journal of American History* in March 2000. Its author, Elizabeth A. Fenn, uses the Fort Pitt incident to explore the role that smallpox played in eighteenth-century warfare. Fenn's work is an excellent example of how a historian uses a journal article to push the analysis of a controversial topic forward, not by settling it once and for all, but by asking new questions and taking new approaches to old sources.

Fenn's article also illustrates the features that make a journal article a "secondary source." "Primary sources" are the raw materials historians use to interpret the past. Any source providing firsthand information about the topic you are studying is a primary source (you have already encountered some of these in the form of woodcuts and engravings, captivity narratives, and runaway advertisements). "Secondary sources" are the result of a historian's interpretation of those primary materials, and they are most commonly found in the form of books and journal articles. Several components make up a successful journal article: it has an introduction that presents a research question and thesis, a body that advances a persuasive argument based on the evidence at hand, footnotes that document that evidence, and a conclusion that summarizes the argument and describes its broader significance.

A journal article offers an excellent model for writing about history, and students can improve their own writing by paying close attention to how historians organize and present their arguments in such articles. For example, the introduction to any piece of persuasive writing must complete certain tasks. It must acquaint the reader with the topic at hand and provide necessary background information, articulate the author's research question, and present the thesis, a brief statement of the argument the author intends to prove. The following introduction from Fenn's article is only two paragraphs long, yet it manages to accomplish all of these jobs, making it a model of concise historical prose.

The opening paragraph introduces the topic, supplies background information, and summarizes the debate over the Fort Pitt incident

Did he or didn't he? For generations, the Amherst–smallpox blanket episode has elicited animated debate both within and beyond academic circles. In books, journals, and now in Internet discussion groups, historians, folklorists, and lay people have argued the nuances of the case. Some have contended that at Gen. Jeffery Amherst's orders, British subordinates at Fort Pitt in 1763 did indeed infect local Indians with items taken from a nearby smallpox hospital. Others have argued that they did not, that the British lacked the knowledge, the ability, or the desire to do so. Still others have claimed that regardless of intent, the timing is wrong, that the Indians around Fort Pitt came down with smallpox well before the damning exchange of letters between Jeffery Amherst and his subordinate Henry Bouquet, and that in fact they were sick even before they received "two Blankets and an Handkerchief" out of the post's smallpox hospital. Finally, and perhaps predictably, a recent article has focused on the incident's genesis as a highly mutable cross-cultural legend that reflects deep anxieties about encounters with the "other."[1]

The author defines the purpose of this article in part by stating explicitly what the article is *not* about

What is this article's research question and thesis?

What follows is not an attempt to condemn or exonerate Jeffery Amherst. The man's documentary record speaks loudly enough regarding his character, if not regarding his ultimate culpability for the smallpox that struck Indians near Fort Pitt in 1763 and 1764. Nor is this essay an exhaustive accounting of all the accusations and incidents of biological warfare in late-eighteenth-century North America. It is, however, an attempt to broaden the debate and to place it in context. Our preoccupation with Amherst has kept us from recognizing that accusations of what we now call biological warfare—the military use of smallpox in particular—arose frequently in eighteenth-century America. Native Americans, moreover, were not the only accusers. By the second half of the century, many of the combatants in America's wars of empire had the knowledge and technology to attempt biological warfare with the smallpox virus. Many also adhered to a code of ethics that did not constrain them from doing so. Seen in this light, the Amherst affair becomes not so much an aberration as part of a larger continuum in which accusations and discussions of biological warfare were common, and actual incidents may have occurred more frequently than scholars have previously acknowledged.

What is this article's research question and thesis?

[1] William Trent, "William Trent's Journal at Fort Pitt, 1763," ed. A. T. Volwiler, *Mississippi Valley Historical Review,* 11 (Dec. 1924), 400. For an excellent appraisal of the Fort Pitt episode that places it in the context of the larger and more complicated struggle for control of the Ohio Valley, see Michael N. McConnell, *A Country Between: The Upper Ohio Valley and Its Peoples, 1724–1774* (Lincoln, 1992), 194–96. For an example of an Internet discussion devoted to biological warfare and smallpox, see the H-OIEAHC discussion log for April 1995, available at http://www.h-net.msu.edu/logs/. For the contention that the attempt at biological warfare was "unquestionably effective at Fort Pitt," see Francis Jennings, *Empire of Fortune: Crowns, Colonies, & Tribes in the Seven Years War in America* (New York, 1990), 447–48, 447n26. On the issue of timing, see Bernhard Knollenberg, "General Amherst and Germ Warfare," *Mississippi Valley Historical Review,* 41 (Dec. 1954), 489–94; Bernhard Knollenberg to editor, "Communications," *Mississippi Valley Historical Review,* 41 (March 1955), 762; and Donald H. Kent, to editor, *ibid.,* 762–63. For a cross-cultural analysis of the incident's place in a pantheon of other such "legends," see Adrienne Mayor, "The Nessus Shirt in the New World: Smallpox Blankets in History and Legend," *Journal of American Folklore,* 108 (Winter 1995), 54–77.

Practically every journal article has one key footnote in the opening pages that demonstrates the author's familiarity with the existing scholarship on the topic

What Can Journal Articles Tell Us?

The rise of Internet listservs, discussion boards, and Web sites devoted to historical topics has made the four-times-a-year publication schedule of most history journals seem slow and antiquated. In our fast-paced society, it may seem strange that historians rely on journals as a method of engaging one another in conversation about the latest research in their fields. But the scholarly journal persists because it has important advantages over other forms of organizing and publishing historical scholarship.

First and most important, scholarly journals are peer-reviewed, which means that articles published by historians in scholarly journals undergo a rigorous editing process. The author of the piece and the reviewers who decide if it merits publication remain anonymous to each other to ensure that all articles published in the journal are evaluated by experts in the field, working as freely as possible from the prejudices and biases that might result if they knew the author's identity. While no review process is foolproof, this method does allow readers of a scholarly journal to assume that any article published in that journal has met professional standards about research, documentation, and writing. This assurance stands in stark contrast to the Internet, where anyone with the technical ability to build a Web site can do so, fill it with whatever content he or she chooses, and label it "history."

A second advantage to working with scholarly articles is that they are concise. Generally, an article published in a history journal will run from 20 to 30 pages. Books written by historians, on the other hand, might run anywhere from 150 to 1,000 pages. Historians write articles and books to accomplish different things: an article is brief and to the point, focused on illuminating a particular question or topic; a book allows room for developing a narrative or synthesizing material with far greater chronological breadth or analytical depth. A good researcher will recognize the merits of each format and use articles and books accordingly. Scholarly articles, because of their brevity and focus, can be especially helpful to you in the early stages of your research, when you are casting your net for potential sources widely and trying to decide what to keep and what to throw back.

This point brings us to the third advantage of using journal articles in your research: their documentation can lead you to the sources you will want to look at next. The quality of documentation on a Web site claiming to contain historical scholarship can vary widely, depending on the creator of the site. All scholarly journals, on the other hand, insist that their authors document their work. The footnotes that accompany a journal article offer you a road map to other sources that might be helpful in your own research. Part of the architecture of any article in a history journal is a review of the relevant scholarship that has preceded it. Within the first few footnotes of an article, its author will identify the most significant previous articles or books on the topic and then situate his or her work in relation to it. Professional historians are avid footnote readers: they are always interested in seeing what new sources the author has identified or what previous interpretations the author is trying to refine or discredit. If you take the time to pay attention to an article's documentation, you will identify the interpretive issues that occupy historians on any given topic more quickly.

The chief disadvantage to working with a journal article or any other secondary source is that someone else is interpreting the facts for you. In one sense, the author has done the reader a service by identifying, collecting, and reading the relevant materials—no small task, even for a thirty-page article—and synthesizing them into a persuasive argument. However, the author has done that in response to his or her own research question; you in all likelihood have a different one.

One other disadvantage of working with journal articles is that they often assume that the reader is already familiar with the topic at hand. Historians publish articles in scholarly journals to engage in conversation with one another, not a popular audience with only a passing interest in history. The authors of journal articles will assume that their readers bring some prior knowledge to the topic and are ready to plunge into finer points of interpretation and analysis. If you find yourself reading an article that has not provided you with enough background information, you may want to read up on the topic first in a textbook, encyclopedia, or other reference work.

Questions to Ask

As mentioned earlier, journal articles tend to share a similar architecture. The author introduces the argument by identifying a research question and thesis and then follows with evidence and documentation in support of that argument.

The conclusion restates the argument, this time as proven fact rather than proposition (think of a lawyer's summation to the jury), and explains its significance in some greater historical context or debate. As you read an article, you should ask questions relevant to each stage of the argument's development.

- What is the research question and thesis?
- What types of evidence is the author presenting?
- Is that evidence appropriately documented?
- Are there weaknesses or flaws in the argument?
- What is the wider significance of the author's conclusion?

Source Analysis Table

Oftentimes, an article's argument and evidence are subdivided into sections marked by subtitles or headings. The following table will help you identify the major points and evidence used in each section of Elizabeth Fenn's article. First, write down the research question and thesis. Then, in the left column note the main point of each section, followed by the evidence used to support it in the middle column, and any comments or questions you have about that evidence in the right column.

72

Introduction
(pp. 73–74)

Research Question:

Thesis:

Section	Evidence Used to Support It	Comments or Questions on the Use of That Evidence
Fort Pitt, 1763 (pp. 74–77) *Main Point:*		
Other Accusations and Incidents (pp. 77–83) *Main Point:*		
Biological Weapons and the Ethics of War (pp. 84–87) *Main Point:*		

To download and print this table, visit the book companion site at **bedfordstmartins.com/brownshannon**.

The Source: An Article from the *Journal of American History,* March 2000

Biological Warfare in Eighteenth-Century North America: Beyond Jeffery Amherst

ELIZABETH A. FENN

Did he or didn't he? For generations, the Amherst–smallpox blanket episode has elicited animated debate both within and beyond academic circles. In books, journals, and now in Internet discussion groups, historians, folklorists, and lay people have argued the nuances of the case. Some have contended that at Gen. Jeffery Amherst's orders, British subordinates at Fort Pitt in 1763 did indeed infect local Indians with items taken from a nearby smallpox hospital. Others have argued that they did not, that the British lacked the knowledge, the ability, or the desire to do so. Still others have claimed that regardless of intent, the timing is wrong, that the Indians around Fort Pitt came down with smallpox well before the damning exchange of letters between Jeffery Amherst and his subordinate Henry Bouquet, and that in fact they were sick even before they received "two Blankets and an Handkerchief" out of the post's smallpox hospital. Finally, and perhaps predictably, a recent article has focused on the incident's genesis as a highly mutable cross-cultural legend that reflects deep anxieties about encounters with the "other."[1]

What follows is not an attempt to condemn or exonerate Jeffery Amherst. The man's documentary record speaks loudly enough regarding his character, if

[1] William Trent, "William Trent's Journal at Fort Pitt, 1763," ed. A. T. Volwiler, *Mississippi Valley Historical Review,* 11 (Dec. 1924), 400. For an excellent appraisal of the Fort Pitt episode that places it in the context of the larger and more complicated struggle for control of the Ohio Valley, see Michael N. McConnell, *A Country Between: The Upper Ohio Valley and Its Peoples, 1724–1774* (Lincoln, 1992), 194–96. For an example of an Internet discussion devoted to biological warfare and smallpox, see the H-OIEAHC discussion log for April 1995, available at http://www.h-net.msu.edu/logs/. For the contention that the attempt at biological warfare was "unquestionably effective at Fort Pitt," see Francis Jennings, *Empire of Fortune: Crowns, Colonies, & Tribes in the Seven Years War in America* (New York, 1990), 447–48, 447n26. On the issue of timing, see Bernhard Knollenberg, "General Amherst and Germ Warfare," *Mississippi Valley Historical Review,* 41 (Dec. 1954), 489–94; Bernhard Knollenberg to editor, "Communications," *Mississippi Valley Historical Review,* 41 (March 1955), 762; and Donald H. Kent, to editor, *ibid.,* 762–63. For a cross-cultural analysis of the incident's place in a pantheon of other such "legends," see Adrienne Mayor, "The Nessus Shirt in the New World: Smallpox Blankets in History and Legend," *Journal of American Folklore,* 108 (Winter 1995), 54–77.

Source: Elizabeth A. Fenn, "Biological Warfare in Eighteenth-Century North America: Beyond Jeffery Amherst," *Journal of American History* 86, no. 4 (March 2000): 1552–80. (To save space, some text and footnotes have been edited.)

not regarding his ultimate culpability for the smallpox that struck Indians near Fort Pitt in 1763 and 1764. Nor is this essay an exhaustive accounting of all the accusations and incidents of biological warfare in late-eighteenth-century North America. It is, however, an attempt to broaden the debate and to place it in context.[2] Our preoccupation with Amherst has kept us from recognizing that accusations of what we now call biological warfare—the military use of smallpox in particular—arose frequently in eighteenth-century America. Native Americans, moreover, were not the only accusers. By the second half of the century, many of the combatants in America's wars of empire had the knowledge and technology to attempt biological warfare with the smallpox virus. Many also adhered to a code of ethics that did not constrain them from doing so. Seen in this light, the Amherst affair becomes not so much an aberration as part of a larger continuum in which accusations and discussions of biological warfare were common, and actual incidents may have occurred more frequently than scholars have previously acknowledged.

Fort Pitt, 1763

The most famous "smallpox blanket" incident in American history took place in the midst of Pontiac's Rebellion in 1763. In May and June of that year, a loose confederation of tribes inspired by the Ottawa war leader Pontiac launched attacks on British-held posts throughout the Great Lakes and Midwest. On May 29, 1763, they began a siege of Fort Pitt, located in western Pennsylvania at the confluence of the Allegheny and Monongahela rivers. The officer in charge at Fort Pitt was the Swiss-born captain Simeon Ecuyer. On June 16, 1763, Ecuyer reported to Col. Henry Bouquet at Philadelphia that the frontier outpost's situation had taken a turn for the worse. Local Indians had escalated the hostilities, burning nearby houses and attempting to lure Ecuyer into an engagement beyond the walls of the well-protected post, where traders and colonists, interlopers on Indian lands, had taken refuge. "We are so crowded in the fort that I fear disease," wrote Ecuyer, "for in spite of all my care I cannot keep the place as clean as I should like; moreover, the small pox is among us. For this reason I have had a hospital built under the bridge beyond musket-fire." Henry Bouquet, in a letter dated June 23, passed the news on to Jeffery Amherst, the British commander in chief, at New York. "Fort Pitt is in good State of Defence against all attempts from Savages," Bouquet reported, but "Unluckily the small Pox has broken out in the Garrison."[3] By June 16, then,

---

[2] A thorough appraisal of the use of biological warfare in the prescientific era can be found in Mark Wheelis, "Biological Warfare before 1914," in *Biological and Toxin Weapons: Research, Development, and Use from the Middle Ages to 1945*, ed. Erhard Geissler and John van Courtland Moon (Oxford, 1999), 8–34.

[3] For a summary of the documentation of this incident, see Knollenberg, "General Amherst and Germ Warfare," 489–94; and Kent to editor, "Communications," 762–63. While my conclusions differ from Knollenberg's, much of the evidence consulted is the same. Simeon Ecuyer to Henry Bouquet, June 16, 1763 [translation], in *The Papers of Col. Henry Bouquet*, ed. Sylvester K. Stevens and Donald H. Kent (30 series, Harrisburg, 1940–1943), series 21649, part 1, p. 153. . . . Bouquet to Jeffery Amherst, June 23, 1763, *ibid.*, ser. 21634, p. 196.

from sources unknown, smallpox had established itself at Fort Pitt. It is likely that Amherst knew of the situation by the end of June.

But it was not Amherst, apparently, who first proposed the use of smallpox against the Delaware, Shawnee, and Mingo Indians surrounding Fort Pitt. Nor was it Amherst who executed the scheme. While the actual provenance of the plan remains unclear, a brief description of the deed itself appears in the diary of William Trent, a trader and land speculator with ties to the more prominent George Croghan. On June 23, the very day that Bouquet penned his letter to Amherst from Philadelphia, Trent reported that two Delaware dignitaries, Turtle's Heart and Mamaltee, visited Fort Pitt late at night and asked to speak with post officials. A conference took place the following day, June 24, in which the Indians urged the British to abandon the fort, and the British, for their part, refused. The parleys came to a close, and the Indians asked for "a little Provisions and Liquor, to carry us Home." The British obliged their request. "Out of our regard to them," wrote William Trent, "we gave them two Blankets and an Handkerchief out of the Small Pox Hospital. I hope it will have the desired effect."[4] He does not mention who conceived the plan, and he likewise does not mention who carried it out, but Fort Pitt account books make it clear that the British military both sanctioned and paid for the deed. The records for June 1763 include this invoice submitted by Levy, Trent and Company:

> To Sundries got to Replace in kind those which were taken from people in the Hospital to Convey the Smallpox to the Indians Viz:
>
> | 2 Blankets | @20/ | £2" | 0" | 0 |
> | 1 Silk Handkerchef | 10/ | | | |
> | & 1 linnen do: | 3/6 | 0" | 13" | 6 |

Captain Ecuyer certified that the items "were had for the uses above mentioned," and Gen. Thomas Gage ultimately approved the invoice for payment, endorsing it with a comment and his signature.[5]

Had Jeffery Amherst known of these actions, he certainly would have approved. From the safety of his New York headquarters, he laid forth his own strategy for biological warfare in early July, prompted no doubt by Bouquet's letter of June 23 informing him that smallpox had broken out at the Monongahela post. In an undated memorandum that is apparently a postscript to a letter of July 7, 1763, Amherst proposed the following to Bouquet: "Could it not be contrived to Send the *Small Pox* among those Disaffected Tribes of Indians? We must, on this occasion, Use Every Stratagem in our power to Reduce them." Bouquet, now at Carlisle en route to Fort Pitt with reinforcements,

---

[4] . . . Trent, "William Trent's Journal at Fort Pitt," ed. Volwiler, 400.

[5] Levy, Trent and Company: Account against the Crown, Aug. 13, 1763, in *Papers of Col. Henry Bouquet,* ed. Stevens and Kent, ser. 21654, pp. 218–19. While the account was submitted for payment in August, the items in it are all listed under the date "1763 June." As Mark Wheelis has pointed out, readers should note that William Trent refers to a single handkerchief in his journal, while the invoice is for two: one silk, one linen. Wheelis, "Biological Warfare before 1914," 23n73.

replied on July 13, also in postscript: "I will try to inocculate the Indians by means of Blankets that may fall in their hands, taking care however not to get the disease myself." To this Amherst responded approvingly on July 16. "You will Do well to try to Innoculate the Indians by means of Blanketts, as well as to try Every other method that can serve to Extirpate this Execreble Race."[6] Unbeknownst to both Bouquet and his commander in chief, their subordinates at Fort Pitt had already conceived and executed the very plan proposed. If the garrison at Fort Pitt perpetrated a second, later act of biological warfare at Amherst's behest, the documents currently available make no mention of it.

What the documents do show, however, is that smallpox struck hard among the Indians around Fort Pitt in the spring and summer of 1763. On April 14, 1764, a man named Gershom Hicks arrived at the British post, having escaped from the Shawnee and Delaware Indians who had held him captive since May 1763. In a deposition taken the day of his arrival, Hicks reported "that the Small pox has been very general & raging amongst the Indians since last spring and that 30 or 40 Mingoes, as many Delawares and some Shawneese Died all of the Small pox since that time, that it still continues amongst them." Five months later, in September 1764, the epidemic continued to wreak havoc among the Shawnees. "Yᵉ poor Rascals are Dieing very fast with yᵉ small pox," reported Col. Andrew Lewis from Virginia's Blue Ridge Mountains; "they can make but Lettle Resistance and when Routed must parish in great Numbers by yᵉ Disordere." . . . As the historian Michael McConnell has pointed out, it is possible and perhaps likely that the epidemic stemmed from multiple sources of infection. John M'Cullough, a fifteen-year-old captive among the Indians, reported that the disease took hold after an attack on some settlers sick with the smallpox along central Pennsylvania's Juniata River. The timing, however, is uncanny: the eruption of epidemic smallpox in the Ohio country coincided closely with the distribution of infected articles by individuals at Fort Pitt.[7]

[6] Memorandum by Sir Jeffery Amherst, [July 7, 1763], in *Papers of Col. Henry Bouquet,* ed. Stevens and Kent, ser. 21634, p. 161. . . . Bouquet to Amherst, Aug. 11, 1763, *ibid.,* 243; Bouquet to Amherst, July 13, 1763, in Jeffery Amherst, *Official Papers, 1740–1783* (microfilm, 202 reels, World Microfilms Publications, 1979), reel 32, frame 305. The published typescript of this last document deviates in important ways from the original. See Bouquet to Amherst, July 13, 1763, in *Papers of Col. Henry Bouquet,* ed. Stevens and Kent, ser. 21634, p. 214. For the July 16 letter, see Amherst to Bouquet, July 16, 1763, in Amherst, *Official Papers,* reel 33, frame 114. . . . See Memorandum by Sir Jeffery Amherst, [July 16, 1763], in *Papers of Col. Henry Bouquet,* ed. Stevens and Kent, ser. 21634, p. 161. . . .

[7] Deposition of Gershom Hicks, April 14, 1764, in *Papers of Col. Henry Bouquet,* ed. Stevens and Kent, ser. 21650, part 1, p. 102. Five days later, under pressure from Fort Pitt officials, Hicks recanted much of his testimony and de-emphasized the Indians' martial intentions. He apparently made no reference to smallpox in his second deposition. William Grant, Re-Examination of Gershom Hicks, in *Papers of Col. Henry Bouquet,* ed. Stevens and Kent, ser. 21651, pp. 7–10. . . . On the Virginia Indians, see Andrew Lewis to Bouquet, Sept. 10, 1764, in *Papers of Col. Henry Bouquet,* ed. Stevens and Kent, ser. 21650, part 2, p. 127. . . . On the possibility of multiple sources of infection, see McConnell, *Country Between,* 195–96. M'Cullough's report is in Archibald Loudon, ed., *A Selection, of Some of the Most Interesting Narratives, of Outrages, Committed by the Indians, in Their Wars, with the White People* (1808; 2 vols., New York, 1977), I, 331. . . .

While blame for this outbreak cannot be placed squarely in the British camp, the circumstantial evidence is nevertheless suggestive.

Usually treated as an isolated anomaly, the Fort Pitt episode itself points to the possibility that biological warfare was not as rare as it might seem. It is conceivable, of course, that when Fort Pitt personnel gave infected articles to their Delaware visitors on June 24, 1763, they acted on some earlier communication from Amherst that does not survive today.[8] The sequence of events, however, makes it more likely that Amherst and Fort Pitt authorities conceived of the idea independently. In each case, the availability of contagious material (thanks to the smallpox epidemic at the post itself) seems to have triggered the plan of infection. Ecuyer reported the outbreak at Fort Pitt on June 16, and the attempt to communicate the disease took place eight days later. Amherst learned of the outbreak in Bouquet's letter of June 23, and the commander in chief proposed his own scheme on July 7. The fact that a single wartime outbreak could prompt two independent plans of contagion suggests that the Fort Pitt incident may not have been an anomaly. Evidence from other fields of battle indicates that in the minds of many, smallpox had an established, if irregular, place in late-eighteenth-century warfare. . . .

Other Accusations and Incidents

Eighteenth-century biological warfare is at best a slippery topic of inquiry. (The term "biological warfare" is itself anachronistic, but it remains well suited for describing what eighteenth-century Americans clearly viewed as a distinctive category of acts and allegations.) The long-standing debate over the Fort Pitt episode — easily the best-documented incident in the period — reveals how very treacherous the historical landscape can be. Even contemporaries could rarely prove culpability beyond refute in a suspicious outbreak of disease; for historians, the task is next to impossible. Accidents happened, and unintentional contagion was common, particularly in wartime. Moreover, in those rare cases where malicious intent was evident, as at Fort Pitt in 1763, the actual effectiveness of an attempt to spread smallpox remains impossible to ascertain: the possibility always exists that infection occurred by some "natural" route.

While all of this complicates the historian's task, it may nevertheless have enhanced smallpox's appeal as a weapon. For unlike rape, pillage, and other atrocities in which the intent and identity of the perpetrator could be made clear, the propagation of smallpox had the advantage of deniability. In the honor-bound world in which eighteenth-century military officials lived, this may well have been biological warfare's greatest attribute. It is possible, given the dearth of ironclad evidence, that biological warfare did not occur beyond the Fort Pitt incident. But another perspective also seems warranted, particularly when smallpox's deniability is taken into account: the shortage of conclusive documentation may simply indicate that perpetrators did not record their deeds.

---

[8] Such a communication might have been either written or oral in form. It is also possible that documents relating to such a plan were deliberately destroyed.

The surviving evidence is rife with ambiguity. Some accusations served propaganda purposes in situations of social or military stress. Others come from oral traditions, at times recorded long after the alleged incidents took place. Many allegations are unsubstantiated, and some are weakly substantiated at best. Nevertheless, the sheer weight of the evidence that follows points to the distinct possibility that eighteenth-century biological warfare was more common than historians have previously believed.

It may well have been Indians, not whites, who used the strategy first. In his voluminous *History and Description of New France,* Pierre-François-Xavier de Charlevoix recounts an Iroquois act of biological sabotage against the English during Queen Anne's War in the early 1700s. The English army, Charlevoix writes, "was encamped on the banks of a little river; the Iroquois, who spent almost all the time hunting, threw into it, just above the camp, all the skins of the animals they flayed, and the water was thus soon all corrupted." The army, Charlevoix continued, suspected nothing. Soldiers "continued to drink this water, and it carried off so many, that Father de Mareuil, and two officers . . . observing the graves where the dead were buried, estimated the number at over a thousand." This account is remarkable not only because it seems to be the only eighteenth-century American incident that did not involve smallpox but also because the perpetrators were Indians. In this regard, the fact that smallpox was *not* the weapon of choice is hardly surprising. Already decimated by repeated epidemics, American Indians everywhere more likely viewed smallpox as a enemy in its own right than as a weapon that might bring down their adversaries.[9] The years that followed would show how true this was.

Amherst aside, smallpox seemed to be everywhere during the Seven Years' War. D. Peter MacLeod has demonstrated elegantly how Indian participation in the conflict with the British waxed and waned according to their simultaneous struggle against smallpox. In 1755–1756 and again in 1757–1758, the disease wreaked havoc among the Indians allied with the French. After the Lake George campaign of 1757, the French-allied Potawatomis suffered greatly in a smallpox outbreak that they believed stemmed from deliberate infection by the British. In July 1767, the British Indian superintendent William Johnson interviewed a man named Cornelius Van Slyke, held prisoner among the Chippewas and the Potawatomis for four years. Van Slyke told Johnson the Potawatomis believed "that the great Number they lost of their People at & returning from Lake George in 1757, was owing to yᵉ. English poisoning the Rum, & giving them the Small Pox, for which they owe them an everlasting ill will." The innuendo here is that the infection was willful, and it is possible that biological warfare occurred. But it is far more likely that the source of the contagion that ravaged the

---

[9] Even the Aztecs may have tried to utilize such a strategy during the Spanish conquest from 1519 to 1521. Motecuhzoma reportedly asked his magicians to work "some charm" against the Spaniards that might "cause them to break out in sores" or even "cause them to fall sick, or die, or return to their own land." Ironically, it was the Aztecs, not the Spaniards, who succumbed en masse to smallpox. Miguel-Leon Portilla, ed., *The Broken Spears: The Aztec Account of the Conquest of Mexico* (Boston, 1966), 34. On Queen Anne's War, see Pierre-François-Xavier de Charlevoix, *History and General Description of New France,* ed. and trans. John Dawson Gilmary Shea (6 vols., New York, 1900), V, 221–22. . . .

Potawatomis was the famous attack (fictionalized in James Fenimore Cooper's *Last of the Mohicans,* 1826) on unarmed prisoners leaving Fort William Henry on August 10, 1757.[10] Many of those prisoners were sick with smallpox.

By the nineteenth century, intentional smallpox infection turned up regularly in Native American oral histories. The Ottawa Indians suffered from smallpox after the 1757 campaign, and their tradition held that the disease came from Montreal, ironically in the possession of the Indians' French allies at the time of the outbreak. "This smallpox," according to Andrew Blackbird's account, "was sold to them shut up in a showy tin box, with the strict injunction not to open the box on their way homeward." When they arrived at their village on the shores of Lake Michigan, the Indians opened the box only to find another box and then another inside. In the end, Blackbird says, the Ottawas "found nothing but mouldy particles in this last little box." Many inspected it, and shortly thereafter, smallpox broke out. According to the story, an enormous Ottawa village, extending for miles west of Mackinac, "was entirely depopulated and laid waste." It is unlikely that the French would have knowingly passed smallpox on to their Indian supporters at this crucial juncture in the Seven Years' War. But the accusation may well reflect a Native American perception that since they had caught the disease while fighting for the French, the French were therefore responsible for the devastation it caused. Eager to retain and appease their Indian allies, French officials laid the blame for the epidemic in the British camp.[11] If further documentation for this alleged incident exists, it remains undiscovered. Nor is it clear how, if at all, this tradition might be linked to the Fort Pitt episode six years later. . . .

The next great conflict to shake the continent was the Revolutionary War. Once again, smallpox erupted repeatedly, and once again, those on the receiving end believed that the outbreaks were not all accidental. Allegations of biological warfare arose in the course of confrontations at Quebec, Boston, and Yorktown, as well as during the mobilization of the Earl of Dunmore's Ethiopian Regiment on the Chesapeake. At Boston, charges of deliberate smallpox propagation by the British cropped up even before the outbreak of hostilities at Lexington and Concord. "The [British] soldiers try all they can to spread the *small-pox,*" wrote an unnamed Bostonian in January 1775. "One of their Officers inoculated his whole family without letting any person know it, — there was a man, his wife, and seven children, under the same roof, and not one of them ever had it." When the American siege of Boston began in April, the disease

---

[10] D. Peter MacLeod, "Microbes and Muskets: Smallpox and the Participation of the Amerindian Allies of New France in the Seven Years' War," *Ethnohistory,* 39 (Winter 1992), 42–64. On the epidemic among the Potawatomis, see *ibid.,* 49; R. David Edmunds, *The Potawatomis: Keepers of the Fire* (Norman, 1978), 55–56; and James A. Clifton, *The Prairie People: Continuity and Change in Potawatomi Indian Culture, 1665–1965* (Lawrence, 1977), 102. . . . For a valuable appraisal of the Fort William Henry affair, see Ian K. Steele, *Betrayals: Fort William Henry & the "Massacre"* (New York, 1990).

[11] Andrew J. Blackbird, *Complete Both Early and Late History of the Ottawa and Chippewa Indians of Michigan, a Grammar of Their Language, Personal and Family History of the Author* (Harbor Springs, Mich., 1897), 2–3. . . . On the French blaming the British, see MacLeod, "Microbes and Muskets," 50–51.

became epidemic among British soldiers and other residents of the city. "The small pox rages all over the Town," wrote George Washington from his headquarters in nearby Cambridge on December 14. "Such of the [British] Military as had it not before, are now under innoculation—this I apprehend is a weapon of Defence, they Are useing against us."[12]

In fact, Washington already suspected that the British, in an effort to infect the vulnerable Continental Army, had inoculated some of the refugees leaving the city. On December 3, 1775, four deserters had arrived at the American headquarters "giving an account that several persons are to be sent out of *Boston,* this evening or to-morrow, that have been lately inoculated with the small-pox, with design, probably, to spread the infection, in order to distress us as much as possible." It was, according to Washington's aide-de-camp, an "unheard-of and diabolical scheme." Washington at first regarded the report with disbelief. "There is one part of the information that I Can hardly give Credit to," he wrote. "A Sailor Says that a number of these Comeing out have been inoculated, with design of Spreading the Smallpox through this Country & Camp."[13]

A week later, however, as the pox erupted among the refugees, the American commander in chief changed his mind. In a letter to John Hancock on December 11, 1775, he explained his reappraisal: "The information I received that the enemy intended Spreading the Small pox amongst us, I could not Suppose them Capable of—I now must give Some Credit to it, as it has made its appearance on Severall of those who Last Came out of Boston." The Americans controlled the outbreak through careful quarantine and disinfection of both refugees and their effects. In the aftermath, the *Boston Gazette* carried a sworn declaration from one refugee, a servant, saying that he had been inoculated and then, as the pustules broke out, ordered by his master to embark on a crowded vessel leaving the city. There he could not avoid communicating the infection to "A Number of said Passengers," as the boat's departure was delayed more than two weeks. According to another report, a Boston physician named Dr. Rand had admitted "that he had effectually given the distemper among those people" quitting the city.[14] . . .

[12] Extract of a letter from Boston, author unknown, *London Evening Post,* March 25–28, 1775, reprinted in Margaret W. Willard, ed., *Letters on the American Revolution, 1774–1776* (Boston, 1925), 57–58; George Washington to John Hancock, Dec. 14, 1775, in *The Papers of George Washington: Revolutionary War Series,* ed. W. W. Abbot and Dorothy Twohig (26 vols., Charlottesville, 1983–), II, 548.

[13] Robert H. Harrison to Council of Massachusetts, Dec. 3, 1775, in *American Archives,* ed. Peter Force, 4th ser. (6 vols., Washington, 1837–1853), IV, 168; Washington to Hancock, Dec. 4, 1775, in *Papers of George Washington: Revolutionary War Series,* ed. Abbot and Twohig, II, 486.

[14] Washington to Hancock, Dec. 11, 1775, in *Papers of George Washington: Revolutionary War Series,* ed. Abbot and Twohig, II, 533; Washington to Hancock, Nov. 28, 1775, *ibid.,* 447; Samuel Bixby, "Diary of Samuel Bixby," *Proceedings of the Massachusetts Historical Society,* 14 (March 1876), 297; Washington to James Otis Sr. [Mass. General Court], Dec. 10, 1775, in *Papers of George Washington: Revolutionary War Series,* ed. Abbot and Twohig, II, 526; John Morgan to Washington, Dec. 12, 1775, *ibid.,* 541–42; Washington to Joseph Reed, Dec. 15, 1775, *ibid.,* 553. On the servant refugee, see *Boston Gazette and Country Journal,* Feb. 12, 1776, p. 4. On Dr. Rand, see Ezekiel Price, "Diary of Ezekiel Price, 1775–1776," *Proceedings of the Massachusetts Historical Society,* 7 (Nov. 1863), 220.

Boston was not the only city besieged by American troops through the winter of 1775–1776. At Quebec another siege was underway, and here again, smallpox emerged as a major player in military affairs. While the American efforts to keep the Continental Army free of smallpox were generally successful at Boston, they failed dismally at Quebec. Here the disease erupted almost immediately upon the Americans' arrival outside the walled city in late November and early December of 1775. What followed was one of the great disasters in American military history. An American attempt on the city failed in a blizzard on the night of December 31, and the army settled in for a miserable, snowbound siege that lasted until the first week of May 1776, when British reinforcements arrived. Riddled with smallpox, the Americans retreated, first to the town of Sorel, where the Richelieu River joins the Saint Lawrence, and then, in midsummer, southward to Ticonderoga and Crown Point. . . .

Many accused the British general, Sir Guy Carleton, of willfully infecting the American camp during the wintry siege of the Canadian city. In the deathbed diary he dictated in 1811, the Pennsylvania rifleman John Joseph Henry recalled that smallpox had been "introduced into our cantonments by the indecorous, yet fascinating arts of the enemy." The Continental Congress held hearings on the debacle even as the Northern Army still suffered from smallpox at Ticonderoga. Thomas Jefferson's abbreviated notes of the testimony reveal that several of the witnesses believed the epidemic was no accident. Capt. Hector McNeal, for example, said "the small pox was sent out of Quebeck by Carleton, inoculating the poor people at government expence for the purpose of giving it to our army." Likewise, according to another witness, it "was said but no proof that Carleton had sent it into the suburbs of St. Roc where some of our men were quartered." The testimony of a Dr. Coates reiterated the theme: "Was supposed Carlton sent out people with it," Jefferson noted in his shorthand. Jefferson, for one, found the testimony credible. "I have been informed by officers who were on the spot, and whom I believe myself," he wrote to the French historian François Soulés, "that this disorder was sent into our army designedly by the commanding officer in Quebec. It answered his purposes effectually."[15]

Smallpox was present at Quebec when the American army arrived, and it seems probable, as they mingled with *habitants* outside the city, that the troops would have picked up the *Variola* virus regardless of any actions on Carleton's part. "The small pox is all around us, and there is great danger of its spreading in the army," wrote the soldier Caleb Haskell on December 6, 1775, shortly after the siege began. "We have long had that disorder in town," observed a British officer on December 9, as the disease made its first appearance among the Americans. Carleton's humane treatment of American smallpox victims

[15] John Joseph Henry, "Campaign against Quebec," in *March to Quebec: Journals of the Members of Arnold's Expedition,* ed. Kenneth Roberts (New York, 1940), 374–75; Thomas Jefferson, "Notes of Witnesses' Testimony concerning the Canadian Campaign, July 1–27, 1776," in *Papers of Thomas Jefferson,* ed. Boyd, I, 435, 437, 447–48; Thomas Jefferson, "Comments on Soulés' *Histoire,* August 8, 1786," *ibid.,* X, 373, 377n24. . . .

taken prisoner when the siege ended would seem to undermine the argument that he deliberately infected the American lines.[16] Nevertheless, it remains possible. By providing a ready supply of inoculees and other contagious patients, the ongoing presence of smallpox in Quebec might in fact have made deliberate infection easier to disguise.

Meanwhile, farther south, more accusations of willful contagion surfaced in Virginia, where some eight hundred African American refugees from slavery had rallied to the British cause in response to a promise of freedom from the colony's royal governor, John Murray, Earl of Dunmore. Written on November 7, 1775, and issued a week later, Dunmore's limited emancipation proclamation inspired African Americans and terrified the slaveholding revolutionaries who spearheaded the American revolt. By May 1776, however, smallpox had infested the governor's little band of freedom fighters in their precarious waterfront camp near Norfolk. Dunmore decided to move to a safe spot and inoculate his men. "His Lordship," according to a rumor in the *Virginia Gazette*, "before the departure of the fleet from Norfolk harbour, had two of those wretches inoculated and sent ashore, in order to spread the infection, but it was happily prevented."[17]

In the end, it was Dunmore's black regiment that suffered most from the disease, dwindling under its impact to 150 effective men and eventually withdrawing from Virginia entirely. "Had it not been for this horrid disorder," wrote Dunmore, "I should have had two thousand blacks; with whom I should have had no doubt of penetrating into the heart of this Colony." When the American rebels questioned one eyewitness to the ravages of smallpox and to Dunmore's final withdrawal, they broached the topic of biological warfare directly: "How long were they inocul[ated] & was it done to communicate it to the People on shore[?]" asked the interrogators. "By no means," was the vague response, "every one in the Fleet was inoculated, that had it not."[18] . . .

---

[16] Caleb Haskell, "Diary at the Siege of Boston and on the March to Quebec," in *March to Quebec*, ed. Roberts, 482–83. . . . When the Americans fled on May 6, 1776, many of the sick were left behind on the Plains of Abraham. Noting "that many of his Majesty's deluded subjects of the neighbouring provinces, labouring under wounds and diverse disorders," were "in great danger of perishing for want of proper assistance," Carleton ordered his men "to make diligent search for all such distressed persons, and afford them all necessary relief, and convey them to the general hospital, where proper care shall be taken of them." Carleton's orders are reprinted in Andrew Parke, *An Authentic Narrative of Facts Relating to the Exchange of Prisoners Taken at the Cedars* (London, 1777), 4–5.

[17] The best account of Dunmore's Ethiopian Regiment remains Benjamin Quarles, *The Negro in the American Revolution* (Chapel Hill, 1961), 19–32. The accusation can be found in Dixon and Hunter's *Virginia Gazette*, June 15, 1776, quoted in *Naval Documents of the American Revolution*, ed. William Bell Clark, William James Morgan, and Michael J. Crawford (10 vols., Washington, D.C., 1964–1996), V, 554. . . .

[18] John Murray, Earl of Dunmore, to the Secretary of State, June 26,1776, in George W. Williams, *History of the Negro Race in America from 1619–1800* (New York, 1885), 342, quoted in Gerald W. Mullin, *Flight and Rebellion: Slave Resistance in Eighteenth-Century Virginia* (New York, 1972), 132; "[James] Cunningham's Examination 18th July 1776," in *Naval Documents of the American Revolution*, ed. Clark, Morgan, and Crawford, V, 1136. . . .

Additional accusations surfaced in 1781, as Gen. Charles Cornwallis's southern campaign came to a close. The British retreat to Yorktown in many ways echoed Lord Dunmore's Virginia campaign five years earlier. Again, African American slaves flocked to British lines seeking freedom from their revolutionary masters. And again smallpox cut them down, for African Americans, like all other Americans, were far more likely to be susceptible to the disease than were troops from Europe.[19]

As early as June 1781, American soldiers in Virginia suspected Cornwallis's army of using smallpox-infected blacks to propagate disease. "Here I must take notice of some vilany," wrote Josiah Atkins as his regiment pursued the British near Richmond. "Within these days past, I have marched by 18 or 20 Negroes that lay dead by the way-side, putrifying with the small pox." Cornwallis, Atkins believed, had "inoculated 4 or 500 in order to spread smallpox thro' the country, & sent them out for that purpose." A Pennsylvania soldier, William Feltman, found a "negro man with the small-pox lying on the road side" on June 25, supposedly left by a British cavalry unit "in order to prevent the Virginia militia from pursuing them." By October, with surrender looming on the horizon, Cornwallis had become desperate. "The British," noted James Thacher in his diary, "have sent from Yorktown a large number of negroes, sick with the small pox, probably for the purpose of communicating the infection to our army." Writing three days after the capitulation, Robert Livingston hoped that reports of such conduct would sway Europeans to the American side. "In Virginia," he wrote, "they took the greatest pains to communicate the Small Pox to the Country; by exposing the dead bodies of those who had died with it, in the most frequented places." Benjamin Franklin later reiterated the charge in his "Retort Courteous."[20]

It may be tempting to dismiss such accusations as so much American hyperbole. But evidence indicates that in fact the British did exactly what the Americans charged. At Portsmouth, Virginia, in July 1781, Gen. Alexander Leslie outlined his plan for biological warfare in a letter to Cornwallis. "Above 700 Negroes are come down the River in the Small Pox," he wrote. "I shall distribute them about the Rebell Plantations." Even if they pardoned their actions by saying they could no longer support so many camp followers, the fact that sick African Americans might communicate smallpox to the enemy could not have been lost on British commanders.[21]

---

[19] . . . S. R. Duncan, Susan Scott, and C. J. Duncan, "The Dynamics of Smallpox Epidemics in Britain, 1550–1800," *Demography,* 30 (Aug. 1993), 405–23.

[20] Josiah Atkins, *The Diary of Josiah Atkins,* ed. Steven E. Kagle (New York, 1975), 32–33; William Feltman, *The Journal of Lt. William Feltman 1781–82* (1853; New York, 1969), 6; Thacher, *Military Journal of the American Revolution,* 337; Robert R. Livingston to Francis Dana, Oct. 22, 1781 (reel 102, item 78, vol. 21, p. 99), Papers of the Continental Congress. . . . Benjamin Franklin, "The Retort Courteous," in *Writings: Benjamin Franklin,* ed. J. A. Leo Lemay (New York, 1987), 1126–27.

[21] Alexander Leslie to Charles Cornwallis, July 13, 1781 (microfilm: frames 280–81, reel 4), Cornwallis Papers, P.R.O. 30/11/6 (Public Record Office, London, Eng.). . . .

Biological Weapons and the Ethics of War

. . . In the seventeenth and eighteenth centuries, many of the widely accepted rules of European warfare had seen codification in Hugo Grotius's *De jure belli ac pacis,* first published in 1625, and Emmerich de Vattel's *The Law of Nations,* published in 1758. Both works established theoretical protections in war for women and children and for the elderly and infirm. They addressed the issue of surrender, and they determined when soldiers should give "quarter" to their enemies. Beyond all this, they also included strictures against the use of poison weapons and "the poisoning of streams, springs, and wells." In an era before microbiology, in which deadly toxins and infectious microbes were hardly distinguishable, it is nearly inconceivable that either Grotius or Vattel would have excluded communicable disease from the general category of poisons."[22] All of these rules applied, theoretically at least, to "civilized" nations engaged in what were termed "just" wars.

For our purposes, ironically, the most important corollary to these customarily determined rules was that in certain situations, they did not apply. Cases in point included not only "unjust" wars but also rebellions, wars against enemies who themselves violated the laws of war, and wars against "savage" or "heathen" people. Vattel used the Turks and Mongols as his example, but his general point is clear: "nations are justified in uniting together as a body with the object of punishing, and even exterminating, such savage peoples." An earlier formulation of this philosophy had allowed the English to pursue brutal policies in Ireland, on the grounds that the Irish were not just rebels but (despite their professed Christianity) barbarians as well. More than one historian has argued that Ireland provided the English with a convenient ideological precedent for their actions in the New World. And colonists did indeed justify their own savage conduct in New England's seventeenth-century Indian wars by touting the "savagery" of the natives they brutalized.[23] In conflicts with "heathen" Indians, European rules of war gave license to unfettered violence, complete annihilation, and, yes, biological warfare. . . .

---

[22] Hugo Grotius, *De jure belli ac pacis libris tres,* ed. James Brown Scott, trans. Francis W. Kelsey (1646; 3 vols., New York, 1964), III, 734–36, 739–40; Emmerich de Vattel, *The Law of Nations: or, Principles of the Law of Nature; Applied to the Conduct and Affairs of Nations and Sovereigns* (1758; New York, 1964), 280, 282–83, 289; Barbara Donagan, "Atrocity, War Crime, and Treason in the English Civil War," *American Historical Review,* 99 (Oct. 1994), 1149–51. . . .

[23] Vattel, *Law of Nations,* 246. . . . On Ireland, see Nicholas Canny, "The Ideology of English Colonization: From Ireland to America," *William and Mary Quarterly,* 30 (Oct. 1973), 575–98; Barbara Donagan, "Codes and Conduct in the English Civil War," *Past and Present* (no. 118, Feb. 1988), 70–71; Donagan, "Atrocity, War Crime, and Treason in the English Civil War," 1139, 1148–49; and Howard Mumford Jones, "Origins of the Colonial Ideal in England," *Proceedings of the American Philosophical Society,* 85 (Sept. 1942), 448–65. On New England, see Jill Lepore, *The Name of War: King Philip's War and the Origins of American Identity* (New York, 1998), 112; Ronald Dale Karr, "'Why Should You Be So Furious?': The Violence of the Pequot War," *Journal of American History,* 85 (Dec. 1998), 888–89, 899–909; and Adam J. Hirsch, "The Collision of Military Cultures in Seventeenth-Century New England," *Journal of American History,* 74 (March 1988), 1187–1212.

Far more ambiguity surrounded the use of smallpox against Americans of European descent—the allegation that surfaced repeatedly during the Revolutionary War. Nothing captured these moral tensions so clearly as a little book titled *Military Collections and Remarks,* published in British-occupied New York in 1777. Written by a British officer named Robert Donkin, the book proposed a variety of strategies the British might use to gain the upper hand in the American conflict. Among them was biological warfare. In a footnote to a two-page section on the use of bows and arrows, Major Donkin made the following suggestion: "Dip arrows in matter of smallpox, and twang them at the American rebels, in order to inoculate them; This would sooner disband these stubborn, ignorant, enthusiastic savages, than any other compulsive measures. Such is their dread and fear of that disorder!"[24]

Such ideas may have been common in verbal banter, but they rarely made it into print. What happened next is therefore revealing, for it shows how controversial the topic of biological warfare was during the American Revolution: Donkin's provocative footnote survives in only three known copies of his book. In all others, it has been carefully excised. The person responsible for this act is unknown, as is the timing. But the fact that only three known copies survived intact seems to indicate that the excision took place close to the time of publication, before the volume was widely distributed.[25] Likely perpetrators include the author, the publisher, or an agent acting on behalf of British high command. Someone may well have found the suggestion morally offensive; or, in the battle for the "hearts and minds" of the American people, someone may have realized that explicit calls for biological warfare could only make enemies.

If the strategy was controversial, those who sought sanction for biological terror could nevertheless find it in customary codes of conduct. Donkin himself called the Americans "savages," and this alone countenanced the repudiation of behavioral constraints in war. The colonists, in fact, even cultivated a symbolic "Indian" identity in episodes such as the Boston Tea Party. But beyond this, the Americans were also "rebels." Sentiments regarding rebellion were changing, but popular insurrection, like savagery, could legitimate a war of unrestrained destruction—a war in which conventional strictures against biological warfare would not apply. . . . But there was no consensus on this among British officers. While some took a conciliatory stance early in the war, it appears that by 1779 a majority of British officers had become what one scholar has termed "hard-liners"—men who believed that "nothing but the Bayonet & Torch" could quell the colonial revolt. Included among them were men such as Banastre Tarleton, notorious for terrorizing the Carolina back-country, and Charles Grey, famous for two nighttime bayonet attacks on

[24] Robert Donkin, *Military Collections and Remarks* (New York, 1777), 190–91, insert.

[25] Some copies of the book contain an engraved insert replicating the missing text. For an example of both the excision and the insert, see the copy of Donkin, *Military Collections and Remarks,* 190n., in the Clements Library, University of Michigan, Ann Arbor. I am grateful to John Dann of the Clements Library for bringing Donkin's book to my attention and for informing me of the recent discovery of a third intact copy.

sleeping American soldiers. In one of these attacks, Grey's men shouted "No Quarters to rebels" as they leapt upon their slumbering foes.[26]

If the mere fact of rebellion was grounds enough for such an attitude, the difficulties presented by long sieges and the Americans' unconventional fighting methods provided additional justification. In the view of many British soldiers, the Americans had themselves violated the rules of war many times over. Some took offense at the effective Patriot sniping during the retreat from Lexington. Others resented the withering musket fire at Bunker Hill, where General Gage's men believed "the Enemy Poisoned some of their Balls." Confronted by rebellion and frustrated by atrocities committed by a "savage" American enemy who often refused to face off head-to-head on the field of battle, British officers may well have believed the propagation of smallpox was justified and put this belief into practice, especially given the fact that the law of nations apparently permitted it. It is worth recalling that Jeffery Amherst, who had found biological warfare so unabashedly justifiable in 1763, was an extremely popular figure in England. According to the historian Robert Middlekauff, he was "probably the most admired military leader in the nation" during the era of the American Revolution.[27] That General Leslie and other British officers may have thought and acted as Amherst did should come as no surprise. . . .

. . . While Native Americans suffered most from smallpox, they were neither the only targets of its use on the battlefield nor the only ones who leveled the charge against others. The Fort Pitt incident, despite its notoriety, does not stand alone in the annals of early American history. Accusations of deliberate smallpox propagation arose frequently in times of war, and they appear to have had merit on at least one occasion—the Yorktown campaign—during the American Revolution. Elsewhere the evidence is often ambiguous. But it nevertheless indicates that the famous Fort Pitt incident was one in a string of episodes in which military officials in North America may have wielded *Variola*

[26] On Indian-as-America symbolism, see Hugh Honour, *The New Golden Land: European Images of America from the Discoveries to the Present Time* (New York, 1975), 84–117, 138–60. . . . On views within the British military, see Stephen Conway, "'The Great Mischief Complain'd of': Reflections on the Misconduct of British Soldiers in the Revolutionary War," *William and Mary Quarterly,* 47 (July 1990), 378–79; Stephen Conway, "To Subdue America: British Army Officers and the Conduct of the Revolutionary War," *William and Mary Quarterly,* 43 (July 1986), 396–97; and Armstrong Starkey, "Paoli to Stony Point: Military Ethics and Weaponry during the American Revolution," *Journal of Military History,* 58 (Jan. 1994), 18. The "Bayonet & Torch" quotation is from Patrick Campbell to Alexander Campbell, July 8, 1778, Campbell of Barcaldine Muniments, G.D. 170/1711/17, S.R.O., quoted in Conway, "To Subdue America," 392. On "hard-liners," see *ibid.,* 404–5; and Conway, "'The Great Mischief Complain'd of,'" 370–90. On Banastre Tarleton and Charles Grey, see Harold E. Selesky, "Colonial America," in *The Laws of War: Constraints on Warfare in the Western World,* ed. Michael Howard, George J. Andreopoulos, and Mark R. Shulman (New Haven, 1994), 80–83.

[27] Selesky, "Colonial America," 81–83. On the poisoned musket balls, see Thomas Sullivan, "The Common British Soldier—From the Journal of Thomas Sullivan, 49th Regiment of Foot," ed. S. Sydney Bradford, *Maryland Historical Magazine,* 62 (Sept. 1967), 236. On Amherst, see Robert Middlekauff, *The Glorious Cause: The American Revolution, 1763–1789* (New York, 1982), 406.

against their enemies. Justification for doing so could be found in codes of war that legitimated excesses even as they defined constraints. Biological warfare was therefore a reality in eighteenth-century North America, not a distant, abstract threat as it is today. Its use was aimed, as one patriot writer accusingly put it in the year of Yorktown, "at the ruin of a whole Country, involving the indiscriminate murder of Women and Children."[28]

Analyzing Journal Articles

1. Briefly describe the incidents of smallpox during the American Revolution that raised suspicions of its use as a weapon. Who made such accusations, and who did they accuse?

2. By her own admission, much of Fenn's evidence is "rife with ambiguity." Where in this article's argument does the evidence consist of rumors or accusations rather than documented cases of the use of smallpox as a weapon? Does Fenn make this distinction clear?

3. Judging from the notes you made in the table on page 72, are any parts of the argument weakened by questionable evidence? Historians often interpret an *absence* of evidence in their primary sources to their advantage; has Fenn done so here?

4. Any piece of persuasive writing relies on the author's command of argument, evidence, and organization. How does the organization of this article reinforce its argument? How has Fenn's evidence shaped the organization and presentation of her argument?

5. Fenn states in the introduction that one of her objectives is to "broaden the debate" over the Fort Pitt incident and "place it in context." Does the article succeed in this regard? If so, explain how Fenn has redefined the significance of the Fort Pitt incident.

6. How did the debate over the use of smallpox as a weapon in the eighteenth century parallel or diverge from debates over the use of weapons of mass destruction (both biological and nuclear) today? Have modern technology and warfare increased or decreased the likelihood of smallpox's use as a weapon?

The Rest of the Story

Shortly after Fenn's article appeared in the March 2000 edition of the *Journal of American History*, historian Philip Ranlet published "The British, the Indians, and Smallpox: What Actually Happened at Fort Pitt in 1763?" in *Pennsylvania History* 67 (2000): 427–41. Ranlet's article is much more skeptical than Fenn's

[28] Robert R. Livingston to Francis Dana, Oct. 22, 1781 (reel 102, item 78, vol. 21, p. 99), Papers of the Continental Congress.

about the use of smallpox as a biological weapon in the eighteenth century, as is evident from his thesis: "Logic, a better understanding of smallpox itself, and another look at the evidence call into question much of the standard rendition of the story and the ways that historians for more than a century have misrepresented the evidence."

Ranlet exonerated Amherst and Bouquet from complicity in the distribution of the infected goods at Fort Pitt, not out of humanitarian or moral principles they may have held dear, but because Bouquet was unwilling to expose himself to the disease (ironically, Bouquet died of yellow fever a few weeks after moving to a British post in Florida in 1765). Ranlet also questioned whether the goods that Trent and Ecuyer gave the Indians on June 24 had their intended effect. Reviewing the available evidence on the reported outbreak of smallpox in the vicinity of Fort Pitt in 1763, Ranlet concluded that the contagion had already been present among the Indians before June 24, most likely as a result of unintentional transmission from their colonial neighbors in the area. By his reading of the same sources used by Fenn, Ranlet found that the "[Fort Pitt] smallpox incident has been blown out of all proportion" by historians.

Fenn further developed her argument about smallpox and biological warfare in the book *Pox Americana: The Great Smallpox Epidemic of 1775–82* (New York: Hill and Wang, 2001). Building on themes found in her article, Fenn's book describes an increasing willingness by the British to use smallpox as a weapon against enemy armies, civilian noncombatants, and Native Americans during the Revolutionary era. Historians who reviewed *Pox Americana* for scholarly journals praised the breadth of her research but varied in their assessment of her conclusions. The reviewer for the *William and Mary Quarterly*, a journal of early American history, heaped praise on the book for "reconstituting the pandemic [of smallpox] for us to behold through a meticulous and imaginative assembly of fragmentary sources." The reviewer for the *Journal of American History* was less impressed, finding the book "great as a story but flawed as historical epidemiology" because in its rush to prove a continental smallpox epidemic, it failed to convey the disease's "early modern profile and narrower geopolitical contexts." Such a range of opinions in book reviews is not uncommon in history journals. Historians are trained to approach evidence and arguments critically, whether their own or those assembled by their peers.

The Fort Pitt incident has become a fixture in American folklore and has been retold countless times in such popular media as movies, television shows, and comic books. Historians still grapple with it because they are constantly reinterpreting the past through the lens of the present. The use of smallpox as a biological weapon raised a host of questions about the ethics of warfare in the eighteenth century. It is no wonder that this particular story retains its hold on our historical consciousness, as modern society deals with similar questions raised by the spread of intercontinental epidemics such as AIDS and the manufacture of biological and nuclear weapons of mass destruction.

To Find Out More

The Internet has made using scholarly journals much easier than it used to be. A good reference librarian can show you any number of online databases that can help you research articles by author, title, subject, keyword, or a variety of other parameters. Two that are particularly well suited for research in American history are *Humanities Abstracts* and *America: History and Life*. Both of these databases will provide a citation and a brief summary, or abstract, of an article's content to help you decide if it is relevant to your research. Once you find a citation for an article in one of these databases, you can check to see if the journal is on shelf in your library or if you need to order it via interlibrary loan. If a journal you want to use is not available in your library, check to see if your library subscribes to *JSTOR* (**jstor.org**), an online database that offers full-text articles from a host of scholarly journals. However, the most recent years of a journal are not usually available on *JSTOR* (for example, the *Journal of American History* lags behind the present date by about three years). In such cases, you can consult the paper copy of the journal on shelf if your library carries it or try a search in another online database.

The footnotes to Fenn's article provide the relevant citations to scholarship on the Fort Pitt incident before 2000. For an excellent recent study of Pontiac's War, see Gregory Evans Dowd, *War under Heaven: Pontiac, the Indian Nations, and the British Empire* (Baltimore, Md.: Johns Hopkins University Press, 2002). A key piece of evidence in the Fort Pitt incident, William Trent's journal, can be found online at **www.hsp.org/default.aspx**. For broader discussions of disease and its role in European expansion in the New World, see Alfred W. Crosby, *Ecological Imperialism: The Biological Expansion of Europe, 900–1900* (Cambridge: Cambridge University Press, 1986), and Noble David Cook, *Born to Die: Disease and New World Conquest, 1492–1650* (Cambridge: Cambridge University Press, 1998).

CHAPTER 5

Toasting Rebellion

Toasts and Songs in Revolutionary America

I n May 1766, the inhabitants of Philadelphia celebrated the repeal of the much despised Stamp Act in grand fashion. Shortly after the ship *Minerva* arrived from England with a copy of the official act of repeal, a local resident "instantly proclaimed the News" by reading the act "aloud at the London Coffee House," a popular haunt of Philadelphia's merchants. The crowd that gathered for this performance expressed its approval by raising "three loud Huzzas [cheers]" and sending a "Deputation from their Number" to escort the captain of the *Minerva* back to the coffeehouse, where a "large Bowl of Punch" awaited them. The crowd and the captain raised their glasses in toasting "Prosperity to America," and then the appreciative colonists presented the captain with a gold-laced hat "for having brought the first certain Account of the Stamp Act being totally repealed."

The celebration was far from over. Philadelphia's leading citizens "appointed the next Evening to illuminate the City," a popular form of civic celebration in which residents placed lighted candles in their windows. According to the newspaper report of this event, the "Ladies" of the city were especially creative in "the different Manner of Placing Lights, Devices, etc." in their windows, adding to the beauty of the event. That same evening, the city's inhabitants enjoyed a bonfire and consumed "many Barrels of Beer," yet no "Riot or Mob" disturbed the peace.

A few days later, Philadelphia's celebration culminated when the "principal Inhabitants" of the city attended "an elegant Entertainment at the State House." Among the three hundred guests were Pennsylvania's governor, military and naval officers, and the city's mayor and aldermen, all of whom conducted themselves with the "greatest Elegance and Decorum." These same guests drank twenty-one toasts, each one punctuated by a cannon salute. The first four toasts honored the king, the queen, and other members of the royal family; most of the remaining ones honored members of Parliament, the king's ministry, or the British Empire. The seventeenth toast was typical in its patriotic sentiments: "May the Interest of Great Britain and her Colonies be always united." The evening concluded with more bonfires, bell-ringing, and "Strong Beer to the Populace."

Seventeen years later, in 1783, Philadelphia witnessed another grand celebration, this one in honor of the Continental Army. Once again, the city's most prominent citizens took the lead, sponsoring a dinner attended by civilian and military officers of the United States. After dinner, Pennsylvania's governor (now styled the "President of the State" according to its new constitution) led the crowd in thirteen toasts, the first several of which honored the United States Congress, the new nation's allies France and Holland, and George Washington and the Continental Army, respectively. Between each toast, a military band played music and soldiers fired salutes. According to the newspaper report of this celebration, all those present conducted themselves "with the utmost order, good honour, and good breeding," and even though the company included people from "every State in the union," they all regarded one another "like members of one great and happy family."

Although separated by seventeen years of political upheaval and revolution, these two events shared elements common to festive culture in eighteenth-century America. Celebration was a full sensory experience. Illuminations and bonfires created spectacles of sight; cannon salutes loudly announced the occasion to all within earshot; the smell and taste of food delighted noses and filled stomachs; and alcohol flowed freely. While reports from both celebrations emphasized widespread participation, distinctions of gender and social rank determined where and how people experienced these events. Prominent male citizens and their guests occupied center stage, attending dinners in taverns or other public buildings. Elite women appeared at public celebrations only fleetingly or in their homes, where the "Ladies" of the city illuminated their windows. The rest of the populace celebrated out-of-doors, in the streets and at bonfires.

Two important features of this festive culture were drink and music. Eighteenth-century Americans—regardless of their race, gender, or class—consumed alcohol regularly and considered it part of a healthy diet. Public drinking, however, followed certain culturally sanctioned patterns that defined who could participate and in what ways. Generally, only free adult white men joined in the communal drinking that occurred at such civic celebrations. Elite women might raise glasses of wine at a toast made during a ball or dinner, but the rules of social decorum would not allow them to indulge in rounds of toasting or public consumption of barrels of beer. Laws passed by local and colonial governments regulated the consumption of alcohol by servants, slaves, Indians, and apprentices, limiting the amount of time they could spend in taverns and the size of the groups in which they could gather for social drinking.

To indulge in drink publicly, in other words, was one of the ways in which free white men in eighteenth-century America expressed their shared identity and set themselves apart from others. Taverns and coffeehouses provided their male customers with social centers and an arena for exchanging news and discussing politics. When the *Minerva* arrived in Philadelphia with word of the Stamp Act's repeal, a crowd of colonists immediately took the captain to the London Coffee House to share the news. In a busy commercial seaport like Philadelphia, such establishments served as a kind of emergency broadcast network, the easiest way to reach an audience as quickly as possible. Likewise, by reading or listening to someone read the newspapers from home and abroad kept at coffeehouses and taverns, patrons could acquaint themselves with current events in the world around them.

Music and song also filled the air at coffeehouses, taverns, and public festivities. Colonial Americans brought a rich musical heritage with them from Europe, and of course, Africans and Indians had their own traditions of music, song, and dance associated with communal celebration. Drinking songs were a part of the folk music tradition in the colonies, and anyone with a knack for rhyming and satire might compose one, often by grafting new lyrics onto a fa-

Figure 5.1 Sign for Gordon's Inn, c. 1790–1830 Tavern and inn signs in early America announced their businesses to potential customers on busy streets and offered visual cues as to what went on inside their doors. This sign, from an inn of unknown location, reveals much about the social significance of drinking in Revolutionary America. The verses read,

> *Gentlemen you are welcome*
> *sit down at your ease*
> *Pay what you call for &*
> *drink what you please*

The bowl and glass suggest plenty of good drink and companionship, but the figure and verses limit that invitation to indulgence to only well-to-do males.

Source: The Connecticut Historical Society, Hartford.

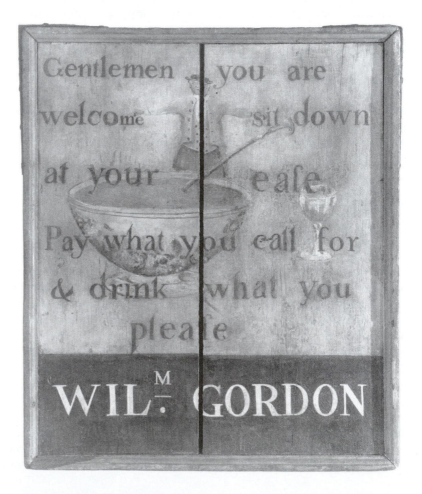

miliar tune. "Yankee Doodle," regarded by subsequent generations as the quintessential patriot song, actually originated in the British army and was sung by redcoats marching toward Lexington, Massachusetts, on the fateful morning of April 19, 1775. It became an American standard only after a parody of it appeared satirizing the British retreat from Lexington and Concord. Singing was also more inclusive during public occasions than drinking: those social groups whose access to alcohol was limited by legal and cultural restraints could nevertheless participate in public gatherings by listening to and joining in the music and song going on around them.

For many eighteenth-century Americans, rituals of public celebration shaped and defined their experience of the Revolution. History books often tell the story of the coming of the Revolution as a series of violent public confrontations between raucous crowds and British soldiers or officials: the Stamp Act riots, the tarring and feathering of customs officials, the Boston Massacre, the Boston Tea Party. However, much more common were crowds that assembled in a peaceful, celebratory fashion to support the patriot cause, their participants more likely to be found carrying wine glasses and punch bowls than clubs and torches. Until the eve of independence, they expressed their political opinions in songs and toasts that venerated the British monarchy and proudly proclaimed their membership in the British Empire. During the Revolutionary era, Americans made changes, some obvious and some subtle, in the way they conducted such celebrations, but the social and political purposes of these events remained much the same. Public festivities were the primary venue in which people affirmed their political identity and displayed their notion of the social order. On such occasions, drink and song served as means by which Americans expressed their transformation from loyal British subjects into citizens of a new nation.

Using The Source: Toasts and Songs

Toasts and drinking songs were part of the masculine drinking culture of eighteenth-century America. Oral tradition transmitted toasts and songs from one generation to the next, and both found their way into printed sources as well. Booksellers in Britain and America published collections of popular toasts, so that the shy and tongue-tied could be prepared to deliver one when in polite company. The association of toasting with refined behavior struck some observers as absurd, considering how the practice encouraged drunkenness. Bumpers, toasts in which each drinker emptied a full glass, were especially damaging to the group's composure but embodied the male bravado associated with drinking. Most toasts were never written down and disappeared along with the alcohol that accompanied them, but newspapers often published in detail the toasts made by prominent men at public celebrations.

Like toasts, drinking songs could be found in book collections or newspapers. Printers also disseminated them on broadsides (also known as ballad sheets), large single sheets of paper that could be shared by a group or posted in public places, such as taverns and coffeehouses. Patriotic songs proclaiming the martial spirit and triumphs of the British were popular among colonial drinkers, but satirical ballads aimed at unpopular public figures also enjoyed a wide audience. Some songs were set to familiar tunes that a crowd would readily recognize. New lyrics could turn the meaning of a popular tune on its head, such as when a New York woman in the 1790s set lyrics titled "The Rights of Women" to the patriotic British anthem "God Save the King." Other songs were little more than poorly metered attempts at patriotic drum-beating, published in newspapers as "curiosities" that reflected the spirit of the times.

While many traditional songs and toasts in eighteenth-century America were too vague and general in the sentiments they expressed to be controversial or confrontational, those with more pointed political content could disrupt the unity of the drinkers who recited them. A drinker who declined to join in a toast or song broke the fellowship symbolized by the communal punch bowl out of which the company drank. Onlookers in a crowded tavern or street might interpret this passive act of refusal as an aggressive challenge to the values and opinions expressed by the group. Toasts and songs could also be an effective way of exerting pressure on a reluctant participant to show solidarity with the rest of the crowd. Consider the case of the captain of the *Minerva*, described on page 90. Did he join enthusiastically or reluctantly in the toasts made in his honor at the coffeehouse? Much of the description provided of this occasion suggests a not-so-subtle form of coercion: members of the crowd retrieved him from his ship, brought him to the coffeehouse, and placed a glass in his hand. What would the consequences have been if he had refused their hospitality and failed to drink to the Stamp Act's repeal?

Using toasts and songs as a source requires being attentive not just to the words used but also to the way in which they were arranged to express the drinkers' and singers' notions of solidarity, allegiance, and social order. Calls to resistance against the king or Parliament were naturally inflammatory, and many eighteenth-century Americans defined political rebellion as a sin, a violation of the biblical commandment to honor your father and mother. Therefore, words and actions taken against Britain's controversial tax policies in the 1760s had to be distanced from outright rebellion by professions of loyalty to the Crown and empire. Notice how the toasts and song lyrics reproduced on pages 99–109 engage in this balancing act.

As recounted in the May 26, 1766, edition of the *Pennsylvania Gazette,* these toasts were made with "flowing glasses" at the Philadelphia dinner in celebration of the repeal of the Stamp Act. As you read them, pay careful attention to the sequence in which they were made.

These opening toasts affirm the colonists' loyalty as British subjects

1. The King
2. The Queen
3. Prince of Wales, and Royal Family
4. May the Illustrious House of Hanover preside over the United British Empire, to the End of Time

5. The House of Lords

6. The House of Commons

7. The present Worthy Ministry

8. The Glorious and Immortal Mr. Pitt

9. That Lover and Supporter of Justice, Lord Camden

Express gratitude to the British Parliament and the king's ministry for repealing the Stamp Act

10. The London Committee of Merchants

11. America's Friends in Great Britain

Honor British merchants who exerted pressure on the Crown and Parliament to repeal the Stamp Act

12. The Virginia Assembly

13. All other Assemblies on the Continent, actuated by the like Zeal for the Liberties of their Country

14. Prosperity to the Spirited Inhabitants of St. Christophers

Toasts to other British colonists in North America and the Caribbean who have resisted the Stamp Act

15. The Navy and Army

16. Daniel Dulany, Esquire

17. May the Interest of Great Britain and her Colonies be always United

18. Trade and Navigation

19. America's Friends in Ireland

20. Prosperity to the Province of Pennsylvania

21. The Liberty of the Press in America

Formulaic tributes to the prosperity of the colony and the British Empire

Potentially controversial tributes to an anti–Stamp Act pamphleteer (16), the printers who published such tracts (21), and political radicals in Ireland sympathetic to the American cause (19)

Like the toasts you just read, the following song lyrics delicately balance the colonists' assertion of their rights with professions of their loyalty as subjects. They are excerpted from "The Liberty Song," written by Pennsylvania patriot John Dickinson and published in the *Boston Gazette* on July 18, 1768 (reprinted in Frank Moore, ed., *Songs and Ballads of the American Revolution* [1856; repr., New York: Arno Press, 1969], 36–40). Dickinson wrote this song to rally support for nonimportation, a boycott movement in which patriots refused to buy goods they thought were unjustly taxed by Parliament.

Come join hand in hand, brave Americans all,
And rouse your bold hearts at fair Liberty's call;
No tyrannous acts, shall suppress your just claims,
Or stain with dishonor America's name.
    In freedom we're born, and in freedom we'll live;
      Our purses are ready,
      Steady, Friends, steady,
    Not as *slaves*, but as *freemen* our money we'll give. . . .

Swarms of placemen and pensioners[1] soon will appear,
Like locusts deforming the charms of the year:

Song begins with very strong language, equating new taxes with tyranny and enslavement

Raises specter of British tax collectors and customs officers robbing colonists of their property

[1] "Placemen" and "pensioners" were derogatory terms for customs officials, military officers, and other officeholders who profited from royal appointments in the colonies.

Calls colonists to
united resistance

Suns vainly will rise, showers vainly descend,

If we are to drudge[2] for what others shall spend.

Then join hand in hand, brave Americans all,

By uniting we stand, by dividing we fall;

In so righteous a cause let us hope to succeed,

For Heaven approves of each generous deed. . . .

Ends, like many
drinking songs,
by calling singers
to a toast, in this
case one affirm-
ing loyalty to
Britain

This bumper[3] I crown for our sovereign's health,

And this for Britannia's glory and wealth;

That wealth, and that glory immortal may be,

If she is but just, and we are but free.

What Can Toasts and Songs Tell Us?

Toasts and songs tell us much about popular political culture in Revolutionary America. In an age before universal adult suffrage or organized political parties, most people expressed their political opinions in ways that did not involve casting votes or supporting particular candidates for office. Unlike the elite males who sat in council chambers and assembly halls to pass laws or draft petitions, most folks practiced their politics out-of-doors, by assembling in crowds to celebrate, commemorate, or protest specific events or policies. A crowd might burn a despised political figure in effigy or bury a hated law, such as the Stamp Act, in a mock funeral procession. A crowd's attendance at a public celebration also lent legitimacy to the political authority of the elites who sponsored it. The toasts and songs that accompanied public events were a part of the experiential nature of politics in Revolutionary America for a much wider cross section of the population than that represented in the official channels of government.

In toasts and songs people also expressed their vision of a well-ordered body politic, in which each part of society occupied a particular place and played a particular role in promoting the unity and welfare of the whole. Multiple toasts, in which participants drank to individuals or groups in descending order of importance, illustrated this hierarchy of political and social relations. Songs likewise celebrated ideal roles and virtues for different groups. By analyzing their lyrics, we can glimpse how patriots mobilized these different groups—women and men, soldiers and civilians—for their cause.

Toasts and songs also offer insights into the origins and development of American nationalism. At the outbreak of the Revolution, regional and cultural differences separated the thirteen colonies. Somehow, the patriots overcame these differences to forge a single nation that withstood not only the war with Britain but also the divisive politics of the postwar period. Toasts and songs of the era allow us to see how the former colonists created a shared political iden-

[2] Labor.

[3] A type of toast in which all drinkers were expected to empty their glasses.

tity in the wake of independence. They tell us much about how colonists formerly connected only by their common status as British subjects manufactured a new inventory of public symbols and rituals to express their new identity as Americans.

The disadvantages of using toasts and songs to study the patriot movement arise from the formulaic and idealized nature of these forms of political expression. Toasts and songs seldom described the world as it was; rather, they described the world as it ought to be, in the eyes of the people who composed them. In toasts, political unity and social harmony always prevailed; in songs, soldiers were always brave, women virtuous, and civilians self-sacrificing. Toasts and songs that promoted social cohesion naturally understated social conflict and political opposition.

One other disadvantage to using toasts and songs has to do with the context in which they were made, sung, and printed. As noted earlier, public drinking in eighteenth-century America was a prerogative of free adult males. We know that women, slaves, and laboring peoples drank, but it is much harder to find descriptions of what political opinions they may have expressed during their consumption. Newspapers did not report songs or toasts associated with these groups. Society did not condone their public consumption of alcohol, associating it with disorder and violence rather than political solidarity and social cohesion. Thus, while songs and toasts associated with the patriot movement claimed to state universally held sentiments, substantial elements of the social order were not invited to join in this form of expression. If those left out did engage in such activity on their own, it was rarely recorded in a way historians can retrieve. The songs and toasts that have survived carry a distinct bias in favor of white, urban men from the middle and upper ranks of society.

Questions to Ask

Eighteenth-century Americans used toasts and songs to promote group solidarity. Thus, when dealing with this source, you need to start by asking about its social context: On what occasion was the toast made or the song sung? Who did the toasting or singing, and what issues, events, or people did they address? Once you have a handle on these questions, you can dissect the meaning of the toast's or song's words or lyrics. What beliefs or practices is it promoting or condemning? How is it defining membership in a particular group, and who is outside of that group? When you have analyzed several toasts and songs, you can compare them across time and place: What evidence do they show of changing political attitudes or social identities over time?

- On what occasion is the toast being made or the song sung?
- Who is making the toast or singing the song?
- What beliefs, practices, or events is the toast or song addressing?
- How is the content of these toasts and songs changing over time?

Source Analysis Table

Toasts	The Occasion of Celebration	The Method of Celebration	The Subjects of the Toasts
1. Wilmington, 1765			
2. Charlestown, 1777			
3. Annapolis, 1788			
Songs	Topic	What Group(s) Are Addressed in the Lyrics?	What Values or Ideas Are the Lyrics Promoting?
4. "To the Ladies"			
5. "The New Recruit/Fare Thee Well, Ye Sweethearts"			
6. "How Stands the Glass Around"			
7. "The Epilogue"			
8. "The Dance"			

To download and print this table, visit the book companion site at **bedfordstmartins.com/brownshannon**.

The Source: Toasts and Songs of the Patriot Movement, 1765–1788

TOASTS

1

Wilmington, North Carolina, 1765

Following the passage of the Stamp Act in early 1765, the Crown appointed a stamp distributor for each of its North American colonies to oversee the collection of the new tax. Colonists used a variety of means to convince these stamp distributors to resign from their posts. The newspaper item below reports on one such instance in North Carolina, in which the stamp distributor was first intimidated and then toasted by a colonial mob.

WILMINGTON, in North Carolina, Nov. 20. — On Saturday, the 16th of this Instant,[1] WILLIAM HUSTON, Esq; Distributor of STAMPS for this Province, came to this Town; upon which three or four Hundred People immediately gathered together, with Drums beating, and Colours flying, and repaired to the House the said STAMP OFFICER put up at, and insisted upon knowing, "Whether he intended to execute the said Office, or not." He told them, "He should be very sorry to execute any Office disagreeable to the People of the Province." But they, not content with such a Declaration, carried him into the Court House, where he signed a Resignation Satisfactory to the Whole.

As soon as the STAMP OFFICER had complied with their Desire, they placed him in an Arm Chair, carried him first round the Court House, giving three Huzzas[2] at every Corner, and then proceeded with him round one of the Squares of the Town, and set him down at the Door of his Lodgings, formed themselves in a large Circle round him, and gave him three Cheers. They then escorted him into the House, where was prepared the best Liquors to be had, and treated him very genteelly. In the Evening a large Bonfire was made, and no Person appeared in the Streets without having LIBERTY, in large Capital Letters, in his Hat. They had a large Table near the Bonfire, well furnished with several Sorts of Liquors, where they drank in great Form, all the favourite AMERICAN Toasts, giving three Cheers at the Conclusion of each. The whole was conducted with great Decorum, and not the least Insult offered to any person.

[1] This month (November).

[2] Three cheers.

Source: Pennsylvania Gazette, January 2, 1766.

2   *Charlestown, South Carolina,* 1777

After the Second Continental Congress declared independence, the American patriots abandoned a calendar of British civic holidays, such as the monarch's birthday or royal weddings. Instead, the new nation created its own civic holidays, aimed at celebrating the break from Britain. The following newspaper item reports on a public celebration of the first anniversary of American independence in Charlestown (Charleston), South Carolina.

CHARLESTOWN, July 19.—Friday last being the first anniversary of the glorious formation of the American Empire, when Thirteen Colonies, driven by necessity, threw off the yoke, and rejected the tyranny of Great Britain, by declaring themselves Free, Independent and Sovereign States, the same was commemorated by every demonstration of joy.

Ringing of bells ushered in the day. At sunrise, American colours were displayed from all the forts and batteries and vessels in the harbour. The Charlestown regiment of militia, commanded by the Hon. Col. Charles Pinckney, and the Charlestown Artillery Company, commanded by Capt. Thomas Grimball, were assembled upon the Parade, and reviewed by his Excellency the President, who was attended, upon this occasion, by his Honour the Vice-President, and the Hon. Members of the Privy Council.[1] At one o'clock the several forts, beginning at Fort Moultrie on Sullivan Island, discharged 76 pieces of cannon, alluding to the glorious year 1776, and the militia and artillery fired three general vollies.

His Excellency the President then gave a most elegant entertainment in the Council Chamber, at which were present all the members of the Legislature then in town, all the public officers, civil and military; the clergy and many strangers of note, to the amount of more than double the number that ever observed the birthday of the present misguided and unfortunate King of Great Britain. After dinner the following toasts were drank, viz.

1. The Free, Independent and Sovereign States of America. 2. The Great Council[2] of America—may wisdom preside in all its deliberations. 3. General Washington. 4. The American army and navy—may they be victorious and invincible. 5. The nations in friendship or alliance with America. 6. The American Ambassadors at foreign courts. 7. The 4th of July, 1776. 8. The memory of the officers and soldiers who have bravely fallen in defence of America. 9. South Carolina. 10. May only those Americans enjoy Freedom, who are ready to die for its defence. 11. Liberty triumphant. 12. Confusion, shame and disgrace to our enemies—may the foes to America (slaves to tyranny) humble and fall before her. 13. May the rising States of America reach the summit of human power and grandeur, and enjoy every blessing.

[1] References to the governor, lieutenant governor, and council of the state of South Carolina.
[2] Second Continental Congress.

Source: Pennsylvania Gazette, July 30, 1777.

Each toast being succeeded by a salute of 13 guns, which were fired by Capt. Grimball's company from their two field pieces with admirable regularity. The day having been spent in festivity and the most conspicuous joy and harmony; the evening was concluded with illuminations, &c. far exceeding any that had ever been exhibited before.

3 *Annapolis, Maryland,* 1788

The battle over ratifying the Constitution threatened to split the new nation apart. In an effort to mobilize public opinion behind the Constitution, supporters sponsored public celebrations of ratification as it occurred in each state. The following news item reports on one such celebration in Maryland.

ANNAPOLIS, April 30.—Monday the 28th instant being the day appointed by the honorable convention of this State, for the ratification of the Federal Government, that solemn, and happy event accordingly took place at Three o'clock in the afternoon.

The Members present at this ceremony amounted to seventy-four, of which number the names of sixty-three were subscribed to the instrument of ratification. The great and important business being completed, the members, preceded by the honorable the President of that body, in consequence of an invitation from the citizens of Annapolis, retired to Mr. Mann's Tavern, where an elegant entertainment was provided, at which were also present many strangers of distinction, and several respectable inhabitants of the city. The company consisted of nearly Two Hundred Persons. The cordiality, and festivity that appeared in the countenance, and conduct of each guest, were the strongest testimonies of the general satisfaction felt on this happy occasion.

After dinner the following Toasts, with a discharge of Thirteen Cannon to each, were given:

1. The United States and Congress.
2. Louis the XVI King of France, and the friendly powers in Europe.
3. The State of Maryland and the present Convention.
4. The late Federal Convention.[1]
5. General Washington.
6. Marquis La Fayette.[2]

[1] The Convention that had drafted the Constitution in Philadelphia in summer 1787.
[2] A French officer and close associate of George Washington who joined the patriot cause.
Source: Pennsylvania Gazette, May 14, 1788.

7. To the memory of the brave officers and soldiers who fell defending America during the late war.

8. May Agriculture, Manufactures and Commerce flourish in the United States.

9. Success to useful Learning and the Arts and Sciences.

10. The late American Army and Navy.

11. The Count Rochambeau,[3] and the French Army and Navy which served in America.

12. May our public councils ever be actuated by wisdom and patriotism.

13. May all the States of America join heartily in adopting and making effectual the proposed Federal Government.

When the fifth toast was proclaimed by the President, a portrait of the Hero, in respect, and in honor to whom that toast was announced, and which had been artfully concealed behind a curtain at the head of the room, was suddenly displayed. The powers of the pen, or the pencil, are inadequate to the description of those feelings that animated the hearts, and glowed in the countenances of the spectators. A general burst of applause testified at once the strong remembrance of past services, and an ardent gratitude for present endeavours and patriotic perseverance.

The entertainment was concluded with a ball at the Assembly-Room, at which the Ladies appeared to partake of the general joy in an equal proportion with the Gentlemen. In a word, all classes of people gave the strongest proofs of their satisfaction on this joyful event.

[3] Commander of French troops at the Battle of Yorktown.

SONGS

 ## To the Ladies

This song appeared in several New England newspapers between 1767 and 1769. It rallied support for the nonimportation movement aimed at overturning the Townshend Duties, a series of taxes imposed by Parliament on colonial imports in 1767. Its tune was borrowed from "Advice to the Ladies," a popular comic song offering advice on what kinds of men women should avoid marrying.

Source: Arthur F. Schrader, *American Revolutionary War Songs to Cultivate the Sensations of Freedom,* audio recording (New York: Smithsonian Folkways No. FH 5279, 1976). To access links to audio recordings of these and several other Revolutionary-era songs, visit the book companion site at **bedfordstmartins.com/brownshannon.**

Young ladies in our town, and those that live round,
Let a friend at this season advise you;
Since money's so scarce, and times are growing worse,
Strange things may soon hap and surprise you.

First, then, throw aside your topknots[1] of pride;
Wear none but your own country linen;
Of economy boast, let your pride be the most
To show clothes of your own make and spinning.

What if homespun they say is not quite so gay
As brocades, yet be not in a passion,
For when once it is known this is much worn in town,
One and all will cry out — 'Tis the fashion!

And, as one, all agree, that you'll not married be
To such as will wear London factory,
But at first sight refuse, tell 'em such you will choose
As encourage our own manufactory.

No more ribbons wear, nor in rich silks appear;
Love your country much better than fine things;
Begin without passion, 'twill soon be the fashion
To grace your smooth lock with a twine of string.

Throw aside your Bohea, and your Green Hyson[2] tea,
And all things with a new-fashion duty;
Procure a good store of the choice Labrador,[3]
For there'll soon be enough here to suit you.

These do without fear, and to all you'll appear,
Fair, charming, true, lovely and clever;
Though the times remain darkish; young men may be sparkish,
And love you much stronger than ever.

[1] Fancy headdresses worn by women of fashion.
[2] Bohea and Green Hyson were types of tea imported into the colonies.
[3] An alternative to foreign tea, made from the red-root bush native to New England.

The New Recruit/Fare Thee Well, Ye Sweethearts

Recruitment was a constant problem for the Continental Army after the disastrous campaign of 1776. Drink and song helped facilitate the process, especially when recruiters appeared at taverns or other public places. It is easy to imagine this song being sung on such an occasion. Like other popular songs, recruitment songs appeared in countless variations. The lyrics below were printed under the title "The New Recruit, or the Gallant Volunteer, A New Song" in a colonial newspaper; the recorded version uses the title "Fare Thee Well, Ye Sweethearts" and has fewer stanzas.

Come on my hearts of tempered steel,
And leave your girls and farms,
Your sports and plays and holidays,
And hark, away to arms!
And to conquest we will go, will go, will go,
And to conquest we will go.

A Soldier is a gentleman,
His honour is his life,
And he that won't stand to his post,
Will never stand by his wife,
And to conquest we will go, &c.

For love and honour are the same,
Or else so near an ally,
That neither can exist alone,
But flourish side by side.
And to conquest we will go, &c.

So fare you well sweethearts a while,
You smiling girls adieu;
And when we drub the dogs away,[1]
We kiss it out with you.
And to conquest we will go, &c.

The spring is up, the winter flies,
The hills are green and gay,
And all inviting honour calls,
Away, my boys, away.
And to conquest we will go, &c.

[1] Send the redcoats retreating.

Source: Pennsylvania Packet, April 8, 1778, and The Committee of Correspondence, *Songs and Ballads of Colonial and Revolutionary America,* audio recording (New York: Smithsonian Folkways No. FH 5274, 1976).

In shady tents, by cooling streams,
With hearts all firm and free,
We chase the cares of life away,
In songs of liberty.
And to conquest we will go, &c.

No foreign slaves shall give us law,
No British tyrants reign;
Tis Independence made us free;
And freedom we maintain.
And to conquest we will go, &c.

We charge the foe from post to post,
Attack their works and lines,
Or by some well laid stratagem,
We make them all Burgoynes.[2]
And to conquest we will go, &c.

And when the war is over, boys,
Then down we sit at ease,
And plow and sow and reap and mow,
And live just as we please.
When from conquest we shall go, &c.

Each hearty lad shall take his lass,
And beaming like a star,
And in her softer arms forget,
The dangers of the war.
When to conquest we did go, &c.

The rising world shall sing of us,
A thousand years to come,
And to their children's children tell,
The Wonders we have done.
When to conquest we did go, &c.

So my honest fellows here's my hand,
My heart, my very soul,
With all the joys of Liberty,
Good fortune and a bowl.[3]
And to conquest we will go, &c.

[2] British general John Burgoyne suffered a humiliating defeat at the Battle of Saratoga in 1777.
[3] A punch bowl.

How Stands the Glass Around

This soldiers' drinking song first appeared in print in 1729 and was popular among British and American soldiers during the French and Indian and Revolutionary wars. It presents a much different view of military life than the recruiting songs sung at the time of enlistment.

How stands the glass around,
For shame ye take no care, my boys,
How stands the glass around,
Let mirth and wine abound,
The trumpets sound,
The colors they are flying, boys.
To fight, kill, or wound,
May we still be found,
Content with our hard fate, my boys,
On the cold ground.

Why, soldiers, why,
Should we be melancholy, boys?
Why, soldiers, why,
Whose business 'tis to die!
What, sighing, fie![1]
Damn fear, drink on, be jolly, boys,
'Tis he, you, or I!
Cold, hot, wet, or dry,
We're always bound to follow, boys,
And scorn to fly!

'Tis but in vain,
I mean not to upbraid you, boys,
'Tis but in vain,
For soldiers to complain.
Should next campaign,
Send us to him who made us, boys,
We're free from pain!
but if we remain,
A bottle and a kind landlady
Cure all again.

[1] An exclamation of disgust.

Source: The Committee of Correspondence, *Songs and Ballads of Colonial and Revolutionary America*, audio recording (New York: Smithsonian Folkways No. FH 5274, 1976).

7   *The Epilogue*

Loyalists also used toasts and songs to express their political opinions, as this song attests. It appeared in October 1778 on ballad sheets published in British-occupied Philadelphia and New York. Its title suggests that the song-writer thought the war almost over and decided in the British favor. The tune is borrowed from the popular British song "Derry Down."

The farce is now finish'd, your sport's at an end,
But ere you depart, let the voice of a friend
By way of a chorus, the evening crown
With a song to the tune of a hey derry down,
CHORUS: Derry down, down, hey derry down . . .

Old Shakespeare, a poet who should not be spit on,
Although he was born in the island called Britain,
Hath said that mankind are all players at best,
A truth we'll admit of, for the sake of the jest.
CHORUS

On this puny stage, we have strutted our hour,
And acted our parts to the best of our power,
That the farce hath concluded not perfectly well,
Was surely the fault of the devil in Hell.
CHORUS

The devil, you know, out of spleen[1] for the church,
Will often abandon his friends in the lurch,
And turn them adrift in the midst of their joy,
'Tis a difficult matter to cheat the old boy.
CHORUS

Our great Independence we give to the wind,
And pray that Great Britain may once more be kind.
In this jovial song all hostility ends,
And Britons and we will for ever be friends.
CHORUS

Once more, here's a health[2] to the King and the Queen!
Confusion to him, who on rancor and spleen,
Refuses to drink with an English good friend,
Immutable amity to the world's end.

[1] Ill temper.
[2] A toast.

Source: Dorothy Messney, *Patchwork and Powder Horn: Songs of the American Revolution,* audio recording (New York: Smithsonian Folkways No. FH 5278, 1975).

8   *The Dance*

This song from 1781 celebrates the American victory at Yorktown, Virginia, the last major battle of the war. Like many songs celebrating military victories, it incorporates the names of each army's commanding officers, lionizing the victors and lampooning the defeated. It is set to the tune of "Yankee Doodle," a popular British song that the patriots adapted to their cause.

Cornwallis[1] led a country dance,
The like was never seen, sir,
Much retrograde and much advance,
And all with General Greene,[2] sir.

They rambled up and rambled down,
Join'd hands, then off they run, sir,
Our General Greene to Charlestown,[3]
The Earl[4] to Wilmington,[5] sir.

Greene, in the South, then danc'd a set,
And got a mighty name, sir.
Cornwallis jigg'd with young Fayette,[6]
But suffer'd in his fame, sir.

Then down he figur'd to the shore,
Most like a lordly dancer,
And on his courtly honor swore,
He would no more advance, sir.

Quoth he, "my guards are weary grown
With footing country dances,
They never at St. James's[7] shone,
At capers, kick or prances."

Though men so gallant ne'er were seen,
While sauntering on parade, sir,
Or wriggling o'er the park's smooth green,
Or at a masquerade, sir.

[1] The British commander at Yorktown.

[2] The commander of the Continental troops who lured Cornwallis into Virginia from the Carolinas.

[3] Charleston, South Carolina.

[4] Cornwallis.

[5] North Carolina.

[6] The Marquis de Lafayette.

[7] St. James's Palace in Britain; that is, they were never skilled dancers at home.

Source: Dorothy Messney, *Patchwork and Powder Horn: Songs of the American Revolution,* audio recording (New York: Smithsonian Folkways No. FH 5278, 1975).

Yet are red heels and long-lac'd skirts,
For stumps and briars meet, sir?
Or stand they chance with hunting-shirts,
Or hardy veteran feet, sir?

Now housed in York,[8]
he challenged all to minuets so sprightly,
And lessons for a courtly ball,
his soldiers studied nightly.

His challenge heard, full soon there came,
a set who knew the dance, sir,
De Grasse and Rochambeau,[9]
whose fame proved certain to advance, sir.

And Washington, Columbia's son,
Who's easy nature taught, sir,
That grace which can't by pains be won,
Nor monarch's gold be bought, sir.

Now hand in hand they circle round,
This ever-dancing peer, sir;
Their gentle movements, soon confound
The Earl, as they draw near, sir.

His music he soon forgets to play—
His feet can no more move, sir,
And all his soldiers curse the day,
They jigged to our shore, sir.

Now Tories all, what can ye say?
Come—is not this a griper,[10]
That while your hopes are danc'd away,
'Tis you must pay the piper.

[8] Yorktown, Virginia.
[9] French officers whose forces aided the Continental Army at the Battle of Yorktown.
[10] A cause for complaint.

Analyzing Toasts and Songs

1. Using your notes from the table on page 98, what were the most significant changes in the occasions and methods of public toast making between 1765 and 1788? Which elements of these rituals remained essentially unchanged?

2. Which of the songs reproduced here invoke social drinking (both alcoholic and nonalcoholic) in their lyrics? How is that drinking defined by gender or occupation, and what political significance is attached to it in these songs?

3. How did references to King George III and other symbols of British power change over time or according to audience in these toasts and songs? Who or what replaced the king as the new focal points of American patriotism?

4. Using your notes from the table on page 98, what do these songs tell you about this society's definitions of male and female roles in public life? How did these songs attempt to mobilize men and women for the patriot cause, and did their messages challenge or reinforce traditional gender roles?

5. Eighteenth-century Americans used toasts and songs to describe who they were as well as who they were not. What individuals or groups were marked as outsiders or exiles from the body politic in these sources? Do you see any evidence here of how rituals of public celebration also intimidated or coerced the reluctant or neutral into supporting a particular cause?

6. Do you think these toasts and songs describe mostly change or stability in American society during the Revolutionary era? How does your answer to that question differ if you look at specific social groups referred to in these sources, such as women, soldiers, or political leaders?

The Rest of the Story

The necessity of mobilizing and maintaining support for the patriot cause during the American Revolution did much to politicize drinking culture in the new nation. During the 1760s and 1770s, patriot leaders were quite liberal with the punch bowl and strong beer during public festivities meant to draw support to their cause. Once the war was over, the Fourth of July and George Washington's birthday became new public holidays that called for parades, illuminations, bonfires, fireworks, military parades, and, of course, drink and song. The rivalry between the Federalists and Democratic Republicans during the 1790s intensified the political partisanship associated with such events, as each side scrambled to use the new symbols and rituals of American civic culture to its own advantage. As the 1790s gave way to the nineteenth century, marginalized groups such as free blacks and women asserted their place in the new nation's political and social order by appropriating the rites of public celebration for their own purposes. In 1796, a group of women in York, Pennsylvania, attending an outdoor tea party made eight toasts honoring President Washington and the federal government, but ended with one to "The Rights of Women." In 1810, free blacks in Boston celebrating the American ban on the transatlantic slave trade made nine toasts to individuals, groups, and nations who supported the abolitionist cause. Interspersed in their list were the names of several honorees probably not typically cited in toasts printed in American newspapers:

> 2. *Mr. Wilberforce*, and other members who advocated the abolition of the slave trade in the British Parliament. . . .
> 4. The Trustees of the African School in *Boston*. . . .

8. Liberty to our African brethren in *St. Domingo* [Haiti, the site of a success-ful slave revolution in the 1790s], and elsewhere.

These African American celebrants had appropriated one of the most common practices in American popular politics to express their own revolutionary cause: the end of slavery.

The political activism associated with public drinking in the new nation put some social reformers ill at ease. They associated tavern going with disorder and contention and demonized public drinking as socially aberrant behavior. Nevertheless, drinking songs and toasts remained fixtures of nineteenth-century American politics, and both survive in modified forms today. Patriotic songs are still an important part of our civic rituals, as anyone who has stood for the performance of "The Star-Spangled Banner" at the start of a sporting event can attest. In the wake of the September 11, 2001, terrorist attacks on the United States, patriotic songs became an important part of how Americans communally acknowledged the tragedy.

To Find Out More

Songs and toasts from the Revolutionary era that addressed the political issues of the day were often reproduced in newspapers. A useful resource for tracking down such items is the online database "Accessible Archives" (**accessible.com**), which provides full-text articles from eighteenth- and nineteenth-century American newspapers. This database is available by subscription only, so you will want to check with a reference librarian to see if you can gain access to it. For more information on using eighteenth-century newspapers, see "To Find Out More" in Chapter 3 (p. 62).

An important nineteenth-century collection of popular political songs from the Revolutionary era is available in a modern edition: Frank Moore, editor, *Songs and Ballads of the American Revolution* (1856; New York: Arno Press, 1969). Researchers interested in ballad sheets will also want to consult the Library of Congress's Web site, "An American Time Capsule: Three Centuries of Broadsides and Other Political Ephemera" at **memory.loc.gov/ammem/rbpehtml/pehome.html**, which includes some examples of Revolutionary-era songs. For audio recordings of colonial and Revolutionary-era songs, visit the Smithsonian Folkways Web site at **folkways.si.edu/index.html**. Travel narratives provide some of the best descriptions of public drinking in early America. Especially useful in this regard are the narratives of Sarah Kemble Knight and Dr. Alexander Hamilton, both of which can be found in Wendy Martin, editor, *Colonial American Travel Narratives* (New York: Penguin Books, 1994).

Two classic articles on the roles of drink and song respectively in the coming of the Revolution are Richard J. Hooker, "The American Revolution Seen through a Wine Glass," *William and Mary Quarterly*, third series, 11 (1954): 52–77, and Arthur M. Schlesinger, "A Note on Songs as Patriot Propaganda,

1765–1776," *William and Mary Quarterly,* third series, 11 (1954): 78–88. More recently, historians have used drinking and tavern-going to explore social and political relationships in early American society. See for example Sharon V. Salinger, *Taverns and Drinking in Early America* (Baltimore, Md.: Johns Hopkins University Press, 2002); Peter Thompson, *Rum Punch and Revolution: Tavern-going and Public Life in Eighteenth-Century Philadelphia* (Philadelphia: University of Pennsylvania Press, 1999); and David W. Conroy, *In Public Houses: Drink and the Revolution of Authority in Colonial Massachusetts* (Chapel Hill: University of North Carolina Press, 1995). For drinking and gender roles in early America, see Jessica Kross, "'If you will not drink with me, you must fight me': The Sociology of Drinking in the Middle Colonies," *Pennsylvania History* 64 (1997): 28–55, and Bruce Dorsey, *Reforming Men and Women: Gender in the Antebellum City* (Ithaca, N.Y.: Cornell University Press, 2002).

A good introduction to the festive culture of the colonial era is Richard L. Bushman, *King and People in Provincial Massachusetts* (Chapel Hill: University of North Carolina Press, 1985). Two studies of the political meaning of festive culture in the early United States are Simon P. Newman, *Parades and Politics of the Streets: Festive Culture in the Early American Republic* (Philadelphia: University of Pennsylvania Press, 1997), and David Waldstreicher, *In the Midst of Perpetual Fetes: The Making of American Nationalism, 1776–1820* (Chapel Hill: University of North Carolina Press, 1997).

CHAPTER 6

Debating the Constitution

*Speeches from the New York
Ratification Convention*

The delegates who attended the Federal Convention in Philadelphia in the summer of 1787 knew that the result of their meeting would be controversial. During the months that followed, as the states organized special conventions to ratify or reject the new plan for a federal government, supporters of the Constitution watched anxiously, like bettors trying to handicap a horse race. One such observer was George Washington, who had come out of his retirement at Mount Vernon to preside over the Federal Convention. Writing to his friend and fellow Federalist Henry Knox in January 1788, Washington noted that of all the states, "the determinations of new York . . . seem the most problematical."

Washington had a gift for understatement. New York had sent three delegates to the Federal Convention, but two of them—Robert Yates and John Lansing—left a few weeks into the proceedings when it became clear that the convention intended to replace rather than revise the Articles of Confederation. Yates and Lansing reported their misgivings to New York governor George Clinton, who shared their displeasure with what was happening at the Federal Convention. A New York City newspaper, the *Daily Advertiser*, printed the first copy of the Constitution in the state on September 21. Other printers quickly followed, even printing the Constitution in translation, so that Dutch-speaking inhabitants could read it in their native language. The Constitution's rapid dissemination throughout the state ensured that it would be the subject of a spirited public debate.

By the time Washington wrote his letter to Knox in early 1788, New York had become a battleground over ratification, with well-organized factions on each side raising money and calling in outside support to make their case. Supporters of ratification were known as Federalists. As was the case in other

Figure 6.1 George Washington Presiding at the Federal Convention, 1787 This 1799
*illustration imagines the delegates at work at the Federal Convention twelve years earlier. No
such images appeared at the time of the convention, in part because the delegates conducted
their work behind closed doors and refused to discuss it in public until they were finished. The
air of secrecy that surrounded the drafting of the Constitution aroused the opposition of some
critics, who believed that a privileged few were trying to impose a new and less democratic
form of government on the many.* Source: Free Library of Philadelphia.

states, they came chiefly from urban and commercial backgrounds and favored
the Constitution because they believed it would create a more centralized and
stable union between the states. They wanted a stronger federal government,
one capable of acting independently of the states, so that the United States
could pursue its economic and diplomatic interests more effectively with foreign powers and Indian nations. They also wanted the federal government to
have its own taxation power, so that it could be financially independent of the
states and pay off its debts at home and abroad. The most famous published
commentary on the Constitution, a series of eighty-five editorials in New York's
newspapers known collectively as *The Federalist*, was a product of their propaganda campaign on behalf of the Constitution in New York.

The Antifederalists, or opponents of the Constitution, met fire with fire,
churning out their own editorials and pamphlets in the battle over ratifica-

tion. As in other states, New York's Antifederalists tended to come from backgrounds more rural and less wealthy than the Federalists. They were more likely than Federalists to be debtors instead of creditors and to be engaged in subsistence agriculture rather than commercial food or craft production. They opposed the Constitution because a strong central government reminded them too much of the government they had rebelled against in 1776. The proposed federal government looked too much like the British Crown and Parliament, distant from and unrepresentative of the common people. They feared that the rich and well-connected could easily monopolize power in such a government, shifting the burden of taxation to the lower and middle classes. Worst of all, the proposed Constitution did not even have a bill of rights, a common feature of the state constitutions, that guaranteed the civil liberties such as freedom of speech and religion that Americans had fought and died for during the Revolution.

When New York's ratification convention finally met in the Hudson River town of Poughkeepsie on June 17, 1788, the Constitution appeared dead on arrival. Governor Clinton, whose Antifederalist sympathies were already well known, chaired the proceedings. More important, of the sixty-five delegates in attendance, forty-six were Antifederalists, a better than two-to-one margin over the Constitution's supporters. The only counties to send Federalist delegations to Poughkeepsie were centered around New York City; every county north of the lower Hudson Valley was represented by Antifederalists. This geographic distribution reflected a division of interests within the state. While lawyers, merchants, and large landowners could be found on each side of the ratification debate, they made up a much larger proportion of the Federalist delegates at the convention (79 percent to 50 percent). From the outset, the New York ratification convention pitted a minority of wealthy, urban Federalists against a majority of Antifederalists from rural counties and more middling social backgrounds.

New York's vote on the Constitution had profound implications for the rest of the United States. When the convention opened, eight of the nine state ratifications necessary for the new government to take effect had already occurred, while contests too close to call were being fought in New Hampshire and Virginia. Regardless of how the votes in New Hampshire and Virginia turned out, the new federal government would not fare well if New York stood apart from the union. New York City had the best harbor in the country and played a central role in the nation's overseas trade. Furthermore, the Hudson and Mohawk rivers provided the nation with its most important route into the continent's interior, and New York was a vital communications link between New England and the South. Without New York, no one expected the new federal government to prosper or endure.

Despite their numerical superiority at the convention, New York's Antifederalists could not afford to reject the Constitution out of hand. Eight states had already ratified, and the Antifederalist delegates were no more interested in seeing their state stand apart from the union than their opponents were. There was even some talk among the Federalists of splitting the state in two, so that the lower Hudson Valley, New York City, and Long Island could join the new federal union if the delegations from the northern counties refused to budge. When news arrived in Poughkeepsie on June 25 that New Hampshire had ratified, it became apparent to all concerned that some version of the Constitution would go into effect, regardless of what the New Yorkers decided. The chief goal of the Antifederalist leadership at that point became securing a conditional ratification, contingent upon the acceptance of amendments to the Constitution before it went into effect. The Federalists opposed this strategy, because conditional ratification would require convening another interstate convention, thereby delaying and perhaps jeopardizing the installation of the new government. Worse yet, the new federal government might form without the New Yorkers on board, locking them out of key decisions on such matters as the location of the new federal capital.

Once deliberations got under way in Poughkeepsie, leaders emerged on both sides of the debate. As presiding officer, Governor Clinton needed to maintain an air of impartiality, so he spoke rarely. Instead, the Antifederalists' most effective speaker was Melancton Smith, a self-educated merchant and lawyer who lived mostly in New York City but attended the convention as a delegate from upstate Dutchess County, where he owned a large estate. Smith's wealth did not make him a typical Antifederalist, but his unpolished manner and firm commitment to democratic principles made him suspicious of privilege and power and naturally sympathetic to the Antifederalist cause. His chief opponent was Alexander Hamilton, a former aide-de-camp to George Washington who had married into one of the state's wealthiest families. Hamilton had been New York's third delegate to the Federal Convention the previous year, but unlike Yates and Lansing, he supported the convention's designs and signed the Constitution when it was finished. With James Madison and John Jay, he coauthored the *Federalist* newspaper editorials in 1787–1788. Observers at the ratification convention recognized the talents and energy of Smith and Hamilton. Poughkeepsie lawyer James Kent called Smith "the most prominent and responsible speaker on the party of the anti-federalist majority . . . Hamilton's most persevering and formidable antagonist." Smith himself described Hamilton as the "champion" of the Federalists: "he speaks frequently, very long and very vehemently." The fate of the Constitution in New York and the nation hinged upon the standoff between these two men and their political allies in a Hudson River courthouse.

Using the Source: The Ratification Debates

The Federal Convention that drafted the Constitution took place in secrecy. The delegates cloistered themselves behind closed doors and did not speak a word to anyone about their proceedings until they presented a completed draft to the public in September 1787. The process of ratification was different. Each state called a special convention solely for the purpose of passing judgment on the document. These conventions were as open and public as the Federal Convention had been closed and secret. New York's ratification convention was no exception: the Poughkeepsie courthouse accommodated 200 spectators in addition to the sixty-five delegates. For the first two weeks of the convention, the *Daily Advertiser* printed each day's debates in full; after July 2 (when news of Virginia's ratification arrived), it printed summaries of each day's proceedings. Like the other state ratification conventions, New York's convention left a substantial public record that has captivated historians ever since.

Each state determined the time and place of its ratification convention and the means by which delegates would be selected for it. Most states held special elections for delegates to their conventions, using the same eligibility requirements for voting that they did for elections to the state legislature. New York differed from this practice by temporarily expanding its franchise, allowing all free adult males to vote for delegates to the ratification convention. This move actually had little impact on the number of votes cast, because the state's 1777 constitution had already significantly lowered the amount of property a man had to own in order to vote, but it did indicate the pervasive belief among Federalists and Antifederalists alike that the power of the proposed federal government would derive directly from the people, and therefore, they would have to be the ultimate arbiters on ratification. Of course, this definition also reflected their consensus that the "people" did not include women, slaves, or other groups traditionally excluded from the political process.

What Can the Ratification Debates Tell Us?

The great advantage to studying the proceedings of the ratification conventions is that they provide the fullest record available of how Americans interpreted the Constitution at the time it was adopted. In other words, this is a source that speaks directly to one of the guiding principles of constitutional interpretation: what was the original intent of the framers of the Constitution? Strict constructionists, those scholars and judges who believe that the power of the federal government should extend no further than is explicitly stated in the Constitution, place great emphasis on original intent and argue that the purposes and ideas of those men who adopted the Constitution should guide our interpretation of the document. Loose constructionists, on the other hand, believe that the Constitution is a "living document" that needs to be reinterpreted by each generation if it is to meet the needs of a changing society. They place less importance on original intent but still argue with strict constructionists about what the framers had in mind when they wrote and ratified the Constitution. Some of the most hotly debated constitutional issues of today, such as gay rights and affirmative action, testify to how far removed our modern society is from the world of Alexander Hamilton and Melancton Smith. Yet, the words they spoke in Poughkeepsie in 1788 are an important part of the textual record lawyers and judges use to interpret the Constitution in our courtrooms.

In arguing over original intent, strict and loose constructionists invariably refer to the same set of sources: the notes kept by James Madison during the

Federal Convention, editorials and pamphlets published during the ratification process in 1787–1788, and the proceedings of the state ratification conventions. Madison's notes are important because he was the primary author of the Constitution, and he left the most complete account of what occurred during the Federal Convention in Philadelphia. The political tracts published during 1787–1788 convey the visceral intensity of the debate over ratification. Neither of these sources, however, compares to the proceedings of the state ratification conventions in presenting the range and depth of the Federalist and Antifederalist positions. Even a cursory review of the state convention records reveals that the debate over original intent should really be one over "original intents," because there was such a variety of opinions expressed among the delegates who decided the ratification issue.

The proceedings of the ratification conventions also illustrate the nature of political expression and ideology in post-Revolutionary America. In our age of modern media politics, in which politicians speak on the evening news in sound bites that are measured in seconds, we may find it strange that convention delegates gave speeches that lasted for hours and commanded the rapt attention of their audiences. As indicated by the following excerpt from a June 21, 1788, speech by Alexander Hamilton, the delegates sprinkled their debates liberally with references to the republics of ancient Greece and Rome.

It was remarked yesterday, that a numerous representation was necessary to obtain the confidence of the people. This is not generally true. The confidence of the people will easily be gained by a good administration. This is the true touchstone. I could illustrate the position by a variety of historical examples, both ancient and modern. In Sparta, the ephori were a body of magistrates, instituted as a check upon the senate, and representing the people. They consisted of only five men; but they were able to protect their rights, and therefore enjoyed their confidence and attachment. In Rome, the people were represented by three tribunes, who were afterwards increased to ten. Every one acquainted with the history of that republic will recollect how powerful a check to the senatorial encroachments this small body proved; how unlimited a confidence was placed in them by the people, whose guardians they were; and to what a conspicuous station in the government their influence at length elevated the plebeians.

One of the city-states of ancient Greece

Representatives of the common people in the Roman republic, who possessed a veto power over other magistrates

The common people of ancient Rome

Elected annually as overseers of Sparta's kings, whom they could impeach and depose if the kings acted contrary to the law

What assumption is Hamilton making here about the education of his audience?

Refers to the Roman Senate, which represented the aristocracy

These references may strike us now as haughty and obscure, but this political language resonated among their listeners. By reading these speeches and trying to unlock their persuasive power, we can gain insight into the political culture and ideology that generated the Constitution in the first place.

A disadvantage arising from the use of this source is the difficulty of measuring how much impact public speeches and debates had on the votes cast at the ratification conventions. Delegates got elected to the New York ratification convention in part because their constituents already knew how they would vote. Then, as now, political debate made for good public theater, but did the eloquence of Alexander Hamilton or Melancton Smith actually convince any of the delegates to change their minds? We know from the final vote tally that some of the Antifederalist delegates did end up voting for ratification, but we do not know if they did so because of the persuasive power of the speeches they heard or because of some other motivation.

Certainly, factors external to New York influenced the proceedings. After news of Virginia's ratification reached Poughkeepsie on July 2, the proceedings changed markedly. As the ratification of the Constitution was now a foregone conclusion, delegates gave fewer speeches and spent most of their time negotiating the wording of proposed amendments and ratification resolutions. How should historians weigh this change in circumstances when trying to determine the impact of the speeches made before July 2? In fathoming the motivations behind the final vote, we must also consider the possibility that some delegates voted for unstated reasons of personal interest, such as the desire for public office in the new federal government, or because of compromises struck with their rivals behind closed doors.

In other words, the ratification debates are a great source for reconstructing the public arguments Federalists and Antifederalists made for and against the Constitution, but we cannot rely on them solely if we wish to reconstruct the thoughts behind the votes cast in the ratification conventions. That is why historians usually supplement their work on the debates with research into the backgrounds and personal writings of the convention delegates. In private letters or recollections, the men who decided the fate of the Constitution were often more plainspoken about the delicate balancing of ideology and interests that determined their votes. Also, research into the economic and social background of the delegates helps to uncover patterns in the voting on ratification that may confirm or contradict the delegates' public statements about the Constitution.

Questions to Ask

When working with the ratification debates, it is good to know as much as you can about the delegates who spoke and voted at the state conventions. Where were they from? What occupations and social positions did they hold? With those facts established, you can turn your attention to the speeches themselves. How do the speeches illustrate the fundamental issues separating the two sides? What elements of the Constitution were the most controversial? Look closely at the language employed by each side. Antifederalists and Federalists used a common political vocabulary but vested different meanings in words like *interests, aristocracy,* and *ambition.* Understanding those words in the context of the speeches will help you comprehend the interests and ideas that separated the two sides in the debate.

- What is the social and economic background of the person giving the speech?
- What elements of the Constitution were most controversial to the delegates?
- What terms and language did each side employ to make its case?
- What do these debates tell you about the economic interests and political ideology behind the ratification of the Constitution?

Source Analysis Table

As you read through the source, use this table to help organize your notes and summarize the Federalist and Antifederalist positions on the following issues.

	Federalists	Antifederalists
Representation in Congress		
Sources of Corruption		
Constitution's Impact on the States		

To download and print this table, visit the book companion site at **bedfordstmartins.com/brownshannon**.

The Source: Speeches Debating the Constitution from the New York Ratification Convention, June 21–28, 1788

The passages that follow are from debates that occurred between June 21 and June 28, when delegates on both sides gave long speeches detailing their contrasting opinions on the Constitution. You will notice that the style of presentation varies from one speech to the next. Some read like verbatim transcriptions, while others read like an editor's narrative summary of the speech's content. These differences resulted from day-to-day variances in how the proceedings were recorded by a newspaper editor who published them in the *Daily Advertiser,* a New York newspaper.

REPRESENTATION IN CONGRESS

One of the Antifederalists' chief objections to the Constitution was that the House of Representatives was not representative enough. The House would be limited in size to no more than one representative for every 30,000 people. Antifederalists believed this would lead to electoral districts much too large to represent the people adequately and that election would be out of the reach of any candidate not rich or famous enough to command reputation over such a wide area. Federalists responded to this argument by questioning whether more representatives actually meant better representation.

1   *Melancton Smith,* June 21, 1788

To determine whether the number of representatives proposed by this Constitution is sufficient, it is proper to examine the qualifications which this house[1] ought to possess, in order to exercise their power discreetly for the happiness of the people. The idea that naturally suggests itself to our minds, when we speak of representatives, is, that they resemble those they represent. They should be a true picture of the people, possess a knowledge of their circumstances and their wants, sympathize in all their distresses, and be disposed to seek their true interests. The knowledge necessary for the representative of a free people not only comprehends extensive political and commercial information, such as is

[1] The House of Representatives.

Source: All of the debate passages reprinted in this chapter are excerpted from Bernard Bailyn, editor, *The Debate on the Constitution: Federalist and Anti-Federalist Speeches, Articles, and Letters during the Struggle over Ratification* (New York: Library of America, 1993), 2:759–835.

acquired by men of refined education, who have leisure to attain to high degrees of improvement, but it should also comprehend that kind of acquaintance with the common concerns and occupations of the people, which men of the middling class of life are, in general, more competent to, than those of a superior class. To understand the true commercial interests of a country, not only requires just ideas of the general commerce of the world, but also, and principally, a knowledge of the productions of your own country, and their value, what your soil is capable of producing, the nature of your manufactures, and the capacity of the country to increase both. To exercise the power of laying taxes, duties, and excises, with discretion, requires something more than an acquaintance with the abstruse[2] parts of the system of finance. It calls for a knowledge of the circumstances and ability of the people in general—a discernment how the burdens imposed will bear upon the different classes.

From these observations results this conclusion—that the number of representatives should be so large, as that, while it embraces the men of the first class, it should admit those of the middling class of life. I am convinced that this government[3] is so constituted that the representatives will generally be composed of the first class in the community, which I shall distinguish by the name of the natural aristocracy of the country. I do not mean to give offence by using this term. I am sensible this idea is treated by many gentlemen as chimerical.[4] I shall be asked what is meant by the natural aristocracy, and told that no such distinction of classes of men exists among us. It is true, it is our singular felicity that we have no legal or hereditary distinctions of this kind; but still there are real differences. Every society naturally divides itself into classes. The Author of nature[5] has bestowed on some greater capacities than others; birth, education, talents, and wealth, create distinctions among men as visible, and of as much influence, as titles, stars, and garters. In every society, men of this class will command a superior degree of respect; and if the government is so constituted as to admit but few to exercise the powers of it, it will, according to the natural course of things, be in their hands. Men in the middling class, who are qualified as representatives, will not be so anxious to be chosen as those of the first. When the number is so small, the office will be highly elevated and distinguished; the style in which the members live will probably be high; circumstances of this kind will render the place of a representative not a desirable one to sensible, substantial men, who have been used to walk in the plain and frugal paths of life.

. . . A substantial yeoman,[6] of sense and discernment, will hardly ever be chosen. From these remarks, it appears that the government will fall into the hands of the few and the great. This will be a government of oppression. I do not mean to declaim against the great, and charge them indiscriminately with

[2] Difficult to comprehend.

[3] The new federal government proposed by the Constitution.

[4] Imaginary.

[5] God.

[6] A middle-class farmer.

want of principle and honesty. The same passions and prejudices govern all men. The circumstances in which men are placed in a great measure give a cast to the human character. Those in middling circumstances have less temptation; they are inclined by habit, and the company with whom they associate, to set bounds to their passions and appetites. If this is not sufficient, the want of means to gratify them will be a restraint: they are obliged to employ their time in their respective callings; hence the substantial yeomanry of the country are more temperate, of better morals, and less ambition, than the great. The latter do not feel for the poor and middling class; the reasons are obvious—they are not obliged to use the same pains and labor to procure property as the other. They feel not the inconveniences arising from the payment of small sums. The great consider themselves above the common people, entitled to more respect, do not associate with them; they fancy themselves to have a right of preeminence in every thing. In short, they possess the same feelings, and are under the influence of the same motives, as an hereditary nobility. I know the idea that such a distinction exists in this country is ridiculed by some; but I am not the less apprehensive of danger from their influence on this account. . . .

2   *Alexander Hamilton,* June 21, 1788

Mr. *Hamilton* then reassumed his argument. . . .

It has been observed, by an honorable gentleman,[1] that a pure democracy, if it were practicable, would be the most perfect government. Experience has proved that no position in politics is more false than this. The ancient democracies, in which the people themselves deliberated, never possessed one feature of good government. Their very character was tyranny; their figure, deformity. When they assembled, the field of debate presented an ungovernable mob, not only incapable of deliberation, but prepared for every enormity.[2] In these assemblies, the enemies of the people brought forward their plans of ambition systematically. They were opposed by their enemies of another party; and it became a matter of contingency, whether the people subjected themselves to be led blindly by one tyrant or by another.

It was remarked yesterday, that a numerous representation was necessary to obtain the confidence of the people. This is not generally true. The confidence of the people will easily be gained by a good administration. This is the true touchstone. I could illustrate the position by a variety of historical examples, both ancient and modern. In Sparta, the ephori were a body of magistrates, instituted as a check upon the senate, and representing the people. They consisted of only five men; but they were able to protect their rights, and there-

[1] Melancton Smith.
[2] Outrage.

fore enjoyed their confidence and attachment. In Rome, the people were represented by three tribunes, who were afterwards increased to ten. Every one acquainted with the history of that republic will recollect how powerful a check to the senatorial encroachments this small body proved; how unlimited a confidence was placed in them by the people, whose guardians they were; and to what a conspicuous station in the government their influence at length elevated the plebeians. Massachusetts has three hundred representatives; New York has sixty-five. Have the people in this state less confidence in their representation than the people of that? Delaware has twenty-one. Do the inhabitants of New York feel a higher confidence than those of Delaware? I have stated these examples to prove that the gentleman's principle is not just. The popular confidence depends on circumstances very distinct from considerations of number. Probably the public attachment is more strongly secured by a train of prosperous events, which are the result of wise deliberation and vigorous execution, and to which large bodies are much less competent than small ones. . . .

It has been further, by the gentlemen in the opposition,[3] observed, that a large representation is necessary to understand the interests of the people. This principle is by no means true in the extent to which the gentlemen seem to carry it. I would ask, Why may not a man understand the interests of thirty as well as of twenty? The position appears to be made upon the unfounded presumption that all the interests of all parts of the community must be represented. No idea is more erroneous than this. Only such interests are proper to be represented as are involved in the powers of the general[4] government. These interests come completely under the observation of one or a few men; and the requisite information is by no means augmented in proportion to the increase of number. . . .

Sir, we hear constantly a great deal which is rather calculated to awake our passions, and create prejudices, than to conduct us to the truth, and teach us our real interests. I do not suppose this to be the design of the gentlemen. Why, then, are we told so often of an aristocracy? For my part, I hardly know the meaning of this word, as it is applied. If all we hear be true, this government is really a very bad one. But who are the aristocracy among us? Where do we find men elevated to a perpetual rank above their fellow-citizens, and possessing powers entirely independent of them? The arguments of the gentlemen only go to prove that there are men who are rich, men who are poor, some who are wise, and others who are not; that, indeed, every distinguished man is an aristocrat. This reminds me of a description of the aristocrats I have seen in a late publication styled the *Federal Farmer*.[5] The author reckons in the aristocracy all governors of states, members of Congress, chief magistrates, and all officers of

---

[3] The Antifederalists.

[4] Federal.

[5] A widely circulated Antifederalist pamphlet.

the militia. This description, I presume to say, is ridiculous. The image is a phantom. Does the new government render a rich man more eligible than a poor one? No. It requires no such qualification. . . .

It is a harsh doctrine that men grow wicked in proportion as they improve and enlighten their minds. Experience has by no means justified us in the supposition that there is more virtue in one class of men than in another. Look through the rich and the poor of the community, the learned and the ignorant. Where does virtue predominate? The difference indeed consists, not in the quantity, but kind, of vices which are incident to various classes; and here the advantage of character belongs to the wealthy. Their vices are probably more favorable to the prosperity of the state than those of the indigent, and partake less of moral depravity. . . .

3 *Melancton Smith*, June 21, 1788

The honorable *Melancton Smith* rose, and observed, that the gentleman[1] might have spared many of his remarks in answer to the ideas he had advanced. The only way to remedy and correct the faults in the proposed Constitution was, he imagined, to increase the representation and limit the powers. He admitted that no precise number could be fixed upon. His object only was to augment the number in such a degree as to render the government more favorable to liberty. . . .

The honorable member[2] had observed, that the confidence of the people was not necessarily connected with the number of their rulers, and had cited the ephori of Sparta, and the tribunes in Rome, as examples. But it ought to be considered, that, in those places, the people were to contend with a body of hereditary nobles; they would, therefore, naturally have confidence in a few men who were their leaders in the constant struggle for liberty. The comparison between the representations of several states did not better apply. New York had but sixty-five representatives in Assembly. But because sixty-five was a proper representation of two hundred and forty thousand, did it follow that it was also sufficient for three millions? The state legislatures had not the powers of the general government, and were not competent to those important regulations which might endanger liberty.

The gentleman, continued Mr. *Smith*, had ridiculed his idea of an aristocracy, and had entered into a definition of the word. He himself agreed to this definition, but the dispute was not of words, but things. He was convinced that in every society there were certain men exalted above the rest. These men he did not consider as destitute of morality or virtue. He only insisted that they could not feel sympathetically the wants of the people.

[1] Alexander Hamilton.
[2] Hamilton.

SOURCES OF CORRUPTION

Both Federalists and Antifederalists believed that corruption in government resulted from the pursuit of individual ambitions for wealth, fame, and power. They disagreed over who was more or less likely to fall prey to such ambitions. The Antifederalists believed that the Constitution gave free rein to the ambitions of the rich and powerful. The Federalists believed that under the Constitution, those seeking office in the federal government were more likely to do so out of a sense of public-spiritedness than personal gain.

 ## *Robert R. Livingston,* June 23, 1788

Robert R. Livingston was a Federalist delegate and chancellor of the New York State Supreme Court. He came from one of New York's wealthiest and most distinguished families.

The honorable gentleman from Dutchess,[1] who has so copiously declaimed against all declamation,[2] has pointed his artillery against the rich and the great. I am not interested in defending rich men: but what does he mean by telling us that the rich are vicious and intemperate?[3] Will he presume to point out to us the class of men in which intemperance is not to be found? Is there less intemperance in feeding on beef than on turtle?[4] or in drinking rum than wine? I think the gentleman does not reason from facts. If he will look round among the rich men of his acquaintance, I fancy he will find them as honest and virtuous as any class in the community. He says the rich are unfeeling; I believe they are less so than the poor; for it seems to me probable that those who are most occupied by their own cares and distresses have the least sympathy with the distresses of others. The sympathy of the poor is generally selfish, that of the rich a more disinterested[5] emotion.

The gentleman further observes, that ambition is peculiarly the vice of the wealthy. But have not all classes of men their objects of ambition? Will not a poor man contend for a constable's staff with as much assiduity and eagerness as a man of rank will aspire to the chief magistracy? The great offices in the state are beyond the view of the poor and ignorant man: he will therefore contemplate an humbler office as the highest alluring object of ambition; he will look with equal envy on a successful competitor, and will equally sacrifice to the attainment of his wishes the duty he owes to his friends or to the public. But, says the gentleman, the rich will be always brought forward; they will

---

[1] Melancton Smith.

[2] Spoken pompously against pompous speech.

[3] Prone to excess, especially in drink.

[4] Turtle was considered a delicacy of the rich.

[5] Concerned for the well-being of others.

exclusively enjoy the suffrages of the people. For my own part, I believe that, if two men of equal abilities set out together in life, one rich, the other of small fortune, the latter will generally take the lead in your government. The rich are ever objects of envy; and this, more or less, operates as a bar to their advancement. What is the fact? Let us look around us: I might mention gentlemen in office who have not been advanced for their wealth; I might instance, in particular, the honorable gentleman who presides over this state,[6] who was not promoted to the chief magistracy[7] for his riches, but his virtue.

. . . We are told that, in every country, there is a natural aristocracy, and that this aristocracy consists of the rich and the great: nay, the gentleman goes further, and ranks in this class of men the wise, the learned, and those eminent for their talents or great virtues. Does a man possess the confidence of his fellow-citizens for having done them important services? He is an aristocrat. Has he great integrity? Such a man will be greatly trusted: he is an aristocrat. Indeed, to determine that one is an aristocrat, we need only be assured he is a man of merit. But I hope we have many such. I hope, sir, we are all aristocrats. So sensible am I of that gentleman's[8] talents, integrity, and virtue, that we might at once hail him the first of the nobles, the very prince of the Senate. But whom, in the name of common sense, will we have to represent us? Not the rich, for they are sheer aristocrats. Not the learned, the wise, the virtuous, for they are all aristocrats. Whom then? Why, those who are not virtuous; those who are not wise; those who are not learned: these are the men to whom alone we can trust our liberties. He says further, we ought not to choose these aristocrats, because the people will not have confidence in them; that is, the people will not have confidence in those who best deserve and most possess their confidence. He would have his government composed of other classes of men: where will we find them? Why, he must go out into the highways, and pick up the rogue and the robber; he must go to the hedges and ditches, and bring in the poor, the blind, and the lame. As the gentleman has thus settled the definition of aristocracy, I trust that no man will think it a term of reproach; for who among us would not be wise? Who would not be virtuous? Who would not be above want? How, again, would he have us to guard against aristocracy? Clearly by doubling the representation, and sending twelve aristocrats instead of six. The truth is, in these republican governments, we know no such ideal distinctions. We are all equally aristocrats. Offices, emoluments,[9] honors, are open to all.

[6] Governor George Clinton, chair of the ratification convention.
[7] Governorship.
[8] Smith's.
[9] The profits of office.

5 | *Melancton Smith,* June 23, 1788

The gentleman[1] wishes me to describe what I meant by representing the feelings of the people. If I recollect right, I said the representative ought to understand and govern his conduct by the true interest of the people. I believe I stated this idea precisely. When he attempts to explain my ideas, he explains them away to nothing; and, instead of answering, he distorts, and then sports with them. But he may rest assured that, in the present spirit of the Convention, to irritate is not the way to conciliate. The gentleman, by the false gloss[2] he has given to my argument, makes me an enemy to the rich: this is not true. All I said was, that mankind were influenced, in a great degree, by interests and prejudices; that men, in different ranks of life, were exposed to different temptations, and that ambition was more peculiarly the passion of the rich and great. The gentleman supposes the poor have less sympathy with the sufferings of their fellow-creatures, for that those who feel most distress themselves, have the least regard to the misfortunes of others. Whether this be reasoning or declamation, let all who hear us determine. I observed, that the rich were more exposed to those temptations which rank and power hold out to view; that they were more luxurious and intemperate, because they had more fully the means of enjoyment; that they were more ambitious, because more in the hope of success. The gentleman says my principle is not true, for that a poor man will be as ambitious to be a constable as a rich man to be a governor; but he will not injure his country so much by the party he creates to support his ambition.

The next object of the gentleman's ridicule is my idea of an aristocracy; and, indeed, he has done me the honor to rank me in the order. If, then, I am an aristocrat, and yet publicly caution my countrymen against the encroachments of the aristocrats, they will surely consider me as one of their most disinterested friends.

[1] Robert R. Livingston.

[2] Explanation.

THE CONSTITUTION'S IMPACT ON THE STATES

One of the chief topics of debate at the New York ratification convention was the impact that the Constitution would have on the powers of the state governments. The Federalists believed the Constitution would elevate the federal government above the state governments, allowing it to operate independently in such realms as international relations, interstate commerce, and taxation. Antifederalists balked at reducing the influence of the state governments within the federal union, because they believed those governments were more democratic and less prone to corruption than the federal one proposed by the Constitution.

6   *Melancton Smith*, June 27, 1788

Sir, I contemplate the abolition of the state constitutions as an event fatal to the liberties of America. These liberties will not be violently wrested from the people; they will be undermined and gradually consumed. On subjects of the kind we cannot be too critical. The investigation is difficult, because we have no examples to serve as guides. The world has never seen such a government over such a country. If we consult authorities in this matter, they will declare the impracticability of governing a free people on such an extensive plan. In a country where a portion of the people live more than twelve hundred miles from the centre, I think that one body cannot possibly legislate for the whole. Can the legislature frame a system of taxation that will operate with uniform advantages? Can they carry any system into execution? Will it not give occasion for an innumerable swarm of officers, to infest our country and consume our substance? People will be subject to impositions[1] which they cannot support, and of which their complaints can never reach the government.

Another idea is in my mind, which I think conclusive against a simple government for the United States. It is not possible to collect a set of representatives who are acquainted with all parts of the continent. Can you find men in Georgia who are acquainted with the situation of New Hampshire, who know what taxes will best suit the inhabitants, and how much they are able to bear? Can the best men make laws for the people of whom they are entirely ignorant? Sir, we have no reason to hold our state governments in contempt, or to suppose them incapable of acting wisely. I believe they have operated more beneficially than most people expected, who considered that those governments were erected in a time of war and confusion, when they were very liable to errors in their structure. It will be a matter of astonishment to all unprejudiced men hereafter, who shall reflect upon our situation, to observe to what a great degree good government has prevailed. It is true some bad laws have been passed in most of the states; but they arose from the difficulty of the times rather than from any want of honesty or wisdom. Perhaps there never was a government which, in the course of ten years, did not do something to be repented of. . . . We all agree that a general government is necessary; but it ought not to go so far as to destroy the authority of the members. We shall be unwise to make a new experiment, in so important a matter, without some known and sure grounds to go upon. The state constitutions should be the guardians of our domestic rights and interests, and should be both the support and the check of the federal government.

[1] Taxes.

7 | *Alexander Hamilton,* June 28, 1788

federalist

The gentleman[1] has made a declaration of his wishes for a strong federal government. I hope this is the wish of all. But why has he not given us his ideas of the nature of this government, which is the object of his wishes? Why does he not describe it? We have proposed a system which we supposed would answer the purposes of strength and safety.—The gentleman objects to it, without pointing out the grounds, on which his objections are founded, or shewing[2] us a better form. These general surmises never lead to the discovery of truth. It is to be desired, that the gentleman would explain particularly the errors in this system, and furnish us with their proper remedies. . . .

The gentleman says, that the operation of the taxes[3] will exclude the states, on this ground, that the demands of the community are always equal to its resources; that Congress will find a use for all the money the people can pay. This observation, if designed as a general rule, is in every view unjust. Does he suppose the general government will want all the money the people can furnish; and also that the state governments will want all the money the people can furnish? What contradiction is this? But if this maxim be true, how does the wealth of a country ever increase? How are the people enabled to accumulate fortunes? Do the burthens regularly augment,[4] as its inhabitants grow prosperous and happy? But if indeed all the resources are required for the protection of the people, it follows that the protecting power should have access to them. The only difficulty lies in the want of resources: If they are adequate, the operation will be easy. If they are not, taxation must be restrained: Will this be the fate of the state tax alone? Certainly not. The people will say no. What will be the conduct of the national rulers? The consideration will not be, that our imposing the tax will destroy the states, for this cannot be effected; but that it will distress the people, whom we represent, and whose protectors we are. It is unjust to suppose that they[5] will be altogether destitute of virtue and prudence. It is unfair to presume that the representatives of the people will be disposed to tyrannize, in one government more than in another. If we are convinced that the national legislature will pursue a system of measures unfavorable to the interests of the people, we ought to have no general government at all. But if we unite, it will be for the accomplishment of great purposes. . . .

I shall conclude with a few remarks by way of apology. I am apprehensive, sir, that, in the warmth of my feelings, I may have uttered expressions which were too vehement. If such has been my language, it was from the habit of using strong phrases to express my ideas; and, above all, from the interesting

[1] Melancton Smith.

[2] Showing.

[3] Taxes levied by the new federal government.

[4] Burdens regularly increase.

[5] Federal officeholders.

nature of the subject. I have ever condemned those cold, unfeeling hearts, which no object can animate. I condemn those indifferent mortals, who either never form opinions, or never make them known. I confess, sir, that on no subject has my breast been filled with stronger emotions, or more anxious concern. If any thing has escaped me, which may be construed into a personal reflection, I beg the gentlemen,[6] once for all, to be assured that I have no design to wound the feelings of any one who is opposed to me.

While I am making these observations, I cannot but take notice of some expressions which have fallen in the course of the debate. It has been said that ingenious men may say ingenious things, and that those who are interested in raising the few upon the ruins of the many, may give to every cause an appearance of justice. I know not whether these insinuations allude to the characters of any who are present, or to any of the reasonings in this house. I presume that the gentlemen would not ungenerously impute such motives to those who differ from themselves. I declare I know not any set of men who are to derive peculiar advantages from this Constitution. Were any permanent honors or emoluments to be secured to the families of those who have been active in this cause, there might be some grounds for suspicion. But what reasonable man, for the precarious enjoyment of rank and power, would establish a system which would reduce his nearest friends and his posterity to slavery and ruin? If the gentlemen reckon me amongst the obnoxious few, if they imagine that I contemplate with ambitious eye the immediate honors of the government, yet let them consider that I have my friends, my family; my children, to whom ties of nature and of habit have attached me. If, to-day, I am among the favored few, my children, to-morrow, may be among the oppressed; these dear pledges of my patriotism may, at a future day, be suffering the severe distresses to which my ambition has reduced them. The changes in the human condition are uncertain and frequent: many, on whom Fortune has bestowed her favors, may trace their family to a more unprosperous station; and many, who are now in obscurity, may look back upon the affluence and exalted rank of their ancestors. But I will no longer trespass on your indulgence. I have troubled the committee with these observations, to show that it cannot be the wish of any reasonable man to establish a government unfriendly to the liberties of the people. Gentlemen ought not, then, to presume that the advocates of this Constitution are influenced by ambitious views. The suspicion, sir, is unjust; the charge is uncharitable.

Analyzing the Ratification Debates

1. Using your notes from the table on page 121, briefly explain the principles upon which Antifederalists objected to the Constitution. How did Federalists answer those objections? How did Antifederalists envision the future of the nation if the Constitution was ratified?

---

[6] His fellow convention delegates.

2. In Sources 1–5 (pp. 122–29), what meanings did the delegates attach to the following words and phrases: *natural aristocracy, ambition, passions,* and *interests*? Did the meanings of these words change depending on whether a Federalist or Antifederalist uttered them?

3. What, if anything, do these passages tell you about the delegates who remained silent during the proceedings? What sort of evidence would you want to see before assuming that they shared the views expressed by their leaders on the floor?

4. Some historians describe the clash between Federalists and Antifederalists as a struggle between economic classes; others emphasize differences in political ideology. Having read these excerpts from the ratification debates, what do you think was the most distinguishing characteristic of the divide between Federalists and Antifederalists? Was the struggle over ratification ultimately about differences in economic interests or political ideas?

5. How should scholars and judges trying to interpret original intent make use of the ratification convention proceedings? Antifederalists were present at the creation of the Constitution, yet spoke—and sometimes voted—against it. How then should modern scholars regard the opinions of the Antifederalists when trying to reconstruct original intent?

6. Having read Federalist and Antifederalist predictions of how the Constitution would work, who do you think was right? Have any of the Antifederalists' fears come true? If you had attended the New York ratification convention, which side do you think you would have taken? Explain your choice.

The Rest of the Story

New York ratified the Constitution by a vote of 30–27, the narrowest margin of victory in any of the state ratification conventions that met in 1787–1788 (Rhode Island, which initially refused to call a ratification convention, finally did so in spring 1790 and ratified the Constitution by an even closer vote of 32–30). If we consider New York along with two other key states, we can get a clearer picture of how narrowly the Constitution passed through the ratification process. Convention delegates in New York, Virginia, and Massachusetts cast a total of 580 votes; the margin of victory in each of those states was 3, 10, and 19 votes respectively. In other words, 32 votes out of 580 cast in those states tilted the balance in favor of ratification, a margin of only 5.5 percent.

In some respects, it might be said that New York's Antifederalists lost the battle but won the war. None of them ever seriously considered making New York an independent republic; after news of ratification in New Hampshire and Virginia reached them, they pegged their hopes on amending the Constitution after it went into effect. As was the case in several other states, the New York Antifederalists thought that the Constitution needed to have a bill of rights that would protect the people's liberties from the power of the new federal government. Alexander Hamilton answered on behalf of the Federalists, calling a federal bill of rights unnecessary because the Constitution did not grant the federal government powers over the rights in question and the state constitutions already guaranteed such rights to their citizens.

The delegates at the New York convention broke their impasse by drafting a resolution that voted for ratification "in full confidence" that a federal convention would be called after the formation of the new government to give "early and mature Consideration" to amendments recommended by the Antifederalists. When Smith and other leading Antifederalist delegates made clear their support for this phrasing, the vote for ratification passed, albeit by only three votes. Smith and his allies formed a political society in the fall of 1788 to pursue a second federal convention, but their objective was preempted by James Madison, who introduced to the first Congress a list of twelve amendments to the Constitution that distilled many of the recommendations made by Antifederalists at the state ratification conventions, including New York's. Madison's proposed amendments dealt chiefly with the civil liberties the Antifederalists were so concerned about protecting: freedom of religion and freedom of the press; the rights to assembly, to bear arms, and to trial by jury; and prohibitions on excessive bail, cruel and unusual punishments, and unreasonable search and seizures. The states ratified ten of those amendments in 1791, and they became known collectively as the Bill of Rights. It is ironic that today, the one part of the Constitution with which Americans are most familiar (who among us has not "taken the Fifth" when faced with an unpleasant question?) would not be there if the Antifederalists had not been so persistent in their demands for a more perfect union.

To Find Out More

The proceedings of the New York ratification convention were first published in the newspaper *The Daily Advertiser* and then as *Debates and Proceedings of the Convention of the State of New-York* (1788; repr., Poughkeepsie, N.Y.: Vassar Brothers Institute, 1905). Nineteenth-century historian Jonathan Elliot included them in his collection of documents related to the state ratification conventions, available in a five-volume reprint as *The Debates in the Several State Conventions on the Adoption of the Federal Constitution* (New York: B. Franklin, 1968). Two other useful reference works on the ratification conventions are Bernard Bailyn, editor, *The Debate on the Constitution: Federalist and Anti-Federalist Speeches, Articles, and Letters during the Struggle over Ratification,* 2 volumes (New York: Library of America, 1993), and Merrill Jensen, John P. Kaminski, and Gaspare J. Saladino, editors, *The Documentary History of the Ratification of the Constitution,* 18 volumes (Madison: State Historical Society of Wisconsin, 1976–). Two online archives of primary sources related to the ratification of the Constitution are the Library of Congress's "American Memory" Web site at **loc.gov/ammem/amlaw**, and the "Avalon Project" at the Yale Law School at **yale.edu/lawweb/avalon/constpap.htm**.

Linda Grant De Pauw provided a complete and engaging retelling of ratification in New York in *The Eleventh Pillar: New York State and the Federal Constitution* (Ithaca, N.Y.: Cornell University Press, 1966). Students looking for a concise retelling of the Constitution's origins might try Carl Van Doren's *The Great Rehearsal: The Story of the Making and Ratifying of the Constitution of the United States* (1948; repr., New York: Penguin Books, 1986), although its bias in favor of the Federalists is quite clear. A good antidote to Van Doren's triumphant tale is Jackson Turner Main's *The Anti-Federalists: Critics of the Constitution, 1781– 1788* (Chapel Hill: University of North Carolina Press, 1961).

Three more recent books have added new vigor to the scholarly debate over ratification. David J. Siemers's *Ratifying the Republic: Antifederalists and Federalists in Constitutional Time* (Stanford, Calif.: Stanford University Press, 2002) and Saul Cornell's *The Other Founders: Anti-Federalism and the Dissenting Tradition in America, 1788–1828* (Chapel Hill: University of North Carolina Press, 1999) reconsider the political thought of the Antifederalists and their enduring influence on American politics. Jack N. Rakove's *Original Meanings: Politics and Ideas in the Making of the Constitution* (New York: Vintage Books, 1996) illuminates the question of original intent by examining the diversity of opinion on several key issues surrounding the Constitution's drafting and ratification.

For an offbeat retelling of the New York ratification convention on film, see *An Empire of Reason*, directed by Muffie Meyer (1988), which recreates the convention as if it were being covered by the modern news media. Actors playing Alexander Hamilton and Melancton Smith express opinions drawn from the original ratification convention proceedings but in the context of television talk shows and news programs. This imaginative film merits viewing, especially for the questions it raises about how our modern media and political system might handle the ratification process if it took place today.

CHAPTER 7

The Question of Female Citizenship

Court Records from the New Nation

William and Anna Martin left home in a hurry. William was an artillery officer in the British army, and when it evacuated Boston in early 1776, he and Anna went with it. They left behind a substantial amount of property. Most of the family's wealth came from Anna, the daughter of a prosperous Boston merchant. When her father died in 1770, she had inherited a house with a wharf and stables in Boston, a farm in Braintree, and more than 800 acres of land in Massachusetts and New Hampshire.

The Martins were just two of the thousands of Americans who went into exile in Britain, Canada, or the West Indies as a result of the Revolution. Many loyalists tried to sit out the war by avoiding public life or military service, but the patriots did not make that easy to do. Local and state governments demanded loyalty oaths from those people they considered suspect and expected adult males to serve in the militia. Many loyalists left home for what they hoped would be temporary stays abroad until the rebellion ended. Others were forced out by neighbors and enemies anxious to seize their property. By the war's end, about 80,000 loyalists had left the United States. They ranged from some of the wealthiest families in British North America to slaves who did not even own the clothes on their backs.

We do not know whether William and Anna Martin intended for their exile to be permanent, but they never returned to Boston. They followed the British army to Nova Scotia and then to New York City, where they stayed until the army evacuated in 1783. From there the Martins resettled in England. In the eyes of the revolutionary government of Massachusetts, the Martins were "absentees," people who had expressed their political allegiance with their feet by leaving the state after the War for Independence broke out on April 19,

1775. Under a law passed in 1779, Massachusetts claimed the right to confiscate the property left behind by such absentees, and the state did so with the Martins' estate in 1781, selling the land and buildings to raise money for the Massachusetts treasury.

In 1801, James Martin, the son and heir of William and Anna (both of whom had since died), sued the state of Massachusetts for restoration of the confiscated property. After losing his case in a lower court, he appealed it to the Massachusetts Supreme Court, which heard the case in 1805. Such legal cases were not uncommon in the aftermath of the Revolution. The peace treaty that ended the war recommended that the states allow loyalists to recover lost property. The novelty of *Martin v. Massachusetts* rested in its focus on the political and legal status of Anna Martin. Both sides agreed that the property in question had belonged to Anna by right of her inheritance from her father. James Martin's attorneys argued that because Anna was a wife, she had no choice but

Figure 7.1 A Female Patriot This woodcut of a woman wearing a tricornered hat and holding a powder horn and a musket appeared in a number of different contexts during the Revolutionary era, usually as testimony to the confusion of the times. The need to choose sides between patriots and loyalists raised many questions about the nature of female citizenship and a woman's right to hold and act on her political opinions. Could a married woman legally express political loyalties contrary to her husband's? What kind of duties, if any, did she owe to the state?

Source: Collection of the New-York Historical Society, id number 48257.

to follow her husband into exile, and therefore, she was not subject to the state's confiscation law. The state's attorneys argued that the law's wording explicitly extended its authority over women as well as men, and therefore, the confiscation was legal and binding. Each side also argued other points about legal jurisdiction and due process, but the case ultimately hinged on the question of Anna Martin's status as a wife and citizen: Did she voluntarily renounce her allegiance to Massachusetts when she left the state, or was she, as a woman and wife, a person who could exercise no option other than to obey her husband's wishes?

Martin v. Massachusetts tells us much about the limits and possibilities of change in women's legal status during the Revolutionary era. In a famous exchange of letters in 1776, Abigail and John Adams debated the extent to which political independence from Great Britain should affect gender relations in the new nation. Abigail urged her husband and his fellow delegates at the Second Continental Congress to "remember the Ladies" in the "new code of laws" they would pass after declaring independence, and she warned him that if they did not, women would not "hold ourselves bound by any laws in which we have no voice, or Representation." John replied dismissively to Abigail's request, noting that the patriots' cause against Britain had "loosened the bands of government everywhere," so that children, apprentices, students, slaves, Indians, and now even wives challenged the authority of their rightful masters. Historians have long used this exchange to illustrate dissension within American society over the meaning of independence. Many Americans previously excluded from the political process hoped that the Revolution would make possible an expansion in their rights and liberties, but many patriot leaders worked to limit the impact that independence from Britain had on the people over whom they claimed authority.

The legal dispute over Anna Martin's property illustrates the questions the Revolution raised about female citizenship. Before the Revolution, the colonists were subjects of the British Crown. A person became a subject to the Crown upon birth, and as the word implies, subjecthood entailed obligations of submission, obedience, and loyalty. When the American patriots declared independence, they disavowed their status as subjects and redefined themselves as citizens of a republic. Then, as now, citizenship implied choice and equality: a person became a citizen by entering into a social contract with others and voluntarily assenting to the laws their government created. This social contract equated property ownership with citizenship: only those individuals who held property had the economic and political independence necessary to enter into the social contract. People without property—children, servants, slaves, the laboring poor—were by definition too dependent on others to live and act independently as fully enfranchised citizens. Under the old system of monarchy, subjecthood was hierarchical and authoritarian, but also inclusive; the British Crown claimed all sorts of people as its subjects, regardless of their race, sex, or ethnic origin. Citizenship in the new nation was egalitarian and contractual, but also exclusive; some people possessed the attributes necessary to become citizens, while others lacked them entirely.

In *Martin v. Massachusetts*, attorneys and judges debated the nature of female citizenship. The case raised all sorts of nettlesome questions about the intersection of property, gender, and a woman's allegiance to her husband and country. The fact that the property in question had belonged to Anna Martin suggested that she had the means to act independently when she chose to give her allegiance to Britain. On the other hand, she was also a wife, bound by personal vows, religious principles, and the law to submit to the will of her husband. The lawyers' arguments and judges' opinions in *Martin v. Massachusetts* raised a host of questions about citizenship in the new nation. What possible obligations could a woman owe to the republic, and could those obligations take precedence over marriage vows? Did independence turn *all* of the former British subjects in the thirteen colonies—or only some of them—into citizens of the new nation? And, if only some subjects became citizens, how did gender figure into that equation?

Using the Source: Court Records

Court cases can be difficult to read because lawyers and judges speak and write in their own specialized language. This problem is compounded when a researcher confronts historical court cases that deal with legal principles and terms no longer commonly used today. Thus, the best place to start when analyzing a source such as *Martin v. Massachusetts* is with making sure you understand the key legal concepts and language involved in the case.

A married woman in eighteenth-century Anglo-American law was known as a "feme-covert" (the plural "femes-covert" is often used in the source on p. 140). This term meant a wife was literally covered by her husband: she could not buy, sell, or own property independently of him; she could not write her own will or enter into contracts; she could not sue or be sued in a court of law; and she could not vote, serve on juries, or hold public office. In short, a woman had no recognized legal identity because the law assumed that her husband spoke and acted for her.

A married woman's status as a feme-covert severely restricted her access to property, yet Anglo-American legal custom did provide certain protections to women in this regard. A woman such as Anna Martin who inherited real estate surrendered its management to her husband upon marriage but retained an interest in it. In legal terms, a husband acquired only a "life estate" in such property: he could lease or rent it and enjoy the profits it generated, but he did not own the property in "fee simple," that is, with no restrictions on transfer of ownership. He could not permanently sell or bequeath the property in question to someone else without his wife's consent. When he died, the management of the property reverted to his wife or her heirs. This legal custom ensured that property the wife brought to the marriage would remain in her family line; her husband could not divert it to the children of a previous or subsequent marriage.

Another important custom that governed female access to property was a woman's "dower right." Anglo-American probate courts, which settled estates when a property owner died without a will, set aside one-third of the estate (both real estate and personal property) to support the widow of the deceased. This reservation was known as a "dower right" or "widow's thirds." Its purpose was to provide for a woman's subsistence during her widowhood. It did not grant her full possession of that property, only the right to the revenues it produced. Upon her remarriage or death, full possession of the property in question reverted to the heirs of her deceased husband.

The legal definitions of a feme-covert and dower right figured prominently in the deliberation of *Martin v. Massachusetts*, as is evident in the following excerpt from the court case. In this passage, Massachusetts Solicitor General Daniel Davis is referring to both a wife's status as a feme-covert and her dower right. Note how he interprets the wording of the Confiscation Act to mean that it applies to absentee women as well as men.

Asks whether a wife can commit any of the offenses that the law identifies as causes for confiscation

Wording of the Confiscation Act that protects the dower right of women who remained in the United States after their loyalist husbands left the country

Argues that the Confiscation Act subjects to confiscation all property held by women who chose to follow their husbands into exile

The question then is: whether a *feme-covert* is capable of committing the offences, or any *one* of the offences specified in the statute?[1] For if a *feme-covert* could commit any one of the offences mentioned, and that offence be well laid in the information, the judgment ought to be affirmed.[2] That a *feme-covert* could perform *one,* at least, of the acts described, that of withdrawing herself from the State into parts and places under the dominion of the King of *Great Britain*, &c. is proved by the *seventh section*—which provides, "that when the *wife* or widow of any of the persons aforedescribed, *shall have remained* within the jurisdiction of any of the said United States &c. she shall be entitled to the improvements and income of one third part of her husband's real and personal estate, after payment of debts, during her life *and continuance within* the said United States; and her dower therein shall be set off to her by the judge of probate in like manner as it might have been if her husband had *died intestate,*[3] within the jurisdiction of this State." The exception proves the rule. *Wives* who *remained here* are mentioned as an exception—the statute therefore embraced all persons who did not remain—who withdrew. The very supposition that *some* persons of this description, some *femes-covert* might remain, implies that all had the *power* of remaining or withdrawing as they pleased—and if *femes-covert* had not been *intended* to be included under the previous *general words* of the statute there could have been no necessity of making the exception in favour of those who remained behind.

[1] The Massachusetts Confiscation Act of 1779.
[2] The judgment of the lower court upholding the confiscation should stand.
[3] Without a will.

The Massachusetts Confiscation Act of 1779 penalized loyalists by seizing the property they left behind when they fled the state. The preamble of the Confiscation Act legitimized such confiscations by claiming that the absentees had broken the social contract by failing to provide assistance to the state during wartime. By fleeing its borders, they renounced their citizenship, freeing the state from its obligation to protect their property and allowing the government to dispose of the abandoned property as it saw fit. This logic became much murkier when applied to women. Most of the states recognized a woman's dower right when they confiscated loyalist estates, preserving one-third of the property to support the dependent women and children of absentees. The Massachusetts Confiscation Act specifically preserved the dower right of loyalist wives who stayed in America, but what about a woman such as Anna Martin who followed her husband into exile? Was she also guilty of breaking the social contract?

In debating this question, the lawyers and judges involved in *Martin v. Massachusetts* had two choices. If the court upheld the confiscation of Anna Martin's property, then it would endorse the idea that a married woman could choose her political allegiance and be held accountable for it independently of her husband. Such a decision would seriously undermine the legal notion of a feme-covert. If the court overturned the confiscation, it would uphold the more traditional view of married women as femes-covert, but it would also give land back to loyalists (or in this case, their heirs), which would undoubtedly prove a politically unpopular decision.

What Can Court Records Tell Us?

Popular images of the law present it as something divinely ordained, neutral, and unchanging, literally carved in stone like the commandments Moses carried down from a mountaintop. The architecture of American courthouses, built in the style of ancient Greek temples and adorned with statues of blind-folded female figures holding the scales of justice, certainly encourage such associations. Legal historians, however, emphasize the social and political context within which laws are made and enforced. Just as Abigail Adams recognized that declaring independence would make necessary a "new code of laws," legal historians find in the law a way of examining how society responds to changing political or social conditions. Legal decisions, from landmark Supreme Court cases such as *Roe v. Wade* to more obscure cases heard in local and state courts, provide a mirror on the critical issues of their day.

Examining court cases also helps historians see how legal abstractions get put into practice. Take for example the republican rhetoric of the American Revolution. The patriots enshrined liberty, equality, and independence as the founding principles of the new nation, but how did these ideas actually affect social relations within the United States, and how did people react when these principles conflicted with traditional ideas about how society should work? In *Martin v. Massachusetts*, the court had to reconsider the meaning of citizenship in light of a clash between a Revolutionary commitment to equality and traditional gender roles that accorded women second-class status to men.

Another advantage to working with court cases and legal documents is their narrative structure. Each court case tells a story with a clear beginning, middle, and end. Anglo-American legal culture emphasizes precedent and logic; lawyers build cases and judges render decisions based on what previous cases have said and the evidence before them. Anyone who has ever watched a film or television show based on a court trial is familiar with the adversarial nature of the American legal process; each side gets to present its case, countering the evidence and arguments presented by the other. Once you comprehend the vocabulary and procedure used in such court cases, you will find that they often render complex ideas in a concise, concrete manner.

Of course, the logic and order evident in a court case can also be a disadvantage if you do not approach the source with a critical eye. It is always important to ask of this type of source, Who made the law in question and why? Who is controlling its interpretation and execution? Legal decisions do not take place in a vacuum; all sorts of external factors influence how lawyers, witnesses, juries, and judges present and interpret evidence. Racism, prejudice, or outright bribery can and do corrupt the legal process. Legal historians must also be aware of more subtle biases that affect the administration of the law.

Consider for example the political affiliations involved in the *Martin v. Massachusetts* case. All four of the judges who rendered written opinions in this case belonged to the Federalist Party, which generally attracted social and political conservatives. As a group, these judges were probably not particularly interested in using this case to rewrite the law on women's rights. James Sullivan, the attorney general of Massachusetts and chief spokesman for the state's case, belonged to the Democratic-Republican Party, which advocated more radical ideas about social and political equality. His argument makes a case for redefining female citizenship in light of the Revolution's commitment to contractual government. At the time of the trial, he was also Massachusetts's Democratic-Republican candidate for governor. How likely do you think it was that the judges listened to Sullivan's arguments without being prejudiced by their opposition to his politics? One does not have to accuse the judges of corruption to recognize that their decision may have been influenced by factors other than the evidence and arguments before them.

Gender bias may also have influenced the decision in the *Martin v. Massachusetts* case. This case was initiated, argued, and decided entirely by men, as was consistent with legal practices at that time. Anna Martin, the central figure in the legal arguments presented, remains mute throughout the entire proceedings. She was of course dead at the time, but neither side in the case seemed particularly interested in trying to retrieve what she thought about her loyalism, property, or status as a wife. Even if she had been alive, the legal system as it was then constructed would have offered her little opportunity to speak for herself in court. You must take into consideration the obvious gender bias built into the legal system that decided this case when determining its usefulness as a source.

Questions to Ask

Much like historians, lawyers and judges build arguments around their interpretation of facts. You can read documents from a court case, therefore, in much the same way you read a journal article or book by a historian. What are the basic facts, and who are the principal figures involved in the case? What specific law or crime does the case address? (For the purposes of this chapter, these questions have already been answered for you.) With a firm grasp of those details, you can turn to how the lawyers and judges present and interpret the facts. What argument is each side making? What evidence is each side using in its argument? How are the judges interpreting the evidence and arguments in their decisions?

- What are the facts of this case?
- What laws or crimes are involved?
- What are the opposing arguments?
- How are judges interpreting the evidence and arguments in their decisions?

Source Analysis Table

As you read the *Martin v. Massachusetts* case, use the tables on page 144 to organize your notes on the lawyers' and judges' interpretations of the Massachusetts Confiscation Act of 1779.

	The Lawyers' Arguments and Evidence
Representing the Plaintiff, James Martin *George Blake* *Theophilus Parsons*	
Representing the Defendant (Commonwealth of Massachusetts) *Daniel Davis* *James Sullivan*	

	The Judges' Opinions
Justice Sedgwick	
Justice Strong	
Justice Dana	

To download and print this table, visit the book companion site at **bedfordstmartins.com/brownshannon**.

The Source: *James Martin (Plaintiff in Error) v. The Commonwealth and William Bosson and Other Ter-tenants*, 1805

James Martin is identified in the case's name as the "plaintiff in error," because he was arguing that he was wronged by an error made in the lower court's decision. "The Commonwealth" identifies the state of Massachusetts as a codefendant in the suit. William Bosson and the other "ter-tenants" were the owners and/or occupants of the property at the time James Martin filed suit. "Ter" means three; thus, Bosson and three other owners and/or occupants were named as codefendants in the suit.

THE LAWYERS' ARGUMENTS

James Martin's lawsuit began in 1801 in a lower court, which upheld the confiscation of his mother's property. He appealed that decision to the Supreme Judicial Court of Massachusetts, which heard the case in 1805. His attorneys argued that the lower court had made four errors in its judgment. These "errors" were the points on which Martin made his case to the state's Supreme Court. The first three dealt with issues of the original right of ownership in the land, due process, and the lower court's jurisdiction. The fourth (referred to in the source text as the "fourth error") concerned whether Anna Martin's status as a feme-covert made her property liable for confiscation under the Massachusetts Confiscation Act of 1779. These excerpts follow the arguments of both sides on this point.

1   *The Fourth Error Identified by James Martin's Attorneys in Their Appeal*

Fourthly. Because, by the information and complaint aforesaid, it doth appear that the said *William Martin* was owner of the estates aforesaid during his natural life only, and that the fee-simple[1] thereof belonged to the said *Anna Martin*, the said *William's* wife, who by the act or law aforesaid, referred to in said information, was not liable to have her estates confiscated as aforesaid, and against whom the process and judgment aforesaid could not by law extend.

[1] Right of ownership.

Source: All of the arguments and opinions reprinted in this chapter are excerpted from *Reports of Cases Argued and Determined in the Supreme Judicial Court of the State of Massachusetts from September 1804 to June 1805—Both Inclusive*, volume 1 (Boston: S. & E. Butler, 1805): 347–99.

2 *George Blake, Attorney for James Martin*

As to the *fourth* error assigned. *Femes-covert* are not within the statute.[1] They are not within the *letter* of the act—almost all the provisions of the act are masculine—nothing is said about females, excepting where provision is made for their dower. It is admitted that there are cases where statutes will extend to females, where the expressions are similar to those used in this act. But it is manifest from the act itself that women were not *intended* to be included under the general description of persons mentioned.

The first *section* of the act says "that every inhabitant and member of the State who &c." Upon the strict principles of law a *feme-covert* is not a member—[she] has no *political* relation to the State any more than an alien—upon the most rigid and illiberal construction of the words she cannot be a member within the meaning of the statute. . . . The legislation[2] *intended* to exclude *femes-covert* and infants from the operation of the act—otherwise the word *inhabitant* would have been used alone, and not coupled with the word *member*. This construction is strengthened by the provision in the same (*the first*) section of the act respecting an oath of allegiance. A *feme-covert* was never holden to take an oath of allegiance. The statute is highly penal—the court therefore will not extend it beyond the express words, or obvious meaning, by an equitable construction. The preamble is a key to unlock the meaning. What says the preamble?

"Whereas every government has a right to command the personal services of all its members, whenever the exigencies of the State shall require it, especially in times of an impending or actual invasion, no member thereof can then withdraw himself from the jurisdiction of the government, and thereby deprive it of *his personal service*,[3] without justly incurring the forfeiture of all *his* property, rights and liberties holden under and derived from that conclusion of government, to the support of which *he* hath refused to afford *his* aid and assistance: and whereas the King of *Great Britain* did cause &c. &c. whereupon it became the indispensable duty of all the *people* of said States forthwith to *unite in defence* of their common freedom, and *by arms* to oppose the fleets and armies of the said King; yet, nevertheless, divers[4] of the *members* of this and the other United States of America, evilly disposed, or regardless of their duty towards their country, did withdraw themselves &c. &c. *aiding* or giving encouragement and countenance to the operations of the fleets and armies of the said King against the United States aforesaid."

It is impossible to read the preamble to the statute without seeing the object and intention of the act. The object was not to punish, but to retain the

[1] The Massachusetts Confiscation Act of 1779.
[2] The Confiscation Act.
[3] Military service.
[4] Many.

physical force of the state, as is evident from the expressions, *personal services in times of actual invasion*— opposing *by arms*— *aiding* the enemy, &c. How much physical force is retained by retaining married women? What are the *personal services* they are to render in opposing by *force* an actual invasion? What *aid* can they give to an enemy? So far are women from being of service in the defence of a country against the attacks of an enemy that it is frequently thought expedient to send them out of the way, lest they impede the operations of their own party.

In construing statutes[5] no rule is better established than that *general* expressions shall be *restrained* by the manifest intent of the legislature to be collected from the whole act taken together.

. . . And can it be supposed, in the case before the court, that the legislature contemplated the case of a wife withdrawing with her husband? It ought not to be, and surely was not, intended that she should be exposed to the loss of all her property for withdrawing from the government with her husband. If he commanded it she was bound to obey him, by a law paramount to all other laws—the law of God.

[5] In interpreting laws.

3   *Daniel Davis, Solicitor General for Massachusetts*

As to the *fourth original* error. It is contended by the counsel for the plaintiff in error, that the statute does not extend to *femes-covert*, that women are not named, are not mentioned in the statute. The *first section* says, *every* inhabitant and member. *Anna Martin* was an inhabitant, and appears by the record to have been so. She is therefore within the statute. The *third section* says, any *person*— this is certainly sufficiently comprehensive to include all persons who could commit any of the offences mentioned in the act. The question then is: whether a *feme-covert* is capable of committing the offences, or any *one* of the offences specified in the statute? For if a *feme-covert* could commit any one of the offences mentioned, and that offence be well laid in the information, the judgment ought to be affirmed. That a *feme-covert* could perform *one,* at least, of the acts described, that of withdrawing herself from the State into parts and places under the dominion of the King of *Great Britain*, &c. is proved by the *seventh section*— which provides, "that when the *wife* or widow of any of the persons aforedescribed, *shall have remained* within the jurisdiction of any of the said United States &c. she shall be entitled to the improvements and income of one third part of her husband's real and personal estate, after payment of debts, during her life *and continuance within* the said United States; and her dower therein shall be set off to her by the judge of probate in like manner as it might have been if her husband had *died intestate,*[1] within the jurisdiction of this State." The exception proves the rule. *Wives* who *remained here* are mentioned as an exception—the statute therefore embraced all persons who did not remain—who withdrew. The very supposition that *some* persons of this description, some *femes-covert* might remain, implies that all had the *power* of remaining or withdrawing as they pleased—and if *femes-covert* had not been *intended* to be included under the previous *general words* of the statute there could have been no necessity of making the exception in favour of those who remained behind. If this be not so, still there is another reason. Where the husband has abjured[2] the realm the relation is dissolved between the husband and wife. This act of the husband, *William Martin,* amounts to an abjuration of the realm—and the consequence is that she became sole seized.[3] If this consequence is not liked, then they may both be considered as having abjured, which is in itself treason—which a *feme-covert* can certainly commit, and by which she forfeits her estate—and this process is sufficient to confiscate her estate for her act of treason.

[1] Without a will.
[2] Renounced his allegiance.
[3] Sole owner of the property.

 ## James Sullivan, Attorney General for Massachusetts

Under the *fourth* error *originally* assigned it has been contended by the counsel for the plaintiff that the statute did not extend to *femes-covert.* And it is said that the *words* of the act do not include them because the words are in the masculine gender—that they are *him, his,* &c. The same reasoning would go to prove that the *Constitution* of the Commonwealth[1] does not extend to women—secures to them no rights, no privileges—for it has no words in the feminine gender: it would prove that a great variety of crimes, made so by statute, could not be committed by women, because the statutes had used only the words *him* and *his.* It is also said that a *feme-covert* is not an *inhabitant* and *member* of the State. Surely a *feme-covert* can be an inhabitant, in every sense of the word. Who are members of the body-politic? Are not all the *citizens,* members; infants, idiots, insane or whatever may be their *relative* situations in society? Cannot a *feme-covert* levy war and conspire to levy war? She certainly can commit treason—and if so, there is no one act mentioned in the statute which she is not capable of performing. In the case before the court she was defaulted[2]—this, as in common civil actions, which may be brought against a *feme-covert,* confesses the facts alleged.

[1] Massachusetts.
[2] Failed to appear in court to contest the original confiscation.

5 Theophilus Parsons, Attorney for James Martin

The real question is whether the statute was intended to include persons who have, by law, no wills of their own. The statute extends to persons who have *freely* renounced their relation to the State. Infants, insane, *femes-covert*, all of whom the law considers as having no will, cannot act *freely*. Can they freely renounce? The statute meant such, and such only, as could. Is the State entitled to the *personal* services of a *feme-covert* to defend it in war? Can she render any? What aid and comfort can she give to an invading enemy? Has she the control of property? Is she ever required to take the oath of allegiance?—As to the provision in the statute for dower; that has no relation to *her* property—it is merely the donation of the State, giving to her a part of that which was absolutely its own. . . . It has been said that the husband abjured the realm, and that this dissolved the marriage contract—this is a strange consequence, and one till now unheard of.

THE JUSTICES' OPINIONS

Like the Supreme Court of the United States, the Supreme Judicial Court of Massachusetts did not use a jury. Rather, it was made up of five justices who heard each case and rendered a decision by vote. The justices then issued written opinions explaining their votes. Five justices heard *Martin v. Massachusetts,* and four of those wrote opinions. Justice George Thacher called for reversing the confiscation because of a procedural error in the lower court, but he did not address the issue of Anne Martin's status as a feme-covert in his opinion. The three remaining written opinions all addressed the "fourth error" concerning Anne Martin's status as a feme-covert, and they are excerpted below.

6 Justice Theodore Sedgwick

. . . By the record before us it appears that *William Martin* and *Anna Martin*, the father and mother of the plaintiff in error, are *jointly* charged with the several acts which are alleged in the libel[1] of the Attorney-General as incurring the forfeiture for which he sued—that, since the 19th day of *April* 1775, they had levied war and conspired to levy war against the provinces, or colonies, or United States: that they had, adhered[2] to the king of *Great Britain* his fleets and armies and had given to them aid and comfort; that since that time they had,

[1] Statement of charges against the Martins.
[2] Pledged their allegiance.

without permission of the legislative or executive authority of any of the United States, withdrawn themselves therefrom into parts and places under the acknowledged authority of the king of *Great Britain*—all these charged as done jointly by the husband and wife—and we are called upon, by matter apparent on the record and by one of the errors expressly assigned, to say whether a *feme-covert* for *any* of these acts, *performed with her husband*, is within the intention of the statute: and I think that she is not.

In construing statutes the great object is to discover from the words, the subject-matter, the mischiefs contemplated and the remedies proposed, what was the true meaning and design of the legislature. In the relation of husband and wife the law makes, in her behalf, such an allowance for the authority of the husband and her duty of obedience, that guilt is not imputed to *her* for actions performed jointly by them, unless of the most heinous and aggravated nature. For instance—the law says, whoever steals shall be punished, and yet if the wife participates in a theft with her husband she is not punishable. Innumerable other instances might be given. She is exempted from punishment, not because she is within the letter of the law if she had sufficient will to be considered as acting voluntarily and as moral agent but, because she is viewed in such a state of subjection and so under the control of her husband that she acts merely as his instrument, and that no guilt is imputable[3] to her.

Compare this with the case under consideration. In a case of great political interest, in which men of great powers and equal integrity, as said by the Attorney-General, divided; and where a *feme-covert* is not expressly included, shall we suppose her to be so by general words? Can we believe that a wife for so respecting the understanding of her husband as to submit her own opinions to his, on a subject so all-important as this, should lose her own property and forfeit the inheritance of her children? Was she to be considered as criminal because she permitted her husband to elect his own and her place of residence? Because she did not, in violation of her marriage vows, rebel against the will of her husband? So hard and cruel a construction, against the general and known principles of law on this subject, could be justified by none but strong and unequivocal expressions. So far is this from being the case in this statute, that it seems to me understood that such was the intention of the legislature—but the contrary. The preamble of the statute has described the persons whom it intended to bring within it. It is that member who "withdraws himself from the jurisdiction of the government and thereby deprives it of the benefit of his personal services." A *wife* who left the country in the company of her husband did not *withdraw* herself—but was, if I may so express it, withdrawn by him. She did not deprive the government of the benefit of her personal services—she had none to render—none were exacted of her. "The member who so withdraws, incurs," says the preamble, "the forfeiture of all his property, right and liberties holden under and delivered from that constitution of government, to the support of which he has refused to afford his aid and assistance." Can any one believe it was the intention of the legislature to demand of *femes-covert* their *aid and assistance* in the support of their constitution and government?

---

[3] Assignable.

The preamble then goes on to particularize the violation of our rights by our former sovereign, and proceeds to declare that it thereupon "became the indispensable duty of all the *people* of said states forthwith to unite in defense of their common freedom, and *by arms* to oppose the fleets and armies of the said King; yet, nevertheless, divers of the *members* of this, and of the other United States of *America*, evilly disposed or regardless of their duty towards their country did withdraw themselves, &c." Now it is unquestionably true that the *members* here spoken of as "evilly disposed" are included in the *people* abovementioned. What then was the duty of these evilly disposed persons, for a violation of which they were to be cut off from the community to which they had belonged, and rendered aliens to it? It was "to unite in defense of their common freedom and *by arms* to oppose" an invading enemy. And can it be supposed to have been the intention of the legislature to exact the performance of this duty from *wives* in opposition to the will and command of their husbands? Can it be believed that an humane and just legislature ever intended that wives should be subjected to the horrid alternative of, either on the one hand, separating from their husbands and disobeying them, or, on the other, of sacrificing their property? It is impossible for me to suppose that such was ever their intention.

The conclusion of the preamble speaks of those who withdrew as thereby "aiding or giving encouragement and countenance to the operations" of the enemy. Were *femes-covert*, accompanying their husbands, thus considered by the legislature? I believe not. So far from believing that *wives* are within the statute, for any acts by them done jointly with their husbands, that a fair construction of the whole *act* together does, to my judgment, clearly exclude them. And I do not discern that the 7th *section* which has been cited to prove that *femes-covert*, for withdrawing with their husbands, were within the act, has the least tendency to that purpose.—This *section* does not contemplate those who withdrew with their husbands, but those who staid behind. The provision which it makes for them is not from their own estates, but from those of their husbands. And I cannot perceive that any inference is to be drawn from the one case which tends to illustrate the other. On the whole I am clearly of opinion that for this error the judgment must be reversed.

7 | *Justice Simeon Strong*

. . . Upon the question whether the estates of *femes-covert* were, by this statute, liable to confiscation, I am of opinion that they were not. The *act* was intended to take the estates of those persons who had voluntarily withdrawn themselves from the country and joined the fleets and armies of *Great Britain* with whom we were then at war. Could a *feme-covert* in any reasonable sense of the words of the *act* do this? I think not. The law considers a *feme-covert* as having no will— she is under the direction and control of her husband—is bound to obey his commands—and in many cases which might be mentioned, indeed in all cases except perhaps treason and murder cannot jointly with her husband act at all—

or at least so as to make herself liable to punishment. She could not even have conveyed this very estate during the coverture[1]—her husband could not have conveyed it so as to have bound her—and therefore I think that she could not forfeit it by any thing which she did or could do against the statute—and that no act of her husband could incur the forfeiture of *her* estate.—I am clearly of opinion that the statute does not extend to *femes-covert*. As to the other points in the cause I give no opinion—it not being necessary for the decision of the case now before us—but for the reasons already given I think that the judgment of the inferior[2] court ought to be reversed.

[1] Time of her marriage.
[2] Lower.

8   *Chief Justice Francis Dana*

. . . Another objection is, that "the statue does not extend to a *feme-covert* leaving the country with her husband." In a former stage of the cause I gave an opinion on this point, (a) and I see no reason to alter it. The words of the statute are general—*femes-covert* are not named—if the statute extends to them it must be by implication.—The statute does not charge a crime—every person had a right to take which side he pleased, in the contest in which we were then engaged. The statute rests on another principle. It is this—that every subject held his lands mediately[1] or immediately[2] from the *Crown*. Then it became a question whether all the *real* property[3] in the country was not holden under the authority of the states. And it was here adopted as a principle of the law that it was so holden. The consequence was that those persons who withdrew themselves from the country, for the purposes mentioned in the statute, lost the right of holding in the manner they would have been entitled to hold if the empire had not been divided. It was not thought fit and right that they should continue to possess and enjoy their property let the issue be what it might. The language of this statute was—go if you please—but if you withdraw we will not protect your property—we will take it. This was fair—they were not to be punished as criminal—but their property was considered as abandoned; and of course, that it belonged to the State. This was a consequence resulting from division of the empire.

. . . I am clearly of opinion that the judgment ought to be reversed . . . because *femes-covert*, having no will, could not incur the forfeiture. And that the statute never was intended to include them—and oblige them either to lose their property or to be guilty of a breach of the duties which by the laws of their country and the law of God they owed to their husbands.

JUDGMENT REVERSED.

[1] Through an intermediary landholder.
[2] Directly.
[3] Real estate.

[Justice] *Sewall* absent—but the Chief Justice said that he perfectly concurred with the rest of the court, on the ground that the statute did not extend to *femes-covert.*

Analyzing Court Records

1. Using your notes from the tables on page 144, summarize the arguments on each side of the case. On what principles or evidence do Martin's attorneys make their case, and how do the attorneys for Massachusetts counter those points? Do the same for the judges' opinions.

2. The lawyers in this case argued about the purposes and uses of the Massachusetts Confiscation Act, but they agreed on certain ideas about the nature of citizenship. According to them, what were the duties of a citizen, and what members of society were fit or unfit to perform them?

3. What are some of the contradictions or tensions between a woman's status as a feme-covert and her role as a citizen that are made evident in this case? How did the judges resolve these contradictions in their decision? How would that resolution have differed if the judges had decided in the state's favor?

4. At several points in this case, lawyers and judges referred to marriage as a relationship governed by law. Which law? How could a woman's adherence to the laws of marriage conflict with her adherence to the laws of the state? Which of the two did these lawyers and judges recognize as the higher law?

5. What implicit or explicit comparisons did the lawyers and judges in this case make between the British king's relationship to his subjects and a husband's relationship to his wife? What does their reasoning in this regard tell you about the impact the patriots' declaration of political independence from Britain had on other patriarchal relationships in American society?

The Rest of the Story

In rendering its decision in *Martin v. Massachusetts*, the court failed to challenge or reinterpret a woman's legal status as a feme-covert in post-Revolutionary America. By reversing the confiscation of Anna Martin's property, the judges endorsed the notion that a married woman could not act independently of her husband in political or economic matters. In the court's view, Anna Martin was bound by her marriage vows to obey her husband and follow him into exile. She could not therefore be subject to the state's confiscation law because she could exercise no choice in her political allegiance independently of her husband.

As this case illustrates, gender and citizenship intersected over the issue of property. In the Declaration of Independence, Thomas Jefferson had changed

John Locke's enumeration of natural rights from "life, liberty, and property" to "life, liberty, and the pursuit of happiness." In the nation that Jefferson and his contemporaries created, a person's freedom to pursue happiness depended in a large part on that person's access to property. Adult male property holders could vote, hold office, and dispose of their labor as they wished. All others — women, children, slaves, servants — were defined legally as dependents ruled over by husbands, parents, or masters.

Some changes occurred in marriage and property laws after the Revolution, but the impact of such changes on women were limited so long as they remained femes-covert. In the 1780s and 1790s, many states liberalized their divorce laws, making it easier for women to divorce husbands who abused or deserted them. State legislatures also abolished primogeniture laws, which favored firstborn sons over daughters and younger sons in settling probate cases. But these changes did not substantially alter a married woman's ability to own property.

Significant changes did not occur in laws governing female property ownership until the Jacksonian era. In the 1830s and 1840s, states passed laws that allowed married women to own and dispose of property independently of their husbands. These new laws originated in circumstances created by the rapidly expanding and highly volatile American economy. As more husbands found themselves entangled in debt, they warmed to the idea of transferring property to their wives, where it would be shielded from creditors in the event of bankruptcy or default. The expansion of industrial production and wage earning in the early nineteenth century also eroded the economic significance of a woman's dower right, and some states reduced or eliminated it altogether. In the face of such economic uncertainty, married women sought greater access and control over a family's real estate and personal property to provide financial stability for themselves and their children. Women's rights advocates supported such legal reforms because they regarded female property rights as one of the foundations of gender equality.

The American Revolution, in short, did not alter women's status as citizens or property holders as dramatically as Abigail Adams had hoped for in 1776. Despite the "new code of laws" drafted by her husband and his peers, the principles and practices behind the feme-covert remained embedded in the legal system. In the American republic, control over property was fundamental to defining citizenship, and the law defined both in masculine terms.

To Find Out More

Court records from the colonial and Revolutionary eras are sometimes available in modern editions. For cases from New England, a good place to start is David Thomas Konig and William Edward Nelson, editors, *Plymouth Court Records, 1686–1859,* 16 volumes (Wilmington, Del.: M. Glazier, 1978–1981). The records of federal courts are deposited in the National Archives in Washington, D.C. State court records are likewise maintained by state archives. Two works that will help you untangle the legal intricacies of inheritance and property laws in early America are Marylynn Salmon, *Women and the Law of Property in Early America* (Chapel Hill: University of North Carolina Press, 1986), and Carole Shammas, Marylynn Salmon, and Michael Dahlin, *Inheritance in America: From Colonial Times to the Present* (New Brunswick, N.J.: Rutgers University Press, 1987). A standard reference work for the meaning of legal terms is Bryan A. Garner, editor, *Black's Law Dictionary,* 7th edition (St. Paul, Minn.: West Group, 1999). Two useful Web sites for accessing primary sources and other materials on women during the Revolutionary era are "American Women's History: A Research Guide," at **mtsu.edu/~kmiddlet/history/women/wh-revol.html**, and "Women and Social Movements in the United States, 1600–2000," at **womhist.binghamton.edu**.

Historians interested in the effects that the American Revolution had on women's lives in the United States have found property law a very fruitful avenue of inquiry. Linda K. Kerber provided a compelling analysis of the legal and political significance of *Martin v. Massachusetts* in the first chapter of *No Constitutional Right to Be Ladies: Women and the Obligations of Citizenship* (New York: Hill and Wang, 1998). See also her article, "The Paradox of Women's Citizenship in the Early Republic: The Case of *Martin v. Massachusetts*, 1805," *American Historical Review* 97 (1992): 349–78. Two useful essays on women's property rights in the Revolutionary era are Carole Shammas, "Early American Women and Control over Capital," and Marylynn Salmon, "Republican Sentiment, Economic Change, and the Property Rights of Women in American Law," both in *Women in the Age of the American Revolution,* edited by Ronald Hoffman and Peter J. Albert (Charlottesville: United States Capitol Historical Society and the University Press of Virginia, 1989), 134–54 and 447–75, respectively. Two studies that focus on women and the law at the state level are Cornelia Hughes Dayton, *Women before the Bar: Gender, Law, and Society in Connecticut, 1639–1789* (Chapel Hill: University of North Carolina Press, 1995), and Norma Basch, *In the Eyes of the Law: Women, Marriage, and Property in Nineteenth-Century New York* (Ithaca, N.Y.: Cornell University Press, 1982).

The case of *Martin v. Massachusetts* also brings to light the difficulties faced by female loyalists, many of whom, like Anna Martin, endured exile and confiscation of property. For more on the fate of loyalist women, see Mary Beth Norton, "Eighteenth-Century American Women in Peace and War: The Case of the Loyalists," *William and Mary Quarterly*, third series, 33 (1976): 386–409. For a case study involving a wife who chose not to follow her loyalist husband into exile, see Wayne Bodle, "Jane Bartram's 'Application': Her Struggle for Survival, Stability, and Self-Determination in Revolutionary Pennsylvania," *Pennsylvania Magazine of History and Biography* 115 (1991): 185–220. A good general history of the loyalists is Wallace Brown, *The Good Americans: The Loyalists in the American Revolution* (New York: William Morrow and Company, 1969).

CHAPTER 8

Family Values

Advice Literature for Parents and Children in the Early Republic

In Philadelphia in 1783, twenty-year-old Nancy Shippen took some time out of her busy day to record how she wanted to raise her seventeen-month-old daughter Peggy. The child was her first, and Shippen, like many new parents, wanted to have some purposeful design behind her parenting. Starting from the premise that her daughter's upbringing should in "some particulars . . . differ from mine," Shippen recorded in her journal a list of points "Concerning a Daughter's Education":

1st. Study well her constitution and genius.
2nd. Follow nature and proceed patiently.
3rd. Suffer not servants to terrify her with stories of ghosts and goblins.
4th. Give her a fine pleasing idea of good, and an ugly frightful one of evil.
5th. Keep her to a good and natural regimen of diet.
6th. Observe strictly the little seeds of reason in her, and cultivate the first appearance of it diligently.

Shippen listed thirty-five points in all. She ended her list with this thought: "When wisdom enters into her heart, and knowledge is made pleasant to her soul, 'discretion shall preserve her, and understanding shall keep her.'"

Almost fifty years later, in 1831, another parent paused to record his thoughts about child rearing. The Reverend Francis Wayland was a New England minister and the father of a fifteen-month-old son named Heman. One Friday morning, Heman began to cry. Francis took from the child a piece of bread, "intending to give it to him again after he became quiet." Heman quieted down, but when his father offered him the bread, the child threw it away in anger. Displeased by this fit of temper, Francis decided it was time to teach his son a lesson. He left the child alone in a room and gave orders that no one was to speak to Heman or give him food or drink until further notice. Every hour or two throughout the day, Francis visited his son, "offering him the bread and putting out my arms to take him," but the child refused to take any food or drink or to embrace him. Heman went to bed that night without having had anything to eat since the previous day; the next morning, the test of wills continued. At 10:00 A.M., Heman took some bread and milk from his father but still refused to embrace him, so Francis continued the child's confinement. Finally, around 3:00 P.M., Heman capitulated and came to his father, "completely subdued." Francis Wayland was so proud of his method of disciplining Heman, which had rendered the child so much more "mild and obedient," that he published a summary of the episode in the *American Baptist Magazine* to serve as a model for other parents.

Between 1780 and 1830, middle-class Americans made child rearing a national project, devoting an enormous amount of time and energy to raising the first generation born after independence. Of course, parents of all times and places have always contemplated the best way to raise their children, and every culture produces a prescribed set of rules for doing so. Shippen and Wayland, however, were representatives of a conscious effort by American parents in the wake of the Revolution to reexamine and experiment with child-rearing practices. Parents such as Shippen and Wayland became self-consciously reflective about their child rearing, often writing about their experiences with an air of scientific observation and detachment. They also felt the urge to share their thoughts on child rearing with others, to read books published by self-appointed experts, or even (as in Wayland's case) to announce their own expertise. Along with this advice literature for parents came a steady flow of books and magazines aimed at children. By 1830, a homegrown genre of children's literature had emerged in America, offering not only instruction in reading and writing but also stories meant to instill habits and values in their young readers appropriate to the gender roles they would assume as adults.

This focus on child rearing and childhood in the early republic had its roots in several important cultural trends associated with American independence. First, the political ideology of the American Revolution, grounded in the scientific and intellectual movement known as the Enlightenment, challenged patriarchal power in all forms, whether it was held by kings or fathers. As a model of family government, patriarchy equated the father's power over the family with a king's power over his subjects: both were absolute and ordained by God. When the colonies disavowed their allegiance to the British Crown, they also dealt a blow to the unlimited power of the father within the family. A significant figure in this regard was the Enlightenment philosopher John Locke, whose *Second Treatise of Government* had inspired Jefferson's language in the Declaration of Independence. Locke also authored two works, *Essay Concerning Human Understanding* (1690) and *Some Thoughts Concerning Education* (1693), that influenced American attitudes about child rearing. Locke posited that an infant's mind was a tabula rasa, or blank slate; children learned and developed personalities according to the circumstances in which they were raised. Locke's ideas challenged long-held beliefs about original sin and the inherent depravity of children, and they were popular among many parents in eighteenth-century America, as evidenced in Nancy Shippen's emphasis on controlling her daughter's environment and nurturing her reason.

Evangelical Protestantism also encouraged a reexamination of child rearing in the new nation, although often on principles much different from those associated with John Locke. When Francis Wayland waged battle with fifteen-month-old Heman, he was following a time-honored practice among many Anglo-American Protestants: "breaking the will" of the child. The Calvinist theology of many Protestant denominations (especially Congregationalists, Presbyterians, and Baptists) taught that original sin corrupted human nature. Left to their own devices, children would follow their natural inclination to do evil rather than good. A parent's job was to break the child of this predisposition early in life, so that a temperament more submissive and obedient to parental and godly authority could be molded in its place. Wayland's episode with his son perfectly illustrates this process and the reasoning behind it. During the early nineteenth century, a wave of religious revivals known as the Second Great Awakening reinvigorated evangelical religion in America, adding to the old Calvinist emphasis on original sin a new message of spiritual perfectionism made possible by God's grace. The evangelists' metaphor of being "born again" into salvation in Christ drew a parallel between spiritual redemption and childhood, inspiring many parents like Wayland to redouble their efforts to raise children who would be fit to respond obediently to God's call when it came.

Economic change and political ideas also influenced family roles and child rearing in the early republic, especially in the Northeast, where urbanization and industrialization were separating the home from the workplace. As fathers took jobs outside the home, the mother's role in child rearing became more pronounced, and the family's domestic life came increasingly under her authority. Middle- and upper-class women redefined their role in society as "republican mothers," charged with the task of raising children capable of governing themselves as productive citizens of the new nation. The notion of Republican Motherhood encouraged female education because mothers had to be capable of instructing their children not only in reading, writing, and arithmetic but also in the moral habits and virtues of a free citizenry: industry, frugality, trustworthiness, public duty, and piety. The "Cult of Domesticity," a phrase used by historians to describe nineteenth-century America's celebration of the home as a refuge from the cold, impersonal world outside, elevated mothers as the central figure in the household. Society praised them for the loving nurture and wise counsel they dispensed to their children. Unlike the patriarchal family model so evident in Francis Wayland's disciplining of his son, Republican Motherhood and the Cult of Domesticity made affection and sentiment, not duty and obedience, the primary bonds of family life. In the South, where slavery persisted after the American Revolution and industrialization occurred much more slowly, patriarchy remained the defining principle behind family roles in white society.

The transformation of child rearing and childhood in the early republic had important ramifications for family and gender roles in American society. Many of the ideas and images associated with our modern debates over family values—the nuclear family, the stay-at-home mother, the "breadwinner" father—have their origins in the world of Nancy Shippen and Francis Wayland. In the half-century after the American Revolution, they made a purposeful effort to redefine the meaning and purpose of family in a democratic society, and their efforts left a lasting imprint on our culture.

Using the Source: Advice Literature for Parents and Children

Before 1800, Anglo-Americans imported their advice on child rearing from Britain or wrote their own imitations of popular English works. Rising literacy rates in eighteenth-century Britain produced a consumer market for children's books in which colonial Americans participated as well. The market for these English works decreased during the Revolutionary era, when Americans rejected much of their cultural patrimony from Britain. Just as many artists thought it important for the new nation to create its own art rather than slavishly imitate Europe's, so too did prominent intellectuals such as Noah Webster, the author of the first American dictionary, urge Americans to reinvent their methods of raising and educating children. By 1830, this impulse had led to a significant surge in magazines and books published by American authors for American parents and children.

What Can Advice Literature Tell Us?

Reading advice literature for parents and children is one of the best ways to reconstruct cultural expectations about roles within the family. All advice literature tells its readers how things ought to be, and parenting literature is no exception. Consider for example this excerpt from a popular parenting book, *The Mother at Home, or, the Principles of Maternal Duty Familiarly Illustrated* by John S. C. Abbott (1833; repr., New York: Harper & Brothers, 1852), in which the author uses the occasion of a boy's question about a pot of boiling coffee to advise parents on how to deal with a child's curiosity:

> "Mother," says the little boy, "what makes the coffee bubble up so?"
> Here the motive is good, and the occasion is proper.[1] And one of the parents explains to the child the chemical process which we call the boiling. The parents have reason to be gratified at the observation of the child, and the

> Note the scientific, experimental tone of author's language

[1] For the child to ask a question.

The author states
a rule of child
rearing

Note which par-
ent intercedes

The rule is ex-
pressed to the
child

explanation communicates to him valuable knowledge. But perhaps a stranger is present, with whom the father is engaged in interesting conversation. Under these circumstances, the child asks the same question. It is, however, now unseasonable.[2] He ought to be silent when company is present. The mother accordingly replies, "My son, you should not interrupt your father. You must be perfectly silent and listen to what he is saying."

This passage calls to mind the adage, "children should be seen and not heard," but closer reading also reveals assumptions the author is making about gender and the division of power within the family. The father is present in this scene, but the mother intercedes when the child speaks before company. What does this vignette tell you about the author's notion of how authority ought to be ordered within a family?

Even children's literature, which at first glance might seem formulaic and transparent in its purposes, reflects the wider cultural currents in which it is produced. Consider the famous illustrated alphabet from *The New-England Primer* (see Figure 8.1), the most commonly used book for teaching spelling and reading to American children before 1850. The images and rhyming couplets that accompany the letters are meant to focus the children's attention as they memorize their ABCs, in much the same way that the "Alphabet Song" is used today. These images and couplets also convey messages that teach moral lessons and proper behavior.

Another advantage to using advice literature to study the family and childhood in the early republic is its inclusion of both male and female voices. Before 1800, advice literature on child rearing was written overwhelmingly by men, usually ministers concerned with the moral instruction of youth. The notion of Republican Motherhood, however, gave women the social authority to write and publish their own opinions on the family and domestic life. Indeed, several of nineteenth-century America's most prominent female public figures first gained recognition for their advice literature on the home and child rearing. By comparing male and female authorship of such works, historians can get a sense of how women reshaped their private and public lives during the early nineteenth century.

When working with these sources, it is also important to bear in mind their shortcomings. First, advice literature on child rearing is prescriptive: its purpose is to tell people what to do, and if they need to be told, then they probably are not doing what the literature recommends. No one should assume, for example, from the glut of diet books available in modern American bookstores that we are a society in which everyone eats right and gets enough exercise. Likewise, nineteenth-century advice literature on parenting does not necessarily reflect how people raised their children, only what certain authors thought about the way people should raise their children. Historians always

---

[2] Untimely.

Figure 8.1 Illustrated Alphabet from **The New-England Primer** *This illustrated alphabet from an early nineteenth-century edition of* The New-England Primer *shows how children learned lessons about morality and proper behavior as they learned to read and write. The letters B, H, I, and S teach submission to the authority of God and parents. A, F, and P warn of the punishments that follow bad behavior. G, R, T, X, and Y remind children of their own mortality: death can come at any time, to the old or young, weak or strong.*

Source: *The New-England Primer Improved, Being an Essay Method to Teach Young Children the English Language* (New York: Daniel D. Smith, 1807), 12–15.

approach prescriptive literature with skepticism, assuming that if everyone acted according to the instructions contained in such books, their authors would not have felt compelled to write them in the first place.

You should also look for regional, class, or racial biases that may be evident in these sources. The authors often presume to speak for everyone, but who actually reads these books? Obviously, the authors wrote for a literate audience, but literacy rates varied widely in early nineteenth-century America. Men were more likely to be literate than women, although this gap closed considerably in the Northeast, the center of the nation's publishing industry. Protestants were more likely to be literate than Catholics, many of whom were poor Irish immigrants working in urban centers, and African American slaves suffered from legal prohibitions against teaching them to read. Literacy also reflected a person's social class, and works on childhood and child rearing enshrined an ideal image of the family that was distinctively middle class, in which fathers were breadwinners, mothers were homemakers, and the nuclear family (parents and children living together under one roof) was the norm. Such an image held little meaning to many working-class, immigrant, and African American families.

This last point brings to mind another caveat about using these sources. Change in family roles and child-rearing practices was hardly uniform in the early republic, even for people living in the same region or in similar material circumstances. If you observe parents and their children at a playground today, you will not have to wait long to witness sharply different models of child rearing practiced by people who in many respects seem alike. The same is true for people of the past. Nancy Shippen and Francis Wayland both lived in northern cities and came from privileged backgrounds, yet each took a very different approach to raising children. As you read these sources, rather than thinking in terms of one type of family or approach to child rearing replacing another, try to identify the different types and approaches that coexisted and influenced each other.

Questions to Ask

When working with any kind of literature as a source, you need to determine the author's intended audience. Is the book or story aimed at adults or children, mothers or fathers, boys or girls? After answering that question, ask what kind of role models the advice literature is establishing for its readers. What is the author's idea of a happy family, of a perfect mother, father, daughter, or son? How do the answers to those questions make clear the conduct or practices in parents and children that the author finds objectionable? Finally, you will want to connect this advice literature to its wider cultural and political context: what values or biases are evident in how it describes family and gender roles?

- Who is the intended audience?
- What set of familial roles does it hold up as ideal?
- What sort of conduct by parents or children does it criticize?
- What wider social values or biases are evident in this literature?

Source Analysis Table

Use the first three columns in the following table to organize your notes on how each of the sources establishes expectations and role models for its intended audience. In the last column, note the values or biases that you think underlie the author's advice.

Source	Intended Audience	Characteristics of Ideal Father, Mother, Daughter, Son	Objectionable Practices or Conduct	Values or Biases Evident in Author's Advice
1. John S. C. Abbott, *The Mother at Home*				
2. Lydia Maria Child, *The Mother's Book*				
3. *The New-England Primer*				
4. *The Busy Bee*				
5. *The Life of George Washington*				

To download and print this table, visit the book companion site at **bedfordstmartins.com/brownshannon**.

The Source: Advice Literature on Child Rearing and Children's Literature, 1807–1833

ADVICE LITERATURE ON CHILD REARING

1 | *The Mother at Home* by John S. C. Abbott, 1833

> John S. C. Abbott was a New England minister who published two of the most widely read books on child rearing in early nineteenth-century America: *The Child at Home* and *The Mother at Home*. These excerpts, from the latter book, concern a topic commonly addressed in such literature: the proper method of disciplining children.

Never Give a Command Which You Do Not Intend Shall Be Obeyed.

There is no more effectual way of teaching a child disobedience, than by giving commands which you have no intention of enforcing. A child is thus habituated to disregard its mother; and in a short time the habit becomes so strong, and the child's contempt for the mother so confirmed, that entreaties and threats are alike unheeded. . . .

Sometimes a child gets its passions excited and its will determined, and it can not be subdued but by a very great effort. Almost every faithful mother is acquainted with such contests, and she knows that they often form a *crisis* in the character of the child. If the child then obtain the victory, it is almost impossible for the mother afterward to regain her authority. . . . When once entered upon, they[1] must be continued till the child is subdued. It is not safe, on *any account*, for the parent to give up and retire vanquished.

The following instance of such a contest is one which really occurred. A gentleman, sitting by his fireside one evening, with his family around him, took the spelling-book and called upon one of his little sons to come and read. John was about four years old. He knew all the letters of the alphabet perfectly, but happened at that moment to be in a rather sullen humor, and was not at all disposed to gratify his father. Very reluctantly he came as he was bid, but when his father pointed with his pencil to the first letter of the alphabet, and said, "What letter is that, John?" he could get no answer. John looked upon the book, sulky and silent.

"My son," said the father pleasantly, "you know the letter *A*."

[1] Such contests.

Source: John S. C. Abbott, *The Mother at Home, or, the Principles of Maternal Duty Familiarly Illustrated* (1833; repr., New York: Harper & Brothers, 1852), 47, 60–66.

"I can not say *A*," said John.

"You must," said the father, in a serious and decided tone. "What letter is that?"

John refused to answer. The contest was now fairly commenced. John was willful, and determined that he would not read. His father knew that it would be ruinous to his son to allow him to conquer. He felt that he must, at all hazards, subdue him. He took him into another room, and punished him. He then returned, and again showed John the letter. But John still refused to name it. The father again retired with his son, and punished him more severely. But it was unavailing; the stubborn child still refused to name the letter, and when told that it was *A*, declared that he could not say *A*. Again the father inflicted punishment as severely as he dared to do it, and still the child, with his whole frame in agitation, refused to yield. The father was suffering from the most intense solicitude. He regretted exceedingly that he had been drawn into the contest. He had already punished his child with a severity which he feared to exceed. And yet the willful sufferer stood before him, sobbing and trembling, but apparently as unyielding as a rock. I have often heard that parent mention the acuteness of his feelings at that moment. His heart was bleeding at the pain which he had been compelled to inflict upon his son. He knew that the question was now to be settled, who should be master. And after his son had withstood so long and so much, he greatly feared the result. The mother sat by, suffering, of course, most acutely, but perfectly satisfied that it was their duty to subdue the child, and that in such a trying hour a mother's feelings must not interfere. With a heavy heart the father again took the hand of his son to lead him out of the room for farther punishment. But, to his inconceivable joy, the child shrunk from enduring any more suffering, and cried, "Father, I'll tell the letter." The father, with feelings not easily conceived, took the book and pointed to the letter.

"*A*," said John, distinctly and fully.

"And what is that?" said the father, pointing to the next letter.

"*B*," said John.

"And what is that?"

"*C*," he continued.

"And what is that?" pointing again to the first letter.

"*A*," said the now humble child.

"Now carry the book to your mother, and tell her what the letter is."

"What letter is that, my son?" said the mother.

"*A*," said John. He was evidently perfectly subdued. The rest of the children were sitting by, and they saw the contest, and they saw where was the victory. And John learnt a lesson which he never forgot—that his father had an arm too strong for him. He learned never again to wage such an unequal warfare. He learnt that it was the safest and happiest course for him to obey.

But perhaps some one says it was cruel to punish the child so severely. Cruel! It was mercy and love. It would indeed have been cruel had the father, in that hour, been unfaithful, and shrunk from his painful duty. The passions which he was then, with so much self-sacrifice, striving to subdue, if left unchecked, would, in all probability, have been a curse to their possessor, and have made him a curse to his friends. It is by no means improbable that upon the decisions of that hour depended the character and happiness of that child for life, and even for eternity. It is far from improbable that, had he then conquered, all future efforts to subdue him would have been in vain, and that he would have broken away from all restraint, and have been miserable in life, and lost in death. Cruelty! The Lord preserve children from the *tender mercies* of those who so regard such self-denying kindness.

2 | *The Mother's Book* by Lydia Maria Child, 1831

Lydia Maria Child was one of the most distinguished women authors of nineteenth-century America, an outspoken advocate for the rights of women, Indians, and African Americans. Early in her career, she edited a successful children's magazine called *Juvenile Miscellany* and published *The Mother's Book,* a best-selling volume of child-rearing advice literature. The excerpts below are from Child's recommendations for dealing with teenage daughters.

The period of twelve to sixteen years of age is extremely critical in the formation of character, particularly with regard to daughters. The imagination is then all alive, and the affections in full vigor, while the judgment is unstrengthened by observation, and enthusiasm has never learned moderation of experience. During this important period, a mother cannot be too watchful. As much as possible, she should keep her daughter *under her own eye;* and above all things she should encourage *entire confidence towards herself.* This can be done by a ready sympathy with youthful feelings, and by avoiding all unnecessary restraint and harshness. I believe it is extremely natural to choose a mother in preference to all other friends and confidants; but if a daughter, by harshness, indifference, or unwillingness to make allowance for youthful feeling, is driven from the holy resting place, which nature has provided for her security, the greatest danger is to be apprehended. Nevertheless, I would not have mothers too indulgent, for fear of weaning the affections of children. This is not the way to gain the perfect love of young people; a judicious parent is always better loved, and more respected, than a foolishly indulgent one. The real secret is, for a mother never to sanction the slightest error, or imprudence, but at the same time to keep her heart warm and fresh, ready to sympathize with all the innocent gayety and enthusiasm of youth. . . .

Source: Mrs. [Lydia Maria] Child, *The Mother's Book* (Boston: Carter, Hendee, and Babcock, 1831), 129–30, 136–40, 145–47, 150–53.

I would make it an object so to educate children that they could in case of necessity support themselves respectably. For this reason, if a child discovered a decided talent for any accomplishment, I would cultivate it, if my income would possibly allow it. Everything we add to our knowledge, adds to our means of usefulness. If a girl has a decided taste for drawing, for example, and it is encouraged, it is a pleasant resource which will make her home agreeable, and lessen the desire for company and amusements; if she marries, it will enable her to teach her children without the expense of a master; if she lives unmarried, she may gain a livelihood by teaching the art she at first learned as a mere gratification of taste. The same thing may be said of music, and a variety of other things, not generally deemed *necessary* in education. In all cases it is best that what is learned should be learned well. In order to do this, good masters should be preferred to cheap ones. Bad habits once learned, are not easily corrected. It is far better that children should learn one thing thoroughly, than many things superficially. . . .

My idea is this—First, be sure that children are familiar with all the duties of their present situation; at the same time, by schools, by reading, by conversation, give them as much *solid* knowledge as you can, no matter how much, or of what kind; it will come in use some time or other; and lastly, if your circumstances are easy, and you can afford to indulge your children in any matter of taste, do it fearlessly, without any idea that it will unfit them for more important duties. Neither learning nor accomplishments do any harm to man or woman if the *motive* for acquiring them be a proper one. . . . I believe a variety of knowledge (acquired from such views as I have stated) would make a man a better servant, as well as a better president; and make a woman a better wife, as well as a better teacher. . . .

It is certainly very desirable to fit children for the station they are likely to fill, as far as a parent can judge what that station will be. In this country, it is a difficult point to decide; for half our people are in a totally different situation from what might have been expected in their childhood. However, one maxim is as safe, as it is true: A well-informed mind is the happiest and the most useful in all situations. Every new acquirement is something added to a solid capital. . . .

A knowledge of domestic duties is beyond all price to a woman. Every one ought to know how to sew, and knit, and mend, and cook, and superintend a household. In every situation of life, high or low, this sort of knowledge is a great advantage. There is no necessity that the gaining of such information should interfere with intellectual acquirement, or even with elegant accomplishments. A well regulated mind can find time to attend to all. When a girl is nine or ten years old, she should be accustomed to take some regular share in household duties, and to feel responsible for the manner in which it is done, such as doing her own mending and making, washing the cups and putting them in place, cleaning the silver, dusting the parlor, etc. This should not be done occasionally, and neglected whenever she finds it convenient; she should consider it her department. When they are older than twelve, girls should begin to take turns in superintending the household, keeping an account of weekly expenses, cooking puddings and pies, etc. To learn anything effectually, they should actually do these things themselves, not stand by and see others do them. It is a great mistake in mothers to make such slaves of themselves, rather than divide their cares with daughters. A variety of employment, and a feeling of trust and responsibility add very much to the real happiness of young people. . . .

There is one subject on which I am very anxious to say a great deal; but on which, for obvious reasons, I can say very little. Judging by my own observation, I believe it to be the greatest evil now existing in education. I mean the want of confidence between mothers and daughters on delicate subjects.[1] Children from books, and from their own observation, soon have their curiosity excited on such subjects; this is perfectly natural and innocent, and if frankly met by a mother, it would never do harm. But on these occasions it is customary to either put young people off with lies, or still further to excite their curiosity by mystery and embarrassment. Information being refused them at the only proper source, they immediately have recourse to domestics,[2] or immodest school-companions; and very often their young minds are polluted with filthy anecdotes of vice and vulgarity. This ought not to be. Mothers are the only proper persons to convey such knowledge to a child's mind. They can do it without throwing the slightest stain upon youthful purity; and it is an imperious duty that they should do it. A girl who receives her first ideas on these subjects from the shameless stories and indecent jokes of vulgar associates, has in fact prostituted her mind by familiarity with vice. A diseased curiosity is excited, and undue importance given to subjects, which those she has been taught to respect think it necessary to envelope in so much mystery; she learns to think a great deal about them, and to ask a great many questions. This does not spring from any natural impurity; the same restless curiosity would be excited by any subject treated in the same manner. On the contrary, a well-educated girl of twelve years old would be perfectly satisfied with a frank, rational explanation from a mother. It would set her mind at rest upon the subject; and instinctive modesty would prevent her recurring to it unnecessarily, or making it a theme of conversation with others. . . .

It is a bad plan for young girls to sleep with nursery maids, unless you have the utmost confidence in the good principles and modesty of your domestics. There is a strong love among vulgar people of telling secrets, and talking on forbidden subjects. From a large proportion of domestics this danger is so great, that I apprehend a prudent mother will very rarely, under any circumstances, place her daughter in the same sleeping apartment with a domestic, until her character is so much formed, that her own dignity will lead her to reject all improper conversation.

[1] Sexuality.

[2] Household servants.

CHILDREN'S LITERATURE

3 *The New-England Primer,* 1807

The New-England Primer was first published in the late seventeenth century, but it remained the most common textbook for teaching children basic lessons in reading, writing, and religion throughout the first half of the nineteenth century. No author was ascribed to it, but the first editions were published by Boston printer Benjamin Harris in the 1690s. Over the next 150 years, many other printers published versions of it, varying the content little from one edition to the next. These excerpts illustrate *The New-England Primer's* moral instructions to boys and girls. Note how the material addressed to boys is rendered in prose form, while that to girls is in verse.

Description of a Good Boy

A Good boy is dutiful to his father and mother, obedient to his master, and loving to all his play fellows. He is diligent in learning his book, and takes a pleasure in improving his mind in every thing which is worthy of praise: he rises early in the morning, makes himself clean and decent, and says his prayers. If he has done a fault, he confesses, and is sorry for it, and scorns to tell a lie, though he might by that means conceal it. He never swears, nor calls names, nor uses any ill words to his companions. He is never peevish nor fretful, but always cheerful and good-humoured; he scorns to steal or pilfer any thing from his companions, and would rather suffer wrong, than to do wrong to any of them. He is always ready to answer when a question is asked of him—to do what he is bidden, and to mind what is said to him. He is not a wrangler nor quarrelsome, and refrains from all sorts of mischief into which other boys run. By this means he becomes, as he grows up, a man of sense and virtue, he is beloved and respected by all who know him; he lives in the world with credit and reputation, and when he dies, is lamented by all his acquaintances.

Description of a Bad Boy

A Bad boy is undutiful to his father and mother, disobedient and stubborn to his master, and ill natured to all his play fellows. He hates his book, and takes no pleasure in improving in any thing. He is sleepy and slothful in the morning, too idle to clean himself, and too wicked to say his prayers. He is always in mischief, and when he has done a fault, will tell twenty lies, in hopes to conceal it. He hates that any body should give him good advice, and when they are out of his sight, will laugh at them. He swears, wrangles, and quarrels with his companions. He will steal whatever comes his way, and if he is not caught,

Source: The New-England Primer Improved, Being an Easy Method to Teach Young Children the English Language (New York: Daniel D. Smith, 1807), 17–20.

thinks it no crime, not considering that God sees what he does. He is frequently out of humour, sullen and obstinate, so he will neither do what he is bid, nor answer any question which is asked him. In short, he neglects every thing which he should learn, and minds nothing but play or mischief, by which means he becomes as he grows up, a confirmed blockhead, incapable of any thing but wickedness or folly, despised by all men, and generally dies a beggar.

The Good Girl

So pretty Miss Prudence,
You've come to the Fair;
And a very good girl
They tell me you are:
Here take this fine Orange,
This Watch and this Knot;
You're welcome my dear,
To all we have got:
For a girl who is good,
And so pretty as you,
May have what she pleases,
Your servant, Miss Prue.

The Naughty Girls

So pert misses, prate-apace, how came you here?
There's nobody wants to see you at the fair;
No Oranges, Apples, Cakes, or Nuts,
Will any one give to such saucy sluts.
For such naughty girls, we here have no room,
You're proud and ill-natur'd—Go hussies, go home.

4   *The Busy Bee,* 1831

The American Sunday School Union, a voluntary association formed by several Protestant denominations in 1824 to promote children's religious education, published thousands of short children's stories aimed at teaching proper values and habits. Like *The New-England Primer,* these stories usually appeared without any attribution to authorship. This typical story features the characters of Fanny and Jane, two eight-year-old orphans who live with a pious old woman, referred to in the story as their mother.

Source: The Busy Bee (Philadelphia: American Sunday School Union, 1831), 11–13, 15–17, 19–24.

The kind lady took the same pains with Fanny as she did with Jane, and taught both these little girls all those things which she thought necessary for children in their station. She endeavoured to teach them to read and write well, to cipher, and to do neatly all kinds of plain work, as well as to understand household business: but though, as I before said, she bestowed the same labour on both children, yet there was great difference in their improvement. Little Jane took every opportunity of profiting, not only by the instructions of her mother, as she called the lady, but like the busy bee, who gathers honey from every flower which comes her way, she strove to gain some good thing, some useful piece of knowledge, from every person she became acquainted with.

Her mother kept only one servant, whose name was Nanny. Nanny was a clever servant, and understood many useful things, though she was often rude and ill-tempered, and spoke in a vulgar manner. But little Jane had sense to know, that although she was not to imitate the manners of Nanny, and her improper way of speaking, yet she might learn many useful things from her: therefore, when she went into the kitchen with the lady, she shut her ears against Nanny's disagreeable way of speaking, and gave her whole mind to learn how to iron, or to make pies and puddings, or whatever useful thing she might be doing.

When any ladies came to drink tea with her mother, Jane would take notice what work they were doing; and if it was pretty or useful, she would try to do something like it for her doll: and thus she taught herself many useful works. . . .

But while Jane was thus daily learning all that is good, Fanny, in the mean time, was gathering all that is evil. Into whatever company she might chance to fall, she always first took notice of what each person was saying or doing wrong, and afterwards tried to do the same. Whenever she went into the kitchen with her mother, instead of learning to do any thing which might be useful from Nanny, she noticed her way of talking or moving, and then tried to do like her. . . .

But I can scarcely tell you (and indeed it would only give you pain if I could) how many naughty things Fanny learned from the young people she met with, when she went with her mother to pay a visit in the town. She came home, I am sorry to say, much worse than she went, and that indeed was bad enough. . . .

One afternoon, at tea, she[1] said to the little girls, "To-morrow will be my birth day, and I mean to give you a feast, in which I intend to consult the taste of each of you."

The little girls said they were very glad to hear it, and the lady told them to come the next evening into her dressing room, where she said the feast would be set out.

When Fanny and Jane came, at the hour which the lady had fixed upon, to the dressing room, they found their mother sitting reading by the fire, and two little round tables were placed in the middle of the room. One of these tables

---

[1] The old woman.

was covered with a neat white napkin and a little dessert set out upon it in doll's dishes, made of white china with blue edges. There were four little dishes on this table: one contained an orange, another a few yellow apples, another a roasted apple, and a fourth a few biscuits; and in the middle was a little covered china cup, made in the shape of a bee-hive, which contained honey in the honey-comb.

The little girls had scarcely time to examine this table, so neatly laid out, before their eyes were caught by the other table, which was set out in a manner so strange, that they stood still with surprise, and were not able to move. This second table was covered with straw instead of a table cloth, and instead of dishes, there was a great empty wooden bowl.

The lady got up when the little girls came in, and, drawing her chair between the two tables, she said, "Come, Fanny, come Jane; come and enjoy yourselves. I have been trying to make a feast suitable to the tastes of each of you." She then pointed to the table neatly set out with china and fine linen, and invited Jane to seat herself at it, and directed Fanny to place herself by the other table. . . .

"And now," said the lady, as soon as they were seated, "I will divide the feast." So saying, she began to peel the oranges, pare the apples, take the roasted apple out of its skin, and pour the honey from the comb. And, as she went on doing these things, she threw the rind of the orange, the parings of the apple, and the other refuse of the feast, into the wooden bowl, while she placed the best parts on the dishes before Jane. When all this was done, she invited the children to begin to eat. . . . Fanny looked very red, and at last, broke into a violent fit of crying.

"What do you cry for?" said the lady. "I know that you heartily love, and have for a long time sought after every thing that is hateful, filthy, and bad; and like a pig, you have delighted in wallowing in mire. I therefore am resolved to indulge you. As you love what is filthy, you shall enjoy it, and shall be treated like a pig."

Fanny looked very much ashamed; and throwing herself on her knees before her mother, begged her to forgive her, and promised that she would never again seek after wickedness, and delight in it, as she had done.

"Fanny," said the lady, "it is very easy for little girls to make fine promises, and to say, 'I will be good,' and 'I am sorry I have behaved ill.' But I am not a person who will be satisfied with words, any more than you can be with orange-peel and skins of apples. I must have deeds, not words. Turn away from your sins, and call upon your God to help you to repent your past evil life. If you do not wish to partake of the portion of dogs and swine and unclean creatures in the world to come, you must learn to hate sin in the present world." . . .

I am happy to say, that this day was the beginning of better things to Fanny: for she at once forsook her evil habits, and, with God's blessing upon her endeavours, and the care of the good old lady, she so far overcame her faults, as to be allowed, by the next birth-day, to feast with little Jane.

The Life of George Washington, 1832

George Washington was a fixture in nineteenth-century children's literature, and his life was used to teach moral lessons about honesty and piety as well as civic lessons about patriotism and citizenship. In children's biographies of Washington, his mother also played a prominent role and served as an exemplar of motherhood for the new nation.

Mrs. Washington was an affectionate parent; but she did not encourage in herself that imprudent tenderness, which so often causes a mother to foster the passions of her children by foolish indulgences, and which seldom fails to destroy the respect which every child should feel for a parent. George was early made to understand that he must obey his mother, and therefore he respected as well as loved her. She was kind to his young companions, but they thought her stern, because they always felt that they must behave correctly in her presence. The character of the mother, as well as that of the son, are shown in the following incident.

Mrs. Washington owned a remarkably fine colt, which she valued very much; but which though old enough for use, had never been mounted; no one would venture to ride it, or attempt to break its wild and vicious spirit. George proposed to some of his young companions, that they should assist him to secure the colt until he could mount it, as he had determined that he would try to tame it. Soon after sunrise one morning, they drove the wild animal into an enclosure, and with great difficulty succeeded in placing a bridle on it. George then sprang upon its back, and the vexed colt bounded over the open fields, prancing and plunging to get rid of its burden. The bold rider kept his seat firmly, and the struggle between them became alarming to his companions, who were watching him. The speed of the colt increased, until at length, in making a furious effort to throw his conqueror, he burst a large blood-vessel, and instantly died.

George was unhurt, but was much troubled by the unexpected result of his exploit. His companions soon joined him, and when they saw the beautiful colt lifeless, the first words they spoke were: "What will your mother say—who can tell her?" They were called to breakfast, and soon after they were seated at the table, Mrs. Washington said, "Well, young gentlemen, have you seen my fine sorrel colt in your rambles?" No answer was given, and the question was repeated; her son George then replied, "Your sorrel colt is dead, mother." He gave her an exact account of the event. The flush of displeasure which first rose on her cheek, soon passed away; and she said calmly, "While I regret the loss of my favourite, *I rejoice in my son, who always speaks the truth.*"

Source: The Life of George Washington (Philadelphia: American Sunday School Union, 1832), 21–23.

Analyzing Advice Literature

1. Using your notes from the table on page 164, compare and contrast the different types of ideal fathers, mothers, sons, and daughters depicted in these sources. How do these ideals complement or contradict one another? How do the parenting philosophies depicted in these sources compare to those of Nancy Shippen and Francis Wayland?

2. How do these sources depict parental discipline? How do the methods of discipline differ between fathers and mothers, and what do those differences tell you about assumptions these sources make about the distribution of power and authority within the family?

3. What sorts of positive and negative examples do these sources present for the behavior of boys and girls? Compare and contrast the language and plots of *The Busy Bee* (Source 4) and *The Life of George Washington* (Source 5): how do they define virtue and character differently for girls and boys? In what ways are the shortcomings of bad boys and bad girls gender specific? For example, compare Child's discussion of sexuality in *The Mother's Book* (Source 2) with *The New-England Primer*'s descriptions of bad behavior (Source 3).

4. What clues do these sources offer about the economic class of their intended audience? How do they depict members of the household who are not biologically related to the parents or children? Where in these sources do you perceive any biases or assumptions that would limit their usefulness for studying the domestic life and family roles of immigrants, slaves, or the urban working class?

5. How do *The New-England Primer* (Source 3), *The Busy Bee* (Source 4), and *The Life of George Washington* (Source 5) compare to the books and stories you read as a child? What does this comparison tell you about the cultural construction of childhood in early nineteenth-century America versus present-day America? What role has television taken in the moral and civic education of present-day American children, and how does it compare in that respect to the efforts of the American Sunday School Union?

The Rest of the Story

In the two decades after 1830, the changes that Republican Motherhood and the Cult of Domesticity wrought in the middle-class American family came into full bloom. Capitalizing on the influence and moral authority that society ascribed to them as mothers and household managers, women stepped out of the home and into public roles by forming female benevolent societies and maternal associations that embraced such causes as Christian missionary work and temperance reform. Lydia Maria Child was on the vanguard of this transformation, giving up her writing on domestic and family topics in the 1830s to promote the antislavery cause. Men continued to publish advice literature on family government and child rearing, but the tone of this literature gradually shifted from its roots in evangelical Protestantism to a more scientific concern for controlling the early childhood environment and promoting public education. A significant work in this regard was Horace Bushnell's *Christian Nurture* (1847), which attacked the practice of breaking the child's will and recommended instead "bending the will" through loving and mild nurture. Bushnell's approach assigned even greater importance to the role of the mother as a teacher and disciplinarian, because it discounted the impact of grand confrontations between parent and child, such as that between Francis and Heman Wayland, in favor of a mother's constant surveillance of children in their earliest years.

As the nineteenth century progressed, American children's literature diverged into gender-specific themes that reflected the boundary between the female world of the household and the male world beyond it. While the exemplary lessons in honesty and manly virtue from George Washington's boyhood remained a mainstay of schoolbooks, young boys in the mid-nineteenth century could also indulge in the tales of a fictional world traveler named Peter Parley or the rags-to-riches stories of Horatio Alger. Young girls were expected to read books that celebrated the roles they would assume as wives and mothers. Women fiction writers dominated the genre of the domestic novel, which featured female characters and mother-child relationships at the center of the plot. Perhaps the most enduring work in this genre is Louisa May Alcott's *Little Women* (1868), the tale of a temporarily fatherless family of four girls and their mother during the Civil War. Harriet Beecher Stowe's *Uncle Tom's Cabin* (1852) was not originally published for young readers, although it did appear in storybook editions for children. Its remarkable influence on its mostly female readership rested in a large part on its sympathetic portrayal of a slave family and its condemnation of slaveholders for violating middle-class domestic values.

The model of family that emerged in middle-class American culture in the early nineteenth century perpetuated itself in future generations through literature that prepared children to assume gender-specific roles as adults. Boys' adventure stories anticipated the ups and downs and geographic mobility they would experience in the competitive marketplace of industrial America, while girls learned the joys and duties of domestic life from idealized fictional versions of themselves. Yet, as the careers of Lydia Maria Child and Harriett Beecher Stowe suggest, society's elevation of women as mothers also gave them an entrée into the public sphere as writers, reformers, and advocates for the political and social causes they embraced.

To Find Out More

Several good documentary collections provide a starting point for research on American childhood and child rearing. Philip J. Greven Jr., editor, *Child-Rearing Concepts, 1628–1861: Historical Sources* (Itasca, Ill.: F. E. Peacock Publishers, 1973), focuses on the colonial era but includes selections from significant nineteenth-century authors. Paula S. Fass and Mary Ann Mason, editors, *Childhood in America* (New York: New York University Press, 2000), deftly combines primary documents and secondary sources. Robert H. Bremner, editor, *Children and Youth in America: A Documentary History, Volume I: 1600–1865* (Cambridge, Mass.: Harvard University Press, 1970), is comprehensive in its coverage of such topics as labor, health, and delinquency. The Web site "Nineteenth-Century American Children and What They Read," at **merrycoz.org/kids.htm**, offers a useful online archive of children's books and parenting manuals. Two editions (1805 and 1807) of *The New-England Primer* can be found online at **public .gettysburg.edu/~tshannon/courses/341/colonialamer.htm**.

Some of the most influential works on child rearing and childhood in the early republic have been written by social historians interested in the domestic life of American families. See especially Nancy F. Cott, *The Bonds of Womanhood: "Woman's Sphere" in New England, 1780–1835* (New Haven, Conn.: Yale University Press, 1977); Philip Greven, *The Protestant Temperament: Patterns of Child-Rearing, Religious Experience, and the Self in Early America* (New York: Alfred A. Knopf, 1977); Jan Lewis, *The Pursuit of Happiness: Family and Values in Jefferson's Virginia* (Cambridge: Cambridge University Press, 1983); and Mary P. Ryan, *Cradle of the Middle Class: The Family in Oneida County, New York, 1790–1865* (Cambridge: Cambridge University Press, 1981). Linda Kerber explains the meaning of Republican Motherhood in *Women of the Republic: Intellect and Ideology in Revolutionary America* (Chapel Hill: University of North Carolina Press, 1980). E. Anthony Rotundo describes male gender roles in the nineteenth-century family in *American Manhood: Transformations in Masculinity from the Revolution to the Modern Era* (New York: Basic Books, 1993).

For a recent survey of childhood and child rearing in the period discussed in this chapter, see Jacqueline S. Reinier, *From Virtue to Character: American Childhood, 1775–1850* (New York: Twayne Publishers, 1996). Another recent survey notable for its attention to childhood outside of the white middle-class experience is Joseph E. Illick, *American Childhoods* (Philadelphia: University of Pennsylvania Press, 2002). Two noteworthy articles on changing child-rearing practices in the nineteenth century are Charles Strickland, "A Transcendentalist Father: The Child-Rearing Practices of Bronson Alcott," *History of Childhood Quarterly* 1 (1973): 4–51, and Daniel T. Rodgers, "Socializing Middle-Class Children: Institutions, Fables, and Work Values in Nineteenth-Century America," *Journal of Social History* 13 (1980): 354–67. For a survey of child-rearing advice literature in the twentieth century, see Ann Hulbert, *Raising America: Experts, Parents, and a Century of Advice about Children* (New York: Alfred A. Knopf, 2003). For historical studies of American children's literature, see Gail Schmunk Murray, *American Children's Literature and the Construction of Childhood* (New York: Twayne Publishers, 1998), and Gillian Avery, *Behold the Child: American Children and Their Books, 1621–1922* (Baltimore, Md.: Johns Hopkins University Press, 1994).

CHAPTER 9

King Cotton

Economic Data on Slavery in the Antebellum South

inton R. Helper had failed as a storekeeper and gold prospector when he tried his hand as an economist in his book *The Impending Crisis of the South: How to Meet It* in 1857. For more than twenty years, Americans had been reading attacks on slavery written by abolitionists and runaway slaves, but Helper's book was different. In the first place, he was a white Southerner, born and educated in backcountry North Carolina before moving to New York and then California to pursue his fortune. Second, his book did not invoke any of the standard arguments found in abolitionist tracts and slave narratives to condemn the South's "peculiar institution." He did not indict masters for the cruelty they inflicted on their slaves, nor did he appeal to Christian morals or divine judgment to convince them to change their ways. He did not sentimentalize slave families as they struggled against forced separations and their masters' sexual abuse. In fact, Helper did not seem particularly concerned with the plight of the slaves at all. Rather, he addressed himself to the nonslaveholding whites of the South, who needed to be liberated from "the secondary degree of slavery" imposed on them by a labor system that cut off their access to opportunity, retarded their economic progress, and kept them mired in poverty and backwardness.

To make his case against slavery, Helper employed a new kind of evidence: economic data he culled from the seventh U.S. census in 1850. As one reviewer of *The Impending Crisis* put it, Helper fired at the walls of slavery with the "heavy artillery of statistics." In table after table of data, he compared free states and slave states in their wealth, mortality rates, mileage of canals and railroads, crops, livestock, farm machinery, and bank capital. He compared Northern and Southern numbers on literacy, public schools, churches, post offices, newspapers, and libraries. "All the free States are alike, and all the slave States are alike,"

Helper concluded. "In the former, wealth, intelligence, power, progress, and prosperity are the prominent characteristics; in the latter poverty, ignorance, embecility [sic], inertia, and extravagance, are the distinguishing features. To be convinced it is only necessary for us to open our eyes and look at the facts, to examine the *statistics* of the country . . . [and] let figures be the umpire."

Helper's critics had statistics of their own. "Cotton *is* king," proclaimed South Carolina senator James Hammond, and trade figures backed him up. Cotton grown on Southern plantations dominated the world market in the mid-nineteenth century and accounted for more than 50 percent of U.S. exports. The world's leading industrial nation of the time, Great Britain, imported more than 70 percent of the cotton used in its textile mills from the American South. Slave prices rose steadily between 1800 and 1860, testimony to the continuing profitability and investment potential of this type of labor. Southern planters, taking their cue from Helper, compared the health, diets, and material circumstances of their slaves with those of free wage laborers in the North and found their slaves to be ahead in all categories. Southern agriculture was vital and expansive in the antebellum era, and Southern farmers moved into new western territories at a rate that outpaced their Northern contemporaries.

Ever since Helper and his critics leveled their statistical artillery at each other, historians have been doing the same, compiling data and crunching numbers in an effort to determine whether slavery had a detrimental or beneficial effect on the South's economic development. Some historians have followed in Helper's footsteps and argued that slavery retarded progress in the South because coerced labor was less efficient than free labor. Masters had to rely on constant supervision to make slaves work, and the slaves had an incentive to sabotage that work by performing it slowly or poorly. Slave owners spent their capital on the purchase of more slaves and land, diverting it from investment in technological improvements that could have increased their productivity.

On the other hand (and in economics, there is always the other hand), some historians have challenged the idea that slavery was inherently inefficient. While not endorsing slavery or the racism it spawned, they have argued that the antebellum Southern economy was more diversified and wealthier than Helper and likeminded critics were willing to admit. Slave prices rose during the antebellum era because slaveholders earned a return on their investment at least on par with that of Northern capitalists investing in textile mills. Slavery also gave slaveholders a distinct advantage over Northern farmers when it came to acquiring labor in an agricultural economy. Northern farmers relied on family members and seasonal hired hands to produce their crops. In the North, where land was plentiful and labor scarce, no free adult male would work for someone else if he could acquire his own farm. Slaveholders, however, controlled a dependent labor force that was constantly growing. The 700,000 slaves counted in the first U.S. census in 1790 had increased to a population of 4 million by 1860. Two factors contributed to that increase. First, the North American slave population achieved a positive rate of natural reproduction during the mid-eighteenth century. Second, the United States continued to import slaves from overseas until Congress banned the international slave trade in 1808 (smuggling meant that the trade did not effectively cease until 1820).

Figure 9.1 Male and Female Field Laborers in the Cotton South *The invention of the cotton gin in the 1790s revolutionized the processing of cotton for sale to textile mills and ignited the rapid expansion of slavery in the American South. Technological change, however, had little impact on planting and reaping cotton, which was still done by male and female slaves toiling for long hours in hot fields. In the decades before the Civil War, Southern planters chose to invest their capital in purchasing more slaves rather than pursuing mechanical innovations in their crop production.* Source: Edward King and James Wells Champney, *The Great South* (American Publishing Co., Hartford, Conn.: 1875).

With no upward limit on the size of their labor force, slaveholders could specialize in a profitable cash crop and realize economies of scale—that is, increases in production above proportional increases in the inputs of land and labor—that Northern farmers could only dream of.

As Helper did in *The Impending Crisis*, economic historians have compared the economic output of the South and the North before the Civil War in an effort to measure the efficiency of slave versus free labor. Efficiency is not the same as profitability. Profitability is a measure of income in excess of outlay; we know slavery was profitable at least in the short run because slaveholders earned enough money to buy more slaves and land. Efficiency is much more difficult to measure. From Helper to the present day, researchers have typically measured the efficiency of slavery relative to that of free labor by trying to determine which of the two labor systems produced more output or higher rates of income. Approaching slavery in this manner may strike you as misleading and unfeeling. After all, this was a racist labor system that brutalized slaves and treated them as property rather than human beings. Asking questions about the economic efficiency of slave labor may seem to minimize or ignore the suffering of those who had to endure this kind of exploitation. Nevertheless, approaching slavery in this manner helps answer important questions about how the economies of the South and the North diverged in the decades before the Civil War and why the resources commanded by each during that conflict differed so substantially.

By no means does this approach exhaust the methods or sources economic historians have used to study slavery, but it does offer a way to frame the questions historians must bring to the evidence. Like all investigators, historians tend to find what they are looking for. In other words, the way in which they approach their evidence profoundly affects what they find. Helper and his critics knew that numbers are not neutral. The way a researcher presents data determines in large part its persuasive power.

Using the Source: Economic Data

Mark Twain once wrote, "There are three kinds of lies: lies, damned lies, and statistics." Historians have typically shared Twain's distrust of statistical data, preferring instead to rely on the more familiar types of textual sources that you have encountered in previous chapters of this book. However, after World War II, the invention of computers that could process enormous quantities of data inspired economic historians to embrace applied mathematics in their reevaluation of American slavery. These scholars described their research methods as "econometrics" or "cliometrics" (Clio was the Muse of history in ancient Greece), a name that signified their emphasis on bringing scientific quantification and precision to the study of history.

Historians who use econometrics to study slavery rely on three main types of evidence. First, they have returned to the census data first used by Helper in 1857 to attack slavery, but rather than simply tallying up totals from the official U.S. census reports, they have gone back into the original manuscript schedules of the census takers and mined them for information as diverse as farm acreage, wealth distribution, and slave birth and marriage patterns. In the same manner, they have used probate records such as wills and estate inventories from county courthouses throughout the South to reconstruct the human and material dimensions of a typical slaveholder's household. The third category of evidence they have used includes textual sources such as slave narratives, travel narratives, and plantation account books and journals. None of these sources were particularly new to historians in the 1950s; previous historians had used them for generations to build their portrait of slavery. But armed with new computer technology, econometricians used these sources differently, bringing a mathematical rigor to their work that rendered in statistical form all sorts of details about day-to-day life in the antebellum South, from the caloric value of the slaves' diet to the average rate of return a planter could expect on his cotton crop.

Some of the evidence and language used in econometrics may be difficult to understand without specialized training in mathematics, but you should confront this data with the same healthy skepticism that you would bring to a more familiar textual source. The mathematics used in compiling the data you will examine in this chapter rarely involved anything more complicated than long division. Even if the mathematical techniques used to compile the data are unfamiliar, you can still ask this source the same questions you would bring to any other source: What is the argument that the author of this data is trying to make? What potential biases or prejudices are evident in that data? Consider for example the two tables that follow, both of which present data concerning the impact slavery had on the development of technology in the South. The first table, from Helper's *The Impending Crisis,* compares the number of patents issued by the federal government for new inventions in free and slave states during 1856. The second table, from econometrician Gavin Wright's *The Political Economy of the Cotton South* (1978), organizes its data on patents in a different manner. Both authors are making a similar point—that slavery retarded technological innovation in the South—but note how Wright's table overcomes some of the problems inherent in Helper's presentation of his evidence.

There is a tendency among people to assume a degree of truthfulness in statistics that they do not automatically grant to written words, but just because the data is generated by someone with knowledge more specialized than yours does not mean you should presume it to be correct and accurate. As Mark Twain knew, numbers as well as words are used to make arguments, and you do not have to be an expert mathematician to approach statistics with a critical eye.

Patents Issued on New Inventions in the Free and Slave States, 1856

Is the use of patent data for one year only a suitable method for collecting information about the antebellum era? Why should the reader assume 1856 was a representative year for such data?

More people lived in the North than in the South in 1856. Should that matter in explaining this discrepancy in patents issued?

Data is divided into two columns, one for free states and one for slave states. The column totals at bottom show a clear discrepancy between the number of patents issued

Where did Helper get his data? Presumably, he looked at the records of the U.S. Patent Office for 1856, but the table lists no source

Free States		Slave States	
California	13	Alabama	11
Connecticut	142	Arkansas	0
Illinois	93	Delaware	8
Indiana	67	Florida	3
Iowa	14	Georgia	13
Maine	42	Kentucky	26
Mass.	331	Louisiana	30
Michigan	22	Maryland	49
N. Hampshire	43	Mississippi	8
N. Jersey	78	Missouri	32
New York	592	N. Carolina	9
Ohio	139	S. Carolina	10
Pennsylvania	267	Tennessee	23
Rhode Island	18	Texas	4
Vermont	35	Virginia	42
Wisconsin	33		
Total	**1,929**		**268**

Patents Granted per Year for Mechanical Devices for Grain and Corn Harvesting, Threshing, and Cutting and for Cotton Harvesting, Picking, and Cutting

	Corn	Grain	Cotton
1837–1849	3.5	6.5	0.2
1850–1860	18.5	10.5	2.6
1866–1879	39.5	38.5	13.2
1880–1890	44.2	59.5	30.5
1891–1900	53.9	56.0	22.9
1901–1914	69.1	52.2	53.6

Source: Jacob Schmookler, *Patents, Inventions, and Economic Change* (Cambridge, Mass.: Harvard University Press, 1972), 100–03.

Margin notes:

This table tells the reader that farmers who grew cotton (grown overwhelmingly in the South with slave labor before 1860) were much less likely to invest in new technologies than farmers who grew corn or grain (mainstays of the North's agriculture)

Wright's table focuses more specifically on patents issued for technology related to agriculture

Presents patent information from 1837 to 1914, allowing the reader to compare data before and after the Civil War

Citation allows readers to go to Wright's source for the data and check Wright's numbers

What Can Economic Data Tell Us?

One of the advantages to working with statistical data is that it allows researchers to organize and process vast quantities of information in a consistent manner. Census data is a good example. The Constitution mandates a census by the federal government every ten years. This process collects information about the U.S. population that is a treasure trove for historians, but working with it requires a researcher to design a consistent method of evaluating the evidence that can be followed by others. Sampling, in which a researcher constructs a small, representative sample for statistical analysis from a much larger pool of evidence, provides one such method. By following commonly accepted formulas and rules for such analysis, econometricians make sure that the results of one researcher can be replicated by others, a standard commonly used by scientists to judge the integrity of one another's work.

Statistical analysis also enables economic historians to circumvent some of the biases found in the traditional textual sources on slavery. Travel narratives written by Northern abolitionists or slave narratives written by runaways appealed to readers in part because of the eyewitness accounts they gave of slavery, but their evidence was by nature anecdotal and subjective. For example, a runaway's slave narrative might tell a harrowing first-person story about a slave auction, but it cannot tell us how many slaves were sold at such auctions over a given period. To answer that sort of question, econometricians have analyzed data from other sources, such as the records of slave sales maintained by the city government of New Orleans between 1804 and 1862, which included thousands of such transactions.

Statistical analysis also helps recover the experience of marginalized groups who left behind few textual sources. The vast majority of slaves in the antebellum South were illiterate because the law prohibited them from learning to read or write. They could not keep journals or write letters detailing their lives for historians to read. Census data and probate records can be used to recover much information about the material circumstances in which they lived: the size of the farms on which they worked, their average marriage ages and family size, their likelihood of being sold and separated from family during their lifetime.

Disadvantages involved in working with statistical data stem from a number of different sources. First, the researcher must determine if the data he or she has on hand is sufficiently complete to produce meaningful conclusions. A sample that is too small or unrepresentative will not produce results that can be easily replicated. Certainly, the U.S. census provided the most complete and reliable record of such data, but it occurred only every ten years and concerned itself chiefly with the vital statistics and material wealth of free whites rather than enslaved African Americans. Recordkeeping by state, county, and municipal governments varied widely in the antebellum era, and such evidence was also susceptible to destruction by fire or flood. Whether they like it or not, econometricians often have to rely on evidence that is fragmentary and incomplete, forcing them to make judgments about the applicability of their conclusions across state or regional boundaries. For example, can conclusions drawn from the New Orleans records on slave sales be applied to slave markets elsewhere in the South? Econometricians may produce very reliable results from analysis of that particular set of data but find their conclusions challenged when they attempt to apply them across the board.

One other disadvantage commonly associated with using statistical data is that it cannot convey the interpersonal and psychological dimensions of slavery. Statistics can provide a wealth of information about a slave's diet, work productivity, and life expectancy, but they cannot plumb the depths of the master-slave relationship. Some econometricians admit this limitation up front, but it does impinge upon their work in a number of significant ways. For example, the question of whether masters relied chiefly on positive or negative incentives to coerce labor from their slaves cannot be fully answered without due consideration of the emotions generated by this relationship. Masters may have been profit seekers, but they were also human beings prone to passions of anger and hostility that affected their use of discipline. Likewise, slaves may have valued rewards offered for their work, but they may have also had non-monetary motives for their behavior, such as solidarity with their kin and friends. In general, statistics can tell us much about the material circumstances of life in the antebellum South, but they cannot explain human behavior within the institution of slavery.

Questions to Ask

A good way to approach economic data is to ask, What point is the author of this information trying to make?: When you comprehend the argument behind a table of statistics, you may then ask more critical questions about the methods used to compile it. What sources is this information coming from? Is it possible for other historians to check its accuracy? Does the presentation of the data hide or obscure information that might challenge the author's argument? If you are convinced of the data's accuracy and relevance, you can then judge what it tells you about the issue at hand (in this case, how slavery affected the South's economy).

- What is the point of this data?
- Has the author identified the sources and methods used to compile this data?
- What questions or problems do you have with the way the data has been collected or presented?
- What does it tell you about the economic impact of slavery on the South?

Source Analysis Table

	What Is the Point of This Data?	What Questions Do You Have About How It Was Collected and Presented?	What Conclusions Can You Draw from This Data About Slavery's Impact on the South's Economy?
OUTPUT			
1. Agricultural Bushel-Measure Products			
2. Value of Farms and Domestic Animals			
3. Crops per Acre			
TECHNOLOGY			
4. Patents Issued on New Inventions			
5. Patents Granted per Year for Mechanical Devices			

	What Is the Point of This Data?	What Questions Do You Have About How It Was Collected and Presented?	What Conclusions Can You Draw from This Data About Slavery's Impact on the South's Economy?
WEALTH AND INCOME			
6. Wealth Per Capita of Cities			
7. Per Capita Income by Region			
8. The Relative Level of the Per Capita Income			
URBANIZATION AND MANUFACTURING			
9. Product of Manufactures			
10. Regional Patterns of Manufacturing			
11. Regional Patterns of Urbanization			

To download and print this table, visit the book companion site at **bedfordstmartins.com/brownshannon.**

The Source: Data Measuring the Economic Efficiency of Slavery in the Antebellum South

Historians have tried to measure the efficiency of slave labor in the antebellum South in a number of ways: output (how much Southern farms produced), technology (how intensively those farms used tools and machines to improve their production), wealth and income (how much that production earned for the South's free and enslaved populations), and urbanization and manufacturing (how rapidly nonagricultural sectors of the economy grew). All of these measures involve comparing the South to other states, regions, or nations, most typically to the free states of the North.

OUTPUT

In *The Impending Crisis*, Hinton Helper included more than fifty tables comparing the economic output of the North and the South. His primary source of data for these tables was the U.S. census of 1850. The following three tables offer examples of how he organized his data to emphasize the difference in outputs between free labor in the North and slave labor in the South.

1   *Agricultural Bushel-Measure Products of Free and Slave States, 1850*

Source: The tables in Sources 1, 2, and 3 are from Hinton R. Helper, *The Impending Crisis of the South: How to Meet It* (New York: Burdick Brothers, 1857), 39.

Free States	Bushels	Price per Bushel	Value
Wheat	72,157,486	1.50	$ 108,236,229
Oats	96,590,371	0.40	38,636,148
Indian Corn	242,618,650	0.60	145,571,190
Potatoes (Irish[1] & Sweet)	59,033,170	0.38	22,432,604
Rye	12,574,623	1.00	12,574,623
Barley	5,002,013	0.90	4,501,811
Buckwheat	8,550,245	0.50	4,275,122
Beans & Peas	1,542,295	1.75	2,699,015
Clover & Grass Seeds	762,265	3.00	2,286,795
Flax Seeds	358,923	1.25	448,647
Garden Products			3,714,605
Orchard Products			6,332,914
Total	**499,190,041**		**$ 351,709,703**

Slave States	Bushels	Price per Bushel	Value
Wheat	27,904,476	1.50	$ 41,856,714
Oats	49,822,799	0.40	19,953,191
Indian Corn	348,992,282	0.60	209,395,369
Potatoes (Irish & Sweet)	44,847,420	0.38	17,042,019
Rye	1,608,240	1.00	1,608,240
Barley	161,907	0.90	145,716
Buckwheat	405,357	0.50	202,678
Beans & Peas	7,637,227	1.75	13,365,147
Clover & Grass Seeds	123,517	3.00	370,551
Flax Seeds	203,484	1.25	254,355
Garden Products			1,377,260
Orchard Products			1,355,827
Total	**481,766,889**		**$ 306,927,067**

[1] White.

2 *Value of Farms and Domestic Animals in Free and Slave States, 1850*

Free States	Value of Livestock	Value of Animals Slaughtered	Cash Value of Farms, Farm Implements, and Machines
California	$ 3,351,058	$ 107,178	$ 3,977,524
Connecticut	7,467,490	2,202,266	74,618,963
Illinois	24,209,258	4,972,286	102,538,851
Indiana	22,478,555	6,567,935	143,089,617
Iowa	3,689,275	821,164	17,830,436
Maine	9,705,726	1,646,773	57,146,305
Mass.	9,647,710	2,500,924	112,285,931
Michigan	8,008,734	1,328,327	54,763,817
N. Hampshire	8,871,901	1,522,873	57,560,122
N. Jersey	10,679,291	2,638,552	124,663,014
New York	73,570,499	13,573,883	576,631,568
Ohio	44,121,741	7,439,243	371,509,188
Pennsylvania	41,500,053	8,219,848	422,598,640
Rhode Island	1,532,637	667,486	17,568,003
Vermont	12,643,228	1,861,336	66,106,509
Wisconsin	4,897,385	920,178	30,170,131
Total	**$ 286,376,541**	**$ 56,990,237**	**$ 2,233,058,619**

Slave States	Value of Livestock	Value of Animals Slaughtered	Cash Value of Farms, Farm Implements, and Machines
Alabama	$ 21,690,112	$ 4,823,485	$ 69,448,887
Arkansas	6,647,969	1,163,313	16,866,541
Delaware	1,849,281	373,665	19,390,310
Florida	2,880,058	514,685	6,981,904
Georgia	25,728,416	6,339,762	101,647,595
Kentucky	29,661,436	6,462,598	160,190,299
Louisiana	11,152,275	1,458,990	87,391,336
Maryland	7,997,634	1,954,800	89,641,988
Mississippi	19,403,662	3,636,582	60,501,561
Missouri	19,887,580	3,367,106	67,207,068
N. Carolina	17,717,647	5,767,866	71,823,298
S. Carolina	15,060,015	3,502,637	86,568,038
Tennessee	29,978,016	6,401,765	103,211,422
Texas	10,412,927	1,116,137	18,701,712
Virginia	33,656,659	7,502,986	223,423,315
Total	**$ 253,723,687**	**$ 54,388,377**	**$ 1,183,995,274**

3   *Crops per Acre on the Average in Free and Slave States, 1850*

Free States	Wheat	Oats	Rye	Indian Corn	Irish Potatoes
Connecticut	0	21	0	40	85
Illinois	11	29	14	33	115
Indiana	12	20	18	33	100
Iowa	14	36	0	32	100
Maine	10	0	0	27	120
Massachusetts	16	26	13	31	170
Michigan	10	26	0	32	140
N. Hampshire	11	30	0	30	220
N. Jersey	11	26	0	33	0
New York	12	25	17	27	100
Ohio	12	21	25	36	0
Pennsylvania	15	0	0	20	75
Rhode Island	0	30	0	0	100
Vermont	13	0	20	32	178
Wisconsin	14	35	0	30	0
Total	**161**	**325**	**107**	**436**	**1503**

Slave States	Wheat	Oats	Rye	Indian Corn	Irish Potatoes
Alabama	5	12	0	15	60
Arkansas	0	18	0	22	0
Delaware	11	20	0	20	0
Florida	15	0	0	0	175
Georgia	5	18	7	16	125
Kentucky	8	18	11	24	130
Louisiana	0	0	0	16	0
Maryland	13	21	18	23	75
Mississippi	9	12	0	18	105
Missouri	11	26	0	34	110
N. Carolina	7	10	15	17	65
S. Carolina	8	12	0	11	70
Tennessee	7	19	7	21	120
Texas	15	0	0	20	250
Virginia	7	13	5	18	75
Total	**121**	**199**	**63**	**275**	**1360**

Recapitulation of Crops per Acre on the Average, 1850

Free States		Slave States	
Wheat	12 bushels per acre	Wheat	9 bushels per acre
Oats	27 bushels per acre	Oats	17 bushels per acre
Rye	18 bushels per acre	Rye	11 bushels per acre
Indian Corn	31 bushels per acre	Indian Corn	20 bushels per acre
Irish Potatoes	125 bushels per acre	Irish Potatoes	113 bushels per acre

TECHNOLOGY

In addition to buying more land and hiring more labor, a farmer may try to increase production through technological innovation. One way historians have tried to measure such change in the nineteenth century is by looking at patent information. The following tables, from Helper's *The Impending Crisis* and historian Gavin Wright's 1978 book *The Political Economy of the Cotton South,* provide comparative data on patents granted in the North and the South. Wright, one of the leading econometricians to study the nineteenth-century South, came to many of the same conclusions as Helper about the negative impact slavery had on technological investment and innovation in the South.

 ## Patents Issued on New Inventions in the Free and Slave States, 1856

Source: Helper, *The Impending Crisis,* 294.

Free States		Slave States	
California	13	Alabama	11
Connecticut	142	Arkansas	0
Illinois	93	Delaware	8
Indiana	67	Florida	3
Iowa	14	Georgia	13
Maine	42	Kentucky	26
Mass.	331	Louisiana	30
Michigan	22	Maryland	49
N. Hampshire	43	Mississippi	8
N. Jersey	78	Missouri	32
New York	592	N. Carolina	9
Ohio	139	S. Carolina	10
Pennsylvania	267	Tennessee	23
Rhode Island	18	Texas	4
Vermont	35	Virginia	42
Wisconsin	33		
Total	**1,929**	**Total**	**268**

| 5 | *Patents Granted per Year for Mechanical Devices for Grain and Corn Harvesting, Threshing, and Cutting and for Cotton Harvesting, Picking, and Cutting* |

Source: Gavin Wright, *The Political Economy of the Cotton South: Households, Markets, and Wealth in the Nineteenth Century* (New York: W. W. Norton, 1978), 108.

	Corn	Grain	Cotton
1837–1849	3.5	6.5	0.2
1850–1860	18.5	10.5	2.6
1866–1879	39.5	38.5	13.2
1880–1890	44.2	59.5	30.5
1891–1900	53.9	56.0	22.9
1901–1914	69.1	52.2	53.6

Source: Jacob Schmookler, *Patents, Inventions, and Economic Change* (Cambridge, Mass.: Harvard University Press, 1972), 100–03.

WEALTH AND INCOME

The following tables compare per capita wealth and income in the South with that of other regions or nations. ("Per capita" means "per person.") The first table is from Helper's *The Impending Crisis*. The second and third tables are the work of econometricians Robert William Fogel and Stanley L. Engerman, whose 1974 book *Time on the Cross: The Economics of American Negro Slavery* challenged many of Helper's conclusions about the inefficiency of slave labor and ignited a controversy among historians about using econometrics to study American slavery.

Wealth Per Capita of Nine Free and Slave Cities

Source: Helper, *The Impending Crisis,* 347.

Nine Free Cities	Population	Wealth	Wealth Per Capita
New York	700,000	$ 511,740,492	$ 731
Philadelphia	500,000	325,000,000	650
Boston	165,000	249,162,500	1,150
Brooklyn	225,000	95,800,440	425
Cincinnati	210,000	88,810,734	422
Chicago	112,000	171,000,000	1,527
Providence	60,000	58,064,516	967
Buffalo	90,000	45,474,476	505
New Bedford	21,000	27,047,000	1,288
Total	**2,083,000**	**$ 1,572,100,158**	**$ 754**

Nine Slave Cities	Population	Wealth	Wealth Per Capita
Baltimore	250,000	$ 102,053,839	$ 408
New Orleans	175,000	91,188,195	521
St. Louis	140,000	63,000,000	450
Charleston	60,000	36,127,751	602
Louisville	70,000	31,500,000	450
Richmond	40,000	20,143,520	503
Norfolk	17,000	12,000,000	705
Savannah	25,000	11,999,015	480
Wilmington	10,000	7,850,000	785
Total	**787,000**	**$ 375,862,320**	**$ 477**

7 | *Per Capita Income by Region for 1840 and 1860 in 1860 Prices*

This table shows the growth in per capita income in several regions of the United States. The reference to 1860 prices in the table's title means that Fogel and Engerman have adjusted the figures in the 1840 column to reflect the dollar's value in 1860. This adjustment eliminates inflation as a factor in explaining the growth of these figures between 1840 and 1860. Fogel and Engerman also noted that their per capita income figures for the South included free and enslaved persons. In other words, if they had calculated per capita income for whites only, the South's would have been much higher than the North's.

Source: The tables in Sources 7 and 8 are from Robert William Fogel and Stanley L. Engerman, *Time on the Cross: The Economics of American Negro Slavery*, 2 volumes (Boston: Little, Brown and Company, 1974), 1:248.

	1840	1860	Average Annual Rates of Change (Percent)
National Average	$ 96	$ 128	1.4
North	**109**	**141**	**1.3**
Northeast	129	181	1.7
North Central	65	89	1.6
South	**74**	**103**	**1.7**
South Atlantic	66	84	1.2
East South Central	69	89	1.3
West South Central	151	184	1.0

Northeast: ME, NH, VT, MA, RI, CT, NY, NJ, PA
North Central: MI, OH, IN, IL, WI, MO, IA, MN, ND, SD, NE, KS
South Atlantic: VA, MD, DE, DC, NC, SC, GA, FL
East South Central: KY, TN, AL, MS
West South Central: OK, AR, LA, TX

8

The Relative Level of the Per Capita Income of the South in 1860

Economists use "relative" measures as a way of creating a common yard-stick for comparing data from different sources. In this case, Fogel and Engerman converted per capita income figures from different nations into U.S. dollars. They assigned the South's per capita income the value of $100 and measured the North's and other nations' per capita incomes relative to it. In other words, think of the $100 value assigned to the South as a bar, the distance over which or under which indicates how another region's or nation's per capita income compared to that of the South in 1860.

Southern Per Capita Income Level = 100

Australia	$144
North	140
Great Britain	126
South	100
Switzerland	100
Canada	96
Netherlands	93
Belgium	92
France	82
Ireland	71
Denmark	70
Germany	67
Norway	54
Italy	49
Austria	41
Sweden	41
Japan	14
Mexico	10
India	9

URBANIZATION AND MANUFACTURING

Economists interested in measuring the efficiency of the South's slave labor system have also studied sectors of the economy other than agriculture. In particular, they have compared the rate of industrialization between the North and the South by looking at each region's production of manufactured goods. They have also used urbanization, or the growth of city populations, as a measure of nonagricultural economic activity, because city dwellers typically earned their living in ways other than farming. These tables, from *The Impending Crisis* and *The Political Economy of the Cotton South,* provide data on such trends.

9 | *Product of Manufactures in the Free and Slave States, 1850*

Source: Helper, *The Impending Crisis,* 284.

Free States	Value of Annual Products	Capital Invested	Hands Employed
California	$ 12,862,522	$ 1,006,197	3,964
Connecticut	45,110,102	23,890,348	47,770
Illinois	17,236,073	6,385,387	12,065
Indiana	18,922,651	7,941,602	14,342
Iowa	3,551,783	1,292,875	1,707
Maine	24,664,135	14,700,452	28,078
Mass.	151,137,145	83,357,642	165,938
Michigan	10,976,894	6,534,250	9,290
N. Hampshire	23,164,503	18,242,114	27,092
N. Jersey	39,713,586	22,184,730	37,311
New York	237,597,249	99,904,405	199,349
Ohio	62,647,259	29,019,538	51,489
Pennsylvania	155,044,910	94,473,810	146,766
Rhode Island	22,093,258	12,923,176	20,881
Vermont	8,570,920	5,001,377	8,445
Wisconsin	9,923,068	3,382,148	6,089
Total	**$ 842,586,058**	**$ 430,240,051**	**780,576**

Slave States	Value of Annual Products	Capital Invested	Hands Employed
Alabama	$ 4,538,878	$ 3,450,606	4,936
Arkansas	607,436	324,065	903
Delaware	4,649,296	2,978,945	3,888
Florida	668,338	547,060	991
Georgia	7,086,525	5,460,483	8,378
Kentucky	24,588,483	12,350,734	24,386
Louisiana	7,320,948	5,318,074	6,437
Maryland	32,477,702	14,753,143	30,124
Mississippi	2,972,038	1,833,420	3,173
Missouri	23,749,265	9,079,695	16,850
N. Carolina	9,111,245	7,252,225	12,444
S. Carolina	7,063,513	6,056,865	7,009
Tennessee	9,728,438	6,975,279	12,032
Texas	1,165,538	539,290	1,066
Virginia	29,705,387	18,109,993	29,108
Total	**$ 165,413,027**	**$ 95,029,879**	**161,738**

10 Regional Patterns of Manufacturing

This table provides regional comparisons of two measures of manufacturing: the per capita (per person) investment in manufacturing and the per capita output of manufacturing. In this table, the "South" includes all slaveholding states. The "Cotton South" refers to a smaller interstate region in which cotton production dominated the economy, primarily South Carolina, Georgia, Alabama, Mississippi, Louisiana, Arkansas, and Texas.

Source: Wright, *The Political Economy of the Cotton South,* 110.

	Capital Invested by Manufacturing per Capita		Value of Manufacturing Output per Capita	
	1850	1860	1850	1860
New England	$57.96	$82.13	$100.71	$149.97
Middle States	$35.50	$52.21	$ 71.24	$ 96.28
Northwest	$11.70	$18.95	$ 26.32	$ 37.33
Pacific States	$10.39	$42.35	$ 84.83	$129.04
South	$ 7.60	$10.54	$ 10.88	$ 17.09
Cotton South	$ 5.11	$ 7.20	$ 6.83	$ 10.47
U.S.	$22.73	$32.12	$ 43.69	$ 59.98

Source: U.S. Bureau of the Census, *Compendium of 1850 Census,* 179; Eighth U.S. Census, *Manufactures,* 725; Ninth Census, *Compendium,* 799.

11 Regional Patterns of Urbanization by Percent of Population

This table shows the growth in the urban population in different regions of the United States between 1820 and 1860.

Source: Wright, *The Political Economy of the Cotton South,* 110.

	1820	1830	1840	1850	1860
New England	10.5	14.0	19.4	28.8	36.6
Middle Atlantic	11.3	14.2	18.1	25.5	35.4
East North Central	1.2	2.5	3.9	9.0	14.1
West North Central	0	3.5	3.9	10.3	13.4
South Atlantic	5.5	6.2	7.7	9.8	11.5
East South Central	0.8	1.5	2.1	4.2	5.9

Source: Douglass North, *The Economic Growth of the United States, 1790–1860* (1961; New York: W.W. Norton, 1966), 258.

Analyzing Economic Data

1. Using your notes on page 186, what types of methods and sources were used in compiling the data presented in these tables? Depending on the types of sources they are using, do you find some of the tables more convincing than others? Why or why not?

2. What factors other than type of labor (slave or free) might have accounted for the differences in Helper's totals for Northern and Southern agricultural output in Sources 1, 2, and 3? Why would or why wouldn't a per acre figure, such as that provided in Source 3, be a more accurate measure of the efficiency of free versus slave labor than state-by-state totals, such as those given in Source 2?

3. Compare Helper's per capita wealth figures in Source 6 with the per capita income figures provided by Fogel and Engerman in Sources 7 and 8. If Helper wanted his figures to prove the superiority of free over slave labor, why was it to his advantage to measure the per capita wealth of urban populations rather than the entire Northern and Southern populations? Likewise, why do you suppose Fogel and Engerman emphasized regional and national comparisons in their per capita income figures?

4. What does the data on patents in Sources 4 and 5 tell you about how Southerners and Northerners chose to invest the capital they put into increasing agricultural production? What sort of incentive did a Northern farmer have for investing in new technology that a Southern farmer did not?

5. What does the data on urbanization and manufacturing in Sources 9, 10, and 11 tell you about the comparative positions of the Northern and Southern economies in these categories? Why would measures of urban population growth and manufacturing output be important in discussions of the efficiency of slave versus free labor?

6. Having reviewed the information provided in these tables, describe the overall economic impact of slavery on the antebellum South. If it was negative, why did Southerners use this labor system for so long?

The Rest of the Story

The divergent paths toward economic development taken by the North and the South during the first half of the nineteenth century had important ramifications for each region. On the eve of the Civil War, the South led the world in cotton production, but it lagged behind the North in population, manufacturing, and wealth. During the war, the North's superior industrial capacity sustained the war effort, while the South's economy withered under a Union naval blockade that closed access to international markets. Cotton planters' profits evaporated during the war, and emancipation destroyed the property value they claimed in their slaves. An economic system that had prospered in the South since the 1790s utterly collapsed by 1865. Recovery came slowly. In the war's aftermath, cotton prices fell and the South's economy stagnated. Yet Southern farmers, white and black alike, continued to cultivate cotton at the expense of other crops. While the rest of the nation experienced unparalleled growth in urbanization, industrialization, and agricultural output, the South remained locked in a cycle of low productivity and profits.

Economic historians debate the reasons for this stagnation as vociferously as they do the efficiency of antebellum slavery. Some attribute it to the destruction the Civil War visited upon the South's economic infrastructure, including its plantations, urban centers, and railroad lines. Others emphasize the loss in property and capital that the planter class faced as a result of emancipation. Still others emphasize external factors, such as the decline in the world demand for cotton, which had little to do with the political or social consequences of the Civil War.

Invariably, studies of the South's postwar economy address the problem of labor and race relations. Planters were stripped of their most valuable asset when the Emancipation Proclamation and Thirteenth Amendment ended slavery. The former slaves were set free with no assets of their own in the form of land, livestock, tools, or cash. Both of these groups needed each other to survive, but their relationship was strained by years of racial antagonism. Planters tried to replicate the old system of slavery as closely as possible by signing the freedmen to labor contracts that tied them to the land for a year or more at a time. The freedmen preferred to work their own land on their own terms, but if that was not an option, they accepted tenancy on white-owned land, so long as they could work free from the white supervision that had been the hallmark of antebellum plantations. Gradually, there evolved in the South a system of sharecropping, in which black farmers lived and worked on land owned by their former masters, paying rent by surrendering a percentage of their crop at the end of the year.

This system gave the freedmen and -women the autonomy they desired, but it also had its drawbacks. Landlords demanded that they cultivate a cash crop, typically cotton, to use as payment for their rent. This led to an intensification of cotton cultivation at a time when its value was declining, drawing precious capital and labor away from the production of livestock and subsistence crops that would have improved the farmers' material welfare. Also, because landlords and local merchants controlled the farmers' access to provisions and supplies, sharecroppers went into debt, which bound them to the land from one generation to the next. Cotton's stranglehold on Southern farmers would not be broken until the twentieth century, when a combination of crop failures caused by boll weevil infestations and black migration to Northern cities finally ended the sharecropping system.

To Find Out More

The seventh U.S. census, which provided the basis of Helper's data in *The Impending Crisis*, was originally published in Washington, D.C., in 1853. A modern edition is United States Census Office, *The Seventh Census of the United States, 1850: Embracing a Statistical View of Each of the States and Territories* (New York:

N. Ross, 1990). The Web site of the U.S. Census Bureau (**census.gov**) is a good place to start Internet searches for census information, but bear in mind that its online data focuses on the most recent U.S. census in 2000. For a Web site that provides access to data from every U.S. census since 1790, see the University of Virginia Geospatial and Statistical Data Center's United States Historical Census Data Browser (**fisher.lib.virginia.edu/census/**). For a useful introduction to the methods of econometrics, see Pat Hudson, *History by the Numbers: An Introduction to Quantitative Approaches* (London: Arnold Publishers, 2000).

The most famous work to apply econometrics to the study of American slavery is Robert William Fogel and Stanley L. Engerman, *Time on the Cross: The Economics of American Negro Slavery,* 2 volumes (Boston: Little, Brown and Company, 1974). Volume 1 presents the book's argument in language aimed at the general reader; Volume 2, *Evidence and Methods,* contains source materials and appendixes useful to anyone interested in the authors' methodology. Fogel and Engerman have since qualified and elaborated on their interpretation of slavery in *Without Consent or Contract: The Rise and Fall of American Slavery* (New York: W. W. Norton, 1989).

Fogel and Engerman's argument that antebellum slavery was economically efficient and provided a higher standard of living for slaves than contemporary wage laborers in the North ignited a firestorm of criticism. Two important works that take aim at Fogel and Engerman's methods and conclusions are Paul A. David, Herbert G. Gutman, Richard Sutch, Peter Temin, and Gavin Wright, *Reckoning with Slavery: A Critical Study in the Quantitative History of American Negro Slavery* (New York: Oxford University Press, 1976), and Herbert G. Gutman, *Slavery and the Numbers Game: A Critique of "Time on the Cross"* (Urbana: University of Illinois Press, 1975). Both of these books make for compelling reading in how historians argue over the meaning of statistical evidence.

The scholarly debate over slavery's efficiency has continued in several important works based on econometrics. Gavin Wright's *The Political Economy of the Cotton South: Households, Markets, and Wealth in the Nineteenth Century* (New York: W. W. Norton, 1978) makes the case for the inefficiency of slave labor. Wright's *Old South, New South: Revolutions in the Southern Economy since the Civil War* (New York: Basic Books, 1986) and Roger L. Ransom and Richard Sutch's *One Kind of Freedom: The Economic Consequences of Emancipation* (Cambridge: Cambridge University Press, 1977) apply econometrics to the study of the Southern economy after the Civil War. Mark M. Smith's *Debating Slavery: Economy and Society in the Antebellum American South* (Cambridge: Cambridge University Press, 1998) provides an excellent, brief overview of the debate over the economics of slavery.

Other significant works that address the economics of slavery in the antebellum South include Eugene D. Genovese's *The Political Economy of Slavery* (New York: Pantheon, 1965), James Oakes's *The Ruling Race: A History of American Slaveholders* (New York: Alfred A. Knopf, 1982), and Walter Johnson's *Soul by Soul: Life inside the Antebellum Slave Market* (Cambridge, Mass.: Harvard University Press, 2000). Peter Kolchin's *American Slavery, 1619–1877* (1993; New York: Hill and Wang, 2003) provides an excellent synthesis of the growth and destruction of the Cotton South.

CHAPTER 10

The West in Jacksonian Arts

George Catlin's Paintings of American Indians

During the Jacksonian era, it was hard to enjoy American arts and literature without bumping into Indians making their final exits. James Fenimore Cooper's novel *The Last of the Mohicans* (1826) popularized the figure of the stoic, lone Indian observing the passing of his people. Theatergoers flocked to see John Augustus Stone's *Metamora; or, The Last of the Wampanoags* (1829), a play that retold the story of Metacom, or King Philip, the doomed leader of a seventeenth-century Indian war in New England. People who preferred seeing real Indians to fictional ones attended lectures given by western Indians touring eastern cities. The most famous of these was Black Hawk, a chief of the Sac and Fox nation in Illinois, who came to the nation's capital in 1833 as a prisoner of war but gained celebrity status after speaking engagements in Baltimore, Philadelphia, and New York. The "vanishing Indian" became a permanent fixture in the cultural landscape of Jacksonian America; as soon as one exited, another appeared to deliver a heartfelt elegy to his people and lament his "last of" status.

An art exhibition that opened in New York City in 1837 did for the vanishing Indian in American painting what *The Last of the Mohicans* and *Metamora; or, The Last of the Wampanoags* had done for him on page and stage. George Catlin's Indian Gallery featured almost 500 paintings of Indians, mostly portraits, but also scenes of hunting, religious ceremonies, and village life. His exhibition also included tools, weapons, clothing, and other artifacts associated with the paintings' subjects. Catlin had painted every single one of the works featured in the exhibition, and he proudly proclaimed their unrivaled authenticity, claiming that he had visited fifty Indian nations from the western reaches of the Missouri River to the southwestern plains of Texas.

Born in Wilkes-Barre, Pennsylvania, in 1796, Catlin spent his formative years in the East, practicing law in Connecticut and then moving to Philadelphia in 1821 to make his living as an artist. He specialized as a painter of miniatures, palm-sized portraits of loved ones in an age before photography, but he longed to devote his talents to a greater purpose. He found his inspiration in 1829 when a delegation of western Indians visited Philadelphia. The exotic appearance and noble carriage of these strangers, so unlike any people Catlin had ever seen before, convinced him to abandon his work and move to St. Louis, where he would seek out and paint Indians still untouched by white society. As Catlin described it in his book *Letters and Notes on the Manners, Customs, and Condition of the North American Indians* (1841), he used his paints and brushes to record "the living manners, customs, and character of an interesting race of people, who are rapidly passing away from the face of the earth, lending a hand to a dying nation who have no historians or biographers of their own to portray with fidelity their native looks and history."

For Catlin, there were two types of Indians: those who retained their "original" character and those who had fallen into their "secondary" character. The difference between the two was exposure to what whites called civilization. In Catlin's view, those Indians who still lived removed from civilization were uncorrupted and worthy of preservation on canvas. Those who traded and lived among whites, even on the frontier, were diminished physically and morally by the evils of "whisky, the small-pox, and the bayonet." Catlin had no doubt that the western expansion of the United States would mean the ultimate extinction of all Indian peoples; those still in their original state were doomed to assume their secondary character before too long. Thus, he undertook his work with great urgency, enlisting the aid of federal Indian superintendent William Clark (of Lewis and Clark fame) to find and paint as many as possible of those Indians still living in their original condition. As Catlin described it, "the traveler who would see these people in their native simplicity and beauty, must needs be hastily on his way to the prairies and Rocky Mountains, or he will see them only as they are now seen on the frontiers, as a basket of *dead game*, harassed, chased, bleeding, and dead."

Between 1832 and 1836, Catlin made five trips into Indian country from his base in St. Louis. The first and longest of these was a steamboat journey of almost 2,000 miles up the Missouri River, to its confluence with the Yellowstone River in modern North Dakota. During this trip, Catlin painted 170 canvases and encountered Indians barely known to Americans outside of a small coterie of fur traders, military personnel, and government agents. In the next five years, Catlin also traveled southwest into the Arkansas Territory and north into the upper Mississippi Valley and western Great Lakes, but none of those trips matched in scale or productivity his first journey up the Missouri. When he returned east with his Indian Gallery in 1837, Catlin had already acquired a reputation (much of it due to his own tireless self-promotion) as an inland Columbus, the first and final witness to the Indians of the Great Plains in their natural state.

Catlin's approach to his Indian subjects reflected the political climate in which he lived and worked. Catlin headed for St. Louis in 1830, the same year

in which Congress, at the urging of President Andrew Jackson, passed the Indian Removal Act. By this legislation, Congress authorized the forced eviction
of Indians east of the Mississippi to reservations in the West. The act was aimed
primarily at several Indian nations in the Southeast that were resisting efforts
by state governments to appropriate their land and extend legal jurisdiction
over them. The Cherokees, Creeks, Choctaws, Chickasaws, and Seminoles—
known collectively as "the Five Civilized Tribes" because of their adoption of
European-style government, farming, and property law after the American Revolution—had no interest in surrendering their lands or sovereignty to Georgia,
Alabama, Mississippi, and Tennessee. Jackson, who had risen to fame fighting
Indians in the 1810s, had no interest in protecting their territorial or political
autonomy.

Supporters of Indian removal justified this policy with language very similar to that used by Catlin to explain why he went west in 1830. They claimed
that Indians and whites could not peacefully coexist; invariably, contact and
trade with whites led to the cultural and physical degeneration of the Indians.
Removal across the Mississippi, where Indians could live free from the corruption of white society, was their only hope for forestalling their extinction. Of
course, the experience of the Cherokees and other Indian nations that had
managed to adapt and even in some cases flourish as whites invaded their
homelands proved otherwise, but in the 1830s, Jackson and his supporters did
not want to recognize such an alternative to removal. In 1831, the Supreme
Court ruled that dispossessing the Cherokees against their wishes was unconstitutional. However, the Supreme Court had no power to enforce its decision;
that job rested with the executive branch of the federal government. As president, Jackson chose to ignore the Supreme Court's ruling, thus enabling the
states to proceed with Indian removal unhindered.

A painter brings more to the canvas than just paints and brushes. In
Catlin's case, the distinction he drew between Indians in their original and secondary character was a product of political and cultural attitudes surrounding
Indian removal in the 1830s. The "vanishing Indian" he took as his subject was
a literary and political invention of his time. Nevertheless, Catlin did go west,
meet hundreds of Indians, and create a rich visual record of their lives.

Using the Source: Paintings

Scholars interested in Catlin's work have always been mindful of his commercial motives. Catlin was an entrepreneur as well as an artist. He took seriously
his self-appointed charge as historian to the Indians, but he also tried constantly to cultivate a paying audience for his Indian Gallery. During his journeys west in the 1830s, he wrote dispatches to eastern newspapers describing
his travels and adventures. As early as 1833, he exhibited selections of his
paintings in Pittsburgh, Louisville, and Cincinnati. And although he told his
audiences that his work was self-financed, he sought the patronage of Indian

agents, military officers, and congressmen who he thought might convince the federal government to purchase his collection for a hefty sum.

Catlin's commercial motives and relentless self-promotion colored the reception of his work from the start. Many of his contemporaries involved in the fur trade found his written accounts of the Indians of the upper Missouri to be exaggerated or misleading, and they ridiculed his claims to being the first white man to visit the sacred pipestone quarries of the Sioux in western Minnesota. One of the pioneering scholars of American anthropology, Henry Rowe Schoolcraft, took issue with Catlin's depiction of the Mandans' O-kee-pa ceremony, calling it sensationalistic and without basis in fact. To counter such attacks, Catlin published statements by other western travelers corroborating his work, and he never missed the opportunity to have a touring group of Indians visit his gallery and testify to its accuracy.

Art historians have also criticized Catlin's work on aesthetic grounds. Catlin placed an obvious priority on quantity over quality in his art and worked at a breakneck pace. The hurried nature of much of his work is evident in the broad strokes he used, especially in his landscapes. As for his portraits, it is important to remember that before painting Indians, Catlin had earned his living as a miniaturist. He preferred to paint sitting figures and was most adept at faces and busts. Many of his full-length portraits are oddly proportioned, featuring improperly sized bodies or limbs. There is no doubt that Catlin was an artist of tremendous output; whether he was one of tremendous skill is debatable.

His defenders emphasize his significance as an innovator in American painting. Previous artists had painted Indian subjects, but always in the comfort of their studios. Catlin was the first to bring his paints and canvases to the Indians in their camps and villages, giving his work an unprecedented realism. His assembly-line style and output also reflected the dynamic quality of Jacksonian society. Catlin was constantly on the move, adapting his work to his surroundings, finding new subjects and trying new ways of painting them. While he may not have been the most technically proficient painter in nineteenth-century America, his work reflected the kinetic, innovative spirit of the Jacksonian era.

It is harder to determine what Catlin's paintings can tell us about the Indians themselves. Indians are ubiquitous in his work, even his landscapes, yet they are silent. Catlin occasionally recorded the reactions his subjects had to his paintings in his letters and journals but with the same air of self-congratulation evident throughout his published writings. Generally, Indians enjoyed the novelty of having their portraits painted by an artist who visited their villages, but some Sioux medicine men warned that Catlin used his craft to capture Indian souls. At the very least, the fact that Catlin conducted his work without threats or injuries to his person or property indicates that his Indian hosts offered no united or sustained resistance to his work.

After taking account of all the biases Catlin brought to his work—his commercial motives, the political climate of Indian removal, his prejudices against Indians who lived among whites, and his idealized vision of those who did not—the reliability of his paintings as a historical source remains in question. Catlin's work ignored the world inhabited by the Five Civilized Tribes and other eastern Indians who had lived for generations among whites, but what can it tell us about those he encountered west of the Mississippi?

What Can Paintings Tell Us?

Few readers are willing to suffer voluntarily through James Fenimore Cooper's novels today, but historians still find them a useful source for understanding the origins of the "vanishing Indian" motif in America literature. So too can Catlin's art help explain the prejudices and assumptions that shaped Indian policy in the Jacksonian era. While it is tempting to evaluate Catlin's paintings by our modern standards of what constitutes good art, it is more fruitful for the historian to ask why an artist wishing to produce commercially viable and historically significant work in the 1830s would have pursued Native Americans as subjects. To understand why Catlin's work appealed to the audiences who paid to see it is to gain insight into American attitudes about the West and Indians at that time.

Another advantage to using Catlin's work is what it can tell us about the life and culture of its subjects. Catlin preferred portraits, but he also painted scenes of Indian religious ceremonies, games, and hunting. These works provide some of the earliest and most complete visual records of Indian life on the Great Plains. In the case of the Mandans, a Missouri Valley tribe practically wiped out by a smallpox epidemic in 1837, Catlin's work is indispensable for documenting Indians that very few other whites ever encountered.

Despite these obvious strengths in Catlin's work, it is important to remember that many contemporaries questioned Catlin's reliability as an eyewitness to Indian cultures. He ranged far and wide during the years he spent in the West, but he did not settle in any one place long enough to learn native languages or knit himself into the fabric of native communities. Unlike fur traders, who often married into Indian families, Catlin developed no kinship ties or other bonds of lasting intimacy among his subjects. He had to rely on traders and government agents as his interpreters, and he lost much of their support when he published reports in newspapers critical of the fur trade, which in Catlin's opinion corrupted Indian morals and society. As noted earlier, his detractors also accused him of engaging in sensationalism whenever it served his commercial purposes. It is useful, therefore, to look for evidence within Catlin's work that contradicts his claim that his Indian subjects lived in a natural state untainted by white contact.

Consider for example the image on page 207, the frontispiece (an illustration that appears at the start of a book) to Catlin's *Letters and Notes on the Manners, Customs, and Condition of the North American Indians.* This self-portrait, titled *The Author Painting a Chief, at the Base of the Rocky Mountains,* depicts Catlin in the process of painting Máh-To-Tóh-Pa, or Four Bears, a chief of the Mandans (see Source 2, p. 212). Careful examination of this image illustrates some of the advantages and disadvantages associated with using Catlin's work

What does this frontispiece tell Catlin's readers about his work?

Catlin has posed his subject in front of Siouan buffalo-hide tipis, rather than the wood and earth lodges of the Mandans

Note the rifle of non-Indian origin

What do the Indians' expressions tell you about the way Catlin promoted himself?

as a historical source. On the one hand, it provides a visual introduction to how Catlin went about his work and how he self-consciously fashioned his identity as an artist (note his confident stance, his awestruck audience). The image, however, also confuses elements of Mandan and Sioux culture in a way that suggests Catlin was more concerned with dramatic effect than factual consistency in this painting. Catlin claimed that his Indian subjects still lived in a natural state untainted by contact with whites, but items of non-Indian origin were often included in his paintings. Besides the rifle, what other evidence in this painting contradicts his claim?

Catlin premised his work on a dichotomy that held very little meaning to his Indian subjects. As an artist, he wanted to freeze time, to capture Indians in their "original" character before they slipped into their degraded "secondary" character. His work shows little interest in documenting the long-term process of cultural adaptation that all Indians experienced in the wake of white contact and that was well under way when he arrived on the Great Plains in the 1830s. Indeed, it may be argued that the Indians Catlin painted never really existed. French, Spanish, and American traders had long preceded him on the Missouri, and the Indians he painted in their supposed natural state showed much evidence of that contact, particularly in their material culture. Historians using Catlin's paintings must bear in mind that many of his subjects were already quite familiar with the world he came from and anxious to expand their trade and diplomacy with it. As living, breathing human beings, they contradicted the very ideas and sentiments Catlin wished to convey in his work.

Questions to Ask

Art may be timeless, but it is also the product of historical circumstances. In other words, any piece of art—be it a painting, sculpture, or poem—may act as a mirror for the social values and cultural assumptions of the people involved in its creation. In the case of Catlin's Indian Gallery, you will want to hold this mirror up to the artist, his subjects, and his audience. What do these paintings tell you about Catlin's motives for going west to paint Indians? What assumptions about Indian life are implicit in his work? What information do these paintings convey about the Indians themselves? What evidence do they present of the impact white contact was having on Native Americans in the Great Plains? Finally, what does Catlin's Indian Gallery tell you about the people who visited it in American and European cities?

- What values or ideas was Catlin expressing in his work?
- What do these paintings tell us about the lives and cultures of the Indians depicted in them?
- Why did Catlin's work appeal to his contemporaries in the United States and Europe?

Source Analysis Table

Painting	What Values or Ideas Is Catlin Expressing in This Painting?	What Information Does This Painting Convey About Indian Culture?	How Do You Think Catlin's Audience Responded to This Painting?
1. Shón-Ka-Ki-He-Ga			
2. Máh-To-Tóh-Pa			
3. La-Dóo-Ke-A			
4. Pshán-Shaw			
5. Jú-Ah-Kís-Gaw			
6. Wi-Jún-Jon			

(continued)

Painting	What Values or Ideas Is Catlin Expressing in This Painting?	What Information Does This Painting Convey About Indian Culture?	How Do You Think Catlin's Audience Responded to This Painting?
7. Fort Pierre			
8. Buffalo Hunt			
9. Buffalo Chase			
10. Bird's-Eye View			
11. Sioux Encamped			
12. The Cutting Scene			

To download and print this table, visit the book companion site at **bedfordstmartins.com/brownshannon**.

The Source: Paintings from George Catlin's Indian Gallery, 1832–1839

Catlin provided a title for each one of his paintings and a brief description of its subject in his exhibition catalog. Each portrait was titled in a similar manner: Catlin rendered the subject's name phonetically, followed by a version in English. In keeping with modern cataloguing practices, the caption for each of the paintings included here also indicates the subject's tribal affiliation as Catlin identified it, followed in some cases by the preferred modern usage (in parentheses), and the year in which Catlin painted it.

1   *Shón-Ka-Ki-He-Ga, Horse Chief, Grand Pawnee Head Chief,* Pawnee, 1832

Catlin's experience as a miniaturist is evident in this portrait, which features only the subject's torso and head. The round object hanging from beads around Shón-Ka-Ki-He-Ga's neck is a peace medal, distributed by the U.S. government to allied Indian chiefs.

Source: Smithsonian American Art Museum: 1985.66.99.

Máh-To-Tóh-Pa, Four Bears, Second Chief, in Full Dress, Mandan (Numakiki), 1832

Máh-To-Tóh-Pa's appearance in this portrait has come to define what novels, films, and other popular media regard as the authentic attire of an Indian chief: a full-length feathered headdress complemented by buffalo horns, beaded leggings and moccasins, and a shirt featuring pictographs of native design. Catlin purchased the outfit from Four Bears and featured it in his Indian Gallery.

Source: Smithsonian American Art Museum: 1985.66.128.

3 | *La-Dóo-Ke-A, Buffalo Bull, A Grand Pawnee Warrior,* Pawnee, 1832

This unfinished portrait (only the torso and head of the subject are complete) tells the viewer about the process of Catlin's work from the field to the exhibit hall. He concentrated on the subject's head and face during a sitting and often left other details to be completed in his studio in St. Louis.

Source: Smithsonian American Art Museum: 1985.66.100.

Pshán-Shaw, Sweet-Scented Grass, Twelve-Year-Old Daughter of Bloody Hand, Arikara (Sahnish), 1832

Catlin's Indian Gallery included far fewer portraits of Indian women than men, an imbalance due in part to his working methods. The traders, agents, and military officers he traveled with transacted most of their business with Indian males. The girl in this portrait was the daughter of Bloody Hand, a chief who also posed for Catlin. Most of Catlin's female subjects were relatives of distinguished males he also painted.

Source: Smithsonian American Art Museum: 1985.66.125.

5   *Jú-Ah-Kís-Gaw, Woman with Her Child in a Cradle,* Ojibwa (Chippewa), 1835

This portrait of an Indian woman and her child also depicts a cradleboard, an object of native manufacture used to hold and carry infants.

Source: Smithsonian American Art Museum: 1985.66.186.

Wi-Jún-Jon, Pigeon's Egg Head (The Light) Going to and Returning from Washington, Assiniboine (Nakoda), 1837–1839

This "before and after" portrait was one of Catlin's most overtly political and frequently reproduced works. Catlin first encountered Wi-Jún-Jon (and painted a portrait of him) in 1831, when the warrior was en route to Washington, D.C., to meet President Jackson. Eighteen months later, Catlin met him again, this time returning from Washington "in the dress and with the airs of a civilized beau." According to Catlin, Wi-Jún-Jon soon fell into disgrace, the stories of his eastern travels earning him the reputation of an "unexampled liar." He was eventually murdered by his own people.

Source: Smithsonian American Art Museum: 1985.66.474.

7 *Fort Pierre, Mouth of the Teton River, 1200 Miles above St. Louis,* 1832

Named for fur trader Pierre Chouteau, this fort was on the Missouri River in Sioux country. The American Fur Company maintained a trading post there. French traders had been active on the upper Missouri since the eighteenth century.

Source: Smithsonian American Art Museum: 1985.66.384.

8   *Buffalo Hunt under the Wolf-Skin Mask,* 1832–1833

Catlin painted several scenes of buffalo and buffalo hunting on the Great Plains. Indians used a variety of methods to hunt buffalo, including driving them into water or snow banks or over bluffs. In this scene, Indian hunters approach a buffalo herd disguised as animals.

Source: Smithsonian American Art Museum: 1985.66.414.

9 *Buffalo Chase, A Surround by the Hidatsa,*
Hidatsa (Minitari), 1832–1833

Note the difference in the hunting techniques used here and in Source 8 on page 218. Several Indian nations on the Great Plains, most notably the Comanche and the Sioux, adopted horses for transportation after Spanish colonists from Mexico brought this animal north of the Rio Grande in the seventeenth century.

Source: Smithsonian American Art Museum: 1985.66.409.

10   *Bird's-Eye View of the Mandan Village, 1800 Miles above St. Louis,* Mandan (Numakiki), 1837–1839

Plains Indian cultures included mobile hunter-gather societies such as the Sioux and more sedentary farming societies such as the Mandans, depicted here with their distinctive dome-shaped lodges.

Source: Smithsonian American Art Museum: 1985.66.502.

11 *Sioux Encamped on the Upper Missouri, Dressing Buffalo Meat and Robes,* Western Sioux (Dakota), 1832

This scene conveys information about the gender division of labor within Plains Indian communities. The female figures in the lower left foreground and right background are dressing buffalo hides, while males return from the hunt with horses loaded with more hides. Buffalo meat is drying on racks arranged around the tipis.

Source: Smithsonian American Art Museum: 1985.66.377.

12   *The Cutting Scene, Mandan O-Kee-Pa Ceremony,* Mandan (Numakiki), 1832

Catlin's paintings of the Mandan O-kee-pa ceremony, an annual initiation and fertility rite, were some of the most controversial in his Indian Gallery. According to Catlin, young men inside a medicine lodge were suspended from cords anchored in their chests and shoulders until they lost consciousness. Catlin's critics claimed that he fabricated many of the gruesome details in his visual and textual descriptions of O-kee-pa, a charge he adamantly denied. The decimation of the Mandans by smallpox in 1837 made corroboration of Catlin's claims difficult, and the debate over the accuracy of his descriptions of this ceremony continued for the rest of his life.

Source: Denver Art Museum, The William Sr. and Dorothy Harmsen Collection.

Analyzing Paintings

1. Catlin claimed that he painted Indians in their natural state, untouched by white contact. Judging from these paintings, what values did Catlin associate with the Indians' "original" character, and how did he think contact with whites altered that character?

2. Using the information you compiled in the table on page 209, briefly describe some of the major cultural elements (such as dress, diet, spiritual practices) of the Plains Indians that Catlin encountered.

3. What evidence do you see in Catlin's paintings of the impact that white contact and exchange was having on the Plains Indians' material culture or subsistence patterns? Would you describe that impact in positive or negative terms?

4. What can you learn from these paintings about Catlin's audiences? Which of these paintings endorse or contradict the notion of the "vanishing Indian" that was so popular in American literature at this time? What commentary do the paintings offer on the political issue of Indian removal?

5. Most of Catlin's paintings were portraits, but he did a fair number of landscapes and village scenes as well. Judging from the works you have examined here, describe the kinds of topics or themes he was trying to address when he painted a landscape or village scene. Do such works have a different impact on the viewer than his portraits?

6. Historians confront potentially unreliable sources all the time yet seldom choose to discard them altogether. Knowing what you do about the methods and motives behind Catlin's work, what do you think are the liabilities of using this source to study American Indians in the Jacksonian era? What do you see as the chief benefits of using Catlin's paintings as a historical source?

The Rest of the Story

When Catlin's efforts to sell his Indian Gallery to the federal government failed, he took it to Europe. In 1839, he sailed for England with more than 500 of his paintings, along with his collection of Indian artifacts, a full-size Crow Indian lodge, and two grizzly bears (both very much alive and not at all pleased with their travel arrangements; one took off the nose of a sailor who got too close). As this inventory might suggest, the European version of the Indian Gallery was one part art exhibit and one part circus. To attract audiences, Catlin dressed himself and a few assistants in Indian costume and reenacted scenes depicted in his paintings. In 1843, a group of Ojibwas already in England joined Catlin's entourage and proved so popular that he hired small parties of Indians to accompany the Indian Gallery to Paris and Brussels.

Despite drawing large audiences, Catlin could not pay his bills, and he ended up in debtors prison in 1852. Bankruptcy forced him to sell off his original collection of paintings. To avoid his creditors, he traveled extensively, including trips to South America to paint Indians there. By 1870, he had completed a second set of 600 paintings, known as the "Cartoon Collection" because much of it was based on sketches he had made of his original paintings before selling them off. In 1870, he returned to the United States to have his work exhibited at the Smithsonian Institution. Once again, he pinned his hopes for solvency on convincing the government to purchase his collection, but those plans were unrealized when he died in 1872.

While Catlin was touring Europe and dodging creditors, great changes were afoot for the Indian peoples he had painted in the 1830s. Catlin may have imagined them as frozen in amber, unspoiled by contact with the outside world, but as his own paintings suggested, they had been in touch with Europeans for quite some time. The pace of change wrought by such contact increased markedly during the 1830s and 1840s, as steamboats, white migration to the West, and the resettlement of Indians evicted from their eastern homelands transformed the landscape of the Great Plains. Smallpox epidemics in the 1830s took a devastating toll on many of the Missouri Valley's sedentary tribes, such as the Mandans, tipping the balance of power there in favor of the horse-powered Sioux. Those Indian nations most adept at using horses to hunt buffalo experienced an increase in power and population between 1830 and 1850 that defied any notion of a "vanishing Indian." However, within a generation they faced the problem of the vanishing buffalo, which was hunted to near extinction by whites and Indians alike after the Civil War. Had Catlin returned to the Great Plains in 1870, he would have encountered a world far different from the one he had left thirty-three years earlier.

Catlin's career may not have gone as planned, but his work had a lasting impact on American cultural attitudes about Indians. In going west to learn about Indians firsthand, he continued an intellectual inquiry initiated by Thomas Jefferson with the Lewis and Clark expedition. By the time of Catlin's death, a new generation of artists were continuing his work, only now with cameras instead of paints and canvas. Anthropologists followed in their wake in the twentieth century, using new technologies in sound recording and filmmaking to document Indian life.

Catlin's career represented another strain of the American cultural fascination with Indians as well, one that equated the "vanishing Indian" with an opportunity to make a buck. The profits that eluded Catlin in the 1830s and 1840s flowed into the hands of promoters like Buffalo Bill Cody between 1880 and 1920, when Wild West shows toured eastern cities and European countries, recreating buffalo hunts, stagecoach raids, and even Custer's Last Stand. By the 1920s, the "vanishing Indian" had made it to the silver screen, giving rise to one of the most popular genres of twentieth-century American film, the Western. *Last of the Mohicans* and *Dances with Wolves*, two films released in the 1990s and now staples of cable television, testify to the enduring appeal of the themes Catlin explored in his art in the 1830s. In the long history of the European-Indian encounter, Catlin stands somewhere between Thomas Jefferson and

P. T. Barnum, a figure who made the Indian an object of both scholarly inquiry and commercial exploitation.

To Find Out More

Catlin never succeeded in his efforts to sell his Indian Gallery to the U.S. government, but the private collector who purchased the first incarnation of the Indian Gallery in 1852 ultimately donated it to the Smithsonian Institution in Washington, D.C. A major exhibit of Catlin's work at the Renwick Gallery of the Smithsonian American Art Museum in 2002–2003 inspired this chapter. The catalog of that exhibit provides an excellent overview of Catlin's life and work, as well as full-color reproductions of his most famous paintings. See George Gurney and Therese Thau Heyman, editors, *George Catlin and His Indian Gallery* (Washington, D.C.: Smithsonian American Art Museum, 2002). The exhibit may be viewed online at **americanart.si.edu/collections/exhibits/catlin/index.html**. Another useful Web site featuring extensive examples and commentary on Catlin's work is "Campfire Stories with George Catlin: An Encounter of Two Cultures" (**catlinclassroom.si.edu**).

Catlin published many works in his lifetime aimed at drawing attention to his Indian Gallery. The most important of these is the two-volume *Letters and Notes on the Manners, Customs, and Condition of the North American Indians* (1841; repr., Minneapolis: Ross and Haines, 1965). It details his western trips in the 1830s and features engravings of his paintings.

Two books useful for exploring the cultural and political climate that produced the "vanishing Indian" theme in American arts are Anthony F. C. Wallace, *Jefferson and the Indians: The Tragic Fate of the First Americans* (Cambridge, Mass.: Harvard University Press, 1999), and Brian W. Dippie, *The Vanishing American: White Attitudes and U.S. Indian Policy* (1982; repr., Lawrence: University of Kansas Press, 1991). Jill Lepore's *The Name of War: King Philip's War and the Origins of American Identity* (New York: Random House, 1998) contains an excellent chapter on the cultural significance of the play *Metamora; or, The Last of the Wampanoags*, and the autobiography of Sac and Fox chief Black Hawk, first published in 1833, provides an important literary complement to Catlin's paintings. For a modern edition, see Donald Jackson, editor, *Black Hawk: An Autobiography* (Urbana: University of Illinois Press, 1955).

For a good overview of the changing circumstances of Plains Indian life during Catlin's lifetime, see Richard White, "The Winning of the West: The Expansion of the Western Sioux in the Eighteenth and Nineteenth Centuries," *Journal of American History* 65 (1978): 319–43. The legacy of Catlin's work in American art and popular culture can be explored in Joy S. Kasson, *Buffalo Bill's Wild West: Celebrity, Memory, and Popular History* (New York: Hill and Wang, 2000); L. G. Moses, *Wild West Shows and the Images of American Indians, 1883–1933* (Albuquerque: University of New Mexico Press, 1996); and Alfred L. Bush and Lee Clark Mitchell, *The Photograph and the American Indian* (Princeton, N.J.: Princeton University Press, 1994).

CHAPTER 11

On and Off the Record

Diplomatic Correspondence on the Eve of the Mexican-American War

President James K. Polk did not like to work on Sundays. A strict observer of his religious principles, he preferred to follow the biblical command to rest on the Sabbath. He had even banned dancing in the White House. Nevertheless, on Sunday, May 10, 1846, he broke from his usual custom and spent the day at his desk. The news he had received the night before was very good, good enough, one might imagine, for Polk to allow himself to dance a private little jig. A courier had arrived late on Saturday to inform the president that U.S. troops under the command of General Zachary Taylor had been attacked by a Mexican military patrol just north of the Rio Grande two weeks earlier. Polk had decided earlier in the day on Saturday to ask Congress for a declaration of war against Mexico, but the news from the Rio Grande was exactly the kind of provocation he needed to clinch his case. And so, on Sunday he revised the message he intended to send to Congress the following day, incorporating the news about General Taylor and stating in no uncertain terms that "Mexico has . . . invaded our territory and shed American blood upon American soil. . . . War exists, and notwithstanding all our efforts to avoid it, exists by the act of Mexico."

Three days later Congress gave Polk the declaration of war he wanted. When the Mexican-American War ended two years later, Mexico ceded one half of its territory to the United States, comprising all or parts of the modern states of California, Arizona, New Mexico, Texas, Nevada, Utah, Colorado, and Wyoming (see Map 11.1). The war with Mexico was the crowning achievement of Polk's administration. During his four years in office (1845–1849), the United States experienced its most significant territorial expansion since the Louisiana Purchase.

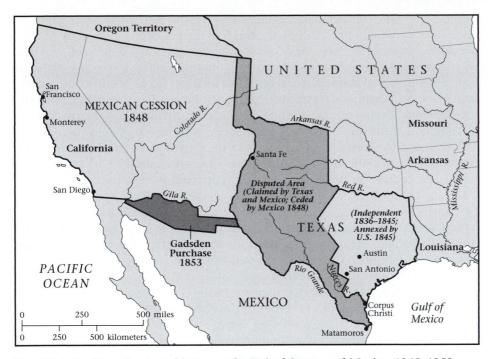

Map 11.1 *Territory Contested between the United States and Mexico, 1845–1853*
The annexation of Texas by the United States in 1845 created the disputed area of possession between Mexico and the United States shown here. The historic border between Mexico and Texas had been the Nueces River, but Texans, backed by President James K. Polk, argued that the border was the Rio Grande. The Mexican-American War (1846–1848) resolved this dispute in the Americans' favor and led to the Mexican cession of California and New Mexico. The Gadsden Purchase in 1853 completed the modern U.S.-Mexican border. Source: Adapted from Bradford Perkins, *The Cambridge History of American Foreign Relations, Vol. 1, The Creation of a Republican Empire, 1776–1865* (Cambridge: Cambridge University Press, 1993), 184.

The rapid unfolding of events in late April and early May 1846 may make it seem as though the Mexican-American War started accidentally. Two military forces, both far removed from their nation's capitals, engaged each other on a remote, contested border. Certainly, the words Polk chose so carefully for his war message conveyed a sense of unanticipated emergency, of hostilities already commenced by a treacherous enemy against unsuspecting Americans. However, the events that preceded Polk's war message were the culmination of an ongoing diplomatic crisis. On Friday, May 8, an envoy Polk had sent to Mexico returned to Washington, D.C., and reported on the Mexican government's refusal to receive him. Before the news arrived of the skirmish on the Rio Grande, Polk intended to make this diplomatic rebuff the centerpiece of his war message to Congress.

The diplomatic showdown between the United States and Mexico had been brewing since the United States annexed Texas a year earlier. A former province of Mexico, Texas had fought a successful war of independence in 1835–1836. Following that conflict, Texas had been a thorn in the side of U.S.-Mexican relations. In 1846, Mexico still regarded Texas as a rebellious province within its borders. While it may have grudgingly accepted the reality of Texan independence, it was loath to accept the idea of Texas joining the United States, which would endanger Mexico's control over its other northern provinces of New Mexico and California. Anglo-Americans in Texas, many of them slaveholders from the southern United States who had migrated there in the 1820s, supported annexation, although a minority of them liked the idea of remaining independent. In the United States, the annexation of Texas was a political hot potato. Southerners generally supported it because it would open new territory for their slave-based plantation economy. Northerners opposed it for exactly the same reason, fearing that the addition of such a large slave state would upset the balance of power between free and slave states within the union. In Europe, Great Britain and France watched the crisis brewing over annexation closely. Both countries were creditors of Mexico and interested in the disposition of its northern territories.

The likelihood of annexation increased when Polk was elected president in November 1844. A Southern Democrat, slaveholder, and ardent expansionist, he made no secret of his desire to see Texas, California, and Oregon incorporated into the union and his willingness to go to war to achieve it. The spirit and rationale behind Polk's aggressive expansionism was summed up in the phrase "manifest destiny," coined by a newspaper editor in 1845 to describe what he believed was God's divine plan for the United States to extend its dominion across the North American continent. Polk skillfully balanced different constituencies to put his plans in motion. To appease Northerners, he pursued the U.S. claim against Britain for the Oregon country, so that the admission of Texas to the union could be balanced with an additional free state. To cement Texans' support for annexation, he endorsed their claim that their border with Mexico extended as far south as the Rio Grande and as far west as Santa Fe, the capital city of New Mexico. Polk knew the Mexican government would find this border unacceptable. Mexico had long maintained that its historic border with Texas was the Nueces River, one hundred miles north of the Rio Grande and far removed from Santa Fe (see Map 11.1 on page 227). The president also kept a close eye on Britain and France, for fear that they would try to use their own diplomacy with Mexico to acquire new colonies in North America.

When Congress voted to annex Texas, Mexico broke off diplomatic relations with the United States and sent troops north to the Rio Grande. Polk ordered a U.S. naval squadron into the Gulf of Mexico to menace the Mexican seaport of Vera Cruz, and he sent troops to occupy the disputed territory between the Nueces River and the Rio Grande. These maneuvers by the Mexican and U.S. governments set the stage for the hostilities that prompted Polk to revise his war message on May 10.

Mexico was not anxious for war, but it did not wish to lose its northern provinces either. Since achieving its independence from Spain in 1821, Mexico had suffered from a succession of weak, poorly financed governments. The chief source of political power in the nation was the army, but it was also the chief source of political instability, as military coups undid one attempt at constitutional government after another. To complicate matters, Mexico's provinces north of the Rio Grande were rich in resources but poor in people. The largest populations in California, New Mexico, and Texas were Native Americans who were not particularly interested in submitting to Mexico or any other foreign power. Spanish missionaries and colonists had established various settlements in the northern provinces before 1800, but these communities were isolated from one another and Mexico City. In brief, Mexico's hold on its territory north of the Rio Grande was tenuous but too valuable to give up.

All of the military posturing between Mexico and the United States was accompanied by quieter efforts to mend the rift between the two nations. Polk, despite his hawkish public demeanor, knew that war with Mexico would not be easy. It would require military organization and spending on a scale unprecedented for the federal government, which had not managed its last major war with a foreign power, the War of 1812 with Britain, very well. Aware of the financial straits of the Mexican government, Polk thought he might be able to purchase a settlement to the dispute over Texas and perhaps even acquire New Mexico and California in the deal. He encouraged his secretary of state, James Buchanan, to pursue this option through both official and unofficial diplomatic channels.

The U.S. declaration of war against Mexico in May 1846 would indicate that Buchanan failed. The two nations did not renew normal diplomatic relations until peace was restored two years later. Describing Buchanan's efforts as a failure, however, raises some important questions about the purposes and methods behind Polk's foreign policy. Was Polk ever genuinely interested in making the sort of compromises that would have been necessary to avoid war? Did he and Buchanan set out to find a solution to this crisis, or did they purposely exacerbate it so they would have justification for going to war? Historians interested in answering these questions look for answers in the documentary record of official and unofficial communications between Buchanan, his foreign agents, and the Mexican government.

Using the Source: Diplomatic Correspondence

During the nineteenth century, the United States conducted its foreign relations according to conventions inherited from Europe and standardized at the Congress of Vienna in 1815. Generally speaking, there were three types of personnel who dealt directly with foreign governments. First, ambassadors carried out official communication between governments. Until the 1890s, the United States avoided using the title "ambassador" because it smacked of Old World aristocracy. Instead, the federal government granted its highest-ranking diplomats the title of "envoy extraordinary and minister plenipotentiary," a mouthful that was usually shortened to "minister." A minister led the embassy or "legation" established in the capital city of a foreign country and typically had several assistants ranked in descending order below him as counselors, secretaries, and agents. Consuls were a second category of foreign service personnel, appointed to protect and assist a nation's citizens traveling, doing business, or living abroad. Consuls kept offices in foreign seaports and commercial centers as well as capitals. Unlike an embassy or legation, a consular office did not conduct official diplomacy, but it did serve as eyes and ears for its government in a foreign nation. Commissioners made up the third category of diplomatic personnel, and they were usually appointed for specific tasks, such as negotiating treaties or initiating relations with another country.

While the minister to a foreign country carried out much of his duties in person, all of his official business was documented in written correspondence. Such business followed an elaborate etiquette observed by the minister and his host government. When an envoy or minister arrived in a foreign country, he presented his credentials, the papers authorizing his appointment, to the foreign secretary (the equivalent of the secretary of state in the United States). If the foreign secretary approved the credentials, he "recognized" the minister, allowing him to conduct business with the government and granting him immunity from its laws. Issues of rank, precedent, and precise language weighed heavily on such occasions. Depending on a diplomat's official title and the wording of his credentials, he might or might not gain access to senior officials of government. If the foreign secretary refused to recognize him, he received no more favor or protection than any other foreign citizen in that country.

Governments also conducted diplomacy through unofficial channels. Confidential agents were hired by their home governments to serve as informants. They received specific instructions with their appointment but were expected to keep such information secret and to assume the character of a private citizen when abroad. They did not carry formal credentials and therefore did not enjoy diplomatic immunity or any other privileges associated with diplomatic rank. Oftentimes, they were businessmen who lived abroad, knew the native language well, and had cultivated relationships with people of influence and power. In an age before international communication by telephone or television, their correspondence with government officials back home gave forthright assessments and advice that contrasted sharply with the highly stylized, restrained language of official diplomatic correspondence. The term "confidential agent" may call to mind images of espionage and skullduggery, but their work was usually more mundane, consisting chiefly of reading the local newspapers and meeting privately with influential officials. Nevertheless, confidential agents provided the primary means of what we call today "intelligence gathering" about foreign governments.

The difference between the official and unofficial diplomacy conducted over the Texas annexation crisis is best grasped through the metaphor of a play or ballet. Official diplomacy between the United States and Mexico was conducted by high-ranking foreign service personnel trained in the specialized language and manners of their profession. Their performance, however, was shaped by the maneuvers of lower-ranking officials and confidential agents, who could express themselves more bluntly because they worked behind the scenes. To reconstruct fully the Texas annexation crisis, the historian must pull back the curtain and scrutinize the unofficial channels of diplomacy as well as the official ones. Only then will the entire process become clear.

Consider the style and tone of the two letters below (from William R. Manning, editor, *Diplomatic Correspondence of the United States: Inter-American Affairs, 1831–1860*, 8:699–700, 760). The first, an example of official diplomatic correspondence, is from the Mexican minister in Washington, D.C., to John C. Calhoun, the secretary of state for President John Tyler, Polk's predecessor in office; in this letter, the Mexican minister formally breaks diplomatic relations with the United States after the congressional vote to annex Texas. The second, an example of unofficial diplomatic correspondence, is from a confidential agent working for the United States in Mexico City, writing to Secretary of State James Buchanan, who succeeded Calhoun when Polk was inaugurated in March 1845.

JUAN N. ALMONTE, MEXICAN MINISTER TO THE UNITED STATES, TO JOHN C. CALHOUN, SECRETARY OF STATE OF THE UNITED STATES, WASHINGTON, D.C., MARCH 6, 1845

WASHINGTON, D.C.

The Undersigned, Envoy Extraordinary and Minister Plenipotentiary of the Mexican Republic, has the honour to address the Honourable John C. Calhoun Secretary of State of the United States of America, with the object of making known to him the profound regret, with which he has seen, that the General Congress of the Union has passed a law, giving its consent, and admitting into the American Confederacy, the Mexican Province of Texas.

> *Note the precise, legalistic tone of this letter*

The Undersigned . . . sees consummated on the part of the American Government, an act of aggression, the most unjust which can be found recorded in the annals of modern history, namely — that of despoiling a friendly nation like Mexico, of a considerable portion of her territory. . . .

> *Stops short of calling the annexation an act of war but makes clear that he sees it as justification for one*

The Undersigned will say in conclusion to the Honourable Secretary of State of the United States, in order that he may be pleased to communicate it to the President of these States; that in consequence of this law against which he has just protested, his mission near this Government has ceased from this day. Wherefore the Undersigned prays the Honourable Secretary of State, to be pleased to deliver to him his

> *He observes the official channel of communication from the secretary of state to the president*

> *Polite request signals the end of formal diplomatic relations*

passports, as he has made arrangements to leave this city without delay for New York.

WILLIAM S. PARROTT, CONFIDENTIAL AGENT OF THE UNITED STATES TO MEXICO, TO JAMES BUCHANAN, SECRETARY OF STATE OF THE UNITED STATES, OCTOBER 11, 1845

Private and Confidential   MEXICO

MY DEAR SIR: Although I am but a neophyte in diplomacy, I am an American, and believe that in every emergency, in which I have been placed, by chance or otherwise, I have not been found wanting—

In the discharge of the important trust confided to me in Mexico, I have followed my instructions to the letter, not my personal desire to see this people well flogged by Uncle Sam's boys, ere we enter upon negotiation—

I have suffered more, perhaps, than any other American citizen, at their [the Mexicans'] hands. I know them better, perhaps, than any other American citizen and I am fully persuaded, they never can love or respect us, as we should be loved and respected by them, until after we shall have given them a positive proof of our superiority.

Parrott intends to speak frankly, in words not meant for public exposure

Before

Beginner. Why would he point out his lack of experience as a diplomat?

Note colloquial, even folksy, tone

Bases his conclusion on his first-hand experience with the Mexicans

Both of these letters refer to a potential military response to the crisis, but they are strikingly different in their language and tone. Almonte maintains an air of formality and politeness even as he breaks diplomatic relations. His carefully chosen words make clear that Mexico sees annexation as an act of aggression. Parrott, on the other hand, offers no pretense of formality. After proudly admitting his lack of diplomatic expertise, he bluntly advises the secretary of state that only war will bring this dispute to a successful resolution.

What Can Diplomatic Correspondence Tell Us?

There are several advantages to working with diplomatic correspondence when studying foreign relations. First, unlike newspaper stories and political speeches intended for public audiences, official diplomatic correspondence was intended for a much smaller audience of officials who controlled the reins of power in foreign affairs. While its specialized language can be difficult to comprehend at first, it does lay out very precisely the issues that divided Mexico and the United States on the eve of war.

A second advantage derives from reading together two types of diplomatic correspondence: that between nations and that between officials and agents of a single nation. The former has the highly stylized, legalistic language one would expect; the latter is much more plainspoken and reveals the ambitions behind the artifice of the first. Instructions from the secretary of state to ministers and agents in the field lay out the objectives of foreign policy in a bare-knuckled way not found in carefully crafted political speeches or official correspondence with other governments. Likewise, the reports that confidential agents and consuls sent back from the field often have an "off-the-record" honesty to them that can be invaluable for revealing the prejudices and assumptions behind foreign policy.

A disadvantage to bear in mind when working with diplomatic correspondence before the twentieth century is the time involved in transmitting it. Communication between the secretary of state and his agents in foreign nations had to be carried by hand in the 1840s, and if a letter was delayed, the information it contained might arrive after important policy decisions had been made. The telegraph was a new technology in 1846 and did not reach beyond cities on the East Coast of the United States. Steamships and specialized courier riders sped the mail, but important communications could still be lost or delayed en route. Most correspondence from U.S. agents in Mexico City to Washington, D.C., first traveled overland to Vera Cruz and then by ship to Havana, Cuba, where it was transferred to another ship headed for New Orleans. After arriving in New Orleans, it took a minimum of three more days to reach Washington, D.C. Agents in the field tried to compensate for the unreliability of long-distance communication by writing many letters, so that if one were lost, another containing similar information might arrive safely. Nevertheless, the delay involved in international correspondence should make you think twice about what role these letters played in decision making at home.

You should also bear in mind the domestic politics that can influence foreign policy. Then as now, high-ranking diplomatic officials were political appointees typically being rewarded for their support of the president and his party. They did not necessarily occupy their posts because of their familiarity or sympathy with the foreign nation to which they were posted; they might in fact be downright ignorant about it. Likewise, career foreign service personnel seldom commanded the political influence necessary to sway policy decisions made by the president and secretary of state.

Diplomatic correspondence will not reveal the full process of decision making in foreign policy. In the case of the Texas annexation crisis, it cannot tell you what sorts of political pressures Polk faced at home: What was the tide of public opinion about war with Mexico? Did some members of Congress want to extract political favors from Polk before agreeing to vote for a declaration of war? How much influence did Buchanan have within Polk's administration? Historians turn to other sources to answer those questions. In studying the origins of the Mexican-American War, they have usually read diplomatic correspondence in conjunction with Polk's diary, his messages to Congress, and the vast literature produced in the popular press about the annexation of Texas.

Questions to Ask

Historians often approach diplomatic correspondence as if they were assembling a jigsaw puzzle. They know what the "picture on the box" is—in this case, the U.S. declaration of war on Mexico—but they read the letters to figure out how the pieces came together to produce that result. To make the most of each piece of this puzzle, you need to ask a series of questions: Who wrote the letter, and what position or special expertise did he have? What sort of letter is it: an official expression of a government's position or an unofficial communiqué intended only for the eyes of the recipient? What sort of information does it contain: news, opinion, instructions? What does the tone of the letter tell us about the author's objectives or biases? When you have read several related letters, you can then start putting them together to explain the outbreak of war with Mexico.

- Who is the letter's author, and what is the purpose of the letter?
- What kind of information is related in the letter?
- What is the tone of the letter?
- How do these letters fit together to explain the outbreak of war?

Source Analysis Table

In the next section, you will read selections from diplomatic correspondence involving U.S.-Mexican relations between March 1845 and March 1846. Much of it deals with Secretary of State James Buchanan's efforts to handle the annexation crisis by gathering information about Mexico's preparedness for war, its willingness to cede California and New Mexico, and the potential for intervention by Great Britain or France.

The letters fall into two general categories: correspondence exchanged between officials of the U.S. and Mexican governments, and correspondence exchanged between Buchanan and his agents in Mexico. As you read them, use this table to organize and record your reactions. The table asks you to describe the tone of the letters, meaning the subtle (and sometimes not so subtle) role that word choice and style played in conveying the author's objectives and designs.

LETTERS BETWEEN U.S. AND MEXICAN OFFICIALS			
Source	Author's Title and Purpose of Writing	Information Contained in Letter	Tone of Letter
1. Buchanan to Almonte			
7. Peña to Black			
11. Castillo y Lanzas to Slidell			
2. Buchanan to Parrott			
6. Buchanan to Black			
8. Buchanan to Slidell			
10. Buchanan to Slidell			

(continued)

LETTERS BETWEEN BUCHANAN AND U.S. AGENTS IN MEXICO			
Source	Author's Title and Purpose of Writing	Information Contained in Letter	Tone of Letter
12. Buchanan to Slidell			
3. Parrott to Buchanan			
5. Parrott to Buchanan			
4. Black to Buchanan			
9. Slidell to Buchanan			
13. Slidell to Buchanan			

To download and print this table, visit the book companion site at **bedfordstmartins.com/brownshannon**.

The Source: Diplomatic Correspondence Concerning the Annexation of Texas, March 10, 1845–March 18, 1846

1 U.S. Secretary of State James Buchanan to Juan N. Almonte, Mexican Minister to the United States, March 10, 1845

When Polk was inaugurated in March 1845, his secretary of state, James Buchanan, inherited the crisis in U.S.-Mexican relations caused by the annexation of Texas.

WASHINGTON, D.C.

The Undersigned, Secretary of State of the United States, has received the note of General Almonte, the Envoy Extraordinary and Minister Plenipotentiary of the Mexican Republic of the 6th instant,[1] addressed to his predecessor, the Honorable John C. Calhoun, protesting, in the name of his Government, against the resolution of the late Congress for annexing Texas to the United States; and he has submitted the same to the President.

In answer, the Undersigned is instructed to say, that the admission of Texas as one of the States of this Union having received the sanction both of the legislative and Executive Departments of the government, is now irrevocably decided, so far as the United States are concerned. Nothing but the refusal of Texas to ratify the terms and conditions on which her admission depends, can defeat this object. It is therefore, too late at present to reopen a discussion which has already been exhausted, and again to prove that Texas has long since achieved her independence of Mexico, and now stands before the world, both *de jure*[2] and *de facto*,[3] as a sovereign and independent State amid the family of nations. Sustaining this character and having manifested a strong desire to become one of the members of our Confederacy, neither Mexico nor any other nation will have just cause of complaint against the United States for admitting her into this Union.

The President nevertheless sincerely regrets that the government of Mexico should have taken offence at these proceedings; and he earnestly trusts that it

[1] This month.
[2] By law.
[3] By fact.

Source: William R. Manning, editor, *Diplomatic Correspondence of the United States: Inter-American Affairs, 1831–1860* (Washington, D.C.: Carnegie Endowment for International Peace, 1937), 8:163.

may hereafter be disposed to view them in a more favorable and friendly light. Whilst entering upon the duties of the Presidential office, he cheerfully declares in advance, that his most strenuous efforts shall be devoted to the amicable adjustment of every cause of complaint between the two Governments, and to the cultivation of the kindest and most friendly relations between the sister Republics.

The Undersigned has the honor to transmit to General Almonte his passport according to his request, and to assure him of his distinguished consideration and regard.

 ## 2   *Secretary of State James Buchanan to William S. Parrott, Confidential Agent of the United States to Mexico,* March 28, 1845

Shortly after the break in formal diplomatic relations between the United States and Mexico, President Polk appointed William S. Parrott a confidential agent in Mexico City. Parrott was a merchant who, like many foreign businessmen, also held an outstanding claim of debt against the Mexican government.

WASHINGTON, D.C.

Sir: All diplomatic intercourse having been suspended between the governments of the United States and Mexico, it is the desire of the President to restore such an intercourse if this can be effected consistently with the national honor. To accomplish this purpose he has deemed it expedient to send a confidential agent to Mexico, and reposing confidence in your abilities and patriotism, has selected you as a proper person to execute this important trust. Your success may mainly depend upon your perfect command of temper in all situations and under all circumstances, and upon your prudence in refraining from the least intimation that you are a Government agent, unless this should become indispensable to the success of your mission. . . . From your long residence in Mexico and your thorough acquaintance with the Mexican people and their language, the President considers you peculiarly qualified for the trust and indulges in favorable anticipation of your success.

You will proceed without delay by the most expeditious route to the City of Mexico, and will there ascertain the temper and tone of the present Mexican Government towards the United States. . . . The great object of your mission and that which you will constantly keep in view in all your proceedings, is to reach the President and other high officers of the Mexican government and

Source: Manning, *Diplomatic Correspondence of the United States,* 8:164–65.

especially the Minister of Foreign Affairs; and by every honorable effort to convince them that it is the true interest of their country, as it certainly is, to restore friendly relations between the two Republics. Should you clearly ascertain that they are willing to renew our diplomatic intercourse, then and not till then you are at liberty to communicate to them your official character and to state that the United States will send a Minister to Mexico as soon as they receive authentic information that he will be kindly received. . . .

Whilst, therefore, you ought not to conceal that the reünion of Texas with the United States is already decreed and can never under any circumstances be abandoned, you are at liberty to state your confident belief that in regard to all unsettled questions, we are prepared to meet Mexico in a most liberal and friendly spirit. . . .

3

William S. Parrott, Confidential Agent of the United States to Mexico, to Secretary of State James Buchanan, April 29, 1845

MEXICO

. . . If it be true that climate forms the character of a nation, that the character of a nation forms its Government, and that the Government forms its manners, morals and institutions, judging from what Mexico has been; it is not probable she will find more repose, hereafter or for years to come, than she has hitherto enjoyed—Prone to revolution and change, as she is; distracted by opposing factions nearly equally balanced, it is hardly reasonable to suppose that, the present Government can be of long duration. . . . The people know not what they want, nor is there, a man in the country, of sufficient moral courage and prestige to establish any stable form of Government, out of the chaos that now exists—Each prominent individual in the country, has his party, and each party is plotting against all others to obtain power, however ephemeral, with a view to personal emolument,[1] at the expense of the nation and happiness of its people. . . .

My instructions are deposited in safety, I keep no copies of my communications to the Department, so as not, under the most unfavorable turn things might take, to be taken by surprise.

---

[1] Profits gained from officeholding.

Source: Manning, *Diplomatic Correspondence of the United States,* 8:712–13.

John Black, U.S. Consul at Mexico City, to Secretary of State James Buchanan, June 21, 1845

> John Black was the American consul in Mexico City. He became the highest-ranking U.S. diplomatic official in Mexico when the U.S. minister there, Wilson Shannon, returned home after the break in formal diplomatic relations in March 1845.

MEXICO

. . . It is not known what course Mexico will take, in respect to the question of Annexation of Texas to the United States, but no doubt she will make some noise, and as far as threats, and words, and paper war will go, we shall no doubt have enough of it, but I do not think the present Government has any serious idea of carrying on any other kind of war, against us, — though forced by the opposition to put itself in a belligerent attitude, to show its patriotism. — Neither do I think, that the opposition who appear to be so eager for war, and are urging on the Government to that extremity, would, if they themselves were in power, or should hereafter get into power, ever seriously think of entering into a war, (in earnest,) with the United States.

It is true our defenceless citizens in different parts of the Country, on account of existing difficulties, will be likely to suffer in their persons and property from unjust and arbitrary acts of the Mexican Authorities, and it is from this kind of depredations we have the most to fear.

Source: Manning, *Diplomatic Correspondence of the United States,* 8:728–29.

 ## William S. Parrott, Confidential Agent of the United States to Mexico, to Secretary of State James Buchanan, August 26, 1845

MEXICO

. . . A declaration of war with the United States is not now spoken of; nor was it ever seriously contemplated—The Government at one time, intended to concentrate a force on the frontier of Texas, sufficient to have annoyed its inhabitants, perhaps to have imprisoned one of its Courts of Justice; but even this is not now contemplated—The face of things have changed, and no additional

Source: Manning, *Diplomatic Correspondence of the United States,* 8:746–47.

force will be sent to the Frontier, unless the Government, intimated as it is, should be compelled to do so by an insincere opposition—There is a desire, even publickly manifested, to receive a commissioner from the United States, and every vessel that arrives . . . is said to have one on board—

I have good reasons to believe that, an Envoy from the United States would not only, be well received; but that his arrival would be hailed with joy—An Envoy possessing suitable qualifications for this Court, might with comparative ease, settle, *over a breakfast,* the most important national question, while such as we have lately had here would make matters worse—An Envoy to this Court, should speak the language of the country, should be accessible and affable in his deportment, to insure the success of his mission. . . .

6   *Secretary of State James Buchanan to John Black, U.S. Consul at Mexico City,* September 17, 1845

WASHINGTON, D.C.

. . . He [President Polk] is anxious to preserve peace, although prepared for war.

Actuated by these sentiments, the President has directed me to instruct you in the absence of any Diplomatic Agent in Mexico, to ascertain from the Mexican Government whether they would receive an Envoy from the United States entrusted with full power to adjust all the questions in dispute between the two Governments. Should the answer be in the affirmative such an Envoy will be immediately despatched to Mexico.

If the President were disposed to stand upon a mere question of etiquette, he would wait until the Mexican Government, which had suspended the Diplomatic relations Between the Two Countries, should ask that they may be restored. But his desire is so strong to terminate the present unfortunate state of our relations, with that Republic, that he has consented to waive all ceremony and take the initiative.

Concerning the most politic and judicious mode of communicating with the Mexican Government, you will consult Dr. Parrott, a Citizen of the United States now in Mexico. He is a discreet man, well acquainted with public affairs and possesses my confidence. . . .

I need scarcely warn you to preserve the most inviolable secrecy in regard to your proceedings, making no communication to any person with the exception of Dr. Parrott, not indispensable to the accomplishment of the object. There will be a vessel of War at Vera Cruz ready to receive your Despatch for this Department, and to convey it to the United States with the least possible delay. . . .

Source: Manning, *Diplomatic Correspondence of the United States,* 8:167–68.

7   *Manuel de la Peña, Minister of Foreign Affairs of Mexico, to John Black, U.S. Consul at Mexico City,* October 15, 1845

On October 10, 1845, John Black met privately with Mexico's foreign minister (the equivalent of the U.S. secretary of state), Manuel de la Peña, to propose that the United States send a commissioner to Mexico to negotiate a settlement to the annexation crisis. Peña responded positively to the idea but insisted that the United States withdraw its naval squadron from the waters off Vera Cruz first.

Confidential   MEXICO

. . . As my Government believes this invitation to be made in good faith, and with the real desire that it may lead to a favourable conclusion, it also hopes that the Commissioner will be a person endowed with the qualities proper for the attainment of this end; that his dignity prudence and moderation, and the discreatness and reasonableness of his proposals, will contribute to calm as much as possible, the just irritation of the Mexicans; and in fine, that the conduct of the Commissioner, on all points, may be such as to persuade them, that they may obtain satisfaction for their injuries, through the means of reason and peace, and without being obliged to resort to those of arms and force.

What my Government requires above all things is, that the mission of the Commissioner of the United States, and his reception by us, should appear to be always absolutely frank and free, from every sign of menace or coercion; and thus Mr. Consul while making known to your Government, the disposition on the part of that of Mexico, to receive the Commissioner, you should impress upon it, as indispensable, the previous recall of the whole naval force, now lying in sight of our port of Vera Cruz. Its presence would degrade Mexico, while she is receiving the Commissioner, and would justly subject the United States to the imputation of contradicting by acts, the vehement desire of conciliation peace and friendship, which is professed and asserted by words. . . .

Source: Manning, *Diplomatic Correspondence of the United States,* 8:763.

8 *Secretary of State James Buchanan to John Slidell, Appointed U.S. Minister to Mexico,* November 10, 1845

After learning of Peña's positive response to Black, Polk appointed John Slidell, a prominent Democrat, Louisiana slaveholder, and ardent expansionist, to serve as his commissioner to Mexico. Buchanan made clear in his instructions to Slidell the president's priorities for negotiating with Mexico.

WASHINGTON, D.C.

. . . In the present crisis of the relations between the two countries, the office for which you have been selected is one of vast importance. To counteract the influence of foreign Powers, exerted against the United States in Mexico & to restore those ancient relations of peace and good will which formerly existed between the Governments and the citizens of the sister Republics, will be principal objects of your mission. The wretched condition of the internal affairs of Mexico, and the misunderstanding which exists between her Government and the Ministers of France and England, seem to render the present a propitious moment for the accomplishment of these objectives. From your perfect knowledge of the language of the country, your well known firmness and ability, and your taste and talent for society, the President hopes that you will accomplish much in your intercourse with the Mexican authorities and people. . . .

In your negotiations with Mexico, the independence of Texas must be considered a settled fact, and is not to be called in question. . . .

It may, however, be contended on the part of Mexico, that the Nueces and not the Rio del Norte,[1] is the true western boundary of Texas. I need not furnish you arguments to controvert this position. You have been perfectly familiar with the subject from the beginning, and know that the jurisdiction of Texas has been extended beyond that river and that representatives from the country between it and the Del Norte have participated in the deliberations both of her Congress and her Convention. Besides, this portion of the territory was embraced within the limits of ancient Louisiana.

The case is different in regard to New Mexico. Santa Fe, its capital, was settled by the Spaniards more than two centuries ago; and that province has been ever since in their possession and that of the Republic of Mexico. The Texans never have conquered or taken possession of it, nor have its people ever been represented in any of the Legislative Assemblies or Conventions.

The long and narrow valley of New Mexico or Santa Fe is situated on both banks of the upper Del Norte, and is bounded on both sides by mountains. It is

---

[1] The Rio Grande.

Source: Manning, *Diplomatic Correspondence of the United States,* 8:172–81.

many hundred miles remote from other settled portions of Mexico, and from its distance, it is both difficult and expensive to defend the inhabitants against the tribes of fierce and warlike savages that roam over the surrounding country. For this cause it has suffered severely from their incursions. Mexico must expend far more in defending so distant a possession than she can possibly derive benefit from continuing to hold it.

Besides, it is greatly to be decided that our boundary with Mexico should now be established in such a manner as to preclude all future difficulties and disputes between the two Republics. A great portion of New Mexico being on this side of the Rio Grande and included within the limits already claimed by Texas, it may hereafter, should it remain a Mexican province, become a subject of dispute and a source of bad feeling between those who, I trust, are destined in future to be always friends.

On the other hand, if in adjusting the boundary, the province of New Mexico should be included within the limits of the United States, this would obviate the danger of future collisions. Mexico would part with a remote and disturbed province, the possession of which can never be advantageous to her; and she would be relieved from the trouble and expense of defending its inhabitants against the Indians. Besides, she would thus purchase security against their attacks for her other provinces West of the Del Norte; as it would at once become the duty of the United States to restrain the savage tribes within their limits and prevent them from making hostile incursions into Mexico. From these considerations and others which will readily suggest themselves to your mind, it would seem to be equally the interest of both Powers, that New Mexico should belong to the United States.

But the President desires to deal liberally by Mexico. You are therefore authorized to offer to assume the payment of all the just claims of our citizens against Mexico, and, in addition, to pay five millions of dollars, in case the countries from the mouth of the Rio Grande, up the principal stream to the point where it touches the line of New Mexico, thence West of the river, along the exterior line of that province and so as to include the whole within the United States until it again intersects the river, thence up the principal stream of the same to its source and thence due north until it intersects the forty second degree of north latitude.

A boundary still preferable to this, would be an extension of the line from the north west corner of New Mexico, along the range of mountains, until it would intersect the forty second parallel. . . .

There is another subject of vast importance to the United States, which will demand your particular attention. From information possessed by this Department, it is to be seriously apprehended that both Great Britain and France have designs upon California. . . . Whilst this Government does not intend to interfere between Mexico and California, it would vigorously interpose to prevent the latter from becoming either a British or a French Colony. You will endeavor to ascertain whether any such design exists, you will exert all your energies to prevent an act which, if consummated, would be so fraught with danger to the best interests of the United States. . . .

The possession of the Bay and harbour of San Francisco, is all important to the United States. The advantages to us of its acquisition are so striking that it would be a waste of time to enumerate them here. If all these should be turned against our country, by the cession of California to Great Britain our principal commercial rival, the consequences would be most disastrous.

The Government of California is now but nominally dependent on Mexico and it is more than doubtful whether her authority will ever be re-instated. Under these circumstances, it is the desire of the President that you shall use your best efforts to obtain a cession of that Province from Mexico to the United States. Could you accomplish this object, you would render immense service to your country and establish an enviable reputation for yourself. Money would be no object when compared with the value of the acquisition. Still the attempt must be made with great prudence and caution, and in such a manner as not to alarm the jealousy of the Mexican Government. Should you, after sounding the Mexican authorities on the subject, discover a prospect of success, the President would not hesitate to give, in addition to the assumption of the just claims of our citizens on Mexico, twenty five millions of dollars for the cession. Should you deem it expedient, you are authorized to offer this sum for a boundary, running due West from the southern extremity of New Mexico to the Pacific ocean, or from any other point on its western boundary, which would embrace Monterey within our limits. . . .

9 John Slidell, Appointed U.S. Minister to Mexico, to Secretary of State James Buchanan, December 17, 1845

MEXICO

. . . The most absurd reasons have been advanced against my recognition,[1] so absurd indeed that they would appear scarcely credible to any one, not upon the spot, unacquainted with the character of the people and ignorant of the manner in which affairs are here conducted — The objections stated were that my credentials did not appear to have been given with the sanction of Congress, that my appointment had not been confirmed by the Senate, that this Government had agreed only to receive a commissioner and that consequently the appointment of an Envoy Extraordinary and Minister Plenipotentiary was not in accordance with the letter of the 15th October from the Minister of Foreign Affairs to Mr. Black,[2] That this letter only contemplated negotiation upon

[1] Slidell is referring to the Mexican government's refusal to accept his credentials.

[2] See Source 7 on page 242.

Source: Manning, *Diplomatic Correspondence of the United States,* 8:777–81.

the subject of Texas, and finally to cap the climax of absurdity, that my powers were not sufficient. I hope before the closing of this despatch, to obtain information of the precise grounds upon which the Council finally decided to recommend that I should not be received . . .

Your instructions direct me to bear & forbear much for the purpose of promoting the great objects of my mission, and caution me against raising any points of honor, with a people so feeble and degraded. . . .

10 | *Secretary of State James Buchanan to John Slidell, Appointed U.S. Minister to Mexico,* January 20, 1846

WASHINGTON, D.C.

. . . Should the Mexican Government, by finally refusing to receive you, consummate the act of folly and bad faith of which they have afforded such strong indications, nothing will then remain for this Government but to take the redress of the wrongs of its citizens into its own hands.

In the event of such a refusal, the course which you have determined to pursue is the proper one. You ought, in your own language, so to conduct yourself as to throw the whole odium of the failure of the negotiation upon the Mexican Government; point out, in the most temperate manner, the inevitable consequences of so unheard of a violation of all the usages which govern the intercourse between civilized nations; and declare your intention to remain in Mexico until you can receive instructions adapted to the exigencies of the case. This sojourn will afford you an honorable opportunity to watch the course of events and avail yourself of any favorable circumstances which, in the mean time, may occur. . . .

In the mean time the President, in anticipation of the final refusal of the Mexican Government to receive you, has ordered the army of Texas to advance and take position on the left bank of the Rio Grande, and has directed that a strong fleet shall be immediately assembled in the Gulph of Mexico. He will thus be prepared to act with vigor and promptitude the moment that Congress shall give him the authority. . . .

Source: Manning, *Diplomatic Correspondence of the United States,* 8:185–86.

11 Joaquín M. de Castillo y Lanzas, Minister of Foreign Affairs of Mexico, to John Slidell, Appointed U.S. Minister to Mexico, March 12, 1846

Joaquín M. de Castillo y Lanzas succeeded Manuel de la Peña as Mexico's foreign minister in December 1845.

MEXICO

The Undersigned, Minister of Foreign Relations and Government of the Republic . . . make[s] known to Mr. Slidell . . . that the Mexican Government cannot receive him as Envoy Extraordinary & Minister Plenipotentiary to reside near it.

And here might the undersigned terminate his note, if reasons of great weight did not convince him of the necessity of making some reflections in this place; not through fear of the consequences which may result from this decisive resolve, but through the respect which he owes to reason and to justice.

It is true that this warlike display, with which the American Union presents herself,—by sea, with her squadrons on both coasts; by land, with her invading forces advancing by the northern frontiers—at the same time, that by her Minister Plenipotentiary propositions are made for conciliation, and accommodation, would be a sufficiently powerful reason for not listening to them, so long as all threatening should not be withdrawn, even to the slightest appearance of hostility. But even this is waived by the Government of the Republic, in order that it may in all frankness & loyalty enter into the discussion, relying solely upon reason and facts. A simple reference to the truth, plainly stated, suffices to show the justice by which Mexico is upheld in the question now under discussion.

The vehement desire of the Government of the United States, to extend its already immense territory at the expense of that of Mexico, has been manifest for many years; and it is beyond all doubt, that in regard to Texas at least, this has been their firm and constant determination: for it has been so declared categorically & officially by an authorized representative of the Union, whose assertion, strange & injurious as was its frankness, has nevertheless not been belied by the United States. . . .

Thus, this incorporation of a territory which had constituted an integral part of that of Mexico during the long period of the Spanish dominion, and after her emancipation for so long a term without any interruption whatever, and which moreover had been recognized & sanctioned by the Treaty limits between the Mexican Republic and the United States of America; this annexation was effected by the reprobated means of violence and fraud. . . .

Civilized nations have beheld with amazement, at this enlightened and refined epoch, a powerful & well consolidated State, availing itself of the internal

Source: Manning, *Diplomatic Correspondence of the United States,* 8:818–22.

dissensions of a neighbouring nation, putting its vigilance to sleep by protestations of friendship, setting in action all manner of springs and artifices, alternately plying intrigue & violence, and seizing a moment to despoil her of a precious part of her territory, regardless of the incontrovertible rights of the most unquestionable ownership and the most uninterrupted possession.

Here, then, is the true position of the Mexican Republic: despoiled, outraged, contemned, it is now attempted to subject her to a humiliating degradation. The sentiment of her own dignity will not allow her to consent to such ignominy. . . .

It follows, that if war should finally become inevitable, and if in consequence of this war the peace of the civilized world should be disturbed, the responsibility will not fall upon Mexico. It will all rest upon the United States, to them will the whole of it belong. Not upon Mexico, who, with a generosity unequalled, admitted the American citizens who wished to colonize in Texas; but upon the United States, who, bent upon possessing themselves, early or late, of that territory, encouraged emigration thither, with that view; in order that, in due time, its inhabitants, converting themselves from colonists into its masters, should claim the country as their own, for the purpose of transferring it to the United States. Not upon Mexico, who having in due season protested against so enormous a transgression, wished to remove all cause for controversy & hostility; but upon the United States, who, to the scandal of the world, and in manifest violation of treaties, gave protection and aid to those guilty of a rebellion so iniquitous. Not upon Mexico, who, in the midst even of injuries so great & so repeated, has shewn herself disposed to admit propositions for reconciliation; but upon the United States, who pretending sincerely to desire a friendly and honourable accommodation, has belied by their acts the sincerity of their words. Finally, not upon Mexico, who, putting out of view her own dearest interests, through her deference for peace, has entertained as long as was wished the propositions which with this view might be made to her: but upon the United States, who, by frivolous pretexts, evade the conclusion of such an arrangement; proposing peace, at the very moment when they are causing their squadrons & their troops to advance upon the ports & the frontiers of Mexico; exacting an humiliation, impossible to be submitted to, in order to find a pretext, if no reason can be found, which may occasion the breaking out of hostilities.

12 *Secretary of State James Buchanan to John Slidell, Appointed U.S. Minister to Mexico,* March 12, 1846

In December 1845, General Mariano Paredes led a military coup in Mexico City and installed himself as the head of the new government. This sudden change in the political climate of Mexico raised the possibility of renewing negotiations over Texas, especially since the Paredes government needed money to solidify its position at home.

WASHINGTON, D.C.

The President [Polk] believes . . . you ought to return to the City of Mexico, if this be practicable consistently with the national honor. . . . It appears from your despatch No. 7, that the Government of Paredes is now tottering for want of money. It would be easy for you to make known to him in some discreet manner that the United States were both able and willing to relieve his administration from pecuniary[1] embarrassment, if he would do us justice and settle the question of boundary between the two Republics. A treaty for this purpose, under your instructions, if ratified by Mexico and transmitted to the United States, could be returned in a brief space with the ratification of the President and Senate. In the meantime, Paredes could command immediately funds on such an assurance. . . .

We have received information from different quarters, in corroboration of your statement, that there may be a design on the part of several European Powers to establish a monarchy in Mexico. It is supposed that the clergy would generally favor such a project and that a considerable party already exists among the people which would give it their countenance and support. It is believed by many that this party will continue to increase in consequence of the successive revolutions which may afflict that country, until at length a majority of the people will be willing to throw themselves into the arms of a monarch for security and protection. Indeed, rumor has already indicated the King, in the person of the Spanish Prince Henry, the son of Francisco de Paula, and the rejected suitor of Queen Isabella.

These may be, and probably are, idle speculations, but they come to us in such a shape that they ought not to be wholly disregarded. It will be your duty to exercise your utmost vigilance in detecting this plot and its ramifications, if any such exists. Should Great Britain and France attempt to place a Spanish or any other European Prince upon the throne of Mexico, this would be resisted by all the power of the United States. In opposition to such an attempt, party distinctions in this country would vanish and the people would be nearly unanimous. It is unnecessary to state to one so well informed upon the subject

[1] Financial.

Source: Manning, *Diplomatic Correspondence of the United States,* 8:189–92.

as yourself, the reasons why the United States could never suffer foreign Powers to erect a throne for a European Prince on the ruins of a neighboring Republic, without our most determined resistance. . . .

13 · John Slidell, Appointed U.S. Minister to Secretary of State James Buchanan, March 18, 1846

Slidell failed in his efforts to negotiate with the Paredes government. He wrote this letter while en route out of Mexico and reached the White House on May 8. The next day, Polk drafted his war message to Congress.

Private   JALAPA[1]

MY DEAR SIR: I have nothing to add to the accompanying dispatches, except to say that while at Vera Cruz, I will make arrangements to convey by express to the Pacific Squadron, any orders which may be sent there. There can be no difficulty in doing this if a steamer convey the first intelligence of war to Vera Cruz, it can be kept secret until the express is well on its way to Mexico. I do not know that I can give any useful information at Washington, but should you think my presence there desirable, I will cheerfully make the journey.

I expect to receive my passports on Thursday next, (24 instant) & in that case I ought to reach New Orleans, about the 5 April. . . . It is no easy matter to preserve one's *sang froid*[2] with these people. Depend upon it, we can never get along well with them, until we have given them a good drubbing.

[1] A Mexican city between Mexico City and Vera Cruz.
[2] Grace under pressure.

Source: Manning, *Diplomatic Correspondence of the United States,* 8:832.

Analyzing Diplomatic Correspondence

1. Briefly describe the nature of the "intelligence" that Parrott, Black, and Slidell provided for Buchanan. On what basis did they make their judgments about the Mexican government and people? How did Buchanan use the information they provided him?

2. How did the subject matter of letters exchanged between the United States and Mexico differ from that in letters exchanged between Buchanan and his agents

in Mexico? What topics or issues were addressed in one that were not addressed in the other?

3. How do the letters written by Mexican officials present Mexico's position on the annexation of Texas? How does their version of events differ from that provided by Buchanan's agents in Mexico?

4. Was there a significant difference in the tone of letters exchanged between Mexican and American officials and those exchanged between Buchanan and his agents in Mexico? If so, how would you describe this difference, and what do you think accounts for it?

5. How did Parrott, Black, and Slidell describe Mexicans? What evidence do you see in their letters of racism or ethnocentrism that may have influenced their advice to Buchanan? Did such prejudices change in any significant ways over time?

6. Judging from the diplomatic correspondence you have read here, what do you think was the ultimate objective of the Polk administration's foreign policy in regard to Mexico? Did Polk want to avoid a war or generate one? Should Buchanan's diplomatic efforts to advance Polk's aims be defined as a failure or a success?

The Rest of the Story

The Mexican-American War proved to be as politically controversial for the Polk administration as was the annexation of Texas. Northern Whigs openly condemned "Mr. Polk's War" as an unjust territorial grab undertaken at the behest of Southern slaveholders. As the war progressed and American troops occupied Mexico City, some American expansionists supported an "All Mexico" movement to incorporate the conquered nation into the United States. Others balked at such a plan, calling the United States a white man's republic that could not possibly assimilate such a large and racially distinct population. Polk did not support the All Mexico movement, but he did want more from the conquered enemy than a Texas border at the Rio Grande. Through the Treaty of Guadalupe Hidalgo, which ended the war in February 1848, the United States acquired California and New Mexico, about one-third of Mexico's national territory, for a payment of $15 million and an agreement to assume any debts owed by Mexico to U.S. citizens.

Victory over Mexico brought its own problems. Despite the successful prosecution of the war, Polk chose not to run for reelection in 1848, and he died shortly after leaving office. He was succeeded by Zachary Taylor, a hero from the Mexican-American War nominated by the Whigs, even though he had no previous connection to the party. Sectional tensions between free and slave states intensified in the wake of Mexico's defeat, as the federal government anticipated the admission of new states carved from its conquests. Everyone knew that Oregon, over which the Polk administration had reached a negotiated settlement with Britain, would enter the union as a free state. New Mexico and much of the rest of the nation's new Southwest were too arid to support a plantation economy, but California beckoned to Northerners and Southerners alike. At the outset of the Mexican-American War, some antislavery congressmen introduced a piece of legislation called the Wilmot Proviso, which stipulated that any territory acquired from the war would be "free soil," or closed to slavery. Southern congressmen believed such a measure violated the property rights of slaveholders. They blocked its passage, but the legislative battle over the Wilmot Proviso led to the creation of the Free Soil Party, which further polarized the sectional debate. As the nation moved into the 1850s, it still had no workable method for resolving the issue of slavery's expansion.

Meanwhile, 11,000 Mexicans in Texas, New Mexico, and California now found themselves living within the borders of the United States. Polk had wanted Mexico's territory, not its people. The presence of even this small number of Mexicans within the newly acquired territory presented a challenge to American race relations, which had for so long been defined by opposing categories of black and white. The fact that many Mexicans were the product of intermarriage between Spanish colonizers and Native Americans aroused the racial prejudices of Anglo-Americans, who legally barred interracial marriage in many states. Social and legal custom in the American West treated Mexican Americans as second-class citizens because in the eyes of the white ruling class, they were a "mongrel" race.

History has a way of turning the tables. According to the 2000 U.S. census, Hispanics are now the largest minority group in the nation, and two-thirds of them are of Mexican heritage. Demographers project that within a few decades, Hispanics will make up the majority of the populations of Texas and California, two of the largest and most politically influential states in the union. While Polk and his contemporaries may have balked at extending citizenship to Mexicans living there in 1848, the reality more than 150 years later is that the American Southwest is defined culturally and politically by historical ties to Mexico that no foreign policy or war could erase.

To Find Out More

The records of nineteenth-century U.S. foreign relations are scattered through a number of institutions, including the U.S. Congress, the National Archives, and the Library of Congress. If you are interested in working in these materials but do not live near Washington, D.C., it is best to consult a number of document collections published in the early twentieth century. The diplomatic correspondence you read in this chapter was selected from William R. Manning, editor, *Diplomatic Correspondence of the United States: Inter-American Affairs, 1831–1860,* 12 volumes (Washington, D.C.: Carnegie Endowment for International Peace, 1932–1939). Another important collection for presidential papers related to diplomatic affairs is James D. Richardson, compiler, *A Compilation of the Messages and Papers of the Presidents, 1789–1902,* second edition, 10 volumes (Washington, D.C.: Bureau of National Literature and Art, 1910). Polk's diary is available in Milo Milton Quaife, editor, *The Diary of James K. Polk during His Presidency, 1845–1849,* 4 volumes (Chicago: A. C. McClurg, 1910).

The most thorough study of the Texas annexation crisis in U.S.-Mexican relations is David M. Pletcher, *The Diplomacy of Annexation: Texas, Oregon, and the Mexican War* (Columbia: University of Missouri Press, 1973). Also see Frederick Merk with Lois Bannister Merk, *The Monroe Doctrine and American Expansionism, 1843–1849* (New York: Alfred A. Knopf, 1967). Charles Sellers explores the origins and operation of Polk's foreign policy in *James K. Polk, Continentalist, 1843–1846* (Princeton, N.J.: Princeton University Press, 1966). An excellent online resource for studying the Mexican-American War, featuring contributions from American and Mexican scholars, is *The U.S.-Mexican War (1846–1848),* available at **www.pbs.org/Kera/usmexicanwar**. The military history of the war is treated in John S. D. Eisenhower, *So Far from God: The U.S. War with Mexico, 1846–1848* (New York: Random House, 1989). A study that measures the cultural impact of the Mexican-American War on the United States is Robert W. Johannsen, *To the Halls of the Montezumas: The Mexican War in the American Imagination* (New York: Oxford University Press, 1985). Two useful studies of Manifest Destiny and American racial attitudes are Reginald Horsman, *Race and Manifest Destiny: The Origins of American Racial Anglo-Saxonism* (Cambridge, Mass.: Harvard University Press, 1981), and Thomas R. Hietala, *Manifest Design: Anxious Aggrandizement in Late Jacksonian America* (Ithaca, N.Y.: Cornell University Press, 1985). Amy S. Greenberg explores the role of gender in the U.S. encounters with Mexico and Central America in *Manifest Manhood and the Antebellum American Empire* (Cambridge: Cambridge University Press, 2005).

CHAPTER 12

Martyr or Madman?

Biographies of John Brown

Late on the night of May 24, 1856, a small band of men led by the abolitionist John Brown visited several homesteads along the Pottawatomie Creek in the Kansas Territory. Brown and his men pounded on the doors of men known in the area for their proslavery sympathies. Those unlucky enough to be home and unarmed were hurried outside, despite the protestations of crying wives and children. Brown asked each one a series of questions about his involvement in the proslavery cause in Kansas. Once Brown was convinced of their guilt, he ordered them killed. Brown's party, which included four of his sons, shot some of their victims at point-blank range and cut others to pieces with broadswords. They left behind five mutilated corpses as a warning to any others who would try to bring slavery to Kansas.

Violence between proslavery and antislavery forces in Kansas was a fact of life in the 1850s. In 1854, Congress had passed the Kansas-Nebraska Act, establishing the doctrine of "popular sovereignty" in this newly organized territory. The brainchild of Illinois senator Stephen Douglas, popular sovereignty sought to sidestep the federal debate over the admission of free and slave states into the union by allowing the settlers within a territory to decide the question for themselves. Douglas may have hoped that the Kansas-Nebraska Act would cool sectional tensions, but it had the opposite effect. In New England and New York, abolitionists created emigrant aid societies to speed the territory's settlement by "free-soilers" opposed to slavery's expansion, while proslavery Missourians poured over their state's western border into Kansas to make sure the territory voted their way. Armed clashes between Missouri "border ruffians" and Northern free-soilers gave the territory a lawless character that earned it the nickname "Bleeding Kansas." Men on both sides formed voluntary brigades and armed themselves to the teeth with Bowie knives, swords, guns, and even cannon. Brown, who had never served in a regular military force, earned the title of "Captain" for organizing some family and neighbors into a company of "Liberty Guards" to defend the free-soil town of Lawrence. They were unsuccessful. Just days before the Pottawatomie murders, a small army of proslavery men sacked Lawrence, putting free-soilers on the defensive. But nothing that had happened in Kansas matched the Pottawatomie murders for cold-blooded ruthlessness. The actions of Brown's band electrified the nation and raised the sectional conflict to a fever pitch.

As news of the Pottawatomie murders reached the national press, everyone was asking the same question: Who was John Brown? He had arrived in Kansas a few months earlier, in October 1855, to help his sons who were homesteading there and to advance the antislavery cause. Brown's family had deep New England roots, and he believed firmly in the same God — the divine, all-seeing judge of human affairs — that his Puritan ancestors had worshipped. He quoted the Bible at length in his verbal attacks on slavery. He did the same with the Declaration of Independence. "All men are created equal" was as much an article of faith for John Brown as the Ten Commandments. This fusion of religious and political principles had made him an abolitionist from an early age. He regarded African Americans as his brothers and sisters and slavery as a grave sin on the nation's conscience.

Figure 12.1 John Brown, 1859 Taken while Brown was traveling in the Northeast to raise money among his abolitionist friends, this photograph captures many of his contradictions. Stern and righteous, he cultivated the appearance of the Old Testament prophets who inspired him. But he was also extraordinarily empathetic to the sufferings of slaves and confident that blacks and whites could live peacefully together in a freer, more democratic America. Finally, it is ironic that a man who supposedly grew a long beard to disguise himself from his enemies was egotistical enough to pose for his portrait.
Source: Library of Congress.

Brown was a man of ambition as well as principle. Before gaining notoriety in Kansas in 1856, he had moved about frequently in New England, New York, Pennsylvania, and Ohio, seeking economic opportunity and stability for his ever-growing family. Born into humble circumstances in Connecticut in 1800, Brown spent most of his adult life in hardscrabble frontier communities, trying his hand at different businesses but often falling prey to debt, lawsuits, and misfortune. He was at various times a farmer, tanner, shepherd, wool merchant, and land speculator. He married twice and fathered twenty children, but only eleven of those survived to adulthood. In 1849, Brown moved his family to a farm in the Adirondack Mountains of northern New York, where they lived among escaped slaves and other free blacks who had been granted land by abolitionist Gerrit Smith. Brown's second wife and several of their children made a home there, but Brown himself remained constantly on the move, going where his business ventures and political convictions led him.

After the Pottawatomie murders, Brown stayed in Kansas and lived for a while as a guerrilla fighter, hiding in swamps and other remote areas with a group of dedicated followers. Territorial officials were unable to capture him, and to proslavery supporters, he became a symbol of "black Republicanism," a radical movement to foment slave rebellion and overthrow the South's racial and economic system. To free-soilers in Kansas, he became something of a folk hero, especially after his band of armed men put up a brave, albeit unsuccessful, defense of the free-soil town of Osawatomie against a much larger proslavery force. One of Brown's sons was killed, and the town was burned to the ground, but many regarded "Osawatomie Brown," as he became known, as a freedom fighter whose bravery helped turn the tide against slavery in Kansas.

Brown took his newfound celebrity east in 1858, touring the drawing rooms of prominent abolitionists in Ohio, New York, and New England and soliciting funding from them for his battle against slavery. Returning west, he led a raid to free several Missouri slaves and helped escort them to safety in Canada. He also met with free blacks in Canada and the northern states to recruit their assistance in money, arms, and men. The famous black abolitionist Frederick Douglass was impressed by Brown's convictions but declined an offer to join him; a group of six prominent white abolitionists, however, opened their pocketbooks to Brown, despite their pacifist convictions.

Brown's militant abolitionism culminated in the raid on Harpers Ferry, Virginia (now West Virginia), in October 1859. Harpers Ferry was a town nestled in the hills of western Virginia along the eastern edge of the Appalachian Mountains. Since the 1840s, Brown had considered it a logical site for starting a slave rebellion that could spread and ultimately engulf every slave state from there to Georgia. It was home to a rifle factory as well as a federal armory that could provide arms to runaway slaves, who could then form guerrilla bands in the nearby mountains. There was not a large slave population near Harpers Ferry, but Brown believed plantation slaves in eastern Virginia and Maryland would flock to his cause once they knew a rebellion was under way.

In the summer and fall of 1859, Brown assembled a force of twenty-one men, about one-quarter of whom were African Americans, for the raid on

Harpers Ferry. On the night of Sunday, October 16, they made their move, seizing the armory and taking many local citizens as prisoners. The following morning, the local militia turned out to do battle with Brown's force. Several men were killed on each side, including two of Brown's sons, but Brown held out in a fire engine house on the armory grounds, expecting assistance from runaway slaves who would help his men escape into the mountains. That night, U.S. Marines under the command of Colonel Robert E. Lee arrived and offered Brown a chance to surrender. Brown refused, and the next morning, Lee's men charged and quickly overcame Brown's defenses. More of Brown's men were killed, but Brown was only wounded and placed under arrest.

Brown's raid on Harpers Ferry was a military disaster. Half of his men were killed, and most of the survivors, including Brown himself, were quickly convicted of treason and executed. Not a single slave had been freed, despite the months of planning, and news of the raid failed to spark any slave rebellions elsewhere in the nation. Brown had failed as an emancipator, but he had succeeded brilliantly as an incendiary. During the six weeks of his imprisonment and trial in Charlestown, Virginia (now Charles Town, West Virginia), the nation's attention was riveted. In his jail cell, he wrote letters and received visitors, sharing with many his belief that "the crimes of this guilty land will never be purged away but with blood." Southern newspapers depicted him as the homicidal madman who lurked at the heart of the abolitionist cause. While leaders of the Republican Party distanced themselves from Brown, other Northerners embraced him as a Christian soldier and martyr. No one doubted that the events at Harpers Ferry had brought the nation one step closer to disunion. Years later, Frederick Douglass said it best: "If John Brown did not end the war that ended slavery, he did, at least, begin the war that ended slavery."

Using the Source: Biographies of John Brown

Who was John Brown? Was he a religious fanatic or a revolutionary? A military genius or a hopeless bungler? A man of conviction or an egomaniac? A visionary advocate of racial equality or a cold-blooded murderer? Was he the first terrorist to carry out an attack on U.S. soil? Like an anxious student facing the blank ovals of a college entrance exam, historians have often found "all of the above" the safest way to answer these questions.

Brown's contemporaries asked these questions about him in the wake of the Pottawatomie murders, and their debate over the meaning of his life and death only intensified after the events at Harpers Ferry in 1859. Most of what was written about Brown in the fifty years after his death was the work of people who wanted to eulogize him as an American hero. James Redpath, an antislavery journalist who had met Brown in Kansas, contributed much to this mythology, as did surviving family members and friends who wished to justify

Brown and their association with him. These narratives of John Brown's life belong in the genre of hagiography, a type of historical writing that originated in the Middle Ages, when monks wrote lives of saints that blended fact and fiction and uncritically celebrated their subjects. It was not until the early twentieth century, a half century after Brown's execution, that the first scholarly biographies of Brown appeared, written by authors using historical methods and sources and claiming to take an even-handed approach to their subject. In the century since, enough biographies have been written about Brown to fill a bookshelf.

Standing in front of that bookshelf, you might ask, "Why would anyone want to write another biography of John Brown?" It is a fair question. At the time of his execution, most of what makes up the standard narrative of his life was already known: his difficult beginnings in frontier Pennsylvania, his intense spirituality, his failed business enterprises, his bloody career as a militant abolitionist. In the absence of any new evidence that challenges that story, why would anyone feel compelled to squeeze yet another Brown biography onto that crowded shelf?

Historians write biographies as much for themselves as they do for their subjects. A historical figure like John Brown is a sort of Rorschach test for historians, an inkblot spread out against an empty background that each viewer interprets differently according to his or her own personality, concerns, or environment. It is not surprising, then, that biographers continue to write about a figure as famous and controversial as Brown. Each generation demands a new interpretation of his life in light of the way contemporary issues constantly affect the interpretation of the past. Any biography of John Brown pulled randomly off a bookshelf will provide the basic facts of his life, but reading and comparing several of them will also reveal how historians have altered their interpretations of Brown to suit their sensibilities and times.

What Can Biographies Tell Us?

Biography is perhaps the most enduring and popular form of historical writing. Most bookstores devote the bulk of their history sections to biographies, and each year, biographies top nonfiction best-seller lists. One reason for this popularity is the inherent narrative structure biographies provide to their writers and readers. A big part of history, after all, is *story*, and whether in the form of a play, film, or book, people like their stories to have clear beginnings, middles, and endings. The story of one person's life neatly fits that structure.

A good biography, however, will do more than merely recapitulate the events of a person's life; it will situate that person in a wider historical context, using the life story told in its pages to illuminate some greater aspect of the world in which its subject lived. How did the subject of a biography shape history, and how was he or she shaped by it? Biographies allow us to explore the role of the individual in society, the intersection of private and public life, and the ways in which personality can shape the broad tide of political and social change.

The disadvantages of working with biographies reflect in some ways the advantages. Biographers often inflate the importance of their subjects and overstate the ways in which their subjects shaped history rather than the ways in which they were shaped by it. Traditional biographies often subscribe to the "great men of history" approach to studying the past: Who was the greatest general of World War II, who was the most indispensable Founding Father, who was the greatest president? "Great women" occasionally get their due in these works, but women in general and other groups that have traditionally been excluded from the corridors of power are shortchanged by this kind of historical writing.

It is also important to remember that biographies are a secondary source. Like the journal articles discussed in Chapter 4, biographies are a product of someone else's interpretation of the facts, and despite their protestations otherwise, biographers are seldom neutral observers of their subjects' lives. After all, biographers are drawn to their subjects for very human reasons of love or hate. They may wish to sing the praises of their subject or to damn that person with the judgment of history. No biographer responds to his or her subject with a shoulder shrug or wants the reader to do so. As with any other type of source, bias plays a role in how a biography gets made, and the attentive reader will take it into account when judging the quality of the work.

Even the most basic facts of a person's life are subject to interpretation and bias in a biography. Consider for example the description of John Brown's marriage to his second wife, Mary Day, found in biographies written by Robert Penn Warren and David S. Reynolds. Each relates the same basic facts. Brown's first wife, Dianthe, died from complications sustained in giving birth to a child who also died. Not long after, Brown became acquainted with the sixteen-year-old sister of his housekeeper and married her. Notice, however, how each author creates a strikingly different picture of Brown and his new bride from these facts.

FROM WARREN'S *JOHN BROWN: THE MAKING OF A MARTYR*[1]

John Brown soon got used to this big-boned, reticent girl who did chores about the house or sat at the spinning wheel, manipulating the yarn with heavy, competent hands. One evening he gave her a letter. This restless, severe man, more than twice her age and looking even older, must have terrified her a little. In any case it was the next morning before she dared read the letter, nor did she dare, when she saw John Brown, to answer the question he had written her. Instead, she took the bucket and went about the customary work of bringing the morning water from the spring. He followed her to the spring and got his answer there. Mary Anne Day married John Brown in July, only a little less than a year after Dianthe and her unnamed son had been buried in the tanyard.[2]

> Is this an attractive portrait of Mary Day?

> How is John Brown portrayed?

[1] Robert Penn Warren, *John Brown: The Making of a Martyr* (1929; Nashville: J. S. Sanders, 1993), 29.

[2] The grounds of Brown's family business, a tannery for processing animal hides into leather.

What is Warren predicting for the marriage here?

But the new wife had in her more of the stuff that made for survival; beneath a certain awkwardness was a great physical vigor, and the embarrassed silences covered a profound, unquestioning devotion to the hard responsibilities of her life. She was ignorant, but possessed a primitive stoicism which meant an efficient if sometimes uncomprehending adaptability to fact. It is doubtful if the grave by the tanyard lay much in her thoughts.

FROM REYNOLDS'S *JOHN BROWN, ABOLITIONIST* [3]

Brown moved back into his own home and took on a housekeeper whose sixteen-year-old sister, Mary Day, came occasionally to spin cloth. Mary caught his eye as she sat at her spinning wheel. Tall and deep bosomed, she had striking black hair and a sturdy frame. The daughter of Charles Day, a blacksmith and farmer in nearby Troy Township, she had had little formal education but impressed Brown as a practical, hard-working woman.

Language suggesting playful romance

It wasn't long before Brown, too bashful to propose verbally, presented her with a written offer of marriage. The girl nervously put his note under her pillow and slept on it a night before opening it. After reading it, she grabbed a bucket and rushed off to a spring to fetch water. Brown followed her. By the time the two returned to the house, he had received the answer he wanted. They were married on June 14, 1833. Ten months later a baby girl, Sarah, arrived.

What is Reynolds predicting for the marriage?

Unlike the erratic Dianthe, Mary would prove to be a rock of stability for John Brown. Staunch and stoical, she set a tone of quiet courage that would influence the whole family.

Warren's version of Brown's second marriage has all the gothic doom and gloom of an Edgar Allan Poe story: an older, overbearing man forces himself on a much younger, powerless woman, while the ghosts of his dead wife and child linger nearby in the family graveyard. Warren's Brown is forceful and bullying, and his Mary Day is a simpleminded stoic, already resigned to the fate of being a martyr's wife. Reynolds, on the other hand, paints a much rosier picture, one that might not be out of place on the cover of a romance novel. The grieving Brown falls hard for the raven-haired beauty at the spinning wheel. After a playful game of cat and mouse, he wins her over, and they get busy making babies. As these short passages indicate, no biography presents an entirely neutral view of its subject. Authors arrange and interpret facts to suit their purposes, nor are they above embellishing details (for example, the grave in the tanyard or Mary's striking black hair) in order to elicit an emotional response from their readers.

[3] David S. Reynolds, *John Brown, Abolitionist: The Man Who Killed Slavery, Sparked the Civil War, and Seeded Civil Rights* (New York: Alfred A. Knopf, 2005), 49.

Questions to Ask

To get more than the simple facts of a person's life out of a biography, it is important to ask questions about the book's own life story: When was it written? What do you know about the author and the era in which he or she wrote? The author's personal background or other publications may give you some sense of why he or she has chosen to write about the biography's subject. Also, read the book carefully for its evidence and argument. Does the author appear to be in control of the facts? Does the author emphasize the subject's virtues or vices? Finally, what does the author think is the subject's historical significance? Why should people still read about this person today?

- When was the biography written and by whom?
- What do you know about the author and the period in which he or she wrote?
- What approach does the author take to the biography's subject?
- What does the author believe to be the subject's historical legacy?

Source Analysis Table

Use the columns in the table on the next page to take notes that will help you compare and contrast how each author depicts Brown, the characters in his life story, and his legacy.

Source	Description of John Brown, His Motives, and His Methods	Description of Brown's Accomplices, Supporters, and Enemies	Historical Significance of Brown
1. DuBois (1909)			
2. Warren (1929)			
3. Reynolds (2005)			

262

To download and print this table, visit the book companion site at **bedfordstmartins.com/brownshannon.**

The Source: Biographies of John Brown

1 | *John Brown* by W. E. B. DuBois, 1909

W. E. B. DuBois was one of the most influential American intellectuals and activists of the twentieth century. He established his reputation as a voice for African Americans with the publication of *The Souls of Black Folks* in 1903 and played a founding role in the National Association for the Advancement of Colored People (NAACP), a pathbreaking civil rights organization. *John Brown* was his second book. The passages below reflect DuBois's interest in the history of American race relations.

So Kansas was free.[1] In vain did the sullen Senate in Washington fume and threaten and keep the young state knocking for admission; the game had been played and lost and Kansas was free. Free because the slave barons played for an imperial stake in defiance of modern humanity and economic development. Free because strong men had suffered and fought not against slavery but against slaves in Kansas. Above all, free because one man hated slavery and on a terrible night rode down with his sons among the shadows of the Swamp of the Swan—that long, low-winding and somber stream "fringed everywhere with woods" and dark with bloody memory.[2] Forty-eight hours they lingered there, and then on a pale May morning rode up to the world again. Behind them lay five twisted, red, and mangled corpses. Behind them rose the stifled wailing of widows and little children. Behind them the fearful driver gazed and shuddered. But before them rode a man, tall, dark, grim-faced and awful. His hands were red and his name was John Brown. Such was the cost of freedom.

Of all this development[3] John Brown knew far more than most white men and it was on this great knowledge that his great faith was based. To most Americans the inner striving of the Negro was a veiled and an unknown tale: they had heard of Douglass,[4] they knew of fugitive slaves, but of the living, organized, struggling group that had made both these phenomena possible they had no conception.

From his earliest interest in Negroes, John Brown sought to know individuals among them intimately and personally. He invited them to his home and he went to theirs. He talked to them, and listened to the history of their trials,

[1] DuBois is referring here to the clinching of a free-soil government for Kansas in 1858.

[2] The site of the Pottawatomie murders.

[3] The growing spirit for rebellion among American slaves.

[4] Frederick Douglass, the leading African American abolitionist of the era.

Source: W. E. B. DuBois, *John Brown* (Philadelphia: G. W. Jacobs and Company, 1909), 247–48, 143–44, 338, 340–41, 374–75.

advised them and took advice from them. His dream was to enlist the boldest and most daring spirits among them in his great plan.

When, therefore, John Brown came East[5] in January, 1858, his object was not simply to further his campaign for funds, but more especially definitely to organize the Negroes for his work. Already he had disclosed his intentions to Thomas Thomas[6] of Springfield and to Frederick Douglass. He now determined to enlist a larger number and he particularly had in mind the Negroes of New York and Philadelphia, and those in Canada. At no time, however, did John Brown plan to begin his foray with many Negroes. He knew that he must gain the confidence of black men first by a successful stroke, and that after initial success he could count on large numbers. His object then was to interest a few leaders like Douglass, organize societies with wide ramifications, and after the first raid to depend on these societies for aid and recruits.

The deed was done.[7] The next day the world knew and the world sat in puzzled amazement. It was ever so and ever will be. When a prophet like John Brown appears, how must we of the world receive him? Must we follow out of the drear, dread logic of surrounding facts, as did the South, even if they crucify a clean and pure soul, simply because consistent allegiance to our cherished, chosen ideal demands it? If we do, the shame will brand our latest history. Shall we hesitate and waver before his clear white logic, now helping, now fearing to help, now believing, now doubting? Yes, this we must do so long as the doubt and hesitation are genuine; but we must not lie. If we are human, we must thus hesitate until we know the right. How shall we know it? That is the Riddle of the Sphinx. We are but darkened groping souls, that know not light often because of its very blinding radiance. Only in time is truth revealed. To-day at last we know: John Brown was right. . . .

Such a light was the soul of John Brown. He was simple, exasperatingly simple; unlettered, plain, and homely. No casuistry of culture or of learning, or well-being or tradition moved him in the slightest degree: "Slavery is wrong," he said, "kill it." Destroy it—uproot it, stem, blossom, and branch; give it no quarter, exterminate it and do it now. Was he wrong? No. The forcible staying of human uplift by barriers of law, and might, and tradition is the most wicked thing on earth. It is wrong, eternally wrong. It is wrong, by whatever name it is called, or in whatever guise it lurks, and whenever it appears. But it is especially heinous, black, and cruel when it masquerades in the robes of law and justice and patriotism. So was American slavery clothed in 1859, and it had to die by revolution, not by milder means. And this men knew. They had known it for a hundred years. Yet they shrank and trembled. From round about the white and blinding path of this soul flew equivocations, lies, thievings and red murders.

---

[5] From Kansas, to raise money for his cause among Northern abolitionists.

[6] A New England free black with whom Brown had shared his plan for inciting slave rebellion.

[7] The raid on Harpers Ferry.

And yet all men instinctively felt that these things were not of the light but of the surrounding darkness. It is at once surprising, baffling, and pitiable to see the way in which men—honest American citizens—faced this light.

Was John Brown simply an episode, or was he an eternal truth? And if a truth, how speaks that truth today? John Brown loved his neighbor as himself. He could not endure therefore to see his neighbor, poor, unfortunate or oppressed. This natural sympathy was strengthened by a saturation in Hebrew religion[8] which stressed the personal responsibility of every human soul to a just God. To this religion of equality and sympathy with misfortune, was added the strong influence of the social doctrines of the French Revolution with its emphasis on freedom and power in political life. And on all this was built John Brown's own inchoate but growing belief in a more just and a more equal distribution of property. From this he concluded, and acted on that conclusion, that all men are created free and equal, and that the cost of liberty is less than the price of repression.

[8] Here DuBois is referring to Brown's Calvinist faith, rooted in Old Testament notions of God as a divine judge and controller of human affairs.

2 ## *John Brown* by Robert Penn Warren, 1929

> Robert Penn Warren was a prominent twentieth-century American author whose work often focused on themes of Southern culture and history. In the 1930s, he associated with a group of like-minded writers known as the Southern Agrarians, who criticized modern industrial society and defended the South as a region of traditional values. Although Warren is most famous for his poetry, literary criticism, and fiction, his first book, written while he was still a student, was a biography of John Brown.

A short while after dark John Brown gave the order to march.[1] The company moved rapidly and quietly northward toward Mosquito Creek. They forded the creek above the Doyle place and soon reached the first cabin. One of the men knocked on the door, while the others stood by waiting. Everything was silent for a moment and then they heard the sound of a gun being rammed through the chinks of the cabin wall. The raiders scattered on the instant; they had not come for a stand-up fight. If that was all they wanted they could have gotten it quickly enough without leaving the militia. . . .

[1] Warren describes in this passage the Pottawatomie murders.

Source: Robert Penn Warren, *John Brown: The Making of a Martyr* (1929; Nashville: J. S. Sanders, 1993), 161–68, 314, 420–21.

They next reached the Doyle cabin, which stood on Mosquito Creek, only a mile or so from where it emptied into the Pottawatomie. As they cautiously approached, two large and savage watchdogs leaped up at them. Frederick[2] swung his short two-edged sword at one of the beasts and Townsley[3] stepped in to dispatch it with a blow of his saber. The first of the Bierce swords[4] was stained with blood. Townsley, Weiner,[5] and Frederick stopped a little way from the house, while John Brown, Thompson,[6] and three of the sons went up to the door and knocked. Doyle's voice answered. There was no saving sound of a rifle being rammed through the cabin chinks, and the gleam of a newly lighted candle shone within. "We want to know where Mr. Wilkinson[7] lives," one of the men said. Doyle replied that he would tell them the way and then opened the door. John Brown and his men pushed inside. "We are from the Northern army. You and your boys must surrender. You are our prisoners." Mahala Doyle cried out in protest; she saw the meaning of the business. Old Doyle must also have understood, but he only said, "Hush, mother, hush." The prisoners of the Northern army were marched out of the house—the father Doyle, the twenty-two-year-old William, and Drury who was only twenty. Mahala Doyle's tears prevailed a little, for the next son, John, was left in the cabin with her and the younger children.

The three victims were hurried a short distance down the road toward Dutch Henry's[8] and there the party halted. John Brown set the example. He presented a revolver to the forehead of old Doyle and fired. It had begun; there was no turning back now. The Brown sons fell on William and Drury Doyle and hacked them down. Drury tried to flee but they pursued and overtook him. In the young grass near a ravine they left his mangled body. The other two lay in a bloody heap by the roadside where they had fallen.

The killing at Doyle's was perforce one of principle, for the family's horses had been out on the prairie. The little group, with their stained swords, hurried forward on foot to Wilkinson's. It was not yet midnight; and the business was far from finished. . . .

Wilkinson was killed in the roadway, to the south of his house. The murderers dragged his body a short distance to one side and left it in some dry bush. It was over neatly and quickly; they proceeded in the direction of Dutch Henry's Crossing. They must have gone along more rapidly now. The saddles could not have been taken from the house for nothing, but at that most of the company had to ride bareback.[9] . . .

---

[2] Frederick Brown, one of Brown's sons who accompanied him on the Pottawatomie raid.

[3] One of Brown's men.

[4] Lucius Bierce was an Ohio abolitionist who supplied Brown with artillery sabers.

[5] One of Brown's men.

[6] One of Brown's men.

[7] One of the proslavery men Brown's party was after that night.

[8] Another proslavery supporter targeted by Brown.

[9] Warren is referring here to horses and saddles that Brown's party stole from their victims.

John Brown and his party returned to their camp between the two deep ravines. The old blades, stained with the blood of five men, were washed in the waters of Pottawatomie Creek. But there remained more important evidence of the crime to be effaced before the gang could confront the world again. Before dawn they were in possession, not of the murdered men's horses, but of fast running horses brought to them and exchanged by their confederates. The terms of the transaction will never be known. The sons who survived John Brown even denied for years his presence on the Pottawatomie on the night of May 25. When the truth was out at last and the world had prepared a motive — a motive which would fit the martyr — there were confessions from the sons. The world had justified the murderer; the Browns knew that it is a little more difficult to justify a horse thief. When daylight came the evidence was gone, for the stolen horses were well on their way north to be sold.

The stooped but still rigid old man[10] with his neat rural dress, his talk about bayonets and bullets and God's will, his immense awkward dignity, immense egotism, his white beard and hard grey-blue eyes which glittered, as one host put it, with a "little touch of insanity," moved impressively about the albums and pleasant china of those New England parlors. Most of the people who sat about him in those parlors, and gave their earnest attention to his words, found something peculiarly congenial to their own prejudices and beliefs. Captain Brown was a "higher law man." He was "superior to any legal tradition" — just as most of these people felt themselves to be — and if he claimed to have a divine commission, they could understand what he meant, for they too were privy to God. The Southerner pointed to the Constitution and said: "There is the law and the bargain; keep them and give us justice." Garrison[11] burned the Constitution and said it was a "covenant with Hell" and many other countrymen of his, if they were not ready to do this, could still call on conscience and the higher law. Unhappily, a corollary of this divine revelation was to make the South pay, and pay again. The disagreement might conceivably have been settled under terms of law, but when it was transposed into terms of theology there was no hope of settlement. There is only one way to conclude a theological argument: bayonets and bullets. And in that last appeal God's hand reached down to prove the "higher law men" perfectly right; as events demonstrated, God was, obviously, not on the side of the South. By the same logic, it may be added, God was not, personally, on the side of John Brown.

Certainly John Brown was not normal — whatever that may mean. His egotism, his enormous force of will, his power of endurance, his deliberate cruelties, his deliberate charities, his intolerance, his merciless ambition, and the element of religious fanaticism which worked regularly as a device of self-justification —

[10] Warren is referring in this passage to John Brown's appearances in the homes of wealthy eastern supporters.

[11] Massachusetts's leading abolitionist, William Lloyd Garrison.

all these things made up an intensity of nature which appeared, beyond doubt, as abnormal. The issue of responsibility remains, and, pragmatically, it is not begging the question to say that John Brown was as responsible for his actions as are the general run of criminals who have suffered similar penalties; that is another problem.

Wise[12] said that John Brown was more sane than his prompters and promoters; certainly he was more intelligent and stronger. If he were insane it is a grave criticism of Sanborn[13] and the other conspirators, and they must assume a horrible weight of responsibility for the whole affair. Sanborn's belief in divinely confirmed missions, especially in his own and John Brown's missions, his absolute certainty that he was right, his irrationality, and his peculiar romanticism give some color to the charge made by Governor Wise; the difference is that Sanborn lacked John Brown's courage and strength, and that difference made the sum total of his other qualities equivalent simply to a habit of rhetoric and a sort of snobbery. If Sanborn had acted out his professions he also might have been called a fanatic. Parker and Higginson were at the same time more rational, more courageous, more intelligent, and stronger than Sanborn, and they were never so well pleased with themselves. As for poor old Gerrit Smith,[14] he went to a lunatic asylum on November 7, 1859.

[12] Governor Henry A. Wise of Virginia, who oversaw Brown's trial and execution.
[13] One of the "Secret Six" abolitionists who funded Brown's attack on Harpers Ferry.
[14] Parker, Higginson, and Smith were all other members of the Secret Six.

3   *John Brown, Abolitionist,* by David S. Reynolds, 2005

David S. Reynolds, a professor at the City University of New York, is a leading scholar of American literature and history of the antebellum era. Before writing about John Brown, he published an award-winning biography of Walt Whitman, a nineteenth-century American poet. The selection below reflects a twenty-first-century perspective on Brown informed by the September 11, 2001, terrorist attacks on the United States.

A crucial question remains: How could John Brown square murder[1] with his religious faith? He was, after all, a Christian, and most Abolitionists of his day used Christianity to endorse pacifism, not violence. Even if we say that Kansas was in a state of war, how could he, as a Christian, commit what amounted to a war crime?

[1] Reynolds is discussing the Pottawatomie murders in this passage.
Source: David S. Reynolds, *John Brown, Abolitionist: The Man Who Killed Slavery, Sparked the Civil War, and Seeded Civil Rights* (New York: Alfred A. Knopf, 2005), 164–67, 502, 503.

By mid-May 1856 the events in Kansas and on the national scene made the Old Testament God of Battles seem more relevant to him than the New Testament's Prince of Peace. In this sense he followed the example of his greatest hero among white Christians, Oliver Cromwell.[2]

. . . The most positive way to view Cromwell's and Brown's crimes is to regard them as what Doris Lessing[3] calls "good terrorism"—that is, terrorism justified by obvious social injustice. Terrorism is violence that avoids combat, is used against the defenseless (often civilians), and is intended to shock and horrify, with the aim of bringing about social change. Cromwell's massacres in Ireland and Brown's Pottawatomie murders may qualify as terrorism on these counts.

It might be argued that excessive force in each case challenged real social injustice: centuries of oppressive British royalty in Cromwell's case and the twin horrors of chattel slavery and Southern violence in Brown's. Just as the populists of late czarist Russia, to whom John Brown was compared in the nineteenth century, are sometimes called "good" terrorists because they envisioned a free, nonviolent society, so Brown is open to a sympathetic interpretation because he used violence in order to create a society devoid of slavery and racism.

Choice of victims is a consideration in gauging whether terrorism is "good." Wholesale slaughter of numerous innocents, as in the September 11, 2001, attack on the World Trade Center, resists this affirmative reading.

Was Brown justified in his choice of victims at Pottawatomie Creek? The most extreme statement he was known to have made on the topic was his declaration to the Free State settler James Hanway that he "proposed to sweep the creek . . . of all the proslavery men on it." If this statement accurately describes Brown's intentions, it avoids the stigma of indiscriminate killing, but just barely. It specifies its victims by politics ("proslavery") and by gender ("men"): but the phrase "sweep the creek" sounds arbitrary, as though he were out to kill any political enemy he could find in the area. If, however, Pottawatomie was a response to long- and short-term proslavery outrages waged against carefully selected targets, it becomes less random and thus more defensible.

Brown's sons Jason and John Jr. insisted that their father did not go on an unsystematic murder spree but instead chose his victims, who were active in proslavery politics and had challenged the Browns personally. As mentioned, three of the victims—James P. Doyle, his son William Doyle, and Allen Wilkinson—had served at the proslavery hearing of Judge Cato, who had issued warrants for the arrest of the Browns. Another victim, William Sherman, was part of the family whose tavern at Dutch Henry's Crossing was the local center for proslavery activities, including Cato's trial. William's brutish brother Henry Sherman had threatened to lynch a merchant who sold lead to Jason Brown.

[2] Leader of the English Civil Wars (1641–1649), responsible for the execution of King Charles I and many atrocities committed by his troops against his opponents in Ireland.

[3] A British writer best known for works sympathetic to the cause of Africans and other indigenous peoples suffering under colonial rule.

The idea that "one man's terrorist is another man's freedom fighter" is no less true now than it was in Brown's day. For some ardent foes of abortion, Paul Hill,[4] who claimed to follow Brown, was a hero. Others thought that Timothy McVeigh[5] carried out justice—Gore Vidal,[6] for instance, disgusted by what he saw as an oppressive American government, compared McVeigh not only to Brown but also to Paul Revere, spreading the alarm that "The Feds are coming, the Feds are coming." Some militant Muslims, appalled by what they regarded as the decadence and corrupt imperialism of the United States, applauded bin Laden's[7] destruction of the World Trade Center. In this sense, contemporary terrorists are no different from Brown, deified by some and demonized by others.

Still, it is misleading to identify Brown with modern terrorists. Actually, Brown would have disapproved of the use of violence by most of those who have proclaimed themselves as his heirs. It is important to recognize that many of the social ills that later bred radical violence plagued the nation in his time, but he went to war only over the issue of slavery. . . .

Why? Because slavery was a uniquely immoral institution that seemed cemented in place by law, custom, and prejudice. Bad economic times came and went. The status of women promised to change. Native Americans, although horribly mistreated, still had a measure of freedom. City conditions were improving as technology progressed. But slavery, the "sum of all evils," was there to stay, at least for the foreseeable future. And slavery was qualitatively different from all other social issues, since it deprived millions of their rights as Americans and their dignity as human beings. No other social phenomenon approached it wickedness. No other problem, Brown believed, called for the use of arms.

Brown had a breadth of vision that modern terrorists lack. He was an *American* terrorist in the amplest sense of the word. He was every bit as religious as Osama bin Laden—but was the Muslim bin Laden able to enlist Christians, atheists, or Jews among his followers? The Calvinistic Brown, reflecting the religious toleration of his nation, counted Jews, liberal Christians, spiritualists, and agnostics among his most devoted soldiers. Bin Laden's ultimate goal was the creation of a Muslim theocracy in which opposing views, especially Western ones, were banned. Brown's goal was a democratic society that assigned full rights to all, irrespective of religious, race, or gender.

[4] Paul Hill was convicted of murdering an abortion provider and executed in 2003.

[5] Timothy McVeigh was convicted of the 1995 Oklahoma City bombing and executed in 2001.

[6] American novelist and journalist.

[7] Osama bin Laden, leader of Al Qaeda.

Analyzing Biographies

1. Briefly summarize how each author describes Brown's motives and methods as an abolitionist. How does each describe Brown's accomplices, supporters, victims, and enemies?

2. Which authors are most similar in their interpretations of Brown? Which author differs the most from the others in his treatment of Brown? Considering what you know about the authors of these biographies and the times in which they wrote, what biases do you think they brought to their work, and where do you see evidence of those biases in these selections?

3. One of these selections refers to Brown as a "terrorist"; do you agree with that assessment? How does Reynolds apply his distinction between bad terrorism and good terrorism to Brown's actions, and do you agree with his conclusion in this regard?

4. The sources in this chapter are from much longer biographies of John Brown. On the basis of the excerpts you have read here, which of these works would you like to read in its entirety? Why?

5. In the concluding pages of his biography of John Brown, DuBois wrote, "Was John Brown simply an episode, or was he an eternal truth? And if a truth, how speaks that truth today?" In light of what you have learned about Brown, how would you answer these questions? What was Brown's significance in 1859, and what is his significance to us today?

The Rest of the Story

John Brown remained as controversial in death as he had been in life. Even before his death at the gallows on the morning of December 2, 1859, he was being ushered into heaven by some and condemned to hell by others. Henry David Thoreau, the New England philosopher and writer who had strong antislavery convictions but generally found abolitionists a tiresome, sanctimonious lot, eulogized Brown while he was still among the living. In "A Plea for Captain John Brown," read before the citizens of Concord, Massachusetts, on October 30, Thoreau compared his subject to the crucified Christ, called him "the most American of us all," and concluded, "He is not Old Brown any longer; he is an angel of light." Other leading intellectuals and reformers of the North chimed in—Henry Ward Beecher, Ralph Waldo Emerson, William Lloyd Garrison—to praise Brown as a man of conviction and action, a martyr whose sacrifice had forced the nation to recognize the sin of slavery.

From the South came protests that Northerners were using their presses and pulpits to make a hero of a man who had committed treason and murder. On the floor of the Senate, Mississippi senator Jefferson Davis voiced the belief of many slaveholders when he accused his Republican colleagues of conspiring with Brown to "wage violent, irreconcilable, eternal warfare upon the institution of American slavery, with the view of its ultimate extinction throughout the land." On the campaign trail, Republican presidential candidate Abraham Lincoln felt it necessary to answer Davis's charge by stating blankly, "John Brown was no Republican," only a deluded man who "fancied himself commissioned by Heaven" to free the slaves.

Five years later, Lincoln might have reconsidered those words when he drafted his Second Inaugural Address. With more blood spilled in the act of ending slavery than Brown or anyone else could have imagined in 1859, Lincoln struggled to make sense of the war that had torn the country apart. He ended up using the same biblical language that Brown had used to explain his actions: God wills it. Lincoln told his countrymen that God had given the war to North and South alike as punishment for their complicity in slavery. Everyone had hoped for a less destructive end to slavery, but if God willed it to continue until "every drop of blood drawn with the lash, shall be paid by another drawn with the sword, as was said three thousand years ago, so still it must be said, 'the judgments of the Lord, are true and righteous altogether.'" John Brown, if he could have heard these words, would have answered with a simple "Amen."

To Find Out More

Primary sources, maps, and other documents and images relevant to John Brown and the raid on Harpers Ferry can be found online at "John Brown and the Valley of the Shadow" at **www3.iath.virginia.edu/jbrown/master.html**. This Web site is part of a larger digital archive sponsored by the University of Virginia that offers a wealth of opportunities for research on the Civil War, "The Valley of the Shadow: Two Communities in the American Civil War," at **valley.vcdh.virginia.edu**.

Besides those featured in this chapter, there are several other notable biographies of John Brown. Oswald Garrison Villard's *John Brown, A Biography, Fifty Years After* (Boston: Houghton Mifflin Company, 1910) was based on thorough historical research and treated its subject sympathetically. It was followed a few years later by Hill Peebles Wilson, *John Brown, Soldier of Fortune* (Lawrence, Kans.: H. P. Wilson, 1913), which set the tone for all subsequent biographies that condemned Brown as a murderous psychopath. Stephen Oates's *To Purge This Land with Blood: A Biography of John Brown* (New York: Harper and Row, 1970) is still widely read and highly regarded as a work of historical scholarship. More recently, Brown's legacy as an abolitionist and catalyst for the Civil War has been reassessed in John Stauffer, *The Black Hearts of Men: Radical Abolitionists and the Transformation of Race* (Cambridge, Mass.: Harvard University Press, 2001); Merrill Peterson, *John Brown: The Legend Revisited* (Charlottesville: University Press of Virginia, 2002); and Peggy A. Russo and Paul Finkelman, editors, *Terrible Swift Sword: The Legacy of John Brown* (Athens: Ohio University Press, 2005). For a fictional treatment of John Brown, see Russell Banks, *Cloudsplitter: A Novel* (New York: Harper, 1998).

CHAPTER 13

The Illustrated Civil War

Photographers on the Battlefield

On September 17, 1862, Union and Confederate armies collided in the small western Maryland town of Sharpsburg. The ensuing Battle of Antietam, named after a nearby creek where much of the action took place, was the bloodiest day of the Civil War. Seventy-five thousand Union troops, led by General George B. McClellan, suffered more than 12,000 casualties. The Confederate army of 52,000 men, led by General Robert E. Lee, suffered almost 14,000 casualties. Put another way, the combined armies of the Union and Confederacy experienced an astounding 20 percent casualty rate: one in five soldiers was either killed, wounded, or missing in action by the end of the day.

The Battle of Antietam was nominally a victory for McClellan because Lee's troops withdrew from the field first. In Washington, D.C., President Abraham Lincoln had been hoping for news of a decisive Union victory to prime public opinion for the Emancipation Proclamation and to improve Republican fortunes in the upcoming congressional election. Instead, Lincoln grew incensed when McClellan failed to pursue Lee's badly damaged army as it retreated into Virginia. His patience worn thin by McClellan's constant foot-dragging, Lincoln traveled to the Antietam battlefield to discuss the matter in person. In a letter to his wife about that meeting, Lincoln noted, "General McClellan and myself are to be photographed . . . if we can be still long enough. I feel General McClellan should have no problem." A few weeks later, Lincoln relieved McClellan of his command.

Lincoln and McClellan did indeed pose for a battlefield portrait (see Source 4 on p. 287), but their photographer took some other pictures as well. About one month after the battle, its horrible cost was brought home to the American public when Mathew Brady opened an exhibit at his New York City gallery of photographs taken at Sharpsburg. Brady and other photographers had been taking pictures related to the war since it had commenced in early 1861, but those were mostly portraits of soldiers. What was different about Brady's Antietam exhibit was the inclusion of images of corpses, horribly twisted, mangled, and bloated from the summer sun, strewn across the fields of Sharpsburg. In a review published on October 20, 1862, the *New York Times* praised Brady for his realism:

> Mr. Brady has done something to bring home to us the terrible reality and earnestness of war. If he has not brought bodies and laid them in our door-yards and along the streets, he has done something very like it. At the door of his gallery hangs a little placard, "The Dead of Antietam." Crowds of people are constantly . . . bending over photographic views of that fearful battle-field, taken immediately after the action. . . . There is a terrible fascination about it that draws one near these pictures, and makes him lo[a]th to leave them. You will see hushed, reverend groups standing around these weird copies of carnage, bending down to look in the pale faces of the dead, chained by the strange spell that dwells in dead men's eyes.

Ironically, Brady had not taken any of the photographs that he exhibited in his gallery that October. Although his name had become synonymous with photography in America during the 1850s, his poor eyesight meant that he rarely operated the cameras that made him famous. Instead, Brady hired and trained others to do much of the work associated with the photographs published under his name. The Antietam images were taken by Alexander Gardner, who managed a gallery owned by Brady in Washington, D.C. A few months before the Battle of Antietam, Gardner joined General McClellan's staff as its official photographer. This appointment enabled him to travel with the army and to photograph battlefields immediately before and after action took place. It was this sort of inside access that gave his Antietam photographs the stunning immediacy and realism that entranced the crowds in Brady's gallery.

Gardner's Antietam photographs were a tremendous commercial success, but Gardner was not pleased that Brady published them without giving him credit. The two men parted ways a few months later and became commercial rivals for the rest of the war, with Gardner working out of his own gallery in Washington, D.C. (see Figure 13.1). Brady, who had made his name in the 1850s as the photographer of the nation's leading citizens, continued to publish photographs of famous figures and landmarks associated with the war. In the meantime, Gardner led a new wave of photographers who focused their work on images of wartime destruction: battlefield dead, blasted buildings, and landscapes transformed by the hard hand of war.

Photographers such as Brady and Gardner produced a rich visual record of the Civil War. Previous wars had been photographed: military portraits and landscapes date to the Mexican-American War (1846–1848) and the British-Russian Crimean War (1854–1856). Both of those conflicts, however, occurred when the technology of photography was in its infancy, and their battlefields

Figure 13.1 Photographer Unknown, "Gardner's Gallery" *This undated photograph shows what the exterior of an urban photographer's gallery looked like. Note the billboards advertising the different types of photographs and photographic services available, as well as the prominent advertisement for "Views of the War."* Source: Library of Congress, Prints and Photographs Division, LC-BH837-207.

were far removed from the cities where photographers worked. The Civil War was different in two significant ways. First, the war's eastern theater of operations was close to urban centers such as Washington, D.C., that already had a commercial photography industry. Second, the consumer market for photographs in the United States had expanded exponentially during the 1850s because of technological improvements that made photographs affordable to just about everyone. Photographs had been a novelty of the well-to-do in the 1840s; by 1860, they were knit into the fabric of American culture, thanks in part to the relentless innovation and promotion of entrepreneurs such as Mathew Brady and Alexander Gardner.

Photography had a profound impact on how Americans experienced the Civil War. As the review of Brady's Antietam exhibit indicates, photography brought the violence and destruction of the battlefield to the doorsteps of the American public and elicited a strong emotional response, even from people far removed from the fighting. Photographers such as Brady and Gardner cultivated their reputations as the war's most accurate and impartial observers, describing their work as a visual record unvarnished by sentimentality or political bias. They also turned the war into a commodity available for purchase. Their claims to rendering the war in objective, unfiltered truthfulness must be weighed against their efforts to market the war for public consumption in a way that suited their own commercial and artistic purposes.

Using the Source: Civil War Photographs

In 1860, there were more than 3,000 photographers working in the United States. During the Civil War, they took tens of thousands of pictures of military subjects: individual and group portraits of soldiers, scenes of camp life and field hospitals, battlefield and city landscapes, railroad depots, fortifications, and shipyards. In order to use these images as a source, you must first familiarize yourself with the history, technology, and terminology of nineteenth-century photography.

The age of photography began with the invention of the daguerreotype in the late 1830s. Named for one of its inventors, Jacques Mandé Daguerre, the daguerreotype was a fixed image produced on a silver-coated copper plate. Shortly after Daguerre introduced his invention in Europe, Samuel F. B. Morse brought the technology to America, where he taught the craft to several students, including Mathew Brady. Daguerreotypists opened studios in U.S. cities during the 1840s, drawing as their customers members of the urban middle and upper classes, who sat for their portraits individually, with their children, or as married couples. A successful daguerreotypist ran a kind of factory, keeping a public gallery/reception area where he displayed samples of his work to attract customers, a studio where he posed his subjects, and backrooms where craftsmen prepared and developed his plates and fit them into handsomely ornamented frames for display at home. As one of many daguerreotypists in New York competing for business, Brady built his reputation by photographing famous politicians, authors, and actors, styling himself the "national historian," and publishing *The Gallery of Illustrious Americans*, an illustrated book based on his daguerreotypes, in 1850.

The next great leap in photography's development came in the mid-1850s with the invention of the wet-plate process. Unlike the daguerreotype, which was a one-time, nonreproducible image, the wet-plate process used glass plates immersed in a solution of photosensitive chemicals to produce negative images from which "positive" paper copies could be made, much like the way negatives from camera film work today. The wet-plate process expanded the market for photography, making possible mass-produced copies and enlargements suitable for exhibit or sale. Two important product innovations based on this improved technology occurred in the years just before the Civil War. The stereograph was a double image produced by fitting two lenses on a single camera. When viewed through a stereoscope, a handheld device that could be purchased from a photographer's studio, it produced a three-dimensional effect. Stereoscopes helped turn the viewing of photographs into a leisure activity that could occur in every home. The carte-de-visite was a small print made by fitting four lenses onto one camera, which produced four identical images on a single plate. Prints from such a negative, when cut into quarters, were used as calling cards. Brady led the way in marketing them as collector's cards (sometimes called album cards), selling cartes-de-visite of famous figures in numbered series much like baseball cards are sold and collected today.

Paper reproduction in such formats made photographs available to even working-class folk. A portrait-size print might cost $1.50, a stereoscope 50 cents, and a carte-de-visite only 25 cents. When Union and Confederate armies mobilized in 1861, soldiers in uniform rushed to have their portraits taken as souvenirs of their service or as keepsakes for loved ones at home. The vast majority of the tens of thousands of Civil War photographs fall into this category. Once photographers realized the demand that the war was creating for their services, they expanded their work to include other subjects that they thought might turn a profit.

What Can Civil War Photographs Tell Us?

The most obvious advantage to using such photographs as a historical source was one immediately realized by the government and military. Photography made possible the recording and communication of visual information with much greater speed and detail. Armies had long relied on sketch artists to record useful information about the scene of battle. During the Civil War, generals added photographers to their staffs so that they could make images of fortifications, bridges, railroads, and natural landmarks, not to mention portraits of themselves as they sallied forth into history. Military photographers also aided in the reproduction of maps. Ever since, historians have used these images to reconstruct the military history of the war, from engagements on rural battlefields like Antietam to scorched-earth attacks on cities such as Richmond and Charleston.

Cultural and social historians find many advantages to working with these photographs as well. How people create visual images of war tells us much about the values and emotions they associate with it. Paintings, drawings, and photographs of battlefields are as much attempts to create meaning out of the violence and death of warfare as are letters home, diary entries, or memoirs. Before the invention of photography, the visual record of American warfare was usually created by painters who worked long after the battle raged. John Trumbull was the most famous battle scene painter of the American Revolution, and the federal government commissioned his work for the new nation's Capitol in the early nineteenth century. Compare his *Death of General*

George Washington leading the Continental Army forward

Compare Mercer's facial expression with that of the dead soldier in the foreground of O'Sullivan's image

Mercer dies in close proximity to the enemy, witnessing the tide of battle around him

Mercer at the Battle of Princeton, New Jersey, 3 January 1777 (above) with the most famous photograph from the Gettysburg battlefield, Timothy O'Sullivan's "A Harvest of Death, Gettysburg, Pennsylvania" (on p. 279). Both depict battlefield carnage, but convey very different messages to their viewers.

Trumbull's painting, which he started ten years after the Battle of Princeton took place, makes Mercer's death heroic: he dies with sword in one hand, his other hand grasping the bayonet that will deliver his fatal wound. He literally stares death in the face, gazing directly into the eyes of his adversary. The worth of his sacrifice is evident by the action occurring behind him. While Mercer dies, General George Washington leads the Continental Army forward to victory.

Now consider O'Sullivan's 1863 photograph "A Harvest of Death," which he took two days after the fighting at Gettysburg had ceased. Corpses litter the battlefield to the horizon. Their horrible disfiguration is most evident on the figure in the foreground, whose mouth gapes open and whose face, stomach, and hands have bloated in the process of decomposing. Off in the distance, a

The photo's title, "A Harvest of Death," calls to mind the fields on which the battle took place and invokes popular images of the Grim Reaper

Compare the shadowy figure on horseback to Washington's figure in Trumbull's painting

No evidence here that these dead soldiers ever saw the faces of their enemy

figure shrouded in mist appears on horseback, but this is not the confident commanding officer of Trumbull's painting. Rather, it is a ghostly presence surveying the battlefield, a Grim Reaper–like figure come to collect his harvest. Unlike Trumbull's painting, this photograph shows no evidence that these soldiers died in hand-to-hand combat or ever stared into their enemies' eyes. They are as anonymous as they are lifeless. This image, one of the most widely reproduced battlefield photographs of the war, challenges the notions of military sacrifice and valor celebrated in Trumbull's painting. It testifies to the crisis that the massive casualties of the Civil War caused in the traditional values nineteenth-century Americans associated with military service.

Studying these photographs also reveals much about how civilians experienced the war. Photographers such as Brady and Gardner sold prints of their work almost as quickly as they made them, constructing a history of the war for public consumption while the conflict was still under way. Stereographs brought the war into the home for viewing the same way television does today, and cartes-de-visite made celebrities out of political and military leaders of the war. By studying the arrangement of photographs in private collections or in the catalogs that advertised them for sale, historians can recover the civilian effort to interpret the war, to make sense of the brutality and destruction the war unleashed.

One disadvantage of working with Civil War photographs is that there was no "blanket coverage" of the war by photographers. Their work favored the North and East at the expense of the South and West. The photography industry in the Confederacy all but collapsed after 1861 as the economic privations of the war increased. Also, the further removed the scene of battle was from eastern urban centers, the less likely it was to be photographed. Antietam and Gettysburg were the most thoroughly photographed battlefields of the war. Not coincidentally, both were within ninety miles of Washington, D.C., where Brady and Gardner had galleries. By contrast, little to no photographic evidence exists of many campaigns west of the Appalachian Mountains.

Another disadvantage to bear in mind when looking at Civil War photographs is the technological limits on photographing battles as they occurred. Cameras had to be mounted on tripods and required exposure time measured in minutes rather than a fraction of a second. Photographers had to bring all of their equipment into the field within darkrooms on wheels, because the glass plates had to be prepared, exposed, and developed in one continuous process, before their chemical coating dried and rendered them useless. As one historian of nineteenth-century photography has noted, these technical limitations meant that we have many "before" and "after" images of Civil War battlefields but no "during," because the photographers and their equipment were not mobile enough to capture the actual battles.

The chief disadvantage to working with Civil War photographs is that the photographers manipulated their subjects, dead as well as living, for commercial purposes. Brady, Gardner, and their peers were businessmen, and they took pictures that they thought would sell. If they could increase sales by posing their subjects in a particular manner, they did not hesitate to do so. Then and now, people invoked the phrase "the camera never lies" to emphasize the impartiality and truthfulness of photography. Knowing something about how Civil War photographs were made, however, should dissuade you from taking that adage too literally when dealing with this source. Of course, when soldiers, officers, and civic leaders posed for their portraits, they assumed postures and carried props meant to broadcast their bravery, leadership, or virtue. But because of the long exposure time required for early photographs, even less formal scenes of camp life or field hospitals had to be carefully arranged by their photographers. One might assume that photographs of corpses on the battlefield were the least posed of the photographer's subjects, but Gardner and his associates moved bodies, added props, and altered backgrounds to achieve the effect they desired.

Questions to Ask

Like any other source, you should begin your analysis of a photograph by asking basic questions about where, when, and how it was produced. Is there a caption or citation that identifies the photographer or the time and place it was taken? If not, does the image itself provide any clues (for example, military uniforms, weaponry, landmarks) that would help you answer these questions? Once you know as much as you can about the photograph's origins, you can turn your attention to its meaning. What did the photographer want to convey in this image? What are the photograph's subjects trying to convey in their poses or props? If you remember that every Civil War photograph was posed in the sense that its creator and subjects went through a long, complicated process to produce it, then you will be less likely to assume that the camera presented an unfiltered representation of reality. Finally, turn your attention to the photograph's viewer: Who do you think saw this image, and how do you think it shaped their experience of the war?

- Where, when, and by whom was the photograph taken?
- Who or what is the photograph's subject?
- What are the photographer and subject(s) trying to convey?
- What do these images tell you about the way Americans experienced the Civil War?

Source Analysis Table

The table on pages 282–283 will help you record your impressions of the photographs you will examine in the next section.

Photograph	What Is the Subject Matter of This Photograph?	What Information, Ideas, or Emotions Are the Photographer and/or Subjects Trying to Convey?	How Do You Think the Photograph Influenced Its Viewers' Experience of the War?
MILITARY PORTRAITS			
1. Lieut. Washington and Capt. Custer			
2. Gen. Potter and Staff			
3. Portrait of a Soldier Group			
4. Lincoln at Antietam			
BATTLEFIELD LANDSCAPES AND CITYSCAPES			
5. Gettysburg			
6. Ruins of Charleston			
AFRICAN AMERICANS IN MILITARY LIFE			
7. Brig. Gen. McLaughlin			
8. Culpeper Contrabands			
9. African American Soldiers and Officers			

Photograph	What Is the Subject Matter of This Photograph?	What Information, Ideas, or Emotions Are the Photographer and/or Subjects Trying to Convey?	How Do You Think the Photograph Influenced Its Viewers' Experience of the War?
BATTLEFIELD DEAD			
10. Antietam, Bodies for Burial			
11. A Contrast			
12. He Sleeps His Last Sleep			
13. Body of Soldier in the Wheat Field			
14. Field Where General Reynolds Fell			
15. Fort Mahone, Petersburgh, Va.			
16. Cold Harbor, Va.			

To download and print this table, visit the book companion site at **bedfordstmartins.com/brownshannon.**

The Source: Photographs of Civil War Battlefields and Military Life, 1861–1866

MILITARY PORTRAITS

Many soldiers posed in uniform for formal portraits before they left home. Photographers also brought their cameras to military camps near battlefields, to capture armies at work.

1   *James F. Gibson, "Lieut. Washington, a Confederate Prisoner, and Capt. Custer, U.S.A.," 1862*

This photograph, published in one of Alexander Gardner's catalogs, has an interesting history. Confederate lieutenant James Barroll Washington (left) was taken prisoner during McClellan's Peninsula Campaign in Virginia. Captain George Armstrong Custer (right), a Union officer who would achieve fame at Gettysburg a year later (and a different kind of notoriety at Little Big Horn in 1876), was an old friend of Washington's. Upon finding the two chatting amiably, James Gibson decided to photograph them. Washington called out for a young African American boy to join them. An illustration based on this image subsequently appeared in *Harper's Weekly* under the title "Both Sides, the Cause."

Source: Library of Congress, Prints and Photographs Division.

2   *Mathew Brady, "Gen. Robert B. Potter and Staff of Seven, Recognized Capt. Gilbert H. McKibben, Capt. Wright, A.A.G. Also Mr. Brady, Photographer,"* c. 1863

Brady owed his reputation in the 1850s to photographing famous people, so it is not surprising that during the war, he devoted much of his work on the battlefield to taking pictures of officers and their staffs. A relentless self-promoter, he also had a penchant for inserting himself into his own work. General Potter is the bareheaded figure at the center of this image. Brady, in civilian clothes, leans against a tree to the right.

Source: National Archives and Records Administration.

3

Photographer Unknown, "Portrait of a Soldier Group," c. 1861–1865

Soldiers often posed for portraits, either individually or in groups. Sometimes, as one soldier does here, they posed with weapons as well. Note that two of the figures in this portrait are holding hands, a sign of intimacy that although rare in such photographs was not scandalous either.

Source: Library of Congress, Prints and Photographs Division, LC-B8184-10694 DLC (b&w film copy neg.).

4 | *Alexander Gardner, "President Lincoln on Battle-Field of Antietam,"* 1862

Gardner took this photograph when President Lincoln traveled to Antietam in October 1862 to confer with General McClellan. McClellan is to the left of Lincoln, standing in profile and facing the president. McClellan's staff forms an arc around the two figures.

Source: Amon Carter Museum, Fort Worth, Texas.

BATTLEFIELD LANDSCAPES AND CITYSCAPES

Photographers often took pictures of battlefield landscapes and cityscapes, juxtaposing civilian and military life or depicting the destructive effects of the war.

5 | Timothy O'Sullivan, "Pennsylvania, Gettysburg 07/1863," 1863

O'Sullivan worked with Gardner in photographing the Gettysburg battlefield. This image, taken from a hill south of the town's center, shows the small remnant of a military camp after most of the Union and Confederate forces had withdrawn. During the Civil War, many small towns saw their farms and fields occupied by armies that dwarfed the local population.

Source: National Archives and Records Administration.

6 | *George P. Barnard, "Ruins of Charleston, S.C.,"* 1866

Photographer George P. Barnard documented the devastating impact of war on the South. This image shows one of the South's greatest cities in ruins, with solitary human figures scattered about, contemplating the destruction.

Source: Beinecke Rare Book and Manuscript Library, Yale University.

AFRICAN AMERICANS IN MILITARY LIFE

African Americans, free and enslaved, worked on and near Civil War battlefields as soldiers and laborers. Slaves who ran away from their masters and sought refuge with the Union army were known
as "contrabands." Before the Emancipation Proclamation, they occupied a limbo between freedom
and slavery. Union officers did not have the legal authority to free them, but neither did they wish
to return them to their former homes, where their labor might benefit the Confederate war effort.
Many contrabands ended up in battlefield and camp photographs.

<table>
<tr><td>7</td><td>

Mathew Brady, "Portrait of Brig. Gen. Napoleon B. McLaughlin, Officer of the Federal Army, and Staff, Vicinity of Washington, D.C.," 1861

</td></tr>
</table>

This photograph from early in the war is typical of Brady's portraits of Union officers and their
staffs (see Source 2 in this chapter). Sometimes these portraits included African Americans, posed in
subservient positions to indicate their status as servants.

Source: Library of Congress, Prints and Photographs Division.

8   *Timothy O'Sullivan, "Culpeper, Va. 'Contrabands,'"* 1863

African Americans worked for Union and Confederate armies in a number of capacities. These two men are pictured outside of a cook's tent at a Union camp.

Source: Library of Congress, Prints and Photographs Division.

9 *Photographer Unknown, "African American Soldiers with Their Teachers and Officers,"* date unknown

Many African Americans, including contrabands, enlisted in the Union army and were photographed in uniform. These recruits posed with their white commanding officers and female teachers. Instead of bearing arms, the recruits hold books.

Source: Library of Congress, Prints and Photographs Division.

BATTLEFIELD DEAD

Battlefield dead made up only a tiny fraction of Civil War photographs, but they became some of the most enduring visual images of the war. To take them, a photographer had to arrive on the battlefield before corpses were buried, usually within two days of the fighting. Gardner's and O'Sullivan's photographs from Antietam and Gettysburg are the most famous of this category, but equally powerful ones were taken after other battles in the war's eastern theater, including Cold Harbor and Petersburg, both in Virginia.

| 10 | *Alexander Gardner, "Antietam, Md. Bodies of Dead Gathered for Burial,"* 1862 |

This image, one of the Antietam series exhibited in Mathew Brady's New York gallery, presents a line of corpses arranged as if in formation. No single soldier is identified; they appear as an anonymous mass. The line running across the photograph is from a crack in the original glass plate.

Source: Library of Congress, Prints and Photographs Division.

11 Alexander Gardner, "A Contrast. Federal Buried; Confederate Unburied, Where They Fell on the Battle Field of Antietam," 1862

This is a stereograph of one of Gardner's Antietam photographs. It juxtaposes the marked grave of Union officer John A. Clark with the unburied corpse of an anonymous Confederate.

Source: Collection of the New-York Historical Society, id number ad18001.

Entered according to Act of Congress, in the year 1863, by Alex. Gardner, in the Clerk's Office of the District Court of the District of Columbia.

12 *Alexander Gardner, "He Sleeps His Last Sleep,"* 1862

As he did with the image shown in Source 11, Gardner sold stereographs and album cards of this Antietam photograph via his catalog. Unlike most of his other photographs of the dead from the Battle of Antietam, this one shows a single casualty far removed from any other fallen soldiers. Gardner's catalog caption for this image read: "A Confederate Soldier, who after being wounded, had evidently dragged himself to a little ravine on the hill-side, where he died."

Source: Collection of the New-York Historical Society, id number ad04002.

Entered according to Act of Congress, in the year 1864, by Alex. Gardner, in the Clerk's Office of the District Court of the District of Columbia.

13 *James F. Gibson, "Battlefield of Gettysburg—Body of a Soldier in 'the Wheat Field,' Evidently Killed by the Explosion of a Shell,"* 1863

Photographers manipulated their subjects, even dead ones, to achieve the desired effect. Gibson accompanied Gardner to Gettysburg to take photographs after the battle. In his catalog, Gardner described this anonymous soldier as a sharpshooter, but a sharpshooter would not have affixed a bayonet to his weapon. Also, by the time photographers reached battlefield corpses, their weapons had usually been collected by the victorious army or by scavengers. The weapon shown here is a "prop gun" placed there by Gibson or Gardner; it shows up in several of their Gettysburg photographs. The photographer has also placed an unexploded shell near the corpse's right knee to suggest the source of the horrible wound in the abdomen. It is more likely that a pig fed on the body shortly after death. The dismembered hand and canteen in the right foreground are also likely props.

Source: Library of Congress, Prints and Photographs Division.

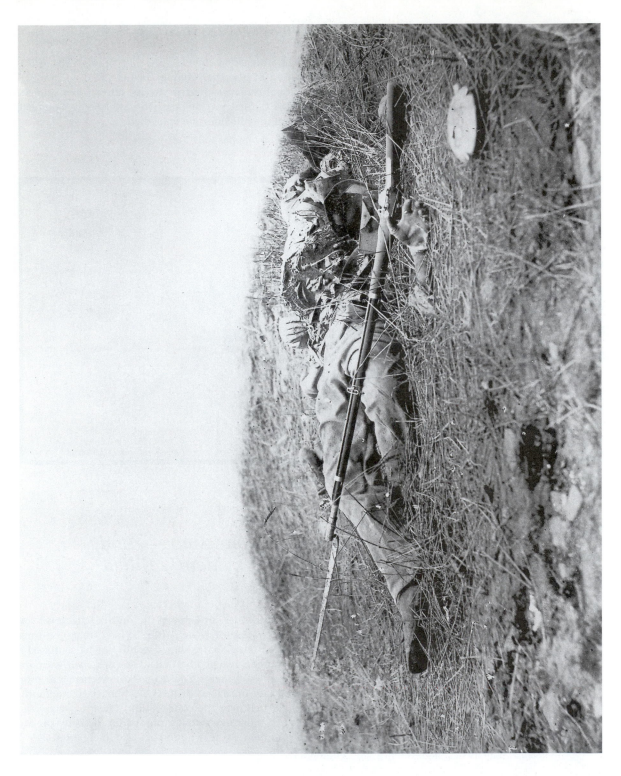

14   *Timothy O'Sullivan, "Field Where General Reynolds Fell, Gettysburg,"* 1863

This image from the Gettysburg battlefield stands in sharp contrast to the caption Gardner chose for it. Reynolds was the highest-ranking Union officer killed at Gettysburg and became in death one of the battle's heroes. This image offers no trace of Reynolds (in fact, he was killed in a wooded area), only anonymous, bloodied, and bloated corpses.

Source: Amon Carter Museum, Fort Worth, Texas.

15   *T. C. Roche, ". . . View of the Covered Ways inside the Rebel Fort Mahone, Called by the Soldiers 'Fort Damnation' . . . Taken the Morning after the Storming of Petersburgh, Va. 1865,"* 1865

T. C. Roche, a former cameraman for Mathew Brady, documented the Union army's assault on Petersburg, a vital railroad junction in Virginia, in April 1865. This stereographic image of a solitary Confederate soldier lying dead in one of the trenches built to defend the city anticipates the photographs that would document trench warfare in World War I. The spiked device in the foreground is a cheval-de-frise, a type of movable fortification designed to slow an enemy advance.

Source: Collection of the New-York Historical Society, id number ad41018.

16 | *John Reekie, "Cold Harbor, Va. African Americans Collecting Bones of Soldiers Killed in Battle,"* 1865

John Reekie was a cameraman for Alexander Gardner and worked with him documenting the final weeks of the war in Virginia in 1865. In this photograph, a burial party made up of African American males is collecting and interring the skeletal remains of soldiers who had died on the Cold Harbor battlefield almost a year earlier. The figures working in the background suggest that Reekie has captured them "in action," but bear in mind that the exposure time required for such a photograph would have meant that they were posed. Likewise, the skull on the far left appears to have been posed to stare directly at the photograph's viewer. The glass plate used to make this image has been damaged, as evidenced by the crack across the photograph and the missing shard on the right-hand side.

Source: Library of Congress, Prints and Photographs Division.

Analyzing Civil War Photographs

1. Overall, would you describe these photographs as critical of the war or supportive of it? Does your answer to this question vary if you ask it of individual groups of photographs (for example, "Military Portraits" or "African Americans in Military Life") rather than the entire lot?

2. How is death presented and interpreted in these photographs? How do the images challenge the notions of military glory and valor embodied in earlier military art such as Trumbull's *Death of General Mercer* (p. 278)? Compare the notes you took on Sources 10, 11, 14, and 16 with those you took on Sources 12, 13, and 15. What messages do you think photographers were trying to convey when they "posed" the dead either as individuals or in groups?

3. How do these photographs present African Americans and the role they played in the Civil War? Did the depiction of African Americans in these images change over time? How does that depiction compare to what you have learned about African Americans and slavery in earlier chapters?

4. Civil War photographers marketed their work to a civilian audience. What needs do you think these images fulfilled for the civilian population during and after the war? How might the visual record of the war have differed if the South had been able to sustain a photography industry as productive as the North's during the war?

5. Compare these images to the visual records you have seen of warfare in the twentieth and twenty-first centuries (for example, photographs, films, documentaries, newscasts). In what ways did the Civil War establish precedents for the ways in which our modern society uses visual images to transmit and document information from the battlefield for the civilian population?

The Rest of the Story

Some Civil War photographers collected the best of their work into albums for sale to the public. Gardner's two-volume *Gardner's Photographic Sketch Book of the Civil War* (first edition, 1865) offered a selection of one hundred of his most popular photographs, arranged to provide a chronological narrative of the war, but its $150 price tag put it far beyond the reach of most American consumers. Such collections had a limited reach because of their expense. For most people, their visual record of the Civil War remained a portrait of a soldier in uniform or a few stereographs or cartes-de-visite purchased from a catalog or at a photographer's gallery.

After the war, Gardner took his camera west to photograph the Union Pacific Railroad expedition of 1867, landscapes, and American Indians. He also pioneered the use of "mug shots," taking photographs of criminals for the police department of Washington, D.C. He died in 1882, leaving behind a reputation as one of the most innovative photographers of the nineteenth century.

Mathew Brady spent much of his career after the Civil War trying to sell off his collection of negatives so that he could lift himself out of debt. Always more of an impresario than an actual working photographer, he continued to live in a high style long after he could afford to do so, seeking out the celebrities who had made his early work famous. In 1872, Congress approved purchasing Brady's collection for $25,000. Despite this deal, he declared bankruptcy a few years later and spent much of the rest of his life shuttling between New York and Washington, D.C., trying to recover his solvency. He died in 1896, regarded as the Civil War's greatest photographer, even though he took very few of the pictures published under his name.

The work of Civil War photographers like Brady and Gardner marked the birth of photojournalism. For the first time, photographers used their craft to convey news of the world around them to a waiting public. The Civil War forever wedded the camera to the civilian experience of American warfare. During the war, the popular press had to rely on images reproduced from engravings, although many of those were based on photographs. By World War I, printing technology allowed for photographic reproductions in newspapers and magazines. During World War II, newsreel footage of Pacific and European battlefields brought the war home to Americans, but these images were heavily edited by the government to limit the public's exposure to the sort of carnage depicted in Civil War battlefield photographs. The Vietnam War was America's first televised war, and much of the public's discontent with that conflict can be traced to the images broadcast into American living rooms every night by photojournalists working half a world away. During the U.S.-Iraq War in 2003, the phrase "embedded journalist" entered the American lexicon, as reporters traveling with military personnel used digital technology to transmit war coverage to American televisions in real time. They are the modern descendants of Alexander Gardner and other Civil War photographers who attached themselves to military units so they could gain access to battlefields. In many respects, however, Gardner and his contemporaries enjoyed greater freedom in deciding what to report and how to publish it than military journalists do today. The camera may never lie, but the constant improvement in photographic technology since the 1860s does not necessarily mean that images produced by it today are any more truthful or complete than those produced during the Civil War.

To Find Out More

The two most significant collections of Civil War photographs may be found at the Library of Congress and the National Archives in Washington, D.C. Both of these institutions have Web sites that will introduce you to their collections and help you navigate them. The Library of Congress's "Selected Civil War Photographs" Web site is part of its American Memory project and is available at **memory.loc.gov/ammem/cwphtml/cwphome.html**. For the National

Archives, see *Pictures of the Civil War* under its "Research Room" Web site, available at **archives.gov/research/civil-war/photos/index.html**.

Many print resources are also available for researching and identifying Civil War photographs. A good place to start in this regard is the six-volume series published by the National Historical Society, *The Image of War* (Garden City, N.Y.: Doubleday, 1981–1984). Alexander Gardner's *Gardner's Photographic Sketch Book of the Civil War,* first published in 1865, is available in a modern edition published by Dover Publications of New York in 1959.

There are thousands of books that include reproductions of Civil War photographs, but few have the background information that will enable you to study them in a scholarly manner. A noteworthy study of Alexander Gardner's work is D. Mark Katz, *Witness to an Era: The Life and Photographs of Alexander Gardner* (Nashville, Tenn.: Rutledge Hill Press, 1991). Mary Panzer provides the same for Mathew Brady in *Mathew Brady and the Image of History* (Washington, D.C.: Smithsonian Institution Press, 1997). William Frassanito's studies of photographs associated with particular Civil War campaigns are based on superior historical detective work—see *Gettysburg: A Journey in Time* (New York: Charles Scribner's Sons, 1975); *Antietam: The Photographic Legacy of America's Bloodiest Day* (1978; repr., New York: Simon and Schuster, 1995); and *Grant and Lee: The Virginia Campaigns, 1864–65* (New York: Charles Scribner's Sons, 1983). For an excellent introduction to the cultural significance of photography in nineteenth-century America, see Alan Trachtenberg, *Reading American Photographs* (New York: Hill and Wang, 1989).

CHAPTER 14

Political Terrorism during Reconstruction

Congressional Hearings and Reports on the Ku Klux Klan

Elias Thomson was an old man in 1871. Born a slave in Spartanburg County, South Carolina, he had lived his entire life on the plantation of Dr. and Mrs. Vernon. When he gained his freedom in 1865, he continued to live there, farming land he rented from his former masters. Thomson's daily life after the war must have gone on much the same as it did before, but freedom did bring some opportunities he was anxious to seize, even at his advanced age. In particular, the ratification of the Fifteenth Amendment in March 1870 guaranteed him the right to vote. Thomson exercised that right in the fall of 1870, casting his ballot in the state and congressional elections for the Republican ticket.

Late one night the following May, a group of men disguised in hoods appeared on his doorstep. They dragged him from his home and told him to start praying, for "your time is short." When Thomson refused, they pointed pistols at his head and asked him, "Who did you vote for?" Thomson responded that he had voted for Claudius Turner, a neighbor whom he held in high esteem. The disguised men told him he had made the wrong choice and whipped him. They told Thomson to remain silent about what had happened and left him with a final warning: "We will have this country right before we get through."

Elias Thomson was one of many Southern men and women to suffer at the hands of the Ku Klux Klan between 1867 and 1871. In fact, his home in Spartanburg, South Carolina, was at the center of one of the most violent and prolonged outbreaks of Klan activity during Reconstruction. The Klan had first appeared there in 1868, using intimidation, arson, whippings, sexual assault, and murder to keep potential Republican voters away from the polls in that year's election. Despite such efforts, the state government remained in the hands of the Republicans, and the Klan temporarily receded as a public threat.

Klan violence rose again, however, with the next election in 1870 and became more intense as white and black Republicans tried to mobilize the vote. In addition to intimidation and physical assaults on potential black voters, Klansmen burned black churches, schools, and homes and murdered black men who had enrolled in the state militia. In several counties of the Carolina up-country, the inland piedmont region, where white and black populations were roughly equal or whites held a slight majority, the Klan conducted these crimes without fear of prosecution. Local sheriffs failed to make arrests, and if they did, white juries refused to render guilty verdicts. In some up-country counties, such as Spartanburg, state Republican officials estimated that practically all of the white adult male population belonged to the Klan or sympathized with it.

The Ku Klux Klan was of very recent origins in 1871 but had spread quickly throughout the former Confederate states. It was founded in 1867 by a group of Confederate veterans in Pulaski, Tennessee, who initially intended for it to be nothing more than a social club, similar in purpose and organization to the Freemasons and other secret fraternal orders popular with American males in the nineteenth century. Like the Freemasons, early Klan members created their own ritual, costume, and hierarchy from a mishmash of precedents in ancient mythology: the name "Ku Klux" was derived from the Greek word *kuklos*, meaning circle, and one of the titles in the organization was "Grand Cyclops," after the Greek mythological figure. As the Klan spread, however, it acquired a different purpose. In Tennessee and the Carolinas in 1868, local "dens" of the Klan began acting as vigilantes, calling themselves "regulators" or "night riders" who enforced law and order according to local custom rather than the dictates of the postwar state governments created by Congress and the Republican Party. Never a centralized organization to begin with, local Klansmen operated autonomously and rarely cooperated with one another beyond the county level. Regardless of that fragmentation, the primary targets of their terrorism remained the same: any blacks who challenged white supremacy by daring to vote, teach, or acquire land, and "carpetbaggers," white Northerners who came to the South after the war to seek their fortunes or to assume office in the Reconstruction state governments.

The violence and intimidation the Klan visited upon freedmen and -women and white Republicans seriously challenged the federal government's plans for the postwar South. After passing the Civil Rights Act of 1866, congressional Republicans had pegged their hopes for Reconstruction on enfranchising the former slaves as full and equal U.S. citizens. In this manner, the freedmen would become a core constituency for the Republican Party in the South and prevent the defeated Confederates from reassuming control of government and society there. The ratification of the Fourteenth Amendment in 1868 made this plan part of the Constitution by granting the freedmen and -women U.S. citizenship and guaranteeing them equal protection under the law. When some Southern states failed to extend their franchise to the freedmen, Republicans in Congress responded with the Fifteenth Amendment, which prohibited states from denying the right to vote to any citizen because of "race, color, or previous condition of servitude."

Republicans had great success in passing their legislative agenda for Reconstruction in Washington, D.C., but the enforcement of those laws in the South

Figure 14.1 Racial Violence in the Reconstruction South *The political cartoonist Thomas Nast condemns the Ku Klux Klan and other perpetrators of racial violence in this illustration from the magazine* Harper's Weekly. *At the center, a black couple kneeling under the words "Worse Than Slavery" cradles their dead child, while a schoolhouse burns and a lynched figure hangs in the background. A hooded Klansman and "White League" supporter clasp hands over their work. The federal government intervened by passing the Ku Klux Klan Act and launching a congressional investigation of racial violence in the South.* *Source:* Library of Cogress.

remained very much in question. The 20,000 federal troops stationed in the South in 1867 were not nearly enough to pacify regions such as the Carolina up-country, where the Klan was at its greatest strength. Furthermore, military officers were reluctant to assume control over matters of law enforcement without specific requests from civilian authorities to do so, lest they alienate the defeated Southern white population even further. As news of the Klan's expansion and pervasive influence in the South made its way to the nation's capital, Republican leaders agreed that further legislation to counteract it was necessary.

In a special message to Congress in December 1870, President Ulysses S. Grant noted that the Klan and similar organizations were using violence to prevent citizens from voting in the Southern states. Acting on a request he had received from the governor of North Carolina for assistance, he asked Congress to investigate the matter. Congress formed a committee to review affairs in North Carolina, and then in April 1871, it created another, much larger committee to expand the investigation into other states. This group, titled the Joint Select Committee to Inquire into the Condition of Affairs in the Late Insurrectionary States, was composed of seven senators and fourteen representatives, thirteen of whom were Republicans and eight of whom were Democrats.

At approximately the same time that it formed the Joint Select Committee to investigate the Klan, Congress also passed the Ku Klux Klan Act. This law gave the president the power to use federal troops and courts to protect the lives, property, and rights of U.S. citizens in the South. For the first time, crimes committed by private persons against other citizens became eligible for prosecution under federal rather than state law. Provisions included in the Ku Klux Klan Act effectively gave the president the ability to declare martial law in any state or region he deemed under Klan influence. The most controversial of these provisions concerned suspension of the writ of habeas corpus, a cornerstone of American civil liberties. The writ of habeas corpus protects citizens from unlawful imprisonment by requiring that any person placed under arrest be charged with a specific crime and placed on trial. By allowing the president to suspend it, Congress made it possible for suspected Klansmen to be jailed indefinitely. Many congressmen, even some Republicans, questioned the constitutionality of this provision and of the Ku Klux Klan Act in general, but the majority who supported the law believed the Klan could not be defeated without such a powerful weapon.

Congressmen formulated and debated this legislation in Washington while freedmen and -women in the South confronted the Klan face to face. Casting a ballot or even expressing an interest in voting could put a former slave's life in jeopardy. Those who joined militias, held office, or tried to improve their economic circumstances faced similar reprisals, while the promise of assistance from Washington must have seemed far off indeed. In 1871, a showdown was brewing between the Ku Klux Klan and the federal government that placed people like Elias Thomson squarely in the middle of the battle to determine Reconstruction's fate in the postwar South.

Using the Source: Congressional Hearings and Reports

The Joint Select Committee undertook one of the most far-reaching congressional investigations ever conducted up to that time. During the summer and fall of 1871, it heard testimony from witnesses in Washington, D.C., and sent subcommittees to interview witnesses throughout the South. Most of its work was concentrated on North Carolina and South Carolina, where the activities and impact of the Klan were reported to be most severe, but committee members also visited Alabama, Florida, Georgia, Mississippi, and Tennessee, compiling a record of testimony that numbered in the thousands of pages. In February 1872, the Joint Select Committee submitted this testimony and its reports to Congress. The majority report, signed by every Republican on the committee, endorsed the Ku Klux Klan Act of 1871 and recommended continuing the president's powers to combat the Klan through the use of federal troops, courts, and suspension of the writ of habeas corpus. The minority report, signed by every Democrat on the committee, did not deny the existence of Klan-related violence but blamed it on misguided federal Reconstruction policy, which had left the Southern states in the hands of carpetbaggers and former slaves.

What Can Congressional Hearings and Reports Tell Us?

Since its publication in 1872, historians have found the thirteen volumes of the Joint Select Committee's report a remarkably detailed and comprehensive source for studying Reconstruction in the South. One of its chief advantages as a source is its sheer size. The committee conducted its work thoroughly, and the hundreds of witnesses who testified before it represented a broad spectrum of Southern society: white and black, rich and poor, male and female, Republican and Democrat. One historian has called their testimony "the richest single source" for understanding Southern society during the Reconstruction era. In the case of freedmen and -women, testimony before the committee provides invaluable first-person narratives of what the transition from bondage to freedom was like.

Another advantage of working with this source has to do with the methods by which the Joint Select Committee collected its evidence. Its procedures resembled legal hearings: oaths were administered to witnesses, and witnesses were subjected to cross-examination, all in meetings open to the public. No witnesses appeared anonymously or gave secret testimony. While those procedures may have prevented many from testifying for fear of reprisals, they nevertheless lent an air of authenticity to the witnesses' descriptions of the Klan that was not necessarily accorded to rumors or sensationalistic stories reported in the press. The Klan conducted its terrorism under cover of night and in disguise. By its very nature, it did not submit willingly to public scrutiny. For the most part, however, the witnesses who appeared before the committee in Southern towns and counties were eyewitnesses to the Klan's activities, making their testimony the most complete and reliable account of this secret organization's operations during Reconstruction.

The disadvantages associated with using the Joint Select Committee's report stem mostly from its inherent political biases. The Republicans who dominated the Joint Select Committee by a two-to-one margin were most interested

308 CHAPTER 14 · Political Terrorism during Reconstruction

in finding evidence that the Klan was a conspiratorial organization bent on depriving black and white Republicans of their civil and political liberties. Such evidence could be used to justify imposing martial law in those regions affected by the Klan. Democrats accused the Republicans of using the committee to drum up stories of Klan brutality and lawlessness that could be publicized to Republican advantage in the upcoming election of 1872. While the Democrats on the committee could not deny the violence of the Klan, they used their questioning of witnesses to cast doubt on its political motives, depicting Klansmen instead as isolated, ill-advised characters pushed to extremes by desperation and offended honor. It is important to remember that Congress had already passed the Ku Klux Klan Act when the Joint Select Committee conducted its work. Given that the committee's majority was made up of the same Republicans who had passed that piece of legislation, how likely was it that the committee's findings would challenge its enforcement? By passing the Ku Klux Klan Act *before* its investigation of the Klan, Congress clearly anticipated the outcome of the Joint Select Committee's work.

As you read the testimony, you will quickly realize that neither the Republicans nor the Democrats on the Joint Select Committee resembled neutral fact finders. Each side brought an agenda to the proceedings that influenced the nature of the testimony before the committee. Consider, for example, these excerpts from the testimony of D. H. Chamberlain, the Republican attorney general of South Carolina, given before the committee in Washington, D.C., on June 10, 1871. A good historian quickly learns to read between the lines of such evidence, looking carefully at the questions as well as the answers to determine what biases and ulterior motives shaped the construction of this source.

D. H. Chamberlain, sworn and examined.

By the Chairman:

Question: How long have you been a resident of the State?
Answer: I have been a resident there since December, 1865.

Question: Please go on and state to the committee the knowledge you have acquired, from your official position, as to the efficiency with which the laws are executed throughout the State of South Carolina, and the protection afforded to life and property in the State. Make your statement in general terms.

Answer: The enforcement of the law has, from time to time, been very much interrupted and disturbed from special causes; lately by what are popularly known as Ku-Klux operations. . . .

An oath to tell the truth similar to that given in a court of law

Republican senator John Scott of Pennsylvania chaired the committee and typically initiated the questioning

Invites Chamberlain to speak freely about law enforcement

By Mr. Van Trump: —————————————————————

Philadelph Van Trump, a Democratic representative from Ohio, typically led the cross-examination

Question: You say you went to South Carolina in 1865?

Answer: Yes, sir.

Question: How long after the termination of the war; what part of the year?

Answer: I went in December, 1865.

Question: From where did you go?

Answer: From Massachusetts. I had been in the Union army during the war. I settled at Charleston in December, 1865, and remained there, and my residence is there now, although I have to be at the capital of the State most of the time.

Returns to the subject of Chamberlain's background, seeking to discredit him as a carpetbagger

One other disadvantage to bear in mind about the Joint Select Committee's report is that while the committee's hearings had the appearance of legal proceedings, they did not work with the same standards of evidence as a court of law. In particular, the Republican majority of the committee was willing to accept hearsay, what someone had heard but not personally witnessed, as evidence. Democrats on the committee objected mightily to this, likening it to accepting rumors and gossip as facts. They equated the two-dollars-a-day allowance the committee paid to witnesses with bribery and accused the local Republican officials of coaching witnesses as well. In the thousands of pages of testimony in the Joint Select Committee's report, some witnesses do appear more reliable than others.

Questions to Ask

Several questions should immediately come to mind as you read the testimony provided to the Joint Select Committee. First, who were the witnesses? Where did they come from, and why were they testifying? Second, what information did the witnesses provide about the Klan's purposes and operations? Third, how reliable was that information? Was their testimony based on firsthand experience, personal opinion, or hearsay and rumor? After analyzing the testimony, you can then try to determine what influence it had on the Joint Select Committee's recommendations to Congress.

- Who were the people testifying before the Joint Select Committee?
- What did they say about the Klan's motives and operations?
- How reliable was their testimony?
- How did the committee use their testimony?

Source Analysis Table

Source	Personal Information	Description of the Klan's Activities and Motives	Reliability of Evidence Provided
WITNESS TESTIMONY			
1. Samuel T. Poinier			
2. D. H. Chamberlain			
3. Elias Thomson			
4. Lucy McMillan			
5. Mervin Givens			

Source	Description of the Klan	Assessment of Federal Response to the Klan
COMMITTEE REPORTS		
6. Majority Report		
7. Minority Report		

To download and print this table, visit the book companion site at **bedfordstmartins.com/brownshannon**.

The Source: Testimony and Reports from the Joint Select Committee to Inquire into the Condition of Affairs in the Late Insurrectionary States

All of the testimony that follows is taken from the Joint Select Committee's investigation of the Ku Klux Klan in South Carolina. Sources 1 and 2 come from testimony heard in Washington, D.C., while Sources 3, 4, and 5 are from testimony heard in Spartanburg, South Carolina. Sources 6 and 7 are excerpts from the committee's majority and minority reports, which were completed after the investigation was over.

1   *Testimony of Samuel T. Poinier,*
Washington, D.C., June 7, 1871

Poinier was a Republican newspaper editor and a federal tax collector in South Carolina at the time of his testimony.

Samuel T. Poinier sworn and examined.

By the Chairman:[1]

> *Question:* Please state in what part of South Carolina you reside.
> *Answer:* In Spartanburg County, the most northern county in the State.
> *Question:* How long have you resided there?
> *Answer:* Since February, 1866; a little over five years.
> *Question:* From what part of the United States did you go to South Carolina?
> *Answer:* I went there from Louisville, Kentucky. . . . I went there in 1866 with no intention whatever of remaining. I went entirely for social reasons, to marry, and I was persuaded to stay there. My wife was a native of Charleston, and I found her up in Spartanburg after the war, where a large number of Charleston people went during the bombardment of the city. . . .
> *Question:* Were you in the Union Army?
> *Answer:* Yes, sir: I went out from Kentucky.
> *Question:* Proceed with your statement.

---

[1] Republican senator John Scott from Pennsylvania.

Source: United States Congress, *Report of the Joint Select Committee to Inquire into the Condition of Affairs in the Late Insurrectionary States,* vol. 2, *South Carolina, Part I* (Washington, D.C.: Government Printing Office, 1872), 25–28, 33–34.

Answer: Just before our last campaign,[2] it was May a year ago, I . . . identified myself publicly with the republican party. I made my paper a republican paper. I did everything I could in the last State election for the reelection of Governor Scott[3] and our other State officers. From that time I have been in very deep water. . . . I was ordered away last fall, immediately after our last election, in November. It was soon after the first appearance of this Ku-Klux organization, or whatever it is. Soon after these outrages occurred in our county I received a note ordering me away from there, stating that I must leave the county; that all the soldiers of the United States Army could not enable me to live in Spartanburg. . . . Two days prior to our election, a party of disguised men went, at night, and took out two white men and three negroes, one of them a colored woman, and whipped them most brutally. Two of them were managers of the box[4] at that election; and the men told them that if they dared to hold an election at that box they would return and kill them. That was the first appearance of any trouble in the State. . . .

Question: Were those people of whom you spoke in disguise?

Answer: They were all in disguise. One of the colored men who were whipped swore positively as to the identity of some of them, and the parties were arrested, but nothing could ever be done with them; they proved an *alibi*, and some of them have since gone to Texas. . . .

Question: Go on and state any similar occurrences in that county since that time. . . .

Answer: Since that time outrages of that nature have occurred every week. Parties of disguised men have ridden through the county almost nightly. They go to a colored man's house, take him out and whip him. They tell him that he must not give any information that he has been whipped. They tell him, moreover, that he must make a public renunciation of his republican principles or they will return and kill him. . . .

Question: Do the facts that have transpired and the manner in which they have occurred satisfy you of the existence of the organization in that portion of South Carolina?

Answer: Yes, sir; I have no doubt of it in the world. I have received anonymous communications signed by the order of "K.K.K.," directing me to leave the county, stating that I could not live there; that I was a carpet-bagger. But personally I have never met with any trouble.

By Mr. Van Trump:[5]

Question: You have a connection with the partisan press there?

Answer: Yes, sir. I am editing a republican paper.

Question: Do you advocate the cause of the negro in your paper?

[2] The election of 1870.

[3] Robert K. Scott was the Republican governor of South Carolina.

[4] Ballot box.

[5] Democratic representative Philadelph Van Trump from Ohio.

Answer: Not the negro especially. I advocate the general principles of republicanism.

Question: You support the whole republican doctrine in your paper?

Answer: So far as general principles go, I do. I do not approve or uphold the State government in many of its acts; but, so far as the general principles of republicanism are concerned, I uphold it very strongly. I advocate the right of the colored people to vote and to exercise their civil and political privileges. . . .

Question: These men who assert that their object is to put down the negro and get possession of the Government are prominent men, are they not?

Answer: Yes, sir.

Question: Can you name a single man?

Answer: Well, I cannot name anybody specially who has made such a remark, but I hear it in the hotels.

Question: Have you yourself heard them make the remark?

Answer: I have heard the remark made; it is a common thing.

Question: Is it not rather an uncommon remark?

Answer: It is not, there.

Question: You cannot recollect the name of a single person who has made that declaration?

Answer: No sir, I cannot recall any now.

2   *Testimony of D. H. Chamberlain,*
Washington, D.C., June 10, 1871

Chamberlain was a Republican and the attorney general of South Carolina.

D. H. Chamberlain, sworn and examined.

By the Chairman:

Question: How long have you been a resident of the State?

Answer: I have been a resident there since December, 1865.

Question: Please go on and state to the committee the knowledge you have acquired, from your official position, as to the efficiency with which the laws are executed throughout the State of South Carolina, and the protection afforded to life and property in the State. Make your statement in general terms.

Answer: The enforcement of the law has, from time to time, been very much interrupted and disturbed from special causes; lately by what are popularly known as Ku-Klux operations. There have been a great many outrages committed, and a great many homicides, and a great many whippings. I speak

Source: Report of the Joint Select Committee, vol. 2, South Carolina, Part I, 48–51.

now, of course, of what I have heard; I have never seen any outrages committed myself; I am simply stating what I believe to be fact. . . .

Question: In what part of the State are these offenses committed which you attribute to the influence of this organization?

Answer: Notably in Spartanburg, Newberry, Union, and York Counties; those are the principal counties that have been the scenes of these disturbances. But they have extended into Laurens, Chester, and Lancaster Counties.[1] . . .

Question: Have there been any convictions for these offenses in the State, so far as your information goes; offenses committed by these organized bands?

Answer: No sir, no convictions, and no arrests, except in the case of this wounded Ku-Klux.[2] . . .

By Mr. Van Trump:

Question: You say you went to South Carolina in 1865?
Answer: Yes, sir.
Question: How long after the termination of the war; what part of the year?
Answer: I went in December, 1865.
Question: From where did you go?
Answer: From Massachusetts. I had been in the Union army during the war. I settled at Charleston in December, 1865, and remained there, and my residence is there now, although I have to be at the capital of the State most of the time.

By Mr. Stevenson:[3]

Question: When did it first come to your knowledge that this organization existed in the State of South Carolina?

Answer: It would be difficult to say. My conviction that there is such an organization has grown up very gradually. . . . I cannot fix the date exactly.

Question: Had you any knowledge of the fact that there were acts of violence and disorders in that State about the time of the election in 1868?

Answer: Yes, sir.

Question: Had you any information of the sending of arms at that time into that State?

Answer: O, I remember that a great many arms were purchased by private individuals, if you refer to that. I know that at the time, during the canvass,[4] there was considerable excitement when it was understood that the democrats,

[1] All seven of these counties were in the piedmont, or up-country, region of South Carolina, where the black and white populations were roughly equal.

[2] Chamberlain is referring to a Klansman wounded during a raid on the Newberry County Courthouse. He was jailed and then released on bail and subsequently either died while in the care of a friend or was spirited away by friends to avoid prosecution.

[3] Republican representative Job Stevenson from Ohio.

[4] Campaigning for votes.

as we call them, were arming themselves with Winchester and Henry rifles, or something of the kind.

Question: Repeating rifles?

Answer: Yes, sir. . . .

By Mr. Blair:[5]

Question: Did you have any actual knowledge of the fact that the democrats were then arming?

Answer: No, sir.

Question: Then you make this statement as a rumor merely?

Answer: Well, yes, sir; I should use, perhaps, a little stronger term than rumor. I had heard it so often that it came to be a belief with me, but it was hearsay. . . .

Question: Was it a common report that those arms all went into the hands of democrats?

Answer: As I heard it, it was understood that those arms were imported into the State upon order of individuals. I do not know but a republican might have had his order filled, but the belief was that they were generally ordered by democrats.

By Mr. Stevenson:

Question: You have no knowledge of any general arming among the republicans at that time?

Answer: No, sir.

Question: You were a republican, then, were you not?

Answer: Yes, sir.

By Mr. Blair:

Question: Did not the republicans have arms?

Answer: O, yes.

By Mr. Van Trump:

Question: Did not the negroes have arms?

Answer: Yes, sir; it is very common for people to have their shot-guns, to have some kind of arms. I suppose that in this instance people thought that there was an unusually large number brought in at a particular time, and that they were not for sporting purposes. They were repeating rifles.

Question: Have you been a politician for any part of your life?

Answer: No, sir; I do not think I have ever been a politician.

Question: Have you never heard a thousand rumors during an election that had no foundation in fact?

Answer: Yes, sir; many of them.

Question: Got up for excitement merely?

Answer: Yes, sir.

[5] Democratic senator Frank Blair from Missouri.

3   *Testimony of Elias Thomson,*
Spartanburg, South Carolina, July 7, 1871

Elias Thomson (colored) sworn and examined.

By the Chairman:

Question: Where do you live?
Answer: Up on Tiger River, on Mrs. Vernon's plantation.[1]
Question: What do you follow?
Answer: Farming.
Question: Do you live on rented land?
Answer: Yes, sir.
Question: How much have you rented?
Answer: I think about fifty acres.
Question: How long have you been living there?
Answer: Ever since the surrender; I never left home.
Question: Have you ever been disturbed any up there?
Answer: Yes, sir.
Question: How?
Answer: There came a parcel of gentlemen to my house one night—or men. They went up to the door and ran against it. My wife was sick. I was lying on a pallet, with my feet to the door. They ran against it and hallooed to me, "Open the door, quick, quick, quick." I threw the door open immediately, right wide open. Two little children were lying with me. I said, "Come in gentlemen." One of them says, "Do we look like gentlemen?" I says, "You look like men of some description; walk in." One says, "Come out here; are you ready to die?" I told him I was not prepared to die. "Well," said he, "Your time is short; commence praying." I told him I was not a praying man much, and hardly ever prayed; only a very few times; never did pray much. He says, "You ought to pray; your time is short, and now commence to pray." I told him I was not a praying man. One of them held a pistol to my head and said, "Get down and pray." I was on the steps, with one foot on the ground. They led me off to a pine tree. There was three or four of them behind me, it appeared, and one on each side, and one in front. The gentleman who questioned me was the only one I could see. All the time I could not see the others. Every time I could get a look around, they would touch me on the side of the head with a pistol, so I had to keep my head square in front. The next question was, "Who did you vote for?" I told him I voted for Mr. Turner—Claudius Turner, a gentleman in the neighborhood. They said, "What did you vote for him for?" I said, "I thought a good deal of him; he was my neighbor." I told them I disremembered who was on the ticket besides, but they had several, and I voted the ticket. "What did you do that for?" they said. Says I, "because I thought it was right."

---

[1] The Vernons were Thomson's former masters.

Source: Report of the Joint Select Committee, vol. 2, South Carolina, Part I, 410–15.

They said, "You thought it was right? It was right wrong." I said, "I never do anything hardly if I think it is wrong; if it was wrong, I did not know it. That was my opinion at the time and I thought every man ought to vote according to his notions." He said, "If you had taken the advice of your friends you would have been better off." I told him I had. Says I, "You may be a friend to me, but I can't tell who you are." Says he, "Can't you recognize anybody here?" I told him I could not. "In the condition you are in now, I can't tell who you are." One of them had a very large set of teeth; I suppose they were three-quarters of an inch long; they came right straight down. He came up to me and sort of nodded. He had on speckled horns and calico stuff, and had a face on. He said, "Have you got a chisel here I could get?" I told him I hadn't, but I reckoned I could knock one out, and I sort of laughed. He said, "What in hell are you laughing at? It is no laughing time." I told him it sort of tickled me, and I thought I would laugh. I did not say anything then for a good while. "Old man," says one, "have you got a rope here, or a plow-line, or something of the sort?" I told him, "Yes; I had one hanging on the crib." He said, "Let us have it." One of them says, "String him up to this pine tree, and we will get all out of him. Get up, one of you, and let us pull him up, and he will tell the truth." I says, "I can't tell you anything more than I have told. There is nothing that I can tell you but what I have told you and you have asked me." One man questioned me all this time. One would come up and say, "Let's hang him a while, and he will tell us the truth"; and another then came up and said, "Old man, we are just from hell; some of us have been dead ever since the revolutionary war." . . . I was not scared, and said, "You have been through a right smart experience." "Yes," he says, "we have been through a considerable experience." One of them says, "we have just come from hell." I said, "If I had been there, I would not want to go back." . . . Then they hit me thirteen of the hardest cuts I ever got. I never had such cuts. They hit me right around my waist and by my hip, and cut a piece about as wide as my two fingers in one place. I did not say a word while they were whipping, only sort of grunted a little. As quick as they got through they said, "Go to your bed. We will have this country right before we get through; go to your bed," and they started away. . . .

Question: Who is Claudius Turner?

Answer: He is a gentleman that run for the legislature here. He was on the ticket with Mr. Scott.

Question: The republican ticket?

Answer: Yes, sir; the radical[2] ticket. . . .

By Mr. Van Trump:

Question: Explain to me, if you can, if the object of this Ku-Klux organization is to intimidate the colored people, why they were so particular as to make you promise, under penalty of death, that you would never disclose the fact that you had been visited; do you understand why that is?

---

[2] Radical Republicans were known for their support of black suffrage and the disenfranchisement of former Confederate military and civilian officers.

Answer: I can explain this fact this far: You know when they said to me to not say anything about this matter, I asked them what I must say, and when I asked, "What must I say? I will have to say something," they said, "What are you going to say?" I said, "What must I say?" He said, "Are you going to tell it?" I told them, "I have to say something, of course, and what must I say; what can I say?" Then they said, looking straight at me—

Question: Why is it that so often in giving your testimony you have to get up and make gesticulations like an orator? Have you been an orator?

Answer: No, sir, but I was showing the way they did me, and what they said to me. They said, "You just let me hear of this thing again, and we will not leave a piece of you when we come back."

Question: To whom have you talked lately about this case, or consulted here in town?

Answer: I have not consulted much about it.

Question: How long have you been waiting to be examined?

Answer: Since Tuesday about 10 o'clock.

Question: Have any white republicans been to see you?

Answer: No, sir; nobody at all.

Question: Did you see them?

Answer: I don't know who the republicans are here. I may have seen some.

Question: Do you pretend to say that since Tuesday you have not talked with any white about your case?

Answer: With none about the Ku-Klux matter.

4   ## *Testimony of Lucy McMillan,*
Spartanburg, South Carolina, July 10, 1871

Lucy McMillan (colored) sworn and examined.

By the Chairman:

Question: Where do you live?

Answer: Up in the country. I live on McMillan's place, right at the foot of the road.

Question: How far is it?

Answer: Twelve miles.

Question: Are you married?

Answer: I am not married. I am single now. I was married. My husband was taken away from me and carried off twelve years ago.

Question: He was carried off before the war?

Answer: Yes, sir; the year before the war; twelve years ago this November coming.

Source: Report of the Joint Select Committee, vol. 3, South Carolina, Part 2, 604–7.

Question: How old are you now?

Answer: I am called forty-six. I am forty-five or -six.

Question: Did the Ku-Klux come where you live at any time?

Answer: They came there once before they burned my house down. The way it happened was this: John Hunter's wife came to my house on Saturday morning, and told they were going to whip me. I was afraid of them; there was so much talk of Ku-Klux drowning people, and whipping people, and killing them. My house was only a little piece from the river, so I laid out at night in the woods. The Sunday evening after Isham McCrary[1] was whipped I went up, and a white man, John McMillan, came along and says to me, "Lucy, you had better stay at home, for they will whip you anyhow." I said if they have to, they might whip me in the woods, for I am afraid to stay there. Monday night they came in and burned my house down; I dodged out alongside of the road not far off and saw them. I was sitting right not far off, and as they came along the river I knew some of them. I knew John McMillan, and Kennedy McMillan, and Billy Bush, and John Hunter. They were all together. I was not far off, and I saw them. They went right on to my house. When they passed me I run further up on the hill to get out of the way of them. They went there and knocked down and beat my house a right smart while. And then they all got still, and directly I saw the fire rise.

Question: How many of these men were there?

Answer: A good many; I couldn't tell how many, but these I knew. The others I didn't. . . .

Question: What was the reason given for burning your house?

Answer: There was speaking down there last year and I came to it. They all kept at me to go. I went home and they quizzed me to hear what was said, and I told them as far as my senses allowed me.

Question: Where was this speaking?

Answer: Here in this town. I went on and told them, and then they all said I was making laws; or going to have the land, and the Ku-Klux were going to beat me for bragging that I would have land. John Hunter told them on me, I suppose, that I said I was going to have land. . . .

Question: Was that the only reason you know for your house being burned?

Answer: That is all the reason. All the Ku-Klux said all that they had against me was that I was bragging and boasting that I wanted the land. . . .

By Mr. Van Trump:

Question: Do you mean to say that they said they burned the house for that reason?

Answer: No sir; they burned the house because they could not catch me. I don't know any other reason. . . .

Question: Who was John Hunter?

Answer: He is a colored man. I worked for him all last summer. I worked with him hoeing his cotton and corn.

---

[1] Another freedman who testified before the committee in Spartanburg.

Question: What was he doing with these Ku-Klux?

Answer: I don't know. He was with them. . . .

Question: How did you come to be named Lucy McMillan?

Answer: I was a slave of Robert McMillan. I always belonged to him.

Question: You helped raise Kennedy and John?[2]

Answer: Not John, but Kennedy I did. When he was a little boy I was with him.

Question: Did he always like you?

Answer: Yes, sir. They always pretended to like us.

Question: That is while you were a slave?

Answer: Yes, sir, while I was a slave, but never afterward. They didn't care for us then.

[2] Sons of Robert McMillan.

5 | *Testimony of Mervin Givens,*
Spartanburg, South Carolina, July 12, 1871

Mervin Givens (colored) sworn and examined.

By Mr. Stevenson:

Question: Your name in old times was Mery Moss?

Answer: Yes, sir; but since freedom I don't go by my master's name. My name now is Givens.

Question: What is your age?

Answer: About forty I expect. . . .

Question: Have you ever been visited by the Ku-Klux?

Answer: Yes, sir.

Question: When?

Answer: About the last of April.

Question: Tell what they said and did.

Answer: I was asleep when they came to my house, and did not know anything about them until they broke in on me.

Question: What time of night was it?

Answer: About twelve o'clock at night. They broke in on me and frightened me right smart, being asleep. They ordered me to get up and make a light. As quick as I could gather my senses I bounced up and made a light, but not quick enough. They jumped at me and struck me with a pistol, and made a knot[1] that you can see there now. By the time I made the light I catched the voice of them, and as soon as I could see by the light, I looked around and saw by the

[1] Bump.

Source: Report of the Joint Select Committee, vol. 2, South Carolina, Part 2, 698–700.

size of the men and voice so that I could judge right off who it was. By that time they jerked the case off the pillow and jerked it over my head and ordered me out of doors. That was all I saw in the house. After they carried me out of doors I saw nothing more. They pulled the pillow-slip over my head and told me if I took off they would shoot me. They carried me out and whipped me powerful.

Question: With what?

Answer: With sticks and hickories. They whipped me powerful.

Question: How many lashes?

Answer: I can't tell. I have no knowledge at all about it. May be a hundred or two. Two men whipped me and both at once.

Question: Did they say anything to you?

Answer: They cursed me and told me I had voted the radical ticket, and they intended to beat me so I would not vote it again.

Question: Did you know any of them?

Answer: Yes, sir; I think I know them.

Question: What were their names?

Answer: One was named John Thomson and the other was John Zimmerman. Those are the two men I think it was.

Question: How many were there in all?

Answer: I didn't see but two. After they took me out, I was blindfolded; but I could judge from the horse tracks that there were more than two horses there. Some were horses and some were mules. It was a wet, rainy night; they whipped me stark naked. I had a brown undershirt on and they tore it clean off. . . .

By Mr. Van Trump:

Question: There were, then, two men who came to your house?

Answer: Yes, sir; that was all I could see.

Question: Were they disguised?

Answer: Yes, sir.

Question: How?

Answer: They had on some sort of gray-looking clothes, and much the same sort of thing over their face. One of them had a sort of high hat with tassel and sort of horns.

Question: How far did John Thomson live from there?

Answer: I think it is two or three miles.

Question: Were you acquainted with him?

Answer: Yes, sir.

Question: Where?

Answer: At my house. My wife did a good deal of washing for them both. I was very well-acquainted with their size and their voices. They were boys I was raised with. . . .

Question: Did you tell anybody else it was John Thomson?

Answer: I have never named it.

Question: Why?

Answer: I was afraid to.

Question: Are you afraid now?

Answer: I am not afraid to own the truth as nigh[2] as I can.

Question: Is there any difference in owning to the truth on the 12th of July and on the 1st of April?

Answer: The black people have injured themselves very much by talking, and I was afraid.

Question: Are you not afraid now?

Answer: No, sir; because I hope there will be a stop put to it. . . .

Question: Do you think we three gentlemen can stop it?

Answer: No, sir; but I think you can get some help.

Question: Has anybody been telling you that?

Answer: No, sir; nobody told me that. . . .

Question: Why did you not commence a prosecution against Thomson and Zimmerman?

Answer: I am like the rest, I reckon; I am too cowardly.

Question: Why do you not do it now; you are not cowardly now?

Answer: I shouldn't have done it now.

Question: I am talking about bringing suit for that abuse on that night. Why do you not have them arrested?

Answer: It ought to be done.

Question: Why do you not do it?

Answer: For fear they would shoot me. If I were to bring them up here and could not prove the thing exactly on them, and they were to get out of it, I would not expect to live much longer.

[2] Near.

---

6   *Majority Report of the Joint Select Committee to Inquire into the Condition of Affairs in the Late Insurrectionary States,* February 19, 1872, Submitted by Luke P. Poland

Poland was a Republican representative from Vermont.

The proceedings and debates in Congress show that, whatever other causes were assigned for disorders in the late insurrectionary States, the execution of the laws and the security of life and property were alleged to be most seriously

Source: Report of the Joint Select Committee, vol. 1, Reports of the Committee, 2–3, 98–99.

threatened by the existence and acts of organized bands of armed and disguised men, known as Ku-Klux. . . .

The evidence is equally decisive that redress cannot be obtained against those who commit crimes in disguise and at night. The reasons assigned are that identification is difficult, almost impossible; that when this is attempted, the combinations and oaths of the order come in and release the culprit by perjury either upon the witness-stand or in the jury-box; and that the terror inspired by their acts, as well as the public sentiment in their favor in many localities, paralyzes the arm of civil power. . . .

The race so recently emancipated, against which banishment or serfdom is thus decreed, but which has been clothed by the Government with the rights and responsibilities of citizenship, ought not to be, and we feel assured will not be left hereafter without protection against the hostilities and sufferings it has endured in the past, as long as the legal and constitutional powers of the Government are adequate to afford it. Communities suffering such evils and influenced by such extreme feelings may be slow to learn that relief can come only from a ready obedience to and support of constituted authority, looking to the modes provided by law for redress of all grievances. That Southern communities do not seem to yield this ready obedience at once should not deter the friends of good government in both sections from hoping and working for that end. . . .

The law of 1871[1] has been effective in suppressing for the present, to a great extent, the operations of masked and disguised men in North and South Carolina. . . . The apparent cessation of operations should not lead to a conclusion that community would be safe if protective measures were withdrawn. These should be continued until there remains no further doubt of the actual suppression and disarming of this wide-spread and dangerous conspiracy.

The results of suspending the writ of *habeas corpus* in South Carolina show that where the membership, mysteries, and power of the organization have been kept concealed this is the most and perhaps only effective remedy for its suppression; and in review of its cessation and resumption of hostilities at different times, of its extent and power, and that in several of the States where it exists the courts have not yet held terms at which the cases can be tried, we recommend that the power conferred on the President by the fourth section of that act[2] be extended until the end of the next session of Congress.

For the Senate:	For the House of Representatives:
JOHN SCOTT, Chairman	LUKE P. POLAND, Chairman
Z. CHANDLER[3]	HORACE MAYNARD[4]

---

[1] The Ku Klux Klan Act.

[2] To suspend the writ of habeas corpus.

[3] Republican senator from Michigan.

[4] Republican representative from Tennessee.

BENJ. F. RICE[5]   GLENNI W. SCOFIELD[6]

JOHN POOL[7]   JOHN F. FARNSWORTH[8]

DANIEL D. PRATT[9]   JOHN COBURN[10]

                                   JOB E. STEVENSON

                                   BENJ. F. BUTLER[11]

                                   WILLIAM E. LANSING[12]

[5] Republican senator from Arkansas.

[6] Republican representative from Pennsylvania.

[7] Republican senator from North Carolina.

[8] Republican representative from Illinois.

[9] Republican senator from Indiana.

[10] Republican representative from Indiana.

[11] Republican representative from Massachusetts.

[12] Republican representative from New York.

7   *Minority Report of the Joint Select Committee to Inquire into the Condition of Affairs in the Late Insurrectionary States,* February 19, 1872, Submitted by James B. Beck

Beck was a Democratic representative from Kentucky.

The atrocious measures by which millions of white people have been put at the mercy of the semi-barbarous negroes of the South, and the vilest of the white people, both from the North and South, who have been constituted the leaders of this black horde, are now sought to be justified and defended by defaming the people upon whom this unspeakable outrage had been committed. . . .

There is no doubt about the fact that great outrages were committed by bands of disguised men during those years of lawlessness and oppression. The natural tendency of all such organizations is to violence and crime. . . . It is so everywhere; like causes produce like results. Sporadic cases of outrages occur in every community. . . . But, as a rule, the worst governments produce the most disorders. South Carolina is confessedly in the worst condition of any of the States. Why? Because her government is the worst, or what makes it still worse,

Source: Report of the Joint Select Committee, vol. 1, *Reports of the Committee,* 289, 463–64, 514–16, 588.

her people see no hope in the future. . . . There never was a Ku-Klux in Virginia, nobody pretends there ever was. Why? Because Virginia escaped carpet-bag rule. . . .

The Constitution was trampled under foot in the passage of what is known as the Ku-Klux law; a power was delegated to the President which could be exercised by the legislative authority alone; whole communities of innocent people were put under the ban of executive vengeance by the suspension of the writ of *habeas corpus* at the mere whim and caprice of the President; and all for what? For the apprehension and conviction of a few poor, deluded, ignorant, and unhappy wretches, goaded to desperation by the insolence of the negroes, and who could, had the radical authorities of South Carolina done their duty, just as easily have been prosecuted in the State courts, and much more promptly and cheaply, than by all this imposing machinery of Federal power, through military and judicial departments. . . .

. . . The antagonism, therefore, which exists between these two classes of the population of South Carolina does not spring from any political cause, in the ordinary party sense of the term; but it grows out of that instinctive and irrepressible repugnance to compulsory affiliation with another race, planted by the God of nature in the breast of the white man, perhaps more strongly manifested in the uneducated portion of the people, and aggravated and intensified by the fact that the Negro has been placed as a *ruler* over him. . . .

We feel it would be a dereliction of duty on our part if, after what we have witnessed in South Carolina, we did not admonish the American people that the present condition of things in the South cannot last. It was an oft-quoted political apothegm, long prior to the war, that no government could exist "half slave and half free." The paraphrase of that proposition is equally true, that no government can long exist "half black and half white." If the republican party, or its all-powerful leaders in the North, cannot see this, if they are so absorbed in the idea of this newly discovered political divinity in the negro, that they cannot comprehend its social repugnance or its political dangers; or, knowing it, have the wanton, wicked, and criminal purpose of disregarding its consequences, whether in the present or in the future, and the great mass of American white citizens should still be so mad as to sustain them in their heedless career of forcing negro supremacy over white men, why then "farewell, a long farewell," to constitutional liberty on this continent, and the glorious form of government bequeathed to us by our fathers. . . .

The foregoing is a hurried, but, as we believe, a truthful statement of the political, moral, and financial condition of the State of South Carolina, under the joint rule of the Negro and the "reconstructive" policy of Congress.

FRANK BLAIR

T. F. BAYARD[1]

S. S. COX[2]

---

[1] Democratic senator from Delaware.

[2] Democratic representative from New York.

JAMES B. BECK

P. VAN TRUMP

A. M. WADDELL[3]

J. C. ROBINSON[4]

J. M. HANKS[5]

[3] Democratic representative from North Carolina.
[4] Democratic representative from Illinois.
[5] Democratic representative from Arkansas.

Analyzing Congressional Hearings and Reports

1. How did the descriptions of the Ku Klux Klan differ between witnesses examined in Washington, D.C. (Sources 1 and 2), and those examined in South Carolina (Sources 3, 4, and 5)? How would you explain those differences?

2. Briefly compare the nature of evidence presented in the testimony: How did it differ between black and white witnesses? In what ways did the Klan's attacks on blacks differ from those on white Republicans? What do you think accounts for such differences?

3. What patterns did you find in the cross-examination of witnesses? How did Van Trump and other Democrats on the committee seek to discredit or shape the testimony they heard, and do you think they succeeded in any instances? Which witnesses do you think were most successful in answering their cross-examinations? Did any of the witnesses contradict themselves?

4. Consider whether the majority and minority reports (Sources 6 and 7) could have been written before the committee heard any witnesses. Using your notes from the second portion of the table on page 311, do you think any of the congressmen sitting on the committee had their minds changed about the Ku Klux Klan or the federal government's response to it by the testimony they heard? What specific examples or passages from the reports would you use to support your answer?

5. What does this source tell you about the limits of federal power during Reconstruction? According to the testimony and reports, what accounted for the breakdown of law and order in South Carolina, and how was it most likely to be restored? How did Republicans and Democrats differ in this regard?

6. Using the testimony you have read here, describe the social and economic conditions faced by the freedmen and -women of the South during Reconstruction. What evidence do Thomson, McMillan, and Givens (Sources 3, 4, and 5) provide of the ways in which African American men and women valued and acted on their freedom after 1865 and of the limits whites tried to impose on that freedom?

The Rest of the Story

As noted in the Joint Select Committee's majority report, the Ku Klux Klan Act of 1871 did succeed in suppressing the Klan's activities in those regions where it was enforced. In October 1871, while the Joint Select Committee was still at work, President Grant suspended the writ of habeas corpus in nine South Carolina counties, including Spartanburg, and sent in federal troops to arrest approximately 1,500 suspected Klansmen. Even more Klansmen fled the region to avoid prosecution. In a series of trials managed by U.S. Attorney General Amos Akerman in late 1871 and in 1872, about ninety Klansmen were sentenced to prison terms ranging from three months to ten years. Most of those given long sentences were released within a year or two, under amnesty offered by President Grant. Overall, very few Klansmen were ever brought to meaningful justice for their crimes, but by the election of 1872, reports of Klan terrorism had declined considerably, and the organization's ability to intimidate black voters appeared to have been broken.

During the 1920s, the Ku Klux Klan was revived by whites who felt threatened by Catholic and Jewish immigrants as well as by African Americans. At its peak, this version of the Klan included three million members and spilled beyond the South into western and northern states. After ebbing in the 1940s, the Klan surged again during the civil rights movement of the 1950s and 1960s. This incarnation was much smaller than its predecessor in the 1920s but more violent in its resistance to racial equality. Today a number of white supremacist organizations continue to call themselves the Ku Klux Klan, but they are poorly organized and constantly at odds with one another and with similar hate groups on the far right of American politics.

In the larger story of Reconstruction, it would seem that the Ku Klux Klan Act and the congressional investigation of the Klan were shining examples of how the federal government and the freedmen and -women of the South acted in partnership to advance the cause of racial justice and equality in the United States. Unfortunately, these successes were short-lived. During his second term, Grant reduced considerably the number of federal troops posted in the South, and the Republicans split between a liberal faction still committed to racial equality and a more conservative faction willing to jettison Reconstruction policies and black voters in return for political compromises with Democrats on other issues.

The third branch of the federal government did not help African Americans in their pursuit of equality either. In two cases from the 1870s, the Supreme Court interpreted the Fourteenth Amendment in such a way that it severely restricted the federal government's ability to intervene on behalf of private citizens when their civil and political rights were violated. In the *Slaughterhouse Cases* (1873), the Court ruled that the Fourteenth Amendment protected only those rights that were derived directly from the federal government, most of which dealt with matters of interstate or foreign travel or business; the civil rights of most concern to blacks in the South still fell under the jurisdiction of state courts and law enforcement. In *U.S. v. Cruikshank* (1876), the Court ruled that the Fourteenth Amendment empowered the federal government only to prosecute violations of civil rights by the states, not by individual persons (violations in that category still fell under state jurisdiction). The combined effect of these two decisions was to place responsibility for protecting the rights of the South's African American population under the authority of the state governments, while making any federal intervention on their behalf similar to that pursued under the Ku Klux Klan Act unconstitutional.

After the last of the former Confederate states had fallen back into Democratic hands in 1877, Southern whites found new ways to confine blacks to second-class citizenship that were far more subtle than the Klan's political terrorism. Insulated from federal intervention by the Supreme Court's decisions and congressional indifference, Southern states passed laws that disenfranchised blacks by imposing poll taxes and literacy tests. They also erected a system of social segregation known as Jim Crow laws that limited black access to education and economic opportunity. When blacks challenged this system, mobs and night riders responded with the same methods used by the Klan, most notably lynching and arson, to prevent any sustained resistance to white rule. Not until the civil rights movement of the 1950s would the federal government again embrace the cause of racial justice in the South with the same vigor it had shown during its battle against the Klan in 1871.

To Find Out More

Like all federal government reports, the Joint Select Committee's report was published by the Government Printing Office in Washington, D.C. In every state, libraries designated as federal repositories receive copies of such publications, and your college or university library may in fact be one. The full citation for the report is *Report of the Joint Select Committee to Inquire into the Condition of Affairs in the Late Insurrectionary States*, 13 volumes (Washington, D.C.: Government Printing Office, 1872). It can also be found under the title *Senate Reports*, 42d Congress, 2d sess., no. 41 (serial 1484–96) or *House Reports*, 42d Congress, 2d sess., no. 22 (serial 1529–41). Some libraries may also catalog it under the title printed on the spine of each volume, *The Ku Klux Conspiracy*. Volume 1 contains the majority and minority reports, and the subsequent volumes contain the verbatim testimony of witnesses before the committee.

For a more accessible selection of the testimony heard by the Joint Select Committee, see Albion W. Tourgée, *The Invisible Empire* (1880; repr., Baton Rouge: Louisiana State University Press, 1989). Tourgée was a disillusioned carpetbagger when he published his autobiographical novel about Reconstruction, *A Fool's Errand*, in 1879. A year later, he published *The Invisible Empire* as an exposé of the Ku Klux Klan.

The *Report of the Joint Select Committee* is not yet available in a digitized format, but several online resources address the experience of freedmen and -women during Reconstruction. The Freedmen's Bureau Online, at **freedmensbureau.com**, is an excellent starting point for conducting Web-based research on the Reconstruction era. It features transcriptions of documents from the National Archives, including a section on "Records Relating to Murders and Outrages" in the Reconstruction South. The Freedmen and Southern Society Project, at **history.umd.edu/Freedmen**, includes primary sources on the experience of emancipation. America's Reconstruction: People and Politics after the Civil War, at **digitalhistory.uh.edu/reconstruction/section4/ section4_presrecon.html**, is an online exhibit on Reconstruction that includes some useful images and primary sources.

For the definitive modern study of the Ku Klux Klan during Reconstruction, see Allen W. Trelease, *White Terror: The Ku Klux Klan Conspiracy and Southern Reconstruction* (New York: Harper and Row, Publishers, 1971). The Klan's place in the wider current of political violence in the Reconstruction-era South is explained in George C. Rable, *But There Was No Peace: The Role of Violence in the Politics of Reconstruction* (Athens: University of Georgia Press, 1984). The best comprehensive history of Reconstruction, Eric Foner's *Reconstruction: America's Unfinished Revolution, 1863–1877* (New York: Harper and Row, Publishers, 1988), also provides a good summary of the Klan's origins and role in Reconstruction. The African American response to the Klan and other forms of political intimidation is addressed in Steven Hahn, *A Nation under Our Feet: Black Political Struggles in the Rural South from Slavery to the Great Migration* (Cambridge, Mass.: Belknap Press, 2003). The film *Birth of a Nation* (1915), directed by D. W. Griffith and based on Thomas Dixon's popular novel *The Clansman* (1905), is a stunning example of how the Klan was mythologized during the Jim Crow era as an organization that defended white Southerners against the depredations of Northern carpetbaggers and black Republicans during Reconstruction.

Avoiding Plagiarism

Acknowledging the Source

Adapted from The St. Martin's Tutorial on Avoiding Plagiarism *by Margaret Price, University of Massachusetts–Amherst*

If you have taken classes that involve writing, particularly writing and research, chances are good that you have heard the term *plagiarism* before. You may have received syllabi that mention plagiarism and describe the penalties for it, such as a failing grade in the course or even suspension from school. You also may have read your school's plagiarism policy, which most likely offers a brief definition of plagiarism and issues dire warnings about what will happen if you plagiarize. And if you read or watch the news, you may have noticed that plagiarism is an important issue not only within academic settings but in the larger world as well. Clearly, plagiarism is serious business. But what is it, exactly? And how do you avoid doing it?

Defined simply, plagiarism is the unattributed use of someone else's words or ideas. However, this apparently simple definition can be quite complicated. It tends to change across contexts and may be understood differently by different readers. Despite the slipperiness of the definition, every writer has the responsibility to learn how to navigate it and to attribute sources accurately and fully. Ethical researchers must acknowledge their sources because writers and readers depend on one another's honesty. To use someone else's words or ideas without sufficient acknowledgment breaks that trust. Writers in academia are interdependent, with each of us depending on everyone else to help uphold the integrity of the group. Every person engaged in academic writing, from the first-time research writer to the seasoned professor, shares this responsibility. For this reason, the penalties for an academic writer who fails to practice academic integrity are severe.

Why Acknowledgment of Sources Is Important

Within the Western academic tradition, new ideas are built on older ones. Writers give acknowledgment in writing to their sources for a number of reasons:

- **To indicate that you are a responsible and careful researcher.** Acknowledging your sources increases your credibility as a researcher.
- **To give your writing added relevance.** When you refer to others' ideas and show how your own ideas fit into that framework, readers can see more easily what is significant about your work.
- **To help define your research project.** Sources help indicate what topic you are addressing, what approach you are taking, with whose ideas you are aligning yourself and from whose ideas you are distancing yourself, and (in some cases) what discipline you are writing in. In sum, citation helps situate *you* as a unique researcher.
- **To give your work added authority.** Your argument is based not only on your own investigation but also on others' investigations.
- **To demonstrate your responsibility as a member of the academic community.** Each of us relies on the others to uphold the values of this community, one of which is attribution of sources.

Keeping Track of Source Materials: The Research Portfolio

As an ethical researcher, you should establish good research habits and stick to them. A research project, even a relatively small one involving only a few sources, quickly accumulates materials. There is no firm rule for how to keep these materials organized, but keeping some form of research portfolio is important. This portfolio should include

- photocopies or electronic copies of your source information
- your notes
- your annotated bibliography
- drafts of the paper or project you are working on
- any feedback you have received

Organize your portfolio so that it is both comprehensive (containing all your materials) and manageable (designed for easy retrieval of information). With experience, you will develop a type of research portfolio that works for you. However, as you collect data, keep in mind some basic principles that will help you organize your research materials and avoid inadvertent plagiarism. Recording your research findings precisely and accurately reduces the chances that you will unintentionally express and claim someone else's idea as your own.

1. Create a structure for your portfolio. One example is the folder system. Hanging file folders represent large categories that can be subdivided using folders to represent smaller categories. As you discover more information through your research, you will add more folders, or perhaps revise the categories altogether. Keep your working bibliography (see the next section) in a separate folder. Also, keep your notes and annotations for each source. Another possible structure for a research portfolio is the notebook system, in which materials are kept in a three-ring binder, with dividers separating the categories. The system you use will be governed by how much material you accumulate as well as your own organizational preferences.

2. Keep backup materials. Your portfolio should include backup copies of everything to guard against loss or computer failure. If a lot of your information resides on a computer, keep hard copies of everything and at least one electronic backup.

3. Make a hard copy of each source for your own use. You should print out any articles that you download from an online periodical database, photocopy articles or chapters of books, and print out all Web sites. (Most printouts of Web sites will automatically note the URL and date of access. If this does not occur, note this information.) These printouts will be very useful for checking quotations, paraphrases, and bibliographic information.

4. Take notes on every source you collect. This step is crucial. If you simply read a source over and then later attempt to include some of its information in the draft of your paper, your chances of plagiarizing are much greater. You cannot truly digest a source's information unless you take notes on what you read. If you fail to take notes, your inclusion of the source's words is likely to sound choppy, with inadequate connectors between the source's ideas and your own.

Maintaining a Working Bibliography

A working bibliography is a list of all the sources you consult as you work on a research project. You may not need to include every source in your project, but you should keep a list of every work you have consulted so that your records are complete. If you develop this habit, you will avoid the problem of wondering where you found certain facts and ideas. A working bibliography also may come in handy for future research projects. After you complete your research, keep your working bibliography so that you can consult it again if necessary.

Your working bibliography should include complete information for each source so that you can write your citations easily (see Appendix II: Documenting the Source). This information includes the author's name, the title of the work, the title of the book or periodical it comes from (if applicable), the volume or issue number, the place of publication, the publishing company, the date of publication, and inclusive page numbers. Note any other information that pertains to the work's publication, such as whether it is a volume in a series, an edition other than the first, or a translation. Write down the information for each source as you begin using it. You can also keep your working bibliography on a computer file; this technique allows you to easily transfer the bibliography into your final draft later on.

Taking Notes: Knowing Where Each Idea and Word Comes From

It is easy to assume that the research process and the writing process are separate—"first I research, and then I write." But in fact, researching and writing should be intimately intertwined. As you read and research, new ideas occur to you. Your research question begins to change shape and sometimes to change direction. The development of your own thoughts in turn leads to a different reading of your sources. Taking notes and writing drafts while you research are essential. If you wait to begin note-taking and drafting until you have "finished" your research, the rich mixture of ideas and thoughts you created while researching will never be captured on paper.

You may be surprised to learn that research involves so much writing before you begin writing your "real" paper. But note-taking is not an optional or extra step. All responsible researchers write notes before (and while) drafting their projects. In fact, you can think of your notes as a first draft, or pre-draft, of your paper. They are crucial building blocks of an effective research project. A detailed note-taking system makes writing a paper much easier.

Taking careful notes while you are researching also makes it easier to figure out which ideas are your own. Any plagiarism policy that you read will say that plagiarism is the act of representing someone else's words or ideas as your own. Summarizing or paraphrasing requires that you take another person's idea and put it into your own words.

Clearly, then, it is better to write as you go rather than to save the writing for the end of a research project. But how do you go about doing it? Here are some concrete note-taking strategies.

- **Write an instant draft.** Before you begin researching, or as early in the research process as possible, write a draft that describes what argument you want to make or what question you want to explore. Writing professors Charles Moran and Anne Herrington call this an "instant draft." An instant draft will be a tentative, somewhat disorganized piece of writing, since you have not yet done your research. Its purpose is to capture what you know about a subject before you begin consulting other people's ideas. In your instant draft, address the following questions: *What do I* *already know about this topic? Where have I gotten my information from so far? Do I have a strong feeling or stance on this topic? What questions do I have about the topic? What is (are) the main thing(s) I want to find out through my research? Where will I begin looking for this information? What do I need help with? Whom can I ask for that help?* An instant draft is a research memo to yourself and is enormously helpful in providing a recorded baseline for your knowledge. As you learn more and more through your research, you will always know where you started out—and hence, which ideas you have acquired through researching.

- **Annotate each source.** Before you begin taking more detailed notes, annotate each source you have just read. That is, write a brief summary of the source's main point and key ideas. It is helpful to include annotations in your working bibliography (which turns it into an *annotated bibliography*). Some instructors will ask you to turn in an annotated bibliography with your final draft.

- **Practice taking notes to avoid patchwriting.** "Patchwriting," a term coined by writing professor Rebecca Moore Howard, means taking notes that are not exact quotations, but that are quite close to the original source's wording. Howard suggests the following system for avoiding patchwriting: First, read a source quickly, just enough to get its main point. Then read it through again, more slowly, taking notes in the margin (perhaps quick questions or key terms) as you go. Wait a bit before moving on to the next step (Howard suggests that half an hour is sufficient). Then, *without looking at the source again*, write a summary of it. Finally, check your summary against the original source. Have you duplicated any of the author's phrases? If so, quote the author directly or adjust the phrasing of your summary. The more often you do this exercise, the more adept you will become at summarizing sources.

Summarizing, Paraphrasing, and Quoting

You can record someone else's words or ideas in your notes by using three techniques: summarizing, paraphrasing, and quoting. Summarizing and paraphrasing involve putting a source's words into your own; quoting involves recording a source's exact words. After you practice these independently, it is a good idea to show your notes to your instructor and to ask for his or her comments on the effectiveness of your note-taking. Is it complete? Is it accurate? When summarizing and paraphrasing, do you put other authors' ideas into your own words effectively?

1. Summarizing. To summarize is to rephrase a relatively large amount of information into a short statement in your own words. While some information will inevitably be lost, your job is to record what you see as the main idea of the passage. Summarizing is useful when you want to give a reader the gist of a relatively lengthy passage without going into every detail.

2. Paraphrasing. To paraphrase is to restate something with your own words and sentence structure. Unlike a summary, a paraphrase is generally about as long as the original passage. Because you are changing the language, you will also inevitably change the meaning of the passage *slightly*, but your job is to keep the meaning as intact as possible. Paraphrasing is useful when you want to convey another author's exact idea, but not his or her exact words—perhaps because the language is highly technical, or perhaps because a quote would be distracting.

3. Quoting. To quote is to state a source's exact words, signaled by the use of quotation marks. If you change a quotation in any way, you must indicate this by including ellipsis points (when you omit part of a quotation) or square brackets (when you make a slight change or addition for clarification). In a final draft, quotations are often less useful than summaries or paraphrases because quotations break up the flow of your writing and often require fairly extensive explanation. Quotations are useful, however, when you want to capture a source's exact wording.

Knowing Which Sources to Acknowledge

Beginning researchers often ask, "Do I have to cite *everything*?" This is a good question because not every piece of information in a research paper must be cited. Figuring out what to cite can be difficult, even for experienced researchers. Generally, if you are unsure, include a citation. It is always better to have an unnecessary citation in your paper than to omit one that is necessary.

Materials That Do Not Require Acknowledgment

Here are some types of materials that usually do not require acknowledgment in research projects:

- **Common knowledge.** It is often easy to spot pieces of common knowledge. The sky is blue, the United States has fifty states, the 1996 presidential candidates were Bill Clinton and Bob Dole—these are all pieces of information that appear in various sources, but because they are known to just about everyone, you do not need to cite a source. Sometimes, however, recognizing common knowledge becomes tricky because common knowledge for one person may not be common knowledge for another. Identifying your audience is the key to recognizing common knowledge. If you know what audience you are writing to, you will have a clearer idea of what your readers would consider common knowledge. As always, if you are unsure, be more conservative rather than less so.

- **Fact.** Uncontested pieces of information that can be found in many different sources—particularly reference sources such as encyclopedias—do not require acknowledgment. In *The St. Martin's Handbook,* writing professor Andrea Lunsford gives an example of one such fact: that most of the Pearl Harbor military base, except oil tanks and submarines, was destroyed on December 7, 1941, by Japanese bombers. She adds an example of information on the same topic that *does* require citation: "a source that argued that the failure to destroy the submarines meant that Japan was destined to lose the subsequent war with the United States" (394). The distinction Lunsford makes here is between fact (something commonly accepted as true) and opinion (something that is arguable).

- **Your own ideas.** Recognizing that an idea is your own can sometimes be difficult, especially during the research process, when you are reading and absorbing so many others' ideas. A good way to capture your own ideas is to write a draft *before* you begin researching.

- **Your own field research.** Knowledge that you create by conducting a field study such as a survey, an interview, or an observation is considered your own work. You do not need to cite this sort of information. However, another kind of ethics guides the field researcher. You should be clear about how you collected the information. In addition, you should be scrupulous about protecting your participants' autonomy (be sure to quote them accurately, and ask for their feedback when possible).

Materials That Do Require Acknowledgment

Anything that you draw from another source, unless it falls into one of the categories described above (common knowledge, fact, your own ideas, and your own field research), must be cited. Your citations should appear in two places: in the body of your paper and in a list at the end of the paper. The style of citation your instructor has asked you to use will affect the formatting of these citations. Complete bibliographic information for each source will appear in a section titled "Bibliography" (see Appendix II: Documenting the Source).

The following list is suggestive, but not exhaustive. New kinds of information are always emerging. Generally speaking, however, here are the types of materials that require acknowledgment in academic writing:

- **Another person's words.** Direct quotations must always be cited.

- **Another person's ideas.** Even if you rephrase someone else's idea by paraphrasing or summarizing it, you must cite it. Citations for paraphrases and summaries look just like citations for quotations, except that no quotation marks are used.

- **Judgments, opinions, and arguments.** Arguable information, such as the idea about the effect of the Pearl Harbor bombing discussed previously, must be cited. Whenever you offer an idea from another source that could be argued, acknowledge that it is this individual's point of view. You should do this even if you thought of the idea and *then* encountered it through your research. You can indicate in your writing that you came to the idea independently of the other author, but you cannot omit mention of the other author.

- **Visual information.** If you use a chart, graph, or picture from another source — or if you use the information from that chart, graph, or picture — acknowledge the source.

- **Information that can be attributed to a company or organization rather than a single person.** Web pages and corporate publications often do not list individual authors. In this case, the organization that sponsored the Web site or publication should be listed as the author. If the author is unknown, your citation should indicate that.

- **Information gathered from class lectures or from another aural source.** If you heard information rather than saw it, you must still cite it. You can cite information you have heard in various ways, including as a lecture, as a personal communication, or as an interview.

- **General help offered by readers.** Sometimes the feedback you receive from readers (such as your teacher, classmates, and friends) will affect the shape of your work, but not its content. For instance, a classmate might offer a suggestion for making your introduction more interesting. In this case, the best way to acknowledge your classmate's contribution is in a note of thanks appended to the paper. Such "Acknowledgments" notes generally appear at the end of academic papers or in a footnote added to the title or first paragraph. If you look at a refereed history journal, you will see examples of less formal acknowledgments of this kind.

Learning these rules and following them appropriately is one of your responsibilities as a member of an academic or writing community. Even if you plagiarize unintentionally, the penalties for plagiarism — which can be very severe — still apply to you. For more information on plagiarism, consult your school's or your department's guidelines. For more detailed and constructive information, speak with your instructor, who probably has a pretty good idea of what sort of citation is expected. You should also find out if your school has a writing center with tutoring available. Tutors can discuss ways of citing information and often can refer you to other sources of information if you need additional help. A third resource to consider is a writing handbook that includes the rules of academic citation as well as guidelines on conducting research, managing information, and citing sources responsibly. For an interactive tutorial on avoiding plagiarism, go to **bedfordstmartins.com/plagiarismtutorial**.

Documenting the Source

Whenever you use another researcher's work as a source in your own writing, whether you quote the researcher's words directly or rely on the researcher's evidence and theories to support your arguments, you must include documentation for that source. This is equally true when using a map, photograph, table, or graph created by someone else. The reasons for this are twofold. First, to avoid any possibility of plagiarism, you must always include proper documentation for *all* source materials (see Appendix I). Second, a proper citation gives important information to your reader about where to find a particular source, be it on a Web site, in a book at the library, or in an archive in your local community.

When documenting sources, historians use a standard form based on the recommendations published in *The Chicago Manual of Style*. All of the following documentation models are based on the guidelines published in the fifteenth edition of *The Chicago Manual of Style* (Chicago: The University of Chicago Press, 2003). These examples are based on the sources that appear in both volumes of *Going to the Source*. The diversity of the examples will give you some sense of the variety of source types that you may encounter in your research. For each source type, you will see a citation style that can be used for either a footnote, which appears at the bottom of the page of text, or an endnote, which appears at the end of a chapter or at the end of the whole text. This will be followed by an example of how this source type would be cited in a bibliography. Two examples are provided because footnote/endnote citation style is slightly different from bibliography citation style.

The examples provided here will help you address many of the documentation issues associated with source types that you come across in your research. However, this guide is not a comprehensive list, and as you dig further into the past, you may uncover source types that are not covered in this brief guide. For additional information about documenting sources in the *Chicago* style, please see **bedfordstmartins.com/resdoc.**

Documentation Basics

The question to keep in mind when you are wondering what to include in a citation is this: what does my reader need to know in order to *find* this source? When citing sources internally, you should use the footnote or endnote style. Footnotes and endnotes are used to document specific instances of borrowed text, ideas, or information. The first time you cite a source, you need to include the full publication information for that source—the author's full name, source title (and subtitle, if there is one), and facts of publication (city, publisher, and date)—along with the specific page number that you are referencing.

> 1. David Paul Nord, *Communities of Journalism: A History of American Newspapers and Their Readers* (Urbana: University of Illinois Press, 2001), 78.

If you refer to that source later in your paper, you need to include only the author's last name, an abbreviated version of the title, and the page or pages cited.

> 4. Nord, *Communities of Journalism,* 110–12.

A bibliography is used in addition to footnotes or endnotes to list all of the works you consulted in completing your paper, even those not directly cited in your footnotes. The sources included in your bibliography should be listed alphabetically, so the citation style for a bibliographic entry begins with the author's last name first.

> Nord, David Paul. *Communities of Journalism*: *A History of American Newspapers and Their Readers.* Urbana: University of Illinois Press, 2001.

BOOKS

■ *Standard format for a book*

The standard form for citing a book is the same whether there is an editor or an author, the only difference being the inclusion of "ed." to indicate that an editor compiled the work.

FOOTNOTE/ENDNOTE:

1. Tim Johnson, ed., *Spirit Capture: Photographs from the National Museum of the American Indian* (Washington, DC: Smithsonian Institution Press, 1998), 102.

BIBLIOGRAPHY ENTRY:

Johnson, Tim, ed. *Spirit Capture: Photographs from the National Museum of the American Indian*. Washington, DC: Smithsonian Institution Press, 1998.

■ *Book with two or more authors or editors*

When citing a source from a book with two or three authors or editors, you need to include the names of all of the authors (or editors) in the order that they appear on the title page. If a work has more than three authors, you need to include all of the names in your bibliography. However, in your footnotes or endnotes, you need only include the name of the lead author followed by "and others" or "et al.," with no intervening comma.

FOOTNOTE/ENDNOTE:

2. Graham Russell Hodges and Alan Edward Brown, eds., *"Pretends to Be Free": Runaway Slave Advertisements from Colonial and Revolutionary New York and New Jersey* (New York: Garland, 1994), 58.

BIBLIOGRAPHY ENTRY:

Hodges, Graham Russell, and Alan Edward Brown, eds. *"Pretends to Be Free": Runaway Slave Advertisements from Colonial and Revolutionary New York and New Jersey*. New York: Garland, 1994.

■ *Edited book with an author*

Sometimes a book will have an author and an editor. In that case, you need to include both the author's and the editor's names.

FOOTNOTE/ENDNOTE:

3. Hilda Satt Polacheck, *I Came a Stranger: The Story of a Hull-House Girl*, ed. Dena J. Polacheck Epstein (Urbana: University of Illinois Press, 1991), 36.

BIBLIOGRAPHY ENTRY:

Polacheck, Hilda Satt. *I Came a Stranger: The Story of a Hull-House Girl*. Edited by Dena J. Polacheck Epstein. Urbana: University of Illinois Press, 1991.

■ *Multivolume book*

If you are referring to a specific volume in a multivolume work, you need to specify which volume you used. This information should come before the page reference toward the end of the citation.

FOOTNOTE/ENDNOTE:

    4. Bernard Bailyn, ed., *The Debate on the Constitution: Federalist and Anti-Federalist Speeches, Articles, and Letters during the Struggle over Ratification* (New York: Library of America, 1993), 2:759–61.

BIBLIOGRAPHY ENTRY:

Bailyn, Bernard, ed. *The Debate on the Constitution: Federalist and Anti-Federalist Speeches, Articles, and Letters during the Struggle over Ratification*. 2 vols. New York: Library of America, 1993.

Sometimes individual volumes in a multivolume work have separate volume titles. When citing a particular volume, you should include the volume title first followed by the name of the complete work.

■ *Book with an anonymous author*

Many books printed in the nineteenth century were published anonymously. If the author was omitted on the title page, but you know from your research who the author is, insert the name in square brackets; if you do not know who the actual author is, begin the citation with the work's title. Avoid using "Anonymous" or "Anon." in citations. As originally published, the author of *The Mother's Book* was listed as "Mrs. Child," so this citation includes that information along with the full name in brackets.

FOOTNOTE/ENDNOTE:

    5. Mrs. [Lydia Maria] Child, *The Mother's Book* (Boston: Carter, Hendee, and Babcock, 1831), 23.

BIBLIOGRAPHY ENTRY:

Child, [Lydia Maria]. *The Mother's Book*. Boston: Carter, Hendee, and Babcock, 1831.

■ *Book-length work within a book*

Sometimes, the source that you are using may be a book-length work that has been reprinted within a longer work. In that case, you need to include both titles along with the editor of the longer work.

FOOTNOTE/ENDNOTE:

6. Álvar Núñez Cabeza de Vaca, *The Narrative of Cabeza de Vaca*, in *Spanish Explorers in the Southern United States, 1528–1543*, ed. Frederick W. Hodge (New York: Charles Scribner's Sons, 1907), 52–54, 76–78, 81–82.

BIBLIOGRAPHY ENTRY:

Cabeza de Vaca, Álvar Núñez. *The Narrative of Cabeza de Vaca*. In *Spanish Explorers in the Southern United States, 1528–1543*, edited by Frederick W. Hodge. New York: Charles Scribner's Sons, 1907.

■ *Chapter from a book*

If you want to cite a particular chapter from a book, you should include the title of the chapter in quotation marks before the title of the book.

FOOTNOTE/ENDNOTE:

7. Vicki L. Ruiz, "The Flapper and the Chaperone," in *From Out of the Shadows: Mexican Women in Twentieth-Century America* (New York: Oxford University Press, 1998), 12–26.

BIBLIOGRAPHY ENTRY:

Ruiz, Vicki L. "The Flapper and the Chaperone." In *From Out of the Shadows: Mexican Women in Twentieth-Century America*. New York: Oxford University Press, 1998.

PERIODICALS

Journals are scholarly publications that are usually published a few times a year. Popular magazines are written for the general public and are most often published on a monthly or weekly basis. Most newspapers are published daily, although some small local papers are published weekly. The following examples demonstrate the style for citing each type of periodical. If you consult an online periodical, the style for citing this source would be the same, with the addition of the URL at the end of your citation.

■ *Journal articles*

When citing an article from a journal, you need to include the volume number, issue number (when given), and date of publication.

FOOTNOTE/ENDNOTE:

8. Elizabeth A. Fenn, "Biological Warfare in Eighteenth-Century North America: Beyond Jeffery Amherst," *Journal of American History* 86, no. 4 (2000): 1552–80.

BIBLIOGRAPHY ENTRY:

Fenn, Elizabeth A. "Biological Warfare in Eighteenth-Century North America: Beyond
    Jeffery Amherst." *Journal of American History* 86, no. 4 (2000): 1552–80.

▪ *Popular magazines*

When citing material from a popular magazine, you need to include only the
magazine title followed by the date of publication and the page number(s) for
the material. If you are citing from a regular feature of the magazine, you
should include the title of the feature in the citation. If there is an author of the
magazine article or the magazine's regular feature, the author's name would appear first in your citation, followed by the name of the feature.

FOOTNOTE/ENDNOTE:

   9. Advertisement for International Realty Corporation, *The Crisis*, October 1911, 262.

BIBLIOGRAPHY ENTRY:

The Crisis. Advertisement for International Realty Corporation. October 1911.

▪ *Newspaper articles*

When citing newspaper articles, you must include the day, month, and year of
publication, and the author if the article had a byline. *Chicago* style allows for
page numbers to be omitted because newspapers often publish several editions
each day and these editions are generally paginated differently.

FOOTNOTE/ENDNOTE:

   10. John Dickinson, "The Liberty Song," *Boston Gazette*, July 18, 1768.

BIBLIOGRAPHY ENTRY:

Dickinson, John. "The Liberty Song." *Boston Gazette*, July 18, 1768.

INTERNET SOURCES

▪ *Internet archives*

Because many older sources like newspapers and letters are rare and fragile, researchers often turn to Internet archives such as that of the Library of Congress
through which digital copies of these documents are made available. Access to
documents on the Internet also allows you to examine materials without having
to travel to the archives in which they are housed. To cite a document found on

an Internet Web site, you need to provide as much of the following information as possible: the author, the name of the document with original date of publication, the name of the site, the sponsor or owner of the site, and the URL. Sometimes a Web archive will include a document number; when available, you should include this cataloging number as well.

FOOTNOTE/ENDNOTE:

11. Civil Rights Act of 1964, Document PL 88-352, *International Information Programs*, U.S. State Department, http://usinfo.state.gov/usa/infousa/laws/majorlaw/civilr19.htm.

BIBLIOGRAPHY ENTRY:

Civil Rights Act of 1964. Document PL 88-352. *International Information Programs*, U.S.
    State Department. http://usinfo.state.gov/usa/infousa/laws/majorlaw/civilr19.htm.

■ An entire Web site

To cite an entire Web site, you need include only the author of the site (if known), the name of the site, the sponsor or owner of the site, and the URL.

FOOTNOTE/ENDNOTE:

12. University of Minnesota College of Liberal Arts, *Immigration History Research Center*, University of Minnesota, http://www.ihrc.umn.edu.

BIBLIOGRAPHY ENTRY:

University of Minnesota College of Liberal Arts. *Immigration History Research Center*.
    University of Minnesota. http://www.ihrc.umn.edu.

OTHER SOURCES

■ Published letters and other forms of correspondence

When citing letters, memoranda, telegrams, and the like, you need to include the name of the sender and the recipient along with the date of the correspondence. Memoranda, telegrams, and other forms of communication should be noted as such in your citation after the recipient's name and before the date, but letters do not need to be specifically noted as such.

FOOTNOTE/ENDNOTE:

13. James Buchanan to Juan N. Almonte, March 10, 1845, in *Diplomatic Correspondence of the United States: Inter-American Affairs, 1831–1860*, ed. William R. Manning (Washington, DC: Carnegie Endowment for International Peace, 1937), 8:163.

BIBLIOGRAPHY ENTRY:

Buchanan, James. James Buchanan to Juan N. Almonte, March 10, 1845. In *Diplomatic Correspondence of ther United States: Inter-American Affairs, 1831–1860*, edited by William R. Manning. Washington, DC: Carnegie Endowment for International Peace, 1937.

■ *Unpublished letters and other forms of correspondence*

Unpublished letters and those that have not been archived should include some indication of this fact, such as "in the author's possession" or "private collection." If the letter was found in an archive, the location of the depository would be included as well. (For information on how to cite material found in an archive, see the section "Photos and other material found in an archive or depository" on p. 347.)

FOOTNOTE/ENDNOTE:

14. Jeff Rogers to William and Adele Rogers, November 10, 1968, in the author's possession.

BIBLIOGRAPHY ENTRY:

Rogers, Jeff. Jeff Rogers to William and Adele Rogers, November 10, 1968. In the author's possession.

■ *Court records*

When you are citing legal cases in historical writing, the name of the plaintiff appears first, followed by the name of the defendant, and both names are italicized. The first time you cite the case, you should also include the court and year in which the case was decided. Supreme Court decisions are published by the government in a series called *United States Reports*. When citing Supreme Court decisions, you need to include the name of the case in italics followed by the number of the volume that contains the particular case, the abbreviation "U.S." for *United States Reports,* page numbers, and the date of the decision.

FOOTNOTE/ENDNOTE:

15. *Korematsu v. United States,* 323 U.S. 242, 242–48 (1944).

BIBLIOGRAPHY ENTRY:

Korematsu v. United States. 323 U.S. 242, 242–48. 1944.

■ *Tables, graphs, and charts*

Whenever you incorporate statistical data into your work, it is important to document your evidence. If you borrow a table, graph, or chart from another source, you must cite it just as you would quoted material in your text. Include a citation in appropriate footnote format to the source of the borrowed information directly below it. If you change the table, graph, or chart in any way (for example, eliminating unnecessary information or adding another element such as a percent calculation to it), use the phrase "adapted from" in your citation, which signals to the reader that you have altered the original. If a number is used to identify the data in the original source, that information should be included as well at the end of the citation.

FOOTNOTE/ENDNOTE:

16. Adapted from Hinton R. Helper, *The Impending Crisis of the South: How to Meet It* (New York: Burdick Brothers, 1857), 71, table XVIII.

Because you wouldn't cite any one particular table in your bibliography, you would follow the style for citing the book, periodical, or Web site where the data you consulted first appeared.

■ *Paintings*

When citing paintings that appear in a catalog, archive, or database, you need to include the artwork's catalog or accession number if available. This documentation will allow other researchers to locate the original source more easily. Generally, specific works of art are not included in your bibliography. However, if a particular painting is important to your research, you may list it in your bibliography by the painter's name first.

FOOTNOTE/ENDNOTE:

17. George Catlin, *Shón-Ka-Ki-He-Ga, Horse Chief, Grand Pawnee Head Chief* (1832, Smithsonian American Art Museum: 1985.66.99).

BIBLIOGRAPHY ENTRY:

Catlin, George. *Shón-Ka-Ki-He-Ga, Horse Chief, Grand Pawnee Head Chief*. 1832.
Smithsonian American Art Museum: 1985.66.99.

■ *Photos and other material found in an archive or depository*

Any material found in an archive or depository, be it a photograph, diary, letter, or map, needs to be cited just as published material would be. The name of the author (or photographer, in the case of photographs) should appear first, followed by the title of the image or document being cited in quotation marks, the date, and the name of the archive or depository. If a source from a collection is important enough to your work, you can mention that source specifically in your bibliography. However, if you make use of more than one photograph or other type of source from a particular collection, you need only cite them generally in your bibliography.

FOOTNOTE/ENDNOTE:

18. George P. Barnard, "Ruins of Charleston, S.C.," 1866, Beinecke Rare Book and Manuscript Library, Yale University.

BIBLIOGRAPHY ENTRY:

Photographs. Beinecke Rare Book and Manuscript Library, Yale University.

■ *Government publications*

The government publishes thousands of pages of documents every year. The format for citing these documents varies slightly from source to source depending on the format of the publication and the source being cited. For example, any testimony given before a congressional committee is usually published in a book. Here the exact name of the committee is given in the title of the work in which the testimony appears. When citing government publications in your bibliography, you would substitute the agency that published the work for the author, unless, of course, a particular author has been specified.

FOOTNOTE/ENDNOTE:

19. United States Congress, *Report of the Joint Select Committee to Inquire into the Condition of Affairs in the Late Insurrectionary States,* vol. 2, *South Carolina, Part I* (Washington, DC: Government Printing Office, 1872), 25–28, 33–34.

BIBLIOGRAPHY ENTRY:

United States Congress. *Report of the Joint Select Committee to Inquire into the Condition of Affairs in the Late Insurrectionary States.* Vol. 2, *South Carolina, Part I.* Washington, DC: Government Printing Office, 1872.

Acknowledgments (continued)

Page 12 (Source 3): *Whale*. Image from André Thevet, *Cosmographie universalle*, fol. 1002r. Courtesy of The John Carter Brown Library at Brown University. Caption text from *André Thevet's North America: A Sixteenth-Century View*, edited by Roger Schlesinger and Arthur P. Stabler. Reprinted with permission of McGill-Queen's University Press.

Page 13 (Source 4): *Alligator*, Erasmus Francisci. Image courtesy of The John Carter Brown Library at Brown University.

Page 14 (Source 5): *Llama*. Image courtesy of The John Carter Brown Library at Brown University. Caption, text from *Discovering the New World: Based on the Works of Theodore de Bry*, edited by Michael Alexander. Reprinted by permission of HarperCollins Publishers.

Page 15 (Source 6): *Birds and Fish of New England*. Image courtesy of The John Carter Brown Library at Brown University. Caption text from *Discovering the New World: Based on the Works of Theodore de Bry*, edited by Michael Alexander. Reprinted by permission of HarperCollins Publishers.

Pages 16–18 (Source 7): *Animals of the Carolinas*. Image from John Lawson, *A New Voyage to Carolina*, 1709. Courtesy of The John Carter Brown Library at Brown University.

Pages 18–19 (Source 8): *Beaver*. Image from Herman Moll, "A New and Exact Map of the dominions of the king of Great Britain on ye Continent of America," 1715, in *The World Discovered*. Courtesy of The John Carter Brown Library at Brown University.

Pages 19–20 (Source 9): *The Vampire, or Spectre of Guiana*. Image from John Gabriel Stedman, *Narrative of a Five Years Expedition against the Revolted Negroes of Surinam*, edited by Richard and Sally Price. Courtesy of The John Carter Brown Library at Brown University.

Pages 20–22 (Source 10): *The Aboma Snake*. From John Gabriel Stedman, *Narrative of a Five Years Expedition against the Revolted Negroes of Surinam*, edited by Richard and Sally Price. Courtesy of The John Carter Brown Library at Brown University.

Chapter 2

Page 26 (Figure 2.1): Detail from the cover of a 1773 Boston Edition of *A Narrative of the Captivity, Sufferings, and Removes of Mrs. Mary Rowlandson*. Courtesy of the Rosenbach Museum & Library, Philadelphia.

Chapter 4

Page 66 (Figure 4.1): Indians talking with Colonel Bouquet. Library of Congress, Prints and Photos Division, Pictorial Americana, Repro # LC-USZ62-104.

Pages 73–87: Elizabeth A. Fenn, "Biological Warfare in Eighteenth-Century North America: Beyond Jeffery Amherst," *Journal of American History* 86, no. 4 (March 2000): 1552–80.

Chapter 5

Page 92 (Figure 5.1): Sign for Gordon's Inn, c. 1790–1830. The Connecticut Historical Society, Hartford, Connecticut.

Chapter 6

Page 114 (Figure 6.1): The Constitutional Congress. Print and Picture Collection, The Free Library of Philadelphia.

Chapter 7

Page 137 (Figure 7.1): A New Touch on the Times by a 'Daughter of Liberty'; Woodcut/Broadside, 1779. Negative number 48257. Collection of The New-York Historical Society.

Chapter 8

Page 161 (Figure 8.1): Illustrated alphabet from *The New-England Primer*. Courtesy of the Special Collections, Musselman Library, Gettysburg College, Gettysburg, Pennsylvania.

Chapter 9

Page 181 (Figure 9.1): Scene on a Cotton Plantation. From Edward King and James Wells Champney, *The Great South; A Record of Journeys in Louisiana, Texas, the Indian Territory, Missouri, Arkansas, Mississippi, Alabama, Georgia, Florida, South Carolina, North Carolina, Kentucky, Tennessee, Virginia, West Virginia, and Maryland*. Used with Permission of Documenting the American South, The University of North Carolina at Chapel Hill Libraries.

Pages 195–196 (Sources 7 and 8): "Per Capita Income by Region for 1840 and 1860 in 1860 Prices" and "The Relative Level of the Per Capita Income of the South in 1860," adapted from Robert William Fogel and Stanley L. Engerman, *Time on the Cross: The Economics of American Negro Slavery*. By permission of W. W. Norton.

Chapter 10
    Page 211 (Source 1): George Catlin, *Shón-Ka-Ki-He-Ga, Horse Chief*, Smithsonian American Art Museum/Art Resource, NY.
    Page 212 (Source 2): George Catlin, *Máh-To-Tóh-Pa, Four Bears, Second Chief, in Full Dress*, Smithsonian American Art Museum/Art Resource, NY.
    Page 213 (Source 3): George Catlin, *La-Dóo-Ke-A, Buffalo Bull, A Grand Pawnee Warrior*, Smithsonian American Art Museum/Art Resource, NY.
    Page 214 (Source 4): George Catlin, *Pshán-Shaw, Sweet-Scented Grass, Twelve-Year-Old Daughter of Bloody Hand*, Smithsonian American Art Museum/Art Resource, NY.
    Page 215 (Source 5): George Catlin, *Jú-Ah-Kís-Gaw, Woman with Her Child in a Cradle*, Smithsonian American Art Museum/Art Resource, NY.
    Page 216 (Source 6): George Catlin, *Wi-Jún-Jon, Pigeon's Egg Head (The Light) Going to and Returning from Washington*, Smithsonian American Art Museum/Art Resource, NY.
    Page 217 (Source 7): George Catlin, *Fort Pierre, Mouth of the Teton River, 1200 Miles above St. Louis*, Smithsonian American Art Museum/Art Resource, NY.
    Page 218 (Source 8): George Catlin, *Buffalo Hunt under the Wolf-Skin Mask*, Smithsonian American Art Museum/Art Resource, NY.
    Page 219 (Source 9): George Catlin, *Buffalo Chase, A Surround by the Hidatsa*, Smithsonian American Art Museum/Art Resource, NY.
    Page 220 (Source 10): George Catlin, *Bird's-Eye View of the Mandan Village, 1800 Miles above St. Louis*, Smithsonian American Art Museum/Art Resource, NY.
    Page 221 (Source 11): George Catlin, *Sioux Encamped on the Upper Missouri, Dressing Buffalo Meat and Robes*, Smithsonian American Art Museum/Art Resource, NY.
    Page 222 (Source 12): George Catlin, *The Cutting Scene, Mandan O-Kee-Pa Ceremony*, 1832, Denver Art Museum Collection, The William Sr. and Dorothy Harmsen Collection, 2001.456. Photo provided by Denver Art Museum.

Chapter 12
    Page 255 (Figure 12.1): Photograph of John Brown. Library of Congress, Prints and Photographs Division, LC-USZ62-2472.
    Pages 265–268: (Source 2) From Robert Penn Warren, *John Brown: The Making of a Martyr*. Copyright © 1929 by Payson & Clarke, Ltd., by permission of Ivan R. Dee, Publisher.
    Pages 268–270 (Source 3): From David S. Reynolds, *John Brown, Abolitionist: The Man Who Killed Slavery, Sparked the Civil War, and Seeded Civil Rights*. Copyright © 2005 by David S. Reynolds. Used by permission of Alfred A. Knopf, a division of Random House, Inc.

Chapter 13
    Page 275 (Figure 13.1): Photographer unknown, "Gardner's Gallery." Library of Congress, Prints and Photographs Division, LC-BH837-207.
    Page 278: John Trumbull, *Death of General Mercer at the Battle of Princeton, New Jersey, 3 January 1777*, Yale University Art Gallery, Trumbull Collection.
    Page 279: Timothy O'Sullivan, "A Harvest of Death, Gettysburg, Pennsylvania," 1863, Albumen silver print, P1984.30.36. Amon Carter Museum, Fort Worth, Texas.
    Page 284 (Source 1): James F. Gibson, "Lieut. Washington, a Confederate prisoner, and Capt. Custer, U.S.A.," 1862. Library of Congress, Prints and Photographs Division, LC-B8171-0428 DLC.
    Page 285 (Source 2): Mathew Brady, "Gen. Robert B. Potter and staff of seven, recognized Capt. Gilbert H. McKibben, Capt. Wright, A.A.G. Also Mr. Brady, photographer," c. 1863. National Archives and Records Administration, 111-B-4.
    Page 286 (Source 3): Portrait of a Soldier Group. Library of Congress, Prints and Photographs Division, LC-B8184-10694 DLC.
    Page 287 (Source 4): Alexander Gardner, "President Lincoln on Battle-field of Antietam," 1862, Albumen silver print, P1984.30.23. Amon Carter Museum, Fort Worth, Texas.
    Page 288 (Source 5): Timothy O'Sullivan, "Pennsylvania, Gettysburg 07/1863," 1863. National Archives and Records Administration, 165-SB-35.
    Page 289 (Source 6): George P. Barnard, "Ruins of Charleston, S.C.," 1866. The Beinecke Rare Book and Manuscript Library, Image # 3610761.
    Page 290 (Source 7): Mathew Brady, "Portrait of Brig. Gen. Napoleon B. McLaughlin, Officer of the Federal Army, and staff, vicinity of Washington, D.C.," 1861. Library of Congress, Prints and Photographs Division, LC-B8171-7180 DLC.
    Page 291 (Source 8): Timothy O'Sullivan, "Culpeper, Va. 'Contrabands,'" 1863. Library of Congress, Prints and Photographs Division, LC-B8171-0221 DLC.
    Page 292 (Source 9): "African American soldiers with their teachers and officers," date unknown. Library of Congress, Prints and Photographs Division, LC-B8184-10061.

Page 293 (Source 10): Alexander Gardner, "Antietam, Md. Bodies of dead gathered for burial," 1862. Library of Congress, Prints and Photographs Division, LC-B8171-0557 DLC.

Page 294 (Source 11): Alexander Gardner, "A Contrast. Federal buried; Confederate unburied, where they fell on the battle field of Antietam," 1863. Collection of the New-York Historical Society, PR-065-788-1.

Page 295 (Source 12): Alexander Gardner, "He Sleeps his Last Sleep," ca. 1861–65. Collection of the New-York Historical Society, PR-065-774-2.

Page 296 (Source 13): James F. Gibson, "Battlefield of Gettysburg—Body of a soldier in 'the wheat field,' evidently killed by the explosion of a shell," 1863. Library of Congress, Prints and Photographs Division, LC-8184-7258.

Page 297 (Source 14): Timothy O'Sullivan, "Field Where General Reynolds Fell, Gettysburg," 1863, Albumen silver print, P1984.30.97. Amon Carter Museum, Fort Worth, Texas.

Page 298 (Source 15): T. C. Roche, ". . . View of the covered ways inside the rebel Fort Mahone, called by the soldiers 'Fort Damnation' . . . taken the morning after the storming of Petersburgh, Va. 1865," E. and H. T. Anthony, Collection of the New-York Historical Society, PR-065-811-18.

Page 299 (Source 16): John Reekie, "Cold Harbor, Va., African Americans collecting bones of soldiers killed in the battle," 1865. Library of Congress, Prints and Photographs Division, LC-B8171-7962 DLC.

Chapter 14

Page 305 (Figure 14.1): Thomas Nast, "The Union as it was. The Lost cause, worse than slavery." Library of Congress, LC-USZ62-128619.

Index

Letters in parentheses following page numbers refer to:
(i)   illustrations
(f)   figures, including charts and graphs
(m)   maps